To Sr. Anne Mary

GOD KEEPS
ON GIVING

You have always
been more than a
good friend.
I hope you
enjoy my books!
always,
Joe Fredericks
1/25/2021

GOD KEEPS ON GIVING

A Thank You to God Who
Has Always Been with
Me and Blessed Me

Joseph B. Frederick Ph.D.

Volume 2

To order additional copies of this book, contact:
Xlibris
844-714-8691
www.Xlibris.com
Orders@Xlibris.com
550111

This book is dedicated and written with love
in memory of our son, Mark.

CONTENTS

PART I: The First Years of Employment in the County Board of Mental Retardation

My first years of employment as a physical education teacher and recreation coordinator (1967–1969).

My challenges as a special services coordinator, classroom consultant, and teacher were many.

Other highlights were writing professional articles, coauthoring a book, and learning the importance of planning, implementing, communicating, and checking on everyone's actions (1969–1975).

PART II: Moving My Workplace from the County to the State Government

This position afforded me the opportunity to come in contact with boards, CEOs, managers, teachers, workshop specialists, social workers, parents, and community organizations (1973–1976).

I was introduced to budget restrictions by having five positions of responsibility with the State Department as well as lawsuits, an $8.2 million construction project, and overseeing several million dollars of state grants for various schools, workshops, and residential projects. The office was being abolished while I was involved with many of these projects (1975–1979).

The staff experienced a Medicaid survey and decertification, reorganization of the service delivery system, and disappearance of a resident, which looked like a kidnapping, to name a few events (1978–1981).

Several group homes were established and opened in Northwest Ohio while the regional offices were being abolished (1981–1983).

PART III: A Second and Third Chance with the
County and Bowling Green State University
(BGSU)

Part IV: Grandchildren

Here comes Zachary and then Joshua to provide fulfillment in our lives.

Part V: Retirement Experience

Experiences with our family, friends, and others, the special people I know.

A continuation of several vacations and other events.

We add more experiences during these retirement years.

PREFACE

Each of us lives our life according to our heredity, living circumstances, and exposure to other people. In my first book, *People + Me*, I covered my background in a small railroad town in Northern Ohio named Willard. The feedback I received from this book was more positive than I could have imagined. People continued to ask me "When will the next book be printed?"

As I reviewed the information that I had collected and the first draft I had written on the second book, I decided to go forward with the second book. The title came easy. As I looked at my professional career and my personal life at that time, it was evident that *God kept on giving* me many blessings.

Like my first, this book is filled with events that I think others will find interesting. There is a great deal of variety and, at times, entertainment in the happenings. There are writings that may be useful for others in living their lives. As I reread the text, I questioned who else was inspiring me as I wrote, for it seems as if forces assisted me in this process. I found many answers about my support system. I still search for answers with God and my twin, who died in utero at three months. I thank you for entering into my world and trust you will find enjoyment in your reading.

ACKNOWLEDGMENTS

I have always appreciated the support of my extremely supportive and loving wife, Kathy, in the time I gave to writing and editing this book for content and other factors. I appreciate the support of my sons Mark and Joe II; my daughter-in-law, Tara; and my grandsons Josh and Zach, as well my family and friends, for allowing me to write about them.

God's gift of life to me is the supreme acknowledgment. My life is really God's life, and my goal is to always use these blessings and gifts to His honor and glory through this book.

My parents taught me that other people's influence through love and giving is an essential part of my life. In following the examples of my parents, I have been fortunate to be involved in several community, educational, and church-related organizations. My parents always encouraged me to "give back" and "leave the world a better place than I found it." It has been my guiding light, telling me that "giving back" to God and the world is essential, and this book is an opportunity to do that.

I wish to give recognition to Jamie Welty for his excellent skills in accomplishing the comprehensive editing of this book and giving helpful suggestions in its content. Without Jamie's and Kathy's suggestions, this book would not have been possible.

In addition, I acknowledge the many people who have shared and contributed a part of their lives, their intellect, their work, and their personal skills with me so that I could be a part of their rich lives as they were part of mine. There have been several people who have had particular effects on my work life. Steve Woitovitch helped me start in my profession as did Walt Solarz. Dr. Rudy Magnony, Dr. Bob Karl, Glen Yoder, Linda Fields, Terry Remer, Cassandra Galbrith, Dr. Maxine Mays, Dr. Norm Nieson, Dr. Roger Gove, Dr. Levester Cannon, Jerry Johnson, Pat Rafter, Ray Anderson, and Dan Housepan were especially helpful in my years of service to the state of Ohio. Special thanks go to Joe Auberger, who was a great professional and also allowed me to live rent-free with him when I was stationed in Columbus.

When I returned to county service, Doug McVey, a friend, coworker, and ultimately my boss, was an outstanding influence on my professional and personal life. Other influences in my Wood County service were Dave Miller, Linda Donley, Rob Spence, Bill Clifford, Liz Sheets, Melinda Slusser, Mary Sehmann, Mark Carpenter, Melanie Stretchbery, Michele Solether, Greg Bair, Steve Foster, and Donna Beam. In Henry County, I cannot forget Jack Boyd, Cheryl Smith, Sherry DeWyer, Kaye Wesche, Verlinda Schantz, Sandy Karmol, Bill Wicks, Paul Oehrtman, John Wilhelm, Robin Small, Rita Franz, John Hanna, Rick Edmonds, and many others.

This book would not have been possible if it had not been for my publisher, Xlibris. Dez Suarez worked with me through the entire process, and I owe much to her hard work. The staff supported my every need to make this book the best it could be.

Introduction and Overview

About the Direction and Title

The direction of this book is to cover the years I spent in the world of work and my associated private life at that time. To say that my years working in my career were enjoyable and challenging would be an understatement. My private life was also enjoyable and challenging. My life in these years was in many ways a mystery. As you read, you will see many eventful happenings and energy whose base was my God and Savior. It is my hope that *God Keeps On Giving* will be a book as good as the book *People +Me*.

The Influence of Others and Me

While this book is about my adult life, I wanted it to be as much as possible about other people's lives. As time passed, another thought about the title of my book struck me. I am but a product of all my experiences, which include all other people, if I am open to them. It works another way. Other people who are open to me would have the capability of showing reflections of me in their lives. We are all more like others than different when we analyze their influence on our lives and ours on theirs.

Our influences on others and theirs on us are at times recognized. Often influences are not recognized, but they do take place. The importance of influences is that they do take place and are often helpful to others, not that people get credit. In these writings, recognition for helpful actions is many times an incomplete act.

Goals

Knowing and getting to where one wishes to be in life is of paramount importance. That is why my life has been driven by goals. I would speculate that some of my major goals are similar to many of your goals: to love God, to obtain an education, to have meaningful relationships, to fall in love, to marry, to have children, and to be successful at one's profession. In the end, we hope to find sources of fulfillment and happiness. One other more unusual goal for me was to write this book based on my experiences. All these goals had one common denominator: to help me live a worthwhile existence and, if possible, in the process, help other people on their life journeys.

Support

In pursuing my goals, I have realized that other people often supported me even when I thought I was trying to help them. Over the years, I have found, and it will be evident as you read, that the greatest help I have received was from God. I feel my twin who died at three months in utero has been another important influence on me.

Writing the Book

As I have grown older and experienced various events, I made it a practice to constantly document and share the many good and not-so-positive times in my life. The passing of people, particularly my father, mother, sister, and especially my son Mark, as well as many friends and neighbors, has always caused me to think about life's journey. My hope is that I can pay homage to the many people and the most influential being in my life, God. When I have a potentially noticeable experience, either in the present or past, I tried to quickly evaluate the happening to see if it is one that I can document and share. It is exciting for me to have the opportunity to share my life and the people in my life with others. It is actually more than exciting; it is a major driving force in my life to develop this book for others' enjoyment and benefit. While it is impossible to sum up one's life in a book, it is possible to leave behind stories about many other wonderful people and myself.

It was never my intention to embarrass, make fun of, or in any way put down anyone in my writings. If I made an error in judgment and hurt someone, I am sorry. You see, writing this book is a risk. The risk is that, at times, I may not convey the information in the best possible manner, and it would be offensive. To guard against this possibility, I have obtained permission from others when appropriate. I would be remiss if I did not acknowledge the unsought encouragement that frequently accompanied many of the permissions that I received from people I was privileged to include in the book.

In writing this book, I have striven to make the text interesting, the contents related to the readers' needs, entertaining yet not dragging on, and one that can be read in either short or longer periods with the use of vignettes. It is important that the text be understood by the intended audience and that the content has some commonality with the readers' lives. I ask you to enjoy the readings and forgive any unintentional errors in the text.

Experiences in our lives are unique to each of us. No other person can go through them as we have. Yet experiences do usually have similarities with other people. For example, when we were into the Halloween holiday, we had the anticipation of obtaining lots of candies. We were also into choosing the right costume and going with our siblings or friends door to door in the neighborhood. When we hear, see, think, or read about Halloween, we identify with these memories. As you read this book, my hope is that you can identify with many of the experiences I have gone through and enjoy parts of your life again.

One Book Becomes Two

I invite you to join me in reliving my life experiences and important lessons I have learned from them. As I began writing the book, the number of pages dictated that two books must be the result. The first volume covers my life from the beginning up to and including my first year of marriage and is titled *People + Me*. The second volume covers my professional career and exemplifies as the title states that *God Keeps On Giving* to me professionally and personally.

Influence of Others

Many people have made a difference in my life. I have seen that everyone I have known or will meet may potentially affect my life in some way. A poem sent to me for Christmas in 2007 by Maxine Mobley, grandmother to my daughter-in-law, Tara, written by an unknown author, captured my sentiments on the influence of other people affecting my life very accurately. Part of the poem went like this:

> *For I am but a total of the many folks I've met*
> *And you happen to be one of those I prefer never to forget,*

And whether I have known you for many years or few,
In some way you have had a part of shaping things I do.

Everyone's life is shaped by others. Please enjoy how mine has been shaped. Possibly by you.

PART I

The First Years of Employment in the County Board of Mental Retardation

CHAPTER 1

Richland County Physical Education
and Recreation Director

Introduction

My first book, *People + Me*, dealt with my life and the influence of people on me in my early year. I had prayed to God in my freshman year at John Carroll University to help me through the challenging studies ahead of me. As my prayers were answered and I graduated from John Carroll, a whole new set of needs began to unfold. It became evident that the world was a happy yet a very challenging place in terms of my education, my profession, and my private life. As these challenges surfaced, I would again and again ask God for help. He would time and again help me, and this set the stage for the title to my second book, *God Keeps On Giving*. The result of God's help in education was four college degrees, ending in a Ph.D. in educational administration and supervision. God's help in my professional career resulted in forty-one years of service in the area of mental retardation, soon to be known as developmental disabilities. My community service has been an enjoyment of several organizations in which I have many times been voted the leader or chairperson. My private life has been blessed with a wonderful wife, two sons, an exceptional daughter-in-law, and thus far two very special grandsons.

I believe God will keep on giving in a way that is not always what I ask. Nevertheless, my family has adjusted to what God has given and been happy.

This chapter covers my first professional year of employment. Our courtship, marriage, and first year together were covered in the first book. Our marriage after January 1969 is covered in this chapter.

As I looked back on my professional career, I saw many actions that turned out to be helpful to many people. As I listened to a homily by Fr. Herb Weber on October 17, 2015, I heard that success is serving others. I knew that what Father Herb said was true, and I knew that this statement was the cornerstone of my life as God kept on giving me the opportunity to serve others as well as my maker, God.

My First Professional Employment After College

I was going through an employment agency, actually the some agency my elder brother, Walt, had used. My reason for finding a job, other than the usual economic reason, was that my future father-in-law had told me that I couldn't marry his daughter, the love of my life, unless I had a full-time job. While I might have somewhat agreed with him, I was confident that there were many jobs out there that I could obtain.

I ended up with two job possibilities from the employment agency, working at Smucker's, a jelly and jam company, or working at the Richland Newhope Center, also known as the Richland County Board of Mental Retardation and Developmental Disabilities Program, located in Mansfield, Ohio. I interviewed in Downtown Mansfield at a nice restaurant in the Leland Hotel. Present was a board member and the superintendent. I can't remember the board member's name, but I do remember that they knew what they were doing as they recommended hiring me. I believe I ordered a hamburger as that was the only thing on the menu I could eat fast. It was familiar to me, and it would allow me time to answer the interview questions.

The job was titled physical education and recreation director. The pay in 1968 was less than $5,000 a year for a nine-month contract. The enrollment in the school and workshop was around two hundred people. The center was one of eighty-eight county programs in the state of Ohio, which served persons with mental retardation and developmental disabilities. Simply put, the programs served individuals with mental retardation or significant subaverage general intellectual functioning existing concurrently with and demonstrated through deficits in adaptive behavior. Adaptive behavior includes the ability to communicate, travel around the community, prepare meal, and more. These deficits are manifested during the developmental period. These adaptive behaviors are essential for us to be able to live out our daily lives.

While people with mental retardation and developmental disabilities could have mental illness involvement, their primary diagnosis was usually mental retardation and developmental disabilities. Mental retardation is a very large subdivision of developmental disabilities. Developmental disabilities is a more broad term and includes areas such as cerebral palsy, epilepsy, or autism. These conditions are closely related to mental retardation and may be eligible for services under the programs offered in Ohio, eventually called the county boards of developmental disabilities. These guidelines depend on being a substantial handicap in areas of significant deficits. The condition originated before age of eighteen and can be expected to continue indefinitely. Mental illness involves a person who is having difficulty in dealing with reality.

Back to the interview, as I stated, it went well. I heard nothing from Smucker's and was offered the job with Richland Newhope Center. This position gave me the opportunity to continue to fulfill my promise to God that I had made in college. That promise was to give back to God somehow and service other human beings for the support in helping me attain a college education. While this promise was not something that had to be repaid immediately upon graduation, it was nice to get an early start.

I immediately enrolled in college to earn my teaching certification. I began to read everything I could put my hands on regarding physical development and the developmental disabilities population. The teachers and other employees were very accepting of me, and I tried to become friends with all of them. I was the only male teacher. I also worked part time at Big Bear grocery store, and Kathy worked at the Mansfield Memorial Nursing Home. I had desires to be an attorney, but my profession went in other directions. Little did I know that in a few years, I would be involved in federal and state courts, dealing with legal matters. It is a good time to look at some of the experiences I had while employed at Richland Newhope Center.

It was very exciting for me to begin my first full-time professional position in Richland County at the Newhope Center. The start of my job was late August to early September 1967. I was to learn that in my professional career, an important part of my work experiences would be linked back to my childhood days and more specifically to my workdays on the farm. While the examples of work, religion, and family that my mother and father gave me were important to me, the long days, physical challenges, and creative thought processes in accomplishing the work tasks on the farm required much physical and mental energy. A quick look at a day on the farm has always given me a good perspective on tools that were helpful in my adult work life.

Programs

Home-Based Specialist and Preschool

The board served around two hundred people in 1967. One of the first philosophies I learned about people with disabilities is "Label jars, not people." In other words, people with mental retardation and developmental disabilities are no different from other people except for their ability to learn and the extent of their learning. Using the word "retards" in any way, especially joking or making fun of people with disabilities, was a put-down where a put-down was not needed. The services offered at the center were growing and were some of the best I have seen in Ohio. The programs offered started from before or at birth and until a person passed. The first program to be offered started with a home-based specialist. When a couple knew it was going to have a developmental delay, counseling services were provided. Once the baby was born, services could be given immediately at the hospital and at home. Services would be to help the parents adjust to a special child and to be able to assess progress and other daily living skills such as motor development.

Up to the age of three, individuals would be eligible for early intervention, and then at the age of three, a preschool option was next. Ancillary services being offered or in the process of being offered were occupational therapy, physical therapy, speech and hearing therapy, and physical development. The saying with early childhood programs is you pay now or you pay later. In other words, if you put money into early childhood programs, children can learn adaptive behaviors and job-related skills such as attending to task, fine and gross motor skills. You will not pay as much later.

School Age

The next phase of the programs was school age programs. The school age program lasted until the student was ready for work. There was a head teacher or experienced teacher who had been involved with the program for many years. Students were divided into classroom by largely age and the number of students in the class. The Individual Program Plan was coming into being at that time, which meant every student must have their own plan to meet their unique individual learning needs. I can remember participating in the conference room with all the other teachers and the superintendent in coming up with a methodology and plans to meet each student's needs. Parents were also to be involved.

Adult Services

Adult programs included a choice of employment programs—supported employment in the community or employment in a sheltered workshop. The sheltered workshop was located behind the school in the same building. At this time, the sheltered workshop was a program that most adults in the program participated. There were assembly jobs and disassembly jobs. One of the disassembly jobs was with the local electric company, and it involved tearing apart meters for the scrap metal. The workshop director oversaw all the programs in the adult center. Another area important in the adult program was the habilitation programs. Habilitation programs are working with individuals so that they can learn new skills. Rehabilitation skills program is the relearning of skills once known but not presently able to be exhibited. Daily living skills such as living in a community setting with other people or by oneself can be either a habilitation or rehabilitation skill.

In 1967, the facilities housing the Newhope programs were completely new. The school, workshop, and administrative offices were completed, and the dedication ceremonies were held in the fall of that year with Muriel Humphrey being the honored guest. Mrs. Humphrey was the wife of the former vice president of the United States Hubert Humphrey, who served from 1965 to 1969 under Pres. Lyndon Johnson.

Physical Development and Recreation

Recreation programs such as parties, gym shows, swimming, and Boy Scouts were some of the options offered to the Newhope participants. At this time, programs for people with mental retardation were growing, and several new programs would emerge in the next few years.

Physical development or physical education and recreation programs were my areas of responsibility. The program consisted of scheduled time for each class and the workshop so that the physical and recreational aspects of their lives were more active than passive. In an unpublished study years earlier I was to conduct with Dr. Robert Blackwell of BGSU, it was shown that inactive activities such as watching television or listening to the radio were by far more frequent activities for people with developmental disabilities and mental retardation than any combination of active activities. Physical activities have a positive effect on the body, and it contributes to a lessening of obesity.

The culmination of the physical activity program each year was a gym show given by the students on a week night during the late spring of the year near the end of the school year. The first gym show was on March 4, 1968, and the second on March 24, 1969. Each class had several skills it would exhibit from the very young to the oldest student. Ball activities, walking activities, and marching to music were some activities exhibited by the younger children. The middle-age students played floor hockey, exhibited skills on the trampoline, and participated in line games, which combined taking one's turn in a skill, and more advanced activities such as dribbling or shooting baskets. The oldest classes would square dance, play basketball games, and exhibit highly developed activities on the trampoline. The gym shows were to take place each year and were one of the highlights of the school year. The show lasted around ninety minutes. After the show, my wife and I were in the habit of having a staff party at our house as a thank-you for all the help the teachers gave to the physical development program.

The lead-up to the second-year gym show did not go as well as the first. I contracted a bug the day before the show, and I was the only person who knew the contents of the show. On the morning of the show, I was home sick. I knew I needed a last practice, so I went in for the last practice and felt pretty good. I went home and almost immediately was sick again. I told the staff I would be there that evening. It came time to leave the show, and I was not feeling so good. I went anyway to the show and felt pretty good, even though I had not eaten much that day. The gym show went well. We had our staff party at our house, and when the last person left the party, I became sick again. I never did figure out how or why I made it through that day. Someone somewhere was helping me.

Writing to Be Published

The superintendent had encouraged me to write articles on some of the various physical development activities. Physical development for people with mental retardation was a developing area, and I was fortunate enough to write on several of these areas and to have them published in a national magazine. One of the articles was on the use of balloons to slow down the motion of an object so that coordination skills were more easily developmentally acquired. This article had significance to me personally as well as professionally because balloons were one of the products that I had been exposed to in my early years at home. The firm my father worked for, the Pioneer Rubber Company, manufactured and marketed balloons. Balloons were a common plaything around our house, and all these factors made the use of balloons in one of my instructional writings very appropriate. The second article written while I was in Mansfield was on walking skills. This article centered on the development of walking skills using bamboo sticks. The sticks were held at various heights and positions so that everyday actions of walking over, through, or around were more easily mastered as a result of this training.

The articles were more visual and understood as a result of our photographer friends, Bill and Rachael Daniels, from rural Willard. Bill and Rachael were more than friends and would never accept any reimbursement for labor or supplies. In those days, I was so green on publishing that I never thought to give credit to Bill and Rachael for their photographic skills!

A curriculum on physical development was another of my writings, and it helped me as a teacher and consultant in working with other teachers in that area. The writing down of information was a skill I used ongoing in my life. Taxing the mind for information was made easier by referring to one's notes.

Swimming with Billy

Richland Newhope Center used the local YWCA pool for its swimming lessons. I had developed check sheets for each student and asked the teachers to help me keep them updated. Instruction started with blowing bubbles and could lead to actually swimming.

It was on one weekday morning that I was in the pool and working with students and teachers on the different skills needed for each of the students' ability levels. After instructing a few students, I noticed one of the newer students, Billy, approaching me from behind. Billy was about sixteen years old, had not been in a school program for most of his life, and was one of the largest and strongest people in the school. He had always been a very happy person and constantly had the biggest smile in the world. Before I could respond to Billy's movement, I noticed that Billy had put his massive arms around me and was pushing me under the water. I lost my footing and was completely under the water. I couldn't scream and was not able to breathe. As they say, my life flashed in front of me.

Since I had taken lifesaving as well as swimming for my Eagle Scout award at the Willard Pool, I had one option to put in place. Since there was no help close to me as probably nobody knew that I was drowning, I immediately swung both of my arms to the side and tried to make contact with the side of Billy's body to prompt the action of him loosening his bear hug. Thank God I was successful as his grip loosened, and I broke free. I don't think Billy knew that he was hurting me. After that experience, I never allowed anyone to come up behind me and have the advantage of pulling me under the water.

Happenings While Living in Mansfield

My Landlady

There was a gap of a few months from the time I started my job in Mansfield until I was married. I needed a place to board from August until December. As I looked around, I found one bedroom in a beautiful house where an older little lady lived. The rent was reasonable, and I was to find out my landlady was the best baker I had known. She would usually bake early in the morning. One of my favorite treats that would wake me up at around six o'clock in the morning was the smell of pecan rolls. These small rolls smelled like a million bucks and tasted the same. The pecan rolls would hit my mouth, and immediately, I would feel there was no taste that could compare. Another baked good that would likely melt in my mouth was her lemon chiffon pie. I had not heard of this type of pie before she offered me a piece. This pie would start with the richest crust known and develop into a never-to-forget-taste treat.

The Afternoon Break

During this time after work, I wasn't married, so I got into the practice of either taking a nap or going over to my sister-in-law's to play cards. Usually, her four children were both napping, so Judy had a little break to play. Both of these practices ceased after I was married. There was far too much activity around my house to either sleep or play cards.

Junkyard

Junkyards have always infatuated me. There are so many different items there that I can spend hours just looking around. When the recycling of one's metal became a big thing, I became even more interested in the junkyard. Before being interested in junkyards, I was interested by the necessity of going to the landfill or the dump in Mansfield. Junkyards are for several types of metal, and landfills or dumps are for waste of all kinds. This interest in dumps came about with two families as each Saturday morning, my brother Walt's family and my family would venture to the landfill to deposit our weekly trash.

One Saturday morning, Kathy received a phone call from Jackie, my brother's eldest girl, who was four years old at the time. She asked Kathy, "What we are you doing?" Kathy said, "We were messing around." Jackie, in a very sincere voice, said, "We don't mess around at our house." The trip to the dump that day centered on the topic of messing around at Joe and Kathy's and not messing around at Walt and Judy's house. It was always a treat to throw out our junk, and then we pulled out of the way of the big equipment and watched the bulldozer push everything over the edge. To this day, going to the landfill is a big treat as they now have a section for metal and other recyclables. It is a real treat with all the big machines and different drop-off points for batteries, tires, water heaters, refrigerators, and more. My dream of being a junkman or recycling specialist who travels the streets with a pickup truck trying to find a treasure is still alive but is fading.

Walt's Neighbor

Next to my brother's house lived a man and a woman and two girls in their late teens or early twenties. The young girls seemed to have an interest in me as they usually came outside and seemed to be looking at me when Kathy and I were visiting Walt, Judy, and the kids.

On a rather warm summer day, we were sitting in the backyard after supper, looking around the yard and the two neighbors' yards. In the one neighbor's yard, as had happened so many times before, my central gaze went to the hearse that they had parked in the backyard. At that time, I saw one of the girls walk out the back door carrying a pan of dishwater and start down the steps. The neighbor girl was so carefully trying to gracefully go down the steps as she glanced over toward me when I saw two feet go into the air and the water from the dish bowl leave the basin and go straight up into the air. At this point, it was apparent that the water and her body in the air must come down. The water came down and hit the neighbor, and then her body hit the stairs. My worst fear was that she had hurt her back. As luck would have it, she merely picked up the water basin, had a brief laugh, and disappeared into the house. It was all that we could do to not laugh about an incident that had elements of being funny and potential elements of injury.

Big Bear and Snyder's Chips

Kathy and I became big fans of the Big Bear grocery store located on Park Avenue West across from Big Bill's discount store. In fact, we liked the store so much that a little less than a year after our marriage, I started working as a stock boy on Friday nights and Saturdays. I also worked with my brother, Walt, doing remodeling jobs in the area. We could use the money as my teacher's salary was around $5,000 a year, and Kathy's part-time wages helped but did not solve our financial needs. We loved to shop at Big Bear because I knew everyone, the prices were reasonable, and the food has always been an interest of Kathy and me.

On a very cold day in January 1969, Kathy and I had purchased our groceries and had pulled the car up our driveway close to our back door to unload our prizes. The weather condition was not only cold, but it was also near blizzard conditions. I had taken in the first two bags of groceries and was bringing in a grocery bag and a four pack of the new glass quart bottles containing 7 Up. As I walked in the kitchen door, the carton containing the bottles broke and hit the floor and shattered. I had not yet closed the door, and the cold air came in on the already very cold spillage. I looked down and began to think how much money I was out because of the faulty cartoon. Bad things got worse because to me and my wife's amazement, the 7 Up had frozen on the kitchen floor. I closed the door and tried to wipe up the sticky mess, only to find out that the frozen 7 Up would allow no clean-up. Eventually, it began to thaw, and I mopped five or six times so that we could walk across the floor without having our shoes stick to it!

I got to thinking about this incident with the 7 Up and decided to write to the Big Bear office and explain to them how one of their products had caused us an unpleasant evening. Not only was the experience unpleasant but also the idea of losing our hard-earned money because of a defect of one of their products did not sit well. I sent the letter and was discussing with Kathy about two weeks later if I should call the company to see if they had received my letter. Kathy thought I should wait a few more days before calling. The very next day, we had just arrived home from work, and I saw someone park their car in the driveway, get out of the car, and pull a bag out of the back seat. The man came to our back door and knocked. I walked over to the door and asked the man to come in. We sat down in the front room. The man explained he was from Big Bear and that they wanted to apologize to us for the experience we had had with the container breaking and the shattered bottles as well as the trouble we had with the floor freezing. He gave us a whole bag of groceries and talked to us for a good fifteen to twenty minutes. We thanked him for his time and the groceries.

That evening, Kathy and I went over to see Walt and his family. During the course of the evening, we explained to Walt and Judy about the free groceries from Big Bear because of the broken pop container and bottles of 7 Up. Almost immediately, Judy began to tell us about some potato chips that she had just thrown out because they were defective. She wrote a letter to the company within a few minutes, and confidently, she told us she was going to get something for her defective chips. She mailed the letter the next day. Two weeks later, she received a letter from the potato chip company. Judy opened the letter and was excited about the prospect of receiving something for her defective chips. She did get something for her chips. She got a letter apologizing for the defective chips and an explanation how they had fixed the process. She did not receive anything other than the letter, and she is still reminded by Kathy and me about the great settlement she received from her defective potato chips.

Gold Label, Leaning Tower of Pizza, and Cards

Walt and Judy introduced us to three of the most cherished activities we experienced in Mansfield. I did not say the most cherished activity; I said two of the most cherished activities. I also want to set the record straight on another area. My sister-in-law's nickname was actually her real last name, Kovach. I do not know if her father, Andy, and mother, Mary, ever knew about this honor. Those cherished activities were eating pizza and drinking beer. Now it was not just any kind of beer or pizza that we liked to experience. It was the Leaning Tower of Pizza and Gold Label Beer. The Leaning Tower of Pizza shop was a well-established business when we came to Mansfield. The pizza was very famous, and it was near impossible to eat too much of it. Actually, it was hard to eat too much pizza because we didn't always have the money to buy a pizza. When we did, there was no comparison. If we went back to Mansfield for any reason, we would find the Leaning Tower Pizza shop to enjoy a pizza that is beat by none. Walt's kids had the most well-tuned noses known. They could be fast asleep in bed, and if a Leaning Tower of Pizza came in the house, they knew it, and they would want a piece.

The second half of our venture was always the Gold Label Beer. Gold Label had a pretty good taste, but the price could be beat by no other as it cost $2.99 a case. It was always a good feeling to have just a few dollars and be able to buy a case of beer. Yes, the price made up for any lack of taste in the beer.

The third most cherished activity at Walt and Judy's house was playing cards. While there was more than one type of cards played, euchre was by far the most played game. For some reason, unknown to Walt and me, Judy and Kathy would accuse us of cheating at cards. Imagine, us cheating at cards. Walt and I had a discussion about this false cheating charge, and it was decided that we really didn't need to cheat because we were just plain good at cards.

Free Gift Day

Judy and Kathy were both "shop until they drop" people. Whenever there were special gifts to be given, always you would find Judy and Kathy. On one occasion, several of the local merchants in Mansfield were giving away special gifts for new residents through the Welcome Wagon coupons who entered their store. For example, the hardware store would give away a small light for entering the store, the gas station would give you a small ice scraper, and the candy store would give a few pieces of candy. Kathy and Judy had hit most of the stores in town and had acquired a large array of nice items. There was one more store that they wanted to go to, and that was a furniture store. The furniture store carried many items, and there were few in the category of being inexpensive. Judy and Kathy were talking to each other as they were driving to the furniture store about the great giveaway that they would receive. They were talking about receiving a small lamp or an inexpensive vase. They composed themselves as they walked in the front door. One of the clerks came up to the pair and asked if they were looking for any special piece of furniture. Judy responded that they were just looking. When they were ready to leave, they asked if there was a giveaway for them. The lady in the business office looked around for a giveaway. Finally, the employee discovered the gift for my wife and Judy. The expensive gift they were to receive turned out to be a very small inexpensive plastic dustpan. Judy and Kathy from that point forward lowered their expectations for giveaway merchandise. From that point on, the plastic dustpan held a place of honor as they could use the dustpan and were forever telling the story of the inexpensive dustpan in a classy furniture store.

The Party

Mary and Tom were friends of ours in Mansfield. One of our mutual activities was having a party. The party was drinks, food, and talk. We met nice couples, and the evening proceeded with a few board games. As the evening wore on, Mary said," There are a lot of people leaving." We all looked around and agreed. Shortly after that, we saw a couple exchanging their apartment key, and we realized we were at one of those swap-your-mate parties. We never actually figured out all the details on how the actual swap of partners happened, but the three other prudes with me being fourth decided that the party was over for us and what we had hoped to be a nice, enjoyable social evening had turned out to be not so nice and too sociable.

Malabar Farms

Near Mansfield was a small town called Lucas, Ohio. One of the distinctions of this area was that the famed novelist and journalist Louis Bromfield had established a scientific farm named Malabar Farms. Malabar Farms was a subject of his writings. Bromfield's novel *Early Autumn* earned the title of being a Pulitzer Prize winner.

It was during the summer of 1968 that my aunt Lucy and uncle Lyle came to Ohio with their five children; age wise, it was twins Kevin and Robin at age eleven on the high end, Rose and Keith in the middle, and the youngest, Kristopher, age four. Lucy, the fourteenth of sixteen children of my mother's siblings was a fun-loving lady, always willing to smile, and had a good laugh. Lyle was like Lucy and me, a shorter person, and he was able to carry on an intelligent conversation with about anyone and always showed a great deal of respect for other people.

Lucy had called me and Kathy and told us that they were in town to visit with us and Walt and his wife. With fourteen people, we needed many cars to go anywhere. It was decided that we would visit Malabar Farms as there were to be many souvenirs to see that Bromfield had brought back to the United States from his extensive travels as a foreign correspondent. A ride in the country was always a welcome activity with young children.

It was rather late in the evening as we began our expedition, but if Lucy and her children were to see anything in the area, it must be done then. It was decided that Walt and I would drive. As I looked at my gas gauge, I noticed that I had a little over a quarter tank of gas. Since there was no time to get gas and I thought I had enough gas, we ventured toward rural Lucas. The directions we had seemed to claim the location of Malabar Farms was diverse. After becoming lost on at least four occasions, we did happen upon the famed Malabar Farms at about dark. Since it was dark, we were not able to enter the grounds, but we did look from our cars and see some older buildings and some cows.

Having concluded our trip to Malabar Farms, we needed to seek our way home. We tried to figure out our best method of leaving the area and concluded it would be with great frustration. As I looked at my gas indicator, I noted that I was now very low. I figured I had gas enough for thirty miles or just enough to find a gas station. We proceeded to retrace our tracks, including being lost four times, to find the closest gas station. We consulted our maps at least eight times, only to find each time we were more lost than the time before and had less gas than our last map check. The night was very dark, and the children had enough of this stop-and-go driving. A prayer was the only logical direction, and we prayed to St. Christopher, patron saint of travelers. We needed a miracle, and that was what we found. When it looked as if running out of gas was our only option, we came out of the rural county to a major highway, and a gas station appeared. We were all happy to pull into the gas station. I was very relieved because I did not know what I would be doing with four children beside the road, no water, no gas, and many mosquitoes. My aunt Lucy to this date still thinks I should have run out of gas.

Wood Street Café

Anyone who lived in the Wood Street area, close to the Mansfield General Hospital, would have the opportunity to visit this neighborhood grill and bar. The bar was noted for its clean atmosphere and the fact that anyone of any background was always welcome to tip a few. Walt and I would once in a while go into the café after we were done with our second job of remodeling homes. After parent meetings at the Richland Newhope Center, some of the staff and parents would have a drink at the cafe. A trademark of one of the parents was to order a splint of champagne. At the time, I was not accustomed to drinking champagne, but as I have grown to make my own champagne, I also drank more champagne, and it is now one of my favorite drinks. The Wood Street Café was an establishment that should have been available in more neighborhoods. While a drink was usually not harmful to the user, the friendships developed and nurtured as a result of this positive communications setting could last a lifetime.

Bob and Bob

Two fellow educators I was to grow to know and respect were Bob and Bob. In my second year at the Richland Newhope Center, I wanted to take coursework to earn my master's degree. It was at that time that I asked the two Bobs if I could ride with them after school from Mansfield to Bowling Green, Ohio. I arranged for a class the same night as theirs, and we left at three o'clock, were at Bowling Green in time for our six o'clock class, and then we ate on our way back before arriving home between twelve and one o'clock in the morning. It was a fun trip because each of the other two riders was very compatible and possessed an array of interesting experiences and a few jokes to lighten up the ride. I would also look for and tell a few jokes so as not to be seen as a freeloader. On the way back, we would stop at a restaurant around Bucyrus for breakfast. The restaurant was a good place to eat until the time we found garbage in the hallway leading to the restroom. It was decided very quickly to change our eating location as our stomachs were forever tainted by this experience.

The Cottage

My mother and father had built a cottage on the Huron River near Huron, Ohio, when I was attending John Carroll University. The cottage was the center for fishing, skiing, swimming, and general relaxation. I remember well many good times we had at the cottage. One memory was a fishing trip with Big Butch and Mildred Rothschild, his son Butch, my father, my brother Mike, Kathy, and me. We had gone fishing for perch, and literally we had caught hundreds. In those days, most fishermen would clean their fish as soon as they were done fishing. With a catch like this, it would take hours to scale the fish and cut the meat from the skeleton. This is exactly what happened this day. We came back from the fishing, dumped all the perch in the boat well, washed the fish, and everyone assumed their role. The role was usually either scaling, filleting, or frying. As the cleaning began to roll down to the finish, Big Butch, Mildred, and my mother began to fry the perch. Fresh perch is a fish in its own class, and that class is one of the best fish meals in the world. With the cleaning complete, we needed to clean up the scales and filleted the bodies of the perch. Drinking a refreshing drink was part of the ritual, and there was always plenty of beer available for the thirsty workers.

I can remember picking up a fish sandwich and taking a big bite out of it. It was scrumptious. At that same time, someone had left an article in the canoe parked next to the boat well in the Huron River, and I was asked to retrieve it. I walked out to the boat eating my sandwich and drinking my beer. As I began to approach the boat, I did not think. I put one foot in the boat and had one on shore. As soon as I put my foot into the canoe, I felt the canoe beginning to separate from the dock. As I began to switch the pressure off the leg in the canoe toward shore, I found that not only could I not move my foot to shore, but the canoe was also widening its distance from the shore, forcing me into what is termed the splits. I was beginning to fall backward into the autumn water. I struggled little as I splashed into the water. I was embarrassed, wet, and suffering a bruised ego. Fortunately, I had dry clothes and was able to change without many people knowing of my foolish move.

An extremely enjoyable game at the cottage in the evening was playing cards. Being more specific, we would find that euchre was the game of choice. It was on one autumn evening that Mike, Kathy, Father, and I were engaged in a hot game of euchre. Euchre is a game in which there are partners. When we played cards, it was not uncommon to fish at the same time. On this evening, I had a few lines out for catfish, sheepshead, or carp. I had just caught a large carp and was starting back to the cabin. There was a sliding door on the back of the cottage. It was dark, and I thought I had left the screen door open. Either I hadn't left the screen door open or someone else had shut it. I tried walking in the door and found that the closed screen door had a very strong screen. I hit the screen as I tried to walk through the door, and I ended up about four feet from the screen door on my back on the lawn. It was easy to see the screen showed me no mercy.

We resumed our playing and noticed that Dad was sitting a short distance from the playing table. This caused him to lean forward and almost leave his seat to make his play. The three of us had an idea employing successive approximation. That is, that a person will learn an act if little by little, the desired behavior is introduced in intervals. In this case, the desired behavior was to have our father leave his chair and go a greater distance each time to reach the table and make his play. Without our father's knowledge, we moved the table and our chairs farther away from Dad. Within a few seconds, Dad was walking a few feet across the room to play his cards. He noticed what was happening, and we decided our fun was over. This single event was to haunt our father for years to come!

Boy Scouts from Richland Newhope School

While living in Mansfield, I had the good fortune to start a Boy Scout troop for the developmentally disabled. Several parents assisted me on various outings with the troop. Some of the boys did not have rides to the evening meetings, so I would pick them up on my way to the meetings. On one occasion, I was to pick up one of the scouts. This boy was my first pickup, so I had gone up to the house and knocked on the door to tell them I was ready to pick up the scout. I was invited in as the boy was not ready. As I walked in the door, I noticed that the scout's three sisters were at the house. Shortly after I went into the house, I heard some people coming in the house. These people turned out to be the husbands of the three sisters. As the men walked in, I saw them stop dead in their tracks and look at me. I felt out of place being in the house with the three sisters. I had to think fast so I could properly tell them why I was there. Without thinking, I shouted out that I was the scoutmaster of the boys troop. Within a split second, the men proceeded to go about their business and leave me to my own business. The scout was ready to leave, and I was also very ready to get out of the house. I often wondered what would have happened to me if I hadn't well explained to the husbands why I was in the house with their wives.

One of the boy's clothes looked like they were hand-me-downs. Whenever I would make small talk with him about his life, he would add that he had just finished a supper of "beans." I couldn't imagine what it must have been like to have beans for many of my meals.

I really enjoyed being the leader of the troop and working with the boys. I was to leave my job at the Richland Newhope School after two years of service. Unfortunately, there was no one who took my place, so I was afraid the troop might have died.

Boy Scouts Blockhouse

Mansfield was close to the Johnny Appleseed Trail. Johnny Appleseed was a pioneer and missionary, and he was most noted for spreading apple seeds, and these seeds would turn into seedlings and eventually apple trees, which would produce fruit for both man and animal. There was a blockhouse in the middle of Mansfield and a Boy Scout troop called the blockhouse troop. My brother, Walt, and I had the honor of him being the scoutmaster and me the assistant scoutmaster of the troop.

Our leadership came about since my brother worked for IBM. He came in contact with some fellow workers who had sons in the troop, and they needed a scoutmaster. The young scouts were teenagers and liked to participate in various adventures common to their age group. One of the activities of the troop was to go for a hike on the Johnny Appleseed Trail. The day of the walk was a beautiful autumn day. The hills were covered with beautiful foliage, and the scouts were into nature. One of the best happenings of the day was a nonhappening. There were no injuries or cuts, and Mother Nature was the boss. This walk was one of the last activities with the troop as both Walt and I were to move out of the Mansfield area shortly after that hike.

The Move Is On

The completion of my master's degree was foremost in our mind, and the two-hour drive to BGSU was demanding. A job advancement at the Lucas County Board of Mental Retardation and Developmental Disabilities in Toledo, Ohio, made a move possible. It was goodbye to the many good people in the Mansfield area.

CHAPTER 2

Lucas County Special
Services Coordinator

We moved to Wood County, Ohio, to attend BGSU and work in the Lucas County Board of Mental Retardation and Developmental Disabilities. Kathy and I were both enrolled in BGSU. My new job was director of physical education and recreation. This was a new job in Lucas County. My job in Richland County was also a new position with me being the first person to fill the job. Mary, a state program consultant, had taken me under her wing, and she encouraged me to interview for the job. Since I was in need of a job near BGSU, I requested an interview. I always had the idea that Mary had put in a good word for me.

Interview with Walt

My interview was scheduled for late in the day as I was traveling from Mansfield to Toledo, a two-hour drive. As we approached the Larc Lane School in South Toledo, I noticed another person leaving their car. The gentleman came over to the car and said, "Who are you trying to find?" I said, "I am looking for Mr. Solarz, the superintendent." He told me he was Walt Solarz and invited me into the building. I introduced myself and my wife, Kathy. As I began getting out of the car, he asked Kathy if she was going to one of the local malls. She explained that she didn't know the area and would just wait in the car. He invited Kathy to come into the building rather than staying in the car. He told Kathy she could be part of the interview process.

The interview was one of the most enjoyable interviews I had ever experienced. Walt felt comfortable that I was the man for the position. At this point in the interview, he asked Kathy if she had plans to work. Kathy explained that she was a nurse and would be looking for work. Since we only had one car, Kathy would need to find a place of employment that I could drop her off in the morning and pick her up at night. Walt explained that he had a position open in the school that would be available to Kathy if she was interested. Kathy had always believed the old saying, "A bird in the hand is worth two in the bush." We had a very profitable meeting that day as both Kathy and I had obtained jobs within a few weeks of moving to Wood County. Both Kathy and I were to have a very long and positive relationship with Walt and the staff.

Finding a New Home near Bowling Green, Ohio

Kathy and I had less than a month to find a dwelling near Bowling Green. I was to start graduate summer school in June, and we had two weekends to find a rental property. The first weekend, we didn't find anything we liked. We went up on a Friday night of the last weekend we had to find a rental and stayed with friends of ours. We went to bed at a respectable time, but one of the apartment neighbors had decided to burn trash. We shut the window, but once smoke is inside, it will not leave.

We got a few hours' sleep and woke up very early on Saturday morning to look for a newspaper that would carry area rental housing listings. We were standing in Downtown Maumee and saw a newspaper container that was empty. We figured the delivery truck would be coming shortly. We were correct. The papers came off the truck, and we gave the correct change and took the newly printed paper. There was one add that caught our attention. It was a home in the country, and the price was right. We called the number on a pay phone and talked to the owner. He said he had other calls, but we were welcome to come out. It took us less than fifteen minutes to get out to the home.

We met the landlord and saw the house. The house was small yet a large enough home for us. The first floor had a bedroom, a bathroom, a kitchen, and a living room. There were two bedrooms upstairs and a full basement. The house was painted white, and there was a block building behind the house for two cars. We said we would take the house. It seems there is almost always a catch to anything one does in life. The landlord said another couple was interested, and he had promised them the home. We established the fact that if the other person didn't come by noon, we got the house. He agreed. We went over to have a quick lunch at Vick's tavern in Lucky, Ohio. The landlord had recommended Vick's restaurant, and he also recommended the fish sandwiches for lunch. We were on pins and needles because this was the house we wished to rent, and we had no other backup. We ate lunch with not too much interest in the food and went back to the house. By this time, he had over fifty calls, and later, we found that he had over two hundred calls for the house. He asked if we had any children. We said no. He said that we had the house. We made the arrangements to move in, and we were on cloud nine.

Leaving Mansfield and Going to Rural Bowling Green

We had rented a U-Haul truck in Mansfield and had pulled it into our driveway on 21 Glenwood Boulevard. It took us a few hours on Friday night in early June to pack the truck, which tells you we didn't have a lot of possessions after a year and a half of marriage. However, we were proud of everything we owned. We had everything on the truck on Friday night. This included our refrigerator, which obtained power from an extension cord. We kept the refrigerator running so all our refrigerated and our frozen products would not spoil. Wasting food was not something in our vocabulary.

The truck was headed into the driveway, so it needed to be turned around so it could go out of the driveway facing the street. We tried backing out the truck, but it had a trailer hitch on it, which began to dig into the pavement. I tried to turn around the truck in the back of the property, but the hills on both sides wouldn't allow me to turn around. Our neighbor Benny and good friend said, "Let me try to turn the truck around." Benny revved up the engine, turned the wheel real sharp, and began to go forward up the lefty hill. One tire of the front wheels and one tire of the back wheels were on the ground because of the two hills. In other words, it was teetering on two wheels, one back and one forth, with all our belongings in the truck. I thought the truck was going to tip over.

Just when we thought all was lost, Benny put the truck into reverse and gave it the juice. At this point, he had the truck half turned around. He turned the wheel toward the road and once again was three-fourths of the way turned around, teetering on a front wheel and a rear wheel. His last reverse placed the truck in a position 180 degrees different from where it first started, and the truck was ready to go down the hill forward. As I got into the driver's seat and Kathy got into our car, we said our last goodbyes to a man who would do anything for us as he just proved in turning around the truck and almost hurting himself. Benny took a chance and allowed us to be able to go toward Bowling Green. If Benny hadn't turned around the truck, we could still be in Mansfield looking at our truck loaded with all our belongings. As I pulled out of the driveway, I noticed that the trailer hitch was very close to hitting the street.

Arriving at 21655 McCutcheonville Road

As we pulled into our new home near Bowling Green with our dog, Missy, in tow, Walt and his family were there to help us unload. Moving people in the Frederick family means you help others and others help you. After we were about done moving everything into the house, my landlord, Norm Brinker, came to the door with a quart of strawberries as a moving-in present. Norm came in and offered us the strawberries. He looked around at my niece and nephew and said, "Are these your children?" I assured him that they were Walt and Judy's kids, and I introduced him to everyone. As he displayed a big smile, the thought occurred to me that we had told him we didn't have any children, and here were children.

Job Responsibilities in Lucas County

From 1969 until 1973, I was employed in the Lucas County Board of Mental Retardation and Developmental Disabilities. Working in a large county with over twenty departments to communicate and cooperate was no small feat. The majority of the workers were very cooperative, so the ability to offer quality programs was shared by many.

There were several areas in which I was responsible for the overall supervision and, in some cases, the direct provision of services as well. The major funding for the position came from a federal grant in the area of recreation for adult consumers with mental retardation, most of them working in the workshop. The associated program for the school age was physical development. In Lucas County, the overall consumer base was 1,250 consumers. The provision of services in the physical therapy program was provided by a contract with physical therapists. The psychological services were provided first by a board employee and then by the Zucker Center under a contract for services. I supervised these two departments and was responsible for the volunteer coordinator. A more specific look at the job responsibilities in each area will now be presented.

Recreation and Physical Education

There were three school locations for people in the school age program, which was the ages of six to twenty-two. At each of these locations, I worked with the teachers and the students in physical development, otherwise known as physical education. The provision of training in the gross and fine motor skills were the major areas of concentration. The use of ball-handling skills, balance, running, and introduction to various games such as hockey, softball, and basketball at various skill levels were some of the areas of exposure.

Many of these skills were also involved in the Special Olympics program for children and adults in the state of Ohio. The Special Olympics program depends on volunteers, and the Toledo Jaycees provided the first funding and volunteers for this program in Lucas County. I had the privilege of being on the first Special Olympics governing board, the Ohio Athletic Association for the Mentally Retarded, in 1971. One of the programs involving basketball gave the students and adults the first chance to compete in this organized sport within Lucas County as well as other counties. In Special Olympics, participation is the important point.

The *Toledo Blade* did a special article on the basketball program on February 28, 1971, thanks to a contact within the Lucas County system. In this article, I am told appeared one of the first pictures of a disabled person in the paper. The other challenge of this feature article was that I told the *Toledo Blade* that I would do the story as long as the basketball coaches and cheerleader advisors were given credit for the program. The article came out on a Sunday.

The next day was a Monday. The coaches and cheerleader advisors felt they were not given enough credit and thought of leaving the program.

This incident did show me that people can understand even when they feel they have been wronged. This is the type of employee one wants on your side. This employee can work through the negatives that all of us experience at one time or another.

Additional public relations came about as a result of the basketball program for the Lucas County Board of Mental Retardation and Developmental Disabilities. Whenever the basketball games were played, I would call in the results of the game to local television stations such as WTOL TV-Channel 11 and WSPD-Channel 13 in Toledo.

One Friday evening after one of our teams, Larc Lane, played a basketball game, Kathy and I were invited over to the superintendent's house, Walt Solarz. Walt was a sports enthusiast, partially based on his talented wrestler son, Chris. As we listened to the sport results reporting all the area high school games, Larc Lane's score came on the air. It was a great feeling to see the whole county being exposed to the fact that people with disabilities were displaying their athletic abilities with their nondisabled peers.

Several people had made this accomplishment possible. Walt had given endless hours to see the physical development program flourish by grant writing and administrative support. The coaches, players, parents, and I had come up with the everyday support to see that the basketball program flourished.

The physical development program offered the opportunity to have the objectives of the physical development and recreation programs incorporated into the individual education program and the individual habilitation programs, which is the formal programs guide for students or adults in a structured program of instruction.

Special Olympics

It is appropriate that additional information on the Special Olympics program be provided at this time. The founder of the Special Olympics program was a remarkable person, Dick Ruff. Dick did not have the full use of all his limbs. Both of his arms were missing—one above and one below his arm joint—and his leg was missing around the knee. Dick could golf, swim, and do about anything you and I could do. I was told that Dick was the place kicker for the Ohio State Buckeyes in his college years. Dick gave so much, and he died prematurely.

Another remarkable person and friend was Doug McVey from the Wood County Board of Mental Retardation. Together, we spearheaded the Northwest Ohio Special Olympics held at BGSU starting in 1971 and had a repeat performance other years. The program was run by students and other organizations such as the Toledo Jaycees and Fred Kossow and the United Commercial Travelers of America. The Northwest Regional Special Olympics allowed the participants to have a chance at competition for the State Special Olympics. I can still remember sitting with Doug and other helpers the night before the first meet. As I sat there, I couldn't help but think, will this really go off as planned? Will the volunteers show? Will the officials show, and will the weather be nice? The trust I had in Doug and the rest of the people running the show paid off. Everyone did their part, and for the first such event, it looked like we had done it for years.

At times, we had special celebrities such a Dave Wottle, Olympic runner and medalist, and Sid Sink, nine-time All-American running star from BGSU, present and interacting with the participants. I never did figure out who had more fun, the participants or the celebrities. McDonald's restaurants served free over 1,300 hamburgers and orange drink through owner Don Michel and manager Ed Ameen from their two restaurants. I didn't see how those two restaurants could serve their regular customers and jointly produce, transport, and serve all those hamburgers and drinks. Over the years, thousands and thousands of McDonald's hamburgers were to be served throughout the state of Ohio for Special Olympics. Cain's Potato Chips of Bowling Green, Ohio, donated chips for the lunch, and the United Commercial Travelers (UCT) insurance was present, serving their special charitable group, the mentally retarded. The UCT members manned a tent with games and prizes so that they were available for all participants. Fred Kossow not only coordinated UCT for the Special Olympics games, but he was also the head person of the scholarship fund for people involved with the developmentally disabled. Using small banks located at various stores, pennies, nickels, dimes, and quarters became dollars and hundreds of dollars so that teachers could be better educated and give better instruction to the developmentally disabled. Scholarships from the UCT were one of the sources of funds I used to obtain my advanced degrees.

One of the lessons I learned at a participant's expense was you cannot be safe enough in any of the events. When we had wheelchair races at the regional Special Olympics meet, the front wheels came off the ground. As the wheels went down, they turned sideways, and the wheelchair turned over with the participant hitting the track on the front of her body. There was no serious accident, but the event was not forgotten by anyone involved.

In the early 1970s, there were organized state training sessions for the Ohio Athletic Association's members. Dick Ruff procured room and board as well as a large hall for the presentations of physical development and recreation training. It was in the evening at a local pub that the members were introduced to a drink containing many different spirits. The drink was called the Killer. The drink almost lived up to its name.

It was at the beginning that I was asked to coordinate meals for the State Special Olympics summer games at Ohio State University. Kathy, sons Mark and Joe, and the Carpenters, Carol and Ron, as well as their children, Mark and Rhonda, were involved for over thirty years in the meals committee. Carol was for years the co-coordinator of this event.

Several years ago, Michele Solether and her niece, Morgan, and nephew, Traver, became regulars. Michele developed systems that allowed over twenty thousand meals to be served for athletes and coaches. Later, Michele and my son Mark became coordinators of the meals committee for the Summer Olympics. I must mention Ron and Mary Jo Bosch as they have worked to provide family volunteers to assemble and serve eight thousand meals. Many challenges such as frozen orange juice, rain, loss of food sponsors, and other conditions were dealt with as they occurred. I marvel at volunteers who keep coming back year after year to work in the hot sun to provide the necessary meals.

One of the most moving parts of the Ohio State Special Olympics is when the law enforcement agencies come together for the Olympic torch light at the Jesse Owens Memorial Stadium. This included the Ohio State Highway Patrol, sheriff departments, and local police agencies from throughout the state. There were around twenty police motorcycles all with their lights on, fifty runners, and fifty bicycle riders who have brought the Olympic torch from all corners of the state. As the last torch runner is on the field, the helicopter representing the Columbus Police Department hovers over the stadium. The Special Olympics torch is light, and one knows for sure at that point that one is part of an incredible happening where everyone involved is honored to be present.

Toledo Jaycees

I had been indoctrinated at a very young age that not only did one owe it to give back to their community but also that giving back from a professional status was good not only for me but also for the organization. No person or organization of a for profit or not for profit can exist in a vacuum, for sooner or later, it will die for lack of business or lack of tax or donation monies. That is why the Toledo Jaycees is spotlighted here. For it to be successful, it is necessary for people to learn from organizations and to give of their time and energy and for each party to be able to profit from each other.

I had been involved with the Jaycees as it had been involved with the Special Olympics program in Lucas County. If the Jaycees had not been involved with the Special Olympics in Lucas County, there may not have been a Special Olympics there for a number of years.

After the Special Olympics in 1971, I was asked by the Toledo Jaycees to be a member. Involvement with organizations, especially organizations that worked closely with the Lucas County Board, was seen as desirable and necessary to the success of the program for people with mental retardation and developmental disabilities. Involvement with organizations would be a theme throughout my employment as these contacts allowed me to open many doors for the population I was to serve. For this reason, among others, I joined and in 1972 was appointed a director in the Toledo Jaycees. In this capacity, I had projects I had the responsibility of seeing through. This fact also gave me management experience with people from several different backgrounds.

One such program in 1972, I was to intimate involvement with the Regional Battle of the Bands. The project was expensive by volunteer organizational standards and was projected to bring in many thousands of dollars. In the beginning, there had been a few issues in the contract. I can remember on more than one occasion that we were meeting on the project, and during the meeting, we would call the company who had the management rights to the National Battle of the Bands. The more we talked, the more frustrating it was because we were getting nowhere in completing the contract. We had already made several commitments and were in no position of pulling out of the program. The bands had been chosen, and we had agreed to have the event. On one call to the management agency for the National Battle of the Bands, we were informed that the director of the agency had had a heart attack. Luckily, it wasn't serious, and we did finalize the contract.

Several meetings were held before the event. On one occasion, we were meeting at an apartment building rented by a Jaycee member when we took a break outside. I had worn sandals that evening and learned very fast not to walk in the grass when there are bees present. The bee hit me with a heavy dose, and we were not able to get the mudpack on fast enough. For about thirty minutes, I was very dizzy and almost was sick enough to go to the hospital. I recovered, and we finished our business for the evening. That was my first and last time that I had a severe reaction to a beesting.

The weekend for the big event came. All the bands had confirmed they would be playing. We received a call from one of the bands, asking that someone come over to its motel room and fill them in on the show. I and another Jaycee went to their room early in the morning. As we walked in, the band members were eating their breakfast in bed. It was their money, so they could spend it the way they wanted. The band members asked when they would be paid. We informed them the payment was between them and the home office. I was feeling a little uncomfortable because the pay arrangements did not seem to be in place, but that was not our responsibility as the home office was responsible for all the band arrangements. We told them we would call the home office and check on it. We didn't want the bands to be in town and not play since they didn't have the money in hand.

The big night came, and we arrived at the Toledo Sports Arena, hoping there would be thousands of fans. There had been good publicity on the event, so we were looking for a big crowd. We walked into the arena and put up displays from one of the sponsors, a chewing gum company. We had hundreds of packs of gum to give away. As we put out the gum, we began to look over the crowd. There were a few hundred fans present, but there were not several thousand. Great, we have a few paying customers, and I also saw the kids having a great time with the bands. I was told the program was done as well as possible, and I shouldn't feel bad about the lack of paying customers. You win a few, and I had just lost one, except for the fans present having a great time.

Recreation

There had been many good recreation programs in place before I arrived in Lucas County, the bowling and swimming programs being two. Field trips had been part of the adult and children's programs, so under the federal grant, the emphasis on field trips to area businesses may help develop interest and possible employment for the mentally retarded and developmentally disabled.

Some additions to the bowling program were trying to be more formal with the instructional program and to vary the awards program. While trophies had been a positive motivator in the past, we looked at the purchase of monogrammed T-shirts. One of the schools' names was Larc Lane. We ordered the T-shirts for all the participating locations in our system. When the shirts came in, they read Lark Lane. My parents had told me that the road to heaven is paved with good intentions.

We had come up with what we thought was a great idea for an award, and now we had a shirt with the wrong spelling. After many hours of developing a sick feeling over this misfortune, we began looking at options to solve our spelling problem. Through some silk screen magic, we were able to correct the shirts, but it hadn't worked out as smooth as we had hoped. After this experience, we ran a double-check on anything we had printed.

As I began to work with other members of the staff, there was a major stumbling block, and that was the fact that no dancing was permitted at board functions. Time and time again, it came to me that there was to be no dancing. The only way we thought we had a chance of changing that policy was that we came up with a questionnaire that showed the board the desire for this activity to be reinstated. This questionnaire involved consumer participation in all types of recreation programs. Within this questionnaire, there was a question if parents thought dancing should be allowed at board functions, and if not, why not. There were hundreds of responses that came back from the 1,250 families who had a son or daughter in the program. After all the results were tallied, there was one person who objected to dancing, and that was from a religious viewpoint.

We went through Superintendent Walt Solarz to ask the board if we could have dancing since there was little objection to this normal activity. We walked into the board meeting with all our findings. Remember that a board meeting is usually a very threatening event for presenters as any question that is asked must have not only an answer but also a good answer. The time came for the presentation on the recreation questionnaire report. We went through many of the findings showing that our population was listening to the radio and watching television many more hours a day than they were exercising. When I said, "I would like to talk a little about dancing because I understand the board does not allow dancing at board functions," I no more than got the words "board functions" out of my mouth, and several board members said, "We never said you can't have dancing." So I said, "That means we can hold dances." All the board members said yes.

I was speechless. I asked no more questions but took their answer and did we ever have dances. If there would have been available a computer program with a statistical multiple regression analysis, Dr. Blackwell and I would have published one of the finest studies ever done on the analysis of recreation programs and the mentally retarded.

Work availability in a sheltered workshop has its ups and downs. When work is available, workers are happy and busy. When work is slack, there is little to do. This point of activity is why the federal grant was written, to offer worthwhile activities for workshop employees during slack times. The solution offered was to have various leisure time activities available that would provide not only activities but also constructive activities. This would mean that people in the workshop were able to enjoy activities and profit skill wise from their involvement. To aid in the instructional portion of the project, the steps to learn the activity were analyzed in a developmental scheme using the developmental task form. With this form, the usefulness and ease in learning would be enhanced.

An example of one of the common activities is playing cards. Its useful skills learned could be eye-hand coordination, finger dexterity, shape and color recognition, and number similarity and differences. Let us look at the first step in learning cards that would be manipulating and dealing cards. In dealing, finger dexterity is learned. The learner would then separate cards according to color using a regular deck. Cards would then be separated by suits and then number or face cards. We are now learning shape, number, and color recognition. A matching game using a few numbers can be learned, and then adding more cards until a person is able to match several cards would be taught. Other card games from simple to complex would be taught. Over fifty various games and activities were analyzed so that examples from less active activities, such as cards, to very active activities, such as basketball, were presented. This information was compiled and published by Mafex Associates, Inc. Publishers in Johnstown, Pennsylvania. The title of the book was *Manual for Constructive Leisure Time Activities*. Dr. Blackwell and I were the coauthors.

One interesting thing behind the scenes is that much of my writing was done while I was squirrel hunting. I have always enjoyed multitasking, and this was no exception. I was a pretty good shot with seven shots producing seven squirrels. The bonus was that I had seven meals from the seven squirrels.

Professional Writings

When I entered my first position in Richland County, I made it a goal to have one professional paper published in a national journal for physical development each year. From 1967 until 1973, I had six articles published. As I reviewed my writings, I found that I had published five articles and coauthored a book in the area of physical development. Much of the credit for my publications goes to Steve Woitovich of Richland County and Dr. Julian Stein with the American Association for Health, Physical Education, and Recreation in Washington, D.C. Dr. Stein was the editor of *Challenge* and always encouraged my publications.

Physical Therapy

The most challenging factor in running a physical therapy program is finding and keeping the physical therapist. The physical therapists we employed were very good with our students, but there were never enough of two factors in this program, the physical therapist and money for the therapy.

Psychology

Much of the time used by psychologists, at this time, was used for psychological or IQ testing. To have the psychologist's time when needed, it became more effective for Lucas County Board of Mental Retardation and Developmental Disabilities to contract with an agency that had access to many psychologists. Zucker Center became that agency. Robert Brown was the administrator of the Zucker Center. The contract with the Zucker Center worked out very well.

Administrator Brown also worked out well because he was to leave the Zucker Center to become a state representative and then the director of the state of Ohio Department of Mental Retardation and Developmental Disabilities (MRDD) at a time the department was under much public scrutiny.

Volunteers

Structuring a volunteer department was the main emphasis of the department at that time. Running volunteers with a part-time staff person was asking a lot. We did what we could and hoped for more volunteers and funding in the future.

Where Do We Go from Here?

While I had been happy in my professional career, there had always been the little voice that urged me to look into employment in the private sector. I had been employed in the government sector for years and had heard that the money was better in the private sector. I had been introduced to a man who was termed a headhunter. He looked for employees for private business and would link up the person with the appropriate agency. I set up a meeting with the headhunter but found that leaving public employment for private business did not always work out well, so I stayed in public employment.

Other Related Happenings in the Lucas County System

A Dance

We have looked at the reintroduction of dancing in the Lucas County system. After the dances had started up, there was one dance that I will never forget. It was a dance in the multipurpose room at the Larc Lane adult workshop. The dance was under way, and the music was very loud, but it was the way the dancers liked to be happy and have fun. Almost everyone was having fun. One of the very large adults, let us call him Jim, was very upset about something and was not having fun. I noticed Jim's behavior and was making my way over to him when I saw a chair flying across the floor. I looked back to the source of the chair, and there was Jim in a very negative mode.

I was concerned about Jim, but I was also concerned about the other dancers. I knew he had his times, but I was in charge, and I needed to get him out of the room. I walked up to him, who was a good foot taller than me, and I said, "Jim, I want to meet you outside right now." I didn't know if he would listen, and I didn't know what he was going to do, but I started to walk out. By this time, the music had stopped, and the crowd of people in the room were watching us. As I started to walk out, I looked out of the corner of my eye and saw Jim coming. I thought that this was good, he would be out of the room, but what was I going to do once I got outside? We walked outside, and I looked at Jim, and he looked at me. Somewhere out of the night, the thought came to "Tell Jim you do not want to fight and ask if he wants to fight." I said, "Jim, I don't want to fight. Do you want to fight?" He looked me square in the eye and said no. Things de-escalated for both of us, and we had a very constructive talk. I bet that if I saw Jim on the street, he would still treat me as nice as he did after our little talk. Sometimes it happens that there is no explanation for the outcome, but there is a chance of something positive if other people trust one another to be understanding.

The Race

One evening I was coming home from work in Toledo, and I was coming through Maumee. There was a bridge that allowed a single lane to pass each way. I saw the light turn green and began to approach the one lane that I was planning on using. As I looked to the side, I saw a car even with me, apparently going to take away from me the right to cross the bridge. I was now on the bridge, and the other driver was alongside me. I thought I'll just pass him, and then I will be safe. As I tried to pass the car, he gave it the gas. I was into the bridge and didn't know how to get out because I wasn't sure where other cars might be. Eventually, I let the other car go around me. I was just happy that I had survived the ordeal. I knew at that point that car racing was not for me.

What Is That Smoking Canister on the Ground?

It was November 5, 1971, and I had made my first solo presentation at a state convention in the Neil House in Downtown Columbus. My friend John McManus was in graduate school in psychology at Ohio State University. Kathy and I arrived at John's ground floor apartment near Ohio State just off High Street in the early evening after the convention. We had a drink when we arrived, and just as I was going to show my slideshow from the day's presentation, it was announced that we were out of beer. The slideshow would have to wait as the beer run took precedence. John, Kathy, and I walked from his apartment to High Street. We walked into a store and bought some beer. As we walked out of the store, we noticed a funny smell. I had never smelled tear gas, but I thought I was smelling tear gas; I was right.

As we looked to our left, there were several policemen in riot gear coming directly toward us. We immediately ran to our right. I thought, *Why am I running? I have done nothing wrong.* As we ran south, we saw a crowd running toward us. Behind these people was another group of police in riot gear. We only had one option, which was to the east. We ran down the side street and hadn't run twenty feet when we saw people running toward us, and behind them was a third group of police in riot gear. At this point, the only option we had was to go north through private property to get back to John's. I took off running and saw a dead end. I saw a balcony that went over the barrier and decided to pull myself up on the balcony and run over the barrier. I successfully ran toward John's house, wondering where John and Kathy had gone as we had been separated as soon as the third set of police came toward us.

I found John's apartment, and John and Kathy were there. He asked me where I went, and I said I went over a barrier by pulling myself onto a balcony that went over the barrier. I stood outside and talked to John and a neighbor. We found out that a Molotov cocktail had been thrown into one of the fast-food restaurants, and it had broken the front window. Police were called, and the rest is history.

As the neighbor finished his story on the start of the riot, I heard a shot from the street. I heard a clink about three feet from me. I looked, and the canister was smoking. My eyes were really watering, and I ran into John's apartment. As I looked out the big picture window in the apartment, I saw a student yelling at a policeman. I never did figure out that conversation. I turned around and began to smell tear gas. Someone said that tear gas was coming in the air conditioner. Everyone cleared out of the apartment, and someone pushed the tear gas canister away from the air conditioner. Everyone went back into the apartment after it cleared, and I finally gave my presentation. After the advent of the riot, my slideshow and speech were not very interesting!

TORCH

In 1972, the Toledo City Department of Recreation called a number of people together who either had a disability or worked in the area of the handicapped. The staff came up with the acronym of TORCH, which stood for Toledo's Organized Recreation for the Community's Handicapped. There were several distinguished community members on the board. I was chosen to be the president of the board. With the guidance of the board and the energy of the staff, the program received notoriety for its several positive programs. This was one of the first such programs of its kind nationally. I also enjoyed serving on this innovative board and program.

In 1976, the *Toledo Blade* printed a feature article on the TORCH program. The program was informative and positive on a summer day program funded by Champion Spark Plug of Toledo. In a letter to the editor, I recognized the *Toledo Blade*'s positive contribution to society made in this article. It was nice to see something other than articles on incidents of crime, violence, and disagreements.

The VW Motor

Around 1971, I was fortunate to be able to hire a physical development specialist. After extensive interviews, John Pristash was hired to work in my department. John was an easygoing person, and his entire body would convey to me his ability to listen to every word I said. His cocked head was my first clue that he was listening, followed by his motionless body. I was always envious yet very appreciative of his listening skills. John made it clear to me that he was from Yonkers, New York.

John was the type of person who was always there to respond to my every need. In fact, you will see in chapter 12 that when I had a presentation in Columbus at a state convention the day after my son Joe was born, John was there to visit my wife in my absence.

John had this love of Volkswagen Bugs. He knew every part of the car and would prove his ability to disassemble and assemble some of the most intimate parts of the car. During the winter, on an occasion, John had a friend whose Volkswagen Bug had lost a working engine. That meant a new one was in order. We had a garage with a wood-burning heater that John felt would be ideal to shelter them as they put a new engine in his buddies VW. The plan was set that on the assigned Saturday John and his friend were to put in a new motor.

John seemed to have a method to his work. Upon arriving at 7:30 a.m., he had brought hot coffee and doughnuts for everyone's breakfast. His buddy must have been in on the plan as not a bit of work was done until the coffee and doughnuts were consumed. One time during the installation of the engine, a candle was produced. It was lit and then placed in a hole where the engine was to be attached. It must have worked because they finished the engine the same day without any negative ramifications. I knew that if I ever purchased a Volkswagen, I would want John to do the mechanical work.

Neighbors on Route 199
Norm and Celia

Landlords and Friends

We had met Norm Brinker when we closed the deal on renting his home. Shortly thereafter, we met Celia, and the four of us became very good friends. In the evening, they liked to play cards, so we would often go over to their house and enjoy their hospitality.

Norm and Celia also owned woods by their house. Those woods were to offer me some prime squirrel hunting and a quiet place for me to study or write a book with Dr. Blackwell on leisure time activities for the mentally retarded. Norm was also a sponge mushroom hunter, so we had a common interest in that area.

In the evening when we played cards (euchre), Norm would offer us a drink. Norm was not stingy with the spirits, so Kathy and I would often ask for a little more 7 UP. Norm and Celia had an endless supply of perch. Perch are a fish native to Lake Erie and are considered the best of the best by many. Norm was an excellent fish fryer, and it was always a treat to have some of his delicious perch sandwiches at the end of a fun night of euchre.

The Hunt

Norm also had a corn bin by our house, and in the late summer, he would clean out the old corn and use the bin for new corn. One day Norm came to the house and asked if he could use our dog. We asked, "What do you want to use her for?" He said he was going to clean out the corn bin and that French poodles like our dog, Missy, are a great hunter of mice and rats. We thought if that is her nature, we should allow her to hunt. We also knew that Norm would never do anything to harm Missy. He told us he would teach her how to hunt.

About an hour went by and we went out to see Missy the hunter. As we approached the corn bin, we saw Missy intently looking at the pile of corn. All at once, we saw her take off and catch a rat. When Missy caught a rat, that was the end of the line for that rat or mouse. By the time Norm was done cleaning out the corn, Missy was done cleaning out the rats and the mice, and her pile of dead rats and mice was about a foot tall!

The End of the Hunt

Norm and Celia had two areas that appeared to be good squirrel and rabbit hunting areas. I had been a hunter since high school. I have hunted birds, rabbits, and squirrels. One of my most memorable experiences was rabbit hunting with Leonard and Lenny Playko. Lenny was my age and had one of the best beagle hunting dogs around. His father, Leonard, was a great hunter and enjoyed spending time with his children. He worked with my father, and our families were good friends. On this particular day, we were hunting near Havana, Ohio, at my sister Mary Lu's house. After the first thirty minutes of hunting and no rabbits, a rabbit was kicked up and almost immediately ran into a large hole. Lenny's dog caught the scent and ran into the hole after the rabbit. The dog went in the hole so far that no part of his body could be seen. After what seemed like an eternity, a rabbit came out of another hole. Since all of us were standing around the hole and the rabbit was running through us, it was impossible to take a shot. Finally, a clear shot was taken, and we bagged the rabbit. We were very concerned about the dog as it appeared it could be stuck in the hole. As we were talking about our next step of trying to dig out the dog, to our surprise, the dog ran out of the hole looking for the rabbit. We never did understand how that dog was able to chase the rabbit out of the hole.

One of the hunting areas Norm and Celia had was a beautiful grove of black walnuts. When I was writing my first book concerning leisure time activities, I would find myself a nice tree, sit down and squirrel hunt, and write on my book. I was using a rifle at that time and had bagged seven squirrels with seven shots. On another occasion, I was hunting with some friends using a shotgun. We had walked into Celia and Norm's woods and were looking for squirrels. I had the sense that there were squirrels in the woods but was not seeing any. Finally, I saw a squirrel on one of the black walnuts and shot it. As soon as I shot the squirrel, eight other squirrels appeared out of nowhere. The woods sounded like a battlefield as all these squirrels ran in several directions. Several shots were not taken because the squirrels had put another hunter in the line of fire of other hunters. We did bag four squirrels and a good memory of squirrels appearing from nowhere.

This squirrel story leads me to the last hunting story. One afternoon I was rabbit hunting in a grove next to the black walnut trees at Celia and Norm's with a 20-gauge shotgun. I enjoyed hunting alone, and that was how I was hunting that day. As I walked through the thicket, one rabbit appeared but disappeared as soon as I saw him. I kicked up another rabbit and had an open shot at the rabbit. I shot and hit the rabbit. It rolled over and then got on his feet and began to run. I saw I had hit it in the head and almost severed his ear. I did shoot the rabbit again. The fact that the rabbit continued to run after enduring a good shot led me to the conclusion that this was not fun. I figured that was the end of my hunting. If I can't bag a rabbit on a hit to the head, I am not going to hunt.

Several years later, I was talking to Shorty Knoll, who was my wife's childhood neighbor, and he described his squirrel hunting like this: "When I go hunting now, I don't take a gun." I interpreted his remark to mean that he didn't feel like shooting squirrel anymore.

Don and Marge Trabbic and Family

True Friends

These neighbors were to play a central part in our new lives on State Route 199 and were to stay in our lives as friends for many years to come. No sooner had we moved into our home than Don and Marge were at our door, trying to see how they could be good neighbors. At the time, they had a daughter, Mary, and were soon to adopt a son, Donny, and after the adoption to give birth to their second son, Joey.

Happenings on the Farm

Don is a farmer and had many market crops such as tomatoes, pickles, and peppers. I have to admit that it was always nice to have produce near the house for a reasonable price.

Don had two brothers, Ken and Jerry. Ken was a farmer in Michigan, and Jerry had a disability. When Jerry moved to Ohio, it was very satisfying to hear Jerry talk about the sheltered workshop, his friends, and his earnings. Unfortunately, Jerry's health only allowed him to enjoy the workshop for a short period. The positive activities Jerry had as a result of the efforts of the Wood Lane adult staff enriched his life immensely.

During the summer, we would usually have a picnic in the labor camp across the road from Trabbic's farmhouse. It was on one of those picnics that we had built a fire on the edge of the field to roast the hot dogs. Within a few minutes after the fire was lit, a wind came along and decided that our fire should be bigger. Well, every spade and every fire equipment implement was put in use. The fire just kept growing instead of dwindling. For a very long period, we fought the fire. Just as we were thinking of calling the fire department, we began to gain on the fire. We put it out, and we were ready to have that picnic to replenish the energy we lost in the firefight.

At Christmas, Don would always find the biggest tree he could that would fit in their front room. I still see Don putting on the tinsel one piece at a time. It could take weeks for Don to apply the tinsel, but it was done right, one piece at a time. At Christmas, Don would always bring out a new bottle of whiskey. I watched Don get ready to open the bottle one evening and saw him hit the bottom of the whiskey bottle with the palm of his hand. I asked him why he hit the bottom of the whiskey bottle before he opened it. He said that it broke lose any grain settlings on the bottom of the bottle, and that made a better bottle of whiskey. I have never been able to disprove his explanation.

Speaking of parties, there were many between the Trabbic and Frederick families. When Don had field-workers, each summer he would have a big Mexican party with Mexican food. There were tamales, taco beans, and don't forget the hot sauce. There was plenty of beer and a few margaritas. The company of all his workers and the Trabbic family made it a very memorable feast. The dancing in the outside garage topped of an excellent celebration.

Wine Making

One day in fall of 1971, Don asked me if I would like to make some wine with him. He had located several bushels of concord grapes, and he knew how to make wine. We had a fifty-five-gallon wooden barrel with one end knocked out of it. We placed straw in the bottom of the barrel to act as a strainer, and we took the grapes off the stem and threw them into the open barrel. When we had placed all the grapes into the barrel, we began to smash the grapes. For a few days, we let the grapes in the barrel to ferment and continued to smash them.

A few days later, we opened the cork at the base of the barrel, and with a large jack placed against the overhead beam, we began to push down a large circular piece of wood so that the juice came out of the bottom of the open barrel and into a new closed barrel. After several attempts, the wine juice was now into the new barrel. We then added the right amount of sugar and put an airlock on the barrel to keep out the fruit flies and the air.

Several months later, the wine was done complete, and we split the it. The wine was very good, and it did not last too long.

Wine and Joe's Baptism

Marge and Don love babies. They were all smiles during Kathy's pregnancy and helpful to both of us as we made this important journey of starting a family complete with a child. At times, I was a little confused as to who was happier, Don and Marge or us. It was a good kind of confusion.

While the details on Joe's birth are provided in chapter 10, it was not coincidental that Joe's baptism happened the same time that my dandelion wine was ready on November 16, 1972. The occasion of my first solo attempt of wine making had a negative side to it. As was reported in the *Sentinel-Tribune* paper in December 2009, my first attempt of making dandelion wine was to be shared with many guests at Joe's baptism. I had used an open method of fermenting, which meant I didn't place the juice in a closed container such as a five-gallon glass jug, but I placed the juice from the dandelions in a crock with a cloth over the top to keep out insects such as the fruit flies.

At the appointed time, I went to the basement, filled up a glass container suitable for serving wine, and decided that I should take the first taste in the basement before the grand unveiling. There was no grand unveiling; in fact, there was no drinking of the wine. The wine, if it could properly be called wine, exited our home through the back door and dumped in the field beside our home. The dandelion wine was not even close to drinkable. Further research showed the green parts of the dandelion flower were thrown in with the yellow part of the dandelion or the good part of the blossom. My first solo adventure, contrary to other wine adventures, became the exception rather than the rule to my wine making. At the time Joey had no idea what was going on with the wine for his baptism.

Joe's Good Wine

After making wine with Don Trabbic and trying to make dandelion wine, I decided to try making some more wine on my own. I always had Don to fall back on if I had questions. I found a wineshop that sold juice for wine and made a couple kinds of very good wine. I wasn't aware that once wine had worked out, there was still yeast in the wine, which could be reactivated, especially if the temperature around the bottle of wine became warm.

On two occasions, that is exactly what happened. One summer day Kathy was home alone, and she heard a few pops in the basement that sounded like a gun. I inspected the basement when I came home and found that the corks had popped out of some of my wine. Not yet fully realizing the power of the yeast in the bottle, a few days later, I walked upstairs in a bedroom we used for storage. In the middle of the room was what used to be a white rug. Next to the rug were two bottles of red wine that had also popped their corks. The rug was now a red wine color. The rug was one of my wife's favorites, and I waited to see if I was still her favorite!

Hoz, Don, Marge, and Spoons

One evening Don and Marge were invited to our house for supper and games. A college roommate of mine from John Carroll University, John McManus, had come in for the evening from wherever he lives, probably Eastern Michigan. John was a person who moved a lot, and he rarely would call ahead to see if we were going to be home. John was a professor in psychology at Eastern Michigan University. After supper, we talked about playing a game. I had learned a new game called spoons from my sister Ann.

Spoons is a very simple game to play. It goes like this. One less spoon than players is set on the table. If there are five players, there would be four spoons. Four cards from a regular deck are dealt to each player. One player picks up a card and either keeps it or gives the picked up card or another card in their hand to the person to their left. The person to the right picks up the card and keeps it or discards the card to the person to their left. This practice continues around the circle. This goes on until one player has four matching cards in their hand. At this point, the cardplayer with the four matching cards quickly picks up a spoon, and this is the signal for other players to do likewise. As in musical chairs, there is always one player who doesn't have a chair, and in this case, it is a spoon. The person without a spoon doesn't play any more in this game. At this point, there could be consequences for the player who is the runner-up. That person could be asked to sing a song or jump around on one leg.

On this evening, the five of us were playing spoons. When the person was declared a runner-up, the remaining group thought up a consequence. At first, the consequences were easy. Calling up a stranger on the phone and asking them a silly question such as their age. Standing on one's head may have been another consequence. Calling a pizza shop and ordering a pizza with worms. Consequences then went from the indoors to the out of doors. The consequence of running around the house with no shoes on or running around the house in twenty seconds took place. One of the more dangerous consequences was to go out on the highway with a flashlight and flag down a car, and then one would tell the flagged down person they were playing a game and they lost so they had to carry out the consequence of stopping a car with a flashlight on a dark night. The later the game went, the more challenging the consequence. One can use their imagination to think up some other consequences. It was a fun game for the winner.

Picking Pickles

During the summer of 1969, I was on a federal grant to earn my master's degree in special education. On one occasion, I was free from school, and Kathy had some time open. Don Trabbic approached us from time to time to help pick pickles as his help was occupied picking other crops.

Kathy and I were to learn that working in the fields was a more challenging activity than we had thought. In the first place, we were picking in an open field with no shade. The second factor we discovered was that we couldn't just pick the pickles using any means possible; we needed to pick in such a way that we left the stem. Why leave the stem? Well, that is where the next pickle sprouts, from the old stem.

The next discovery we made was that our backs became very sore and stiff after we bent over picking pickles for many hours. The other discovery was that our fingertips became very sore as we picked.

The last discovery was that the smaller the pickle, the better the price we received. We found it also took many small pickles to obtain a decent monetary return. We only picked pickles a few times.

Bruce and Kathy Travis

Travis Family

Another family in the neighborhood was Bruce and Kathy Travis and their dog, Molly. We spent many good times with Bruce and Kathy. One of the more memorable times was when the Trabbic, Travis, and Frederick families spent the weekend on the Huron River at my parents' cottage. The cottage was a nice size A-frame with the upstairs being one open room with roughly five to six beds. The downstairs had a kitchen, living room, and two bedrooms. On that weekend, we had spent the greater part of a day fishing for crappies in the lagoon. We had caught several dozen fish, and Don distinguished himself by catching the largest fish. Bruce or "Big Fellow" had been out most of the day, and the water and sun had him pretty tired. Bruce went to bed early, and Don got the bright idea of tying him to the bed with the several marine ropes that were stored in the cottage. Bruce was successfully tied up and had a real surprise when he woke. Bruce didn't struggle long as we felt a little sorry for him.

Halloween

A fun time in our neighborhood was Halloween time. A favorite activity was called corning. Corning was the practice of shelling corn into a pail and then making a sneak attack upon the neighbor's house by throwing corn at their window, more specifically in the evening, when it was dark. One would park their car a distance from the house to be corned and then slowly and quietly sneak up to the house. To get the full effect of corning, it is best to position oneself near the house so that one can see the effects of the corning. When everyone is in position outside the house, a signal is given so that everyone throws the corn at the exact time. This will give the effect to the people in the house that a mass attack is taking place.

A short time after the attack, it is necessary to pull back from the house so the throwers are not seen when the lights are turned on outside the house. After a decent time of waiting, the corners will give themselves up so that the people in the corned house do not call the law on them.

One time we were at the Travis house, and we were in the process of corning their house. Bruce evidently knew that we were coming to his house, and he decided to have a scare of his own. He worked his way behind the corners and shot his shotgun into the air after the corning. He did scare us and taught us a lesson in corning.

Mel Wicks

Shortly after moving into our home on McCutcheonville Road, Don and Marge introduced us to Melvyn Wicks. Mel was an up-and-coming financial planner, and we were to form a lasting relationship with Mel and his then partner, George Able.

The management of our fiscal resources was always of great interest and concern to us since financial security was not an area we wished to find we were severely lacking. For this reason, we had many life insurance policies and had always been involved in savings programs. When Don and Marge told us about Mel, we felt it would be a good investment of our time and money to have one person who could plan, guide, and help us execute our financial plan. The execution of our plan was a process that has to date been an ongoing process. Our finances constantly change, and our ability to be flexible and effective in dealing with our resources has been challenging. While we are sure we were never one of the most well-heeled of Mel's clients, enough money—not tons of money—has been our goal. With Mel, we always felt that we were receiving the best guidance we could possibly receive. Mel's mild approach and friendly mannerisms made our experiences the most pleasant we felt we could obtain with any financial planner.

Over the years, Mel handled of our savings, insurance policies, legal affairs such as wills and durable power of attorney, and other essential actions. Mel was a quiet yet forceful pusher on those areas that he and we agreed must be accomplished.

We did reach a crisis decision in the early 2000s because our son became a financial planner, and we toyed with the idea of switching our business to him. The fact that we had over twenty years with Mel and a son who understood how hard it would be to switch financial planners helped us make up our mind. To this date, Mel is still our financial planner and has done a yeoman's job of managing our finances.

Jim and Aggie Lewis

Aggie and Jim were a delightful couple. Each of them had their interests and respected each other's. I can remember walking in their house one day and seeing Jimmy in the dining room working on his dog race statistics, and Aggie (I called her Gaggie) was in the living room reading her Bible. In addition to their three offspring—Annie, Sarah, and Randy—they had a dog named Jake. The first time I saw Jake, I had to look close because Jake was a small dog, and he ran on three legs. It was a sight to behold.

The Lewises had a beautiful garden. When I would see Jim sitting out by the garden, I would tease him that he was just waiting for a weed to come up so he could pull it. Actually, there was some truth to this story as the garden was weedless.

After Jim passed, we visited Gaggie at least once a year. It doesn't sound like much, but it seems we are always busy. Now that Aggie has passed, we are glad we did visit her.

A food that Jim was responsible for was his famous Tucker Treats. The dessert was made from marshmallows, milk, Rice Krispies, coconut, and an unknown ingredient. These treats would last about the time it took to set them on the table.

Winter Activities with Norb and Grace Stang

There were many favorite winter activities that the Stangs and Fredericks enjoyed. The two most memorable were the skating trip down the river by the Stang property, and the other would be the camping trip at the Fredericks' in near zero degrees.

The skating trip went something like this. As Kathy was speeding on her ice skates down the river with the Stang men and me in hot pursuit, she came across a wet spot that she did not judge as a soft spot. Her knowledge of the hole was made complete as her feet went through into the icy water.

The color of her pants went from dry to wet. Norb had a great laugh about this mishap. Little did he know that around the next corner, he would make a miscalculation on the depth of the ice and also end up with a foot and hip deep into the river. It was time for Kathy to laugh as she had already experienced the frigid water. Thank heaven there were some warm spirits present to take the nip off the frigid temperature.

The next event was the campout behind Fredericks' house. The Stang boys—Richard, Roger, Russell, Tommy, and Leroy—were there. Joe was there with his little brother through Big Brothers of Northwest Ohio, Herb. The tent was pitched, the fire was made, and everyone had their bed made up except Norb. Where was Norb going to sleep? Well, you better ask him.

The boys and Joe stayed outside freezing until two or three o'clock in the morning, and then it seemed too unsafe to continue the camp out. It was most interesting to go inside and see Norb sleeping; you got it, beside the fireplace.

There were many other fish fries, euchre games, and a glass or two of beer. Where have all those great times gone with such a great family?

Life on North River Road

Buying and Remodeling Our House on North River Road

In the four years we were looking for a house to buy, there was only one house we saw that we were interested in buying. Eastwood Schools had a great reputation, and whenever a house came up for sale, it sold. Most times, it never made it to the open market. Kathy and I saw a farmhouse advertised in the local paper the *Sentinel-Tribune*, and within minutes, we were at the house that was for sale. We took a tour of the home and asked what the purchase price would be. The purchase price was within our range in 1973. Our savings at that time were minimal, and we knew we would need a down payment. Kathy's father and mother loaned us the money, interest free.

We talked to the owners further about purchasing the property in New Rochester, Ohio, and a few days after our initial contact, we agreed on a price. When Kathy and I came into the closing meeting, we thought we had money to cover all the costs. During the meeting, other costs were added on, and we both became very concerned if we had enough money to cover these costs, and thankfully we did. Everyone seemed happy, especially me and Kathy, for this was the first house we had ever bought, and we were very excited when the house was in our name and the First Federal Bank's name.

As soon as the house was in our name, the first of many remodelings began. The walls were covered with an institutional green and lavender paint in the two large front rooms. Beneath the paint were many coats of wallpaper. The only effective manner of removing the wallpaper and paint was with many razor blades. One of the downfalls of using razor blades is that at times, the blades dig into the plaster on the wall, and then they needed to be repaired.

Another job that needed to be done was to remove the base of a chimney in the front room. I remember being home from work with the flu when Kathy announced that she was going to take out the chimney. I was going to wallpaper the rooms when they were cleaned and wasn't sure how to wallpaper around the chimney as it had several corners and round areas. Kathy made her way to the garage, found the sledgehammer, and proceeded to demolish the chimney. It didn't take too long to rip out the chimney. I had the repair job of filling the hole in the wall as well as the one in the ceiling. Over the next few years, we proceeded to remodel the three rooms downstairs as well as a bathroom and a kitchen. A back room or mudroom of the kitchen also needed attention. Upstairs there were four bedrooms and a built-in bathroom eventually needing attention. All these rooms were remodeled over the years more than once so that our soon-to-be century home was in the updated category.

Paying off the Rest of the Debt

When we negotiated the sale of the house from Melvyn and Dalene Dierksheide, they informed us that they had already paid the taxes for a time. I asked them if I could work off the money we owed them as I would rather work than pay out monies from our ongoing income. It was decided that I would help Melvyn clear the site of an old barn so that a new building could be built. On the assigned date, I showed up on time and was told what my job would be. I was to clear the area of rocks by pulling out the rocks and laying them outside the perimeter of where the new barn was to be built. I worked all morning in the hot sun and cleared out the rocks by hand and with a backhoe. There were several vines that were in the way, and I pulled them out by hand, and those that were too large to be pulled by hand I used the backhoe. I finished the job, and Melvyn and I thought we were even.

The trouble began the next day when I started to itch. I put on several medicines, alcohol, hydrogen peroxide, and other anti-itch remedies. I took another shower and went to bed. In the middle of the night, I began to itch without any relief. After a brief conversation with Kathy at one o'clock, we decided that I had contracted poison ivy from the vines of the barn project I had worked on two days ago. I had a bad case of poison ivy when I was younger, and it didn't take us too long to work out the culprit. We slept in an air-conditioned room, so heat was not a problem. I had used calamine lotion on my poison ivy a few years ago, and we had a full bottle in our medicine chest. Kathy covered the areas that were itching the most, and when she was done, I still had the better part of a half bottle. I began to cover pretty much the rest of my body. We went to sleep only to have me awake a few hours later. I was not awake because of my itching ivy; I was awakened because my whole body was covered with the calamine lotion, and my skin could not breathe. I quickly took a shower and washed off the calamine lotion. We used another itch reducer on the itchiest part of my body, and we were able to sleep for a few hours. I was in the doctor's office the next day and received a shot for the poison ivy. The shot took effect rather quickly, and I was on the way to an itchless body.

Fish Cemetery

We were somewhat slow in buying our plots in the cemetery behind our house. This cemetery is located on Zeppernick Road and is called Fish Cemetery. Interestingly enough, a nearby cemetery on Fish Road is called Pemberville Cemetery. I never understood why Fish Cemetery was not located on Fish Road, but there have been more baffling incidents in my life. The choosing of our cemetery plot was to last for the rest of eternity, so Kathy and I spent a considerable amount of time choosing our plot. It has always been our belief that nobody is better than us, and we are no better than anyone else. Just as we never want an abundance of money, we did not want what could be viewed as a special place in the cemetery. After much soul-searching and discussion, we decided that we would choose our lot in the new section. Actually, there are few plots available in the front section or old, and we decided that we would find the middle of the cemetery so that when we were laid to rest, our location would not be far to the side or near the back or front. The middle would satisfy our philosophy of being in the middle or not better or worse than others. Coincidentally, the plot in the middle of the new cemetery was located by our good friend Gene Walston. As years were to go by, our friends, the Rucks, John and Pat (Peanuts), were to be on the other side of our plot. We always kidded one another that we could have a good game of cards.

Since we are talking about the Fish Cemetery, it seems appropriate to talk about the high points of the cemetery.

The first high point in the Fish Cemetery is located on the south side of the cemetery about two-thirds of the way to the back of the cemetery. It is a tombstone marker in the form of a dead tree with a few cut-off branches. On the tombstone is the following inscription:

Oh where oh where are my wandering children today
Oh where oh where can they be
The children of my hopes and past
The children of my dreams
Mother has gone at last
Went with a broken heart

Every time I read this inscription, chills go up my spine. When we first visited, we inquired of people what the story was behind this tombstone. Our neighbor lady, Edna Restemeyer, gave us the following story. The lady buried beneath the tree was a lady who lived on Route 199 in a house to the north and west of Housekeeper Road. As the story goes, the children did not often visit their mother, and so the mother took in a man who did the farming for her. Upon her death, all the inheritance went to the hired hand.

Another unusual factor of the Fish Cemetery was that some tombstones had their writings in German. Since the area was settled by Germans, the German writings were to be understood. Unfortunately for someone like me who is not well versed in the German language, it is impossible to understand the German writings.

Another unusual tombstone is the picture of a little girl placed on a piece of porcelain. The girl was eleven years old when she died in 1945. I am not sure when the picture was placed on the tombstone, but it has been there ever since.

Our Neighbors near North River Road in New Rochester

Our second dwelling in Wood County turned out to be our home for over fifty years and the longest single dwelling of our life. We were to retain many of the neighbors from Route 199 and develop new relatives around New Rochester.

Aunt Edna

The lady who was to influence the lives of our children, especially Joey, and became one of our best friends was Edna Restemeyer. Edna was married to Clarence, and they had been married later in life and had no children. Before and after Clarence's death, it was not unusual for Edna to invite us to her house for dinner. Sometimes it was us, and sometimes it was other friends of Edna and Clarence whom we had grown to know over the years. Edna was a good cook, a great gardener, a religious being, and a very good person.

Edna's flowers tended to come to a climax every year at the Pemberville Fair. She would pick all the good flower specimens in her yard, and all evening and much of the night, her cellar light would be on while she arranged her flowers. Every year the family would go to Edna's basement and see her beautiful flowers. She would always win prizes and sometimes felt she should have won more prizes.

Joey learned much from Edna about how to care for the outdoors. Edna taught Joey the right way to cut bushes. She taught how to cut bushes so they looked natural by having uneven rather than even shoots. Joe learned about plants in the garden and around the yard. It was a sad day when Edna passed on in her sleep, and Mark and especially Joey sat out by the yard looking at Edna's house and thinking about Edna. We missed Edna and still do because she was a person who was in the know and would make sure that she shared her knowledge with us.

Aunt Edna taught us about many happenings in the community. One evening I heard the church bell toll. I heard Aunt Edna say that someone had died. I asked her how she knew that, and she informed me that the church bells always were rung when someone died, and the number of times the bell rang equaled the age of the deceased. It was not unusual for me to hear the bells and then for me to say a prayer for the deceased.

The Mysterious Car

It was around eleven o'clock in a summer evening in 1973 when the phone in our bedroom rang. I picked up the phone and heard a voice whispering at the other end. I discovered that it was our neighbor girl Carol Welty. I asked her why she was whispering. She informed me that outside her bedroom window was a car sitting in Aunt Edna's driveway, and a person was in the car, just sitting there. She had no idea who was in the car, but it looked very suspicious. She thought Aunt Edna wasn't home and was afraid the person might be waiting for her to come home.

After looking out our bedroom window, I talked the situation over with Kathy. The only conclusion we came up with was the same conclusion Carol had made, and that was to call the sheriff and get to the bottom of this matter. I told Carol she needed to call the sheriff and ask them to investigate the matter.

A few minutes later, Kathy remembered that Aunt Edna and her friend Mildred had gone to a meeting together and that the person sitting in Aunt Edna's driveway was probably Mildred's husband, Walter. I immediately called Carol to fill her in on what Kathy had told me. Carol was going to call the sheriff and tell them not to come to New Rochester as the matter was solved.

We looked out our bedroom window and discovered that Carol's call was too late. The sheriff had pulled into the driveway, and immediately following the sheriff were Edna and Mildred. The sheriff was talking to

Walter while Aunt Edna and Mildred were looking at the investigation. All I could think about was the mass confusion of everyone in the driveway, especially Walter, Aunt Edna, and Mildred. Eventually everything was straightened out after many questions from all the participating parties. This happening was an item of conversation for some time and eventually became more an item of laughter than of a serious investigation!

Jim Moore

Jim was the "mayor" of New Rochester. There had never been an election, but Jim was known as the mayor. Jim was a plumber by trade, and from time to time, he would help us out with a plumbing need if we were in a pinch. Jim was also a very well-known and liked person by the neighbor children. He was so well-known and liked that our son Joey invited him to his fourth birthday party, along with about ten other neighborhood boys and girls. Jim came to the party, brought his gift, and played all the children's games such as "London Bridge." Jim was a right jolly man. Little did I know that several years later, when Jim passed on, I would without an election be known as the "mayor" of New Rochester.

Gene Walston

Gene was an all-time great person. I served on the Black Swamp Humanitarian Awards Committee with Gene, and he was involved in many farm-related organizations such as the National Soybean Association. When Gene was involved, he was involved. He was vice president of the Humanitarian Awards Committee and president of the National Soybean Association. He was active in the Lions Club and Boy Scouts of America and was an Eagle Scout.

Gene's most notable gifts to others were his acts of kindness. I remember when one of the field-workers was picking tomatoes, and after his basket was emptied, a marker was placed into the basket so he could be paid for his work. On this particular occasion, the basket was thrown down from the truck with the marker, and it fell under the truck. The worker jumped down to retrieve the basket and marker under the truck, but he didn't pull one of his legs clear fast enough, and his leg was run over and broken. It was late in the season, and there were not too many camps with open beds. Gene was asked if the man with the broken leg could live at his camp. Gene said he had paid for his license, but the license was never sent to him. If the man needed a place to stay, he would offer his camp. Shortly after the man moved in, an inspector from the state came and asked for Gene's license. Gene explained he paid his money and had the proof, and he had contacted the licensing agent, and they still hadn't sent the license. Gene was cited, went to court, and paid a hefty fine for essentially being a nice guy. Because of the licensing agency's inability to issue a license, Gene paid.

Farming can be a dangerous occupation. I remember one time when a field-worker was setting stakes with a pole pounder and the stake broke while being set and went through the worker's foot.

Gene had been a famer his entire life. For years, he had breathed the chemicals that he was applying to the crops. He was having some difficulty with his lungs and had a scan done. A few months after he had the scan, he called the doctor and asked for the results. The office informed him that they had sent out a postcard telling him to make an appointment as there were some complications with the lung test. Gene never received the postcard. Gene died of lung cancer less than a year after his communication with his doctor.

A Dinner Invitation

We had known some neighbors in the New Rochester area for some time. One evening when we had met them at a party, they had asked us over for dinner the following Friday at their home. Kathy and I had our plans set and proceeded over to their house the next Friday for dinner. We parked our car in the driveway and proceeded to the front door. We knocked on the door, and no one answered.

We knocked harder on the front door as we knew they must be home if they had invited us for supper. Soon, the door opened, and the lady of the house greeted us in her bathrobe. She looked at us confused and then said, "What's up?" She then followed up with "Did we invite you over for the evening?" Shyly, we said that they had. She explained that they had the flu and had forgotten about the engagement. We decided on a date for the future and hoped for better health. Kathy and I went out to eat at a fast-food restaurant and enjoyed some time with each other. We vowed to make a special effort to keep our records straight when we invited anyone to dinner.

CHAPTER 3

The Early Years of Our Sons Joe and Mark

While our sons Joe and Mark will be in other chapters, this chapter will provide information specifically relative to their new lives. The first few years of their lives are provided here. It is my hope that you will experience the joys of these two new births.

Joe Is First

The Grand Announcement

In an office communication dated May 8, 1972, to the staff of the Lucas County Board of Mental Retardation and Developmental Disabilities titled "All Interested Parties" from Joe and Kathy Frederick, the following message was distributed: "In an attempt to dispel any rumors, it is our pleasure to announce that a bundle of joy will be arriving in the Frederick Household sometime in December. The baby will be our first in over four and one-half years of marriage. For further information you may contact either Kathy or Joe on Cloud 9." The message was received with many smiles and congratulations.

The Class on Bringing Our Baby into the World

We had been doctoring for years to have a baby as we were married and had no offspring to show for our efforts. St. Vincent Hospital was the site that our gynecologist had chosen to deliver our babies.

Kathy had gone to Dr. Hillabrand since she moved to Wood County in 1969. She had received the tip from her good friend and neighbor after she had asked Marge Trabbic who she was seeing as a gynecologist. Marge had responded that her doctor was the best. The matchup between Kathy's doctor and St. Vincent made it mandatory that if I wished to go in the delivery room with Kathy, I needed to take the course. At that time, it was unusual for fathers to be in the delivery room. The course lasted several weeks, and by the end, we had our breathing techniques and our understanding of the delivery pretty well in line. The next step would be the delivery.

Joe's Birth

It was three o'clock in the morning on November 16, 1976, and Kathy told me that she felt she was beginning labor. At this time, we lived in our home on McCutcheonville Road on State Route 199 near State Route 582. I immediately reached for my stopwatch I kept on the nightstand and asked her to tell me when the contractions started. They were around fifteen minutes apart.

She informed me that she had plenty of time before the birth, but she was done sleeping. Kathy went about cleaning the house and then took a shower. I continued to check the contractions, and they had not changed too much. After that, she continued to keep herself busy by checking on the status of her suitcase to be taken to the hospital and updating her phone numbers so that I would be prepared to call relatives and friends after the birth. Finally, Kathy ran out of tasks around the house and decided that we might as well go the hospital, even though she knew that the baby was not going to come for hours.

We packed Kathy's suitcase into the car, and off we went in the middle of the night to have the baby. As we drove toward St. Vincent Hospital in Toledo, we found no traffic anywhere. In Downtown Toledo, there were only a few cars and fewer people on the streets. I pulled into the emergency room and parked the car. The attendant allowed us to park in a very special close spot since Kathy was in labor. We checked in, and before I knew it, she was in her hospital bed. She wished she had stayed at home in bed as it was more comfortable. The time got to be around eight o'clock in the morning, and I was getting itchy about breakfast. My big personal plan for this event was eating breakfast at the hospital cafeteria. Kathy began to have harder labor at about this time, so I stayed with her instead of leaving her for my breakfast. After nine o'clock, Kathy's contractions slowed down. At about this time, some jackhammers were heard about three stories above Kathy's window. The noise was so loud and so annoying that I could hardly hear Kathy talk. Finally, she said that I should eat breakfast as there was nothing of significance happening in the baby to be born area. I agreed and told her that I would be back soon. As a result of my comment, Kathy reminded me that she was not going anywhere, and she might as well be home for all that was happening here at the hospital. I said nothing other than "Goodbye, I love you, and I will be back soon." I also asked Kathy to not have the baby when I was gone. She reminded me that there was not a chance of that happening. Under my breath, I was reminding myself that I was so hungry that I could eat two bears.

I went down to the cafeteria and walked straight into the serving area, only to find out that there was no one in the serving area and no food either. I had made a big mistake. The cafeteria had closed at nine o'clock for breakfast and would not be serving any food at that time regardless of how hungry I was or how long I planned to eat this breakfast. The excuse that I missed breakfast because my wife was in labor was of no help in trying to procure that breakfast. I found the gift shop and bought some small powdered doughnuts, which did not in the least taste like eggs and bacon. I dutifully walked up to my wife's room and reported my miscalculation on the timing of breakfast. She said it was her fault, and I reminded her that I was a grown man and ought to be able to check the cafeteria times so that I could go there to eat when it was open.

Again, I heard the jackhammers, which seemed even closer now to Kathy's room than before. "OK," I said to Kathy, "I have had just about enough of this noise." I walked out to the nurses' station and informed her that the jackhammering was annoying my wife who was here to deliver a baby, not to be involved in a construction crew. The nurse informed me that they had complained to the proper person and were told that the workers were going to be paid regardless if they were working or not working, and the hospital preferred them to be paid for working. I informed the nurse that it would be nice if the noise were a little quieter for all the ladies experiencing the discomfort of pregnancy. I did not mention my discomfort as I knew it would be of no significance. It was early afternoon, and even though hard labor had not begun, Dr. Hilldabrand, her gynecologist, had been informed that Kathy was in labor, and he wanted to see how she was coming. As Dr. Hilldabrand began to examine Kathy, he asked, "How long have they been making that noise?" I informed him that the noise from the jackhammer had been going on since early this morning. He said something to the effect that he was going to check into the noise that was disturbing his patients.

The noise continued in the early afternoon and was continuing into the late afternoon. Things started to happen with Kathy's contractions about four o'clock. Kathy's water had broken, and her contractions were becoming closer together, and the discomfort in her back was increasing. (I had learned in my prenatal class that there is not a place in the labor rooms for the word "pain" as it actually makes the discomfort worse.) At this time, there was an extremely huge traffic pattern developing in the delivery area as it seemed everybody and their brother decided to have a baby that day. I had mentioned to the nurses that I thought Kathy had squatters right to a delivery room as she had been in labor more time than anyone else, and I was concerned about the availability of a delivery room when she needed it. I heard the nurses talking that there had been more babies born this day than any other day that year so far. I knew at that point that there would never be a delivery room available and asked Dr. Hillabrand if I needed to be doing something to one that was available. He laughed and told me not to worry about a delivery room as he would take care of that detail at the right time.

I was given a gown to wear because I was to go into the delivery room as I had taken the prenatal course on the delivery of a baby. Kathy was being wheeled out, and I told her everything was going to be OK and I would be right beside her. As I got the words out of my mouth about being beside her in the delivery room, Dr. Hillabrand walked into the room, looked at me, and said, "I am sorry, but there have been complications with another birth, and no husbands are being allowed in the labor room at this time."

I was crushed. I had waited my entire life to see the birth of my first child, and now something had prevented me from going into the delivery room. I kissed Kathy and watched everybody but me go toward the delivery room. As I looked out the door and began to go to my chair, I noticed that Dr. Hillabrand had left his cigarette by the sink. I picked up the cigarette and, without thinking, began to puff on the few puffs left. Since I was having a good time celebrating a new son, that evening, I forgave myself as I had given up cigarettes when I had married Kathy in 1968, and this was the first time since then that I had smoked. It tasted really good!

Around five o'clock, I was more than concerned that things were processing very fast. Joey was born shortly thereafter, and when I held him for the first time, I knew this was a miracle. I stayed with Kathy in the recovery room until they said it would be best if she would go to her room and get some rest and instruction on nursing the baby. I went down to the pay phone and began calling our relatives and friends. Since we lived many miles away from our relatives, nobody was expecting a call saying that Joey was born. Several of my sisters and brothers said, "This is a joke, isn't it?" or "You are kidding, aren't you?" Kathy's due date was in December. When I talked to Kathy's parents, my father-in-law acted happier about the birth of this baby than anything I have ever seen him experience. He told me that they were going to a Christmas party at Faulhabers (a factory my mother-in-law had worked in for many years). I later found that he was really having a great time celebrating a new grandson that evening.

Presentation at the Superintendent Conference

The day after the birth of Joe, November 17, 1972, I was scheduled to make a presentation to the Superintendent's Association of the County Boards of Mental Retardation and Developmental Disabilities in Columbus on my programs involving physical development. I asked Kathy if she would mind if I went. Although she wanted to see me the day after the birth of Joe, she knew it was important for me to give the presentation. I told her that I would arrange for someone to take my place and visit her since I would be in Columbus. My right-hand man at the time was John Pristash. John had worked for me for a few years; I trusted him to visit Kathy. The presentation went well, and John visited Kathy in Toledo. When I came back from Columbus, I immediately went to see Kathy. From that point on, we began to realize a little bit more every day that the addition to the Frederick family was to produce more changes in all phases of our lives than we had ever begun to imagine.

Our First Thanksgiving with Joey

The following week was Thanksgiving. We celebrated the holiday at home with our new baby. At a local turkey farm, I bought a fresh twelve-pound turkey. We took a picture of our baby and the turkey. The baby weighed six pounds and the turkey was twelve! Our good friends Marge and Don brought down mashed potatoes and gravy. Our first Thanksgiving as a family was wonderful.

Haircuts

Joey's first haircut was on September 5, 1973, and was given by Kathy. He wondered what that snipping noise was. When he was two and Kathy had her haircut, he observed how her hair had grown short on her head when it was cut.

The First Six Months

Joey was a very good baby. During this time, we had several neighbor visits from the Lewis, Trabbic, and Brinker families. Several friends and family also visited. Butch Rothschild was the first visitor from Willard.

Joey was baptized on December 3, 1972, at St. Thomas Moore Parish. Godparents were Uncle Joe Schlotterer and Agnes Clayton.

Grandma Frederick said, "He was a doll and looked like Uncle Bob."

It was during these first six months that we were looking to purchase our first house. We purchased our present home in New Rochester and moved in with our new baby.

Christmases

Joey's first Christmas was in 1972, and it was also his first trip to Willard. In 1974, Joey was very excited about Christmas as he received a homemade barn from his daddy. He opened some gifts that were not his, but opened they were. In 1976, we also had Mark and went to Ann and Mark Martin's house on Christmas Eve. Christmases were so much more fun with children!

Friends

Joey had many friends—Josh and Jamie Myers, Aaron Martin, Jamie Welty, Michelle Lopez, Jason Danielson, and the Winkleman children. His babysitter was Carol Welty, and they did many activities together.

Favorite Activities

In the winter, Joey loved to build forts out of snow. We had an old chicken coop, and Joey loved to sit in the boxes where the chickens laid their eggs. If there was a puddle, Joey would always find the nearest one.

Toys

Joey loved his toys, and he liked them to be put back in the shelves he had chosen for them. When friends would be leaving, the parents would tell their children to put Joey's toys away. Joey would usually have to adjust them in the toy room so that they met his expectations. John Deere tractors and Legos were always two of his favorites.

Ring Bearer

June 1980 was when Joey's babysitter, Carol Welty, was married to James Biddle Jr. Joey was the ring bearer and did an excellent job at St. Paul's Lutheran Church in New Rochester.

Mark Was Next

Elvis Presley

It was New Year's Eve 1976, and we were invited by our friends Carol and Ron Carpenter and a few of Carol's relatives to attend a concert by "the King" Elvis Presley with fifty thousand fans. After the opening acts, we were all ready to see a great performance. As Elvis was to come on stage, the entire Pontiac Stadium in Detroit went dark. The introductory music came on loud, and the spotlight focused on the main stage. It was so exciting that all I could see on the other side of the stage was thousands of camera bulbs go off. As Elvis came to our side of the stage, I began taking pictures. I didn't want to miss a shot. It was then I noticed that I had my lens cap on my camera. I did miss a few shots. Then an unexpected event happened—Elvis had split his pants. By accident, I caught the split on my camera.

The evening was one of the most entertaining we have ever experienced. Elvis was truly "the King." The performance was great, and the encore nine months later was a very personal experience as Mark was to come into our lives. This was because of the fact that Kathy and I had attended the Elvis Presley concert, and as a result of attending the performance, it was projected that "We Were All Shook Up."

Birth of Mark

Mark was to be born at St. Vincent in Toledo. Since we had one child, Joe, the events leading up to the delivery were much more contained than those similar events with Joe's birth.

It was September 18, 1976, when Mark decided that he was to come into this world. Our neighbor, Edna Restemeyer, was watching Joey until my parents arrived at our house to do their grandparent duty of child watching. I remember Kathy's warning that her water was breaking as we were walking through a parking lot at St. Vincent Hospital. I kidded her a bit by saying I would have brought my fishing pole had I known that there was going to be a lake in the parking lot. I don't think Kathy was in the mood for a fishing joke.

Upon entering St. Vincent, I looked at all the pregnant ladies and their spouses walking the halls or in the waiting or labor room in the hospital. I could not remember seeing one of these couples at the Elvis Presley concert, so it might have been that Elvis inspired only Kathy and me.

Once again, I was to spend the better part of the day with Kathy in labor. The delivery went well, and I was to see the birth of our son. We wanted to thank Kathy's doctor, and so I brought in a couple of bottles of wine. The doctor took the bottles and gave them to the nurse to store somewhere.

The story got better as the nurse put them in the storage area. Unfortunately, the storage area was close to a light bulb. The longer the bulb was on, the hotter the wine became until the wine could take it no more. The cork on the wine popped, and there was a stream of red all over the nurses' station. The doctor had no chance to sip either of the bottles of wine.

After a few days, we brought Mark home, and he was introduced to his big brother. We adjusted to family life with two beautiful boys. Mark was also baptized in a few weeks, and his godparents were Diane Long and Fred Eldred.

Earache

I was away on business, and Mark had developed an earache in the middle of the night. This gave Kathy the responsibility of dealing with Mark's earache and trying to keep Joey from being the second child awake.

As the night went on, Mark's ear got worse as his crying and ear pulling increased.

At about three o'clock in the morning, Kathy decided to call her pediatrician for help. She called the doctor, but she couldn't hear what he was saying over Mark's crying. The doctor suggested taking Mark into the next room, placing him in the far corner, and running back to the telephone so she could talk to the doctor. Kathy took Mark into the next room and picked up the telephone in the adjacent room. Kathy began to talk to the doctor, but it wasn't long before Mark had worked his way back into the room with the telephone.

Since Kathy had not finished her conversation with the doctor, she had to take Mark to another room a few times before she knew the directions the doctor had given her. The doctor asked Kathy if I had any whiskey in the house. She said that she did. He instructed her to take a small amount of the whiskey, place it into a bottle, and add water. She did as he instructed, gave the bottle to Mark, and he was asleep within a few minutes. The other good happening that evening was that Joey slept through the whole noisy night.

The Penny

To this day, we have not been able to figure how a penny got on Mark's changing table. It was there because as Kathy began to change Mark, we saw he pick up something and put it in his mouth. As soon as it went into his mouth, he began to choke, and we knew we had to act fast. We put him upside down and tapped on his back to dislodge the penny. The penny came out faster than it went in, and the appearance of the stray penny is a mystery to this date.

The Toilet

Mark had a great interest in shoes. Mark also had an interest in toilets. One day as Mark was enjoying his terrible twos, he decided that he was going to walk around the house with his new shoes. These were the kind of shoes that all kids wore in those days. They were white, and they had high sides on them, so they looked like a shoe boot. Mark's tour of the house stopped in the bathroom. Kathy and I knew that Mark was in the bathroom because we heard the toilet flush and Mark's laugh. Immediately after hearing this noise, Kathy and I walked in the bathroom. What a sight! Mark had combined his interest in shoes and toilets by standing in the toilet bowl with his shoes on and holding on to the toilet reservoir with the right and flushing the toilet with his left hand. It must have been a funny sensation of having the cold water flow over one's new shoes. It was to be an experience that Kathy and I are never to enjoy.

The Boots

Mark was to have a babysitter as Kathy and I were to spend the evening out, and Joey was with a friend. We asked the neighbor boy, Andrew, if he could child sit, and he said he would. As we were about to leave the house, we had a bit of uncomfortable feeling because about a week earlier, Kathy had walked in the front room and smelled a funny smell like sulfur. She looked over at the bookcase and saw yellow egg running down the front onto the rug. The eggs were our beautiful Ukrainian Easter eggs. The keyword is "were beautiful eggs." Mark finally admitted that he had broken the eggs while trying to reach an item on the bookcase. He was not to be playing on the bookcase. Kathy was trying a new technique to correct behavior called time-out.

As we were about to leave the house, we told Andrew that if Mark misbehaved, put him on the church bench in the kitchen and set the timer for five minutes. If Mark was really bad, he should set the timer for ten minutes. When Mark was with Andrew, he found something to occupy his time that led to trouble. Andrew told Mark he needed to go to the bench. Andrew set the timer and almost immediately began to hear strange noises. Andrew checked out the house and then came into the kitchen. As he came into the kitchen, Andrew thought the noise was coming from Mark. Andrew listened closer and soon discovered that it was Mark saying under his breath, "I hate the timer."

When we came home, we asked Andrew if Mark had been good. Andrew answered that he had a few problems. We found out that while Mark was on the bench, he had urinated into Andrew's boots beside the bench. I think that was the last time Andrew babysat.

The Magazines

While Mark was playing with his friend Edwin Winkleman, they came to Kathy and asked her if he could look at *Playboy* magazines. Kathy asked where he would find these magazines. The boys answered that a friend had some and said he could see them. Kathy knew she needed to think fast and answered, "Mark, you need to read *Ranger Rick* magazines, not those *Playboy* magazines."

The Large Gumball

We were at the IGA grocery store in Pemberville shopping when Joey ran up to me and said, "Mark has a gumball in his mouth, and he can't breathe!" Without thinking, I ran to Mark and gave him the Heimlich maneuver, and the gumball jetted out of his mouth and traveled ten feet before it hit the floor. We usually controlled the gumballs the boys had because we didn't want them to choke on them. Where the large gumball came from is a mystery because we steered away from this type of candy. We were happy Joey was looking out for his little brother.

Corn

There is yet another unusual happening that required our intervention with Mark. Joey once again came to us from his bedroom and informed me and Kathy that Mark had put something in his nose, and he couldn't breathe from his nose. We looked at each other and rushed up the stairs to Mark's bedroom. We looked into his nose, and sure enough, Mark had something in his nose, and we couldn't pull it out. I was still working on my doctorate and had some work to finish, so I stayed home with Joey, and Mark went to the hospital with his mother.

A few hours later, in walks Mark and Kathy. I found that the obstruction in Mark's nose was field corn. The corn had begun to sprout as a result of the moisture in his nose. Once again, the question came up about the origination of the corn. All we could conclude was that Mark must have taken a stroll in the cornfield beside our house.

Joe and Mark's Experiences in Common

Stickers and Contracts

Both Kathy and I agreed on positive reinforcement for our boys. We developed a chart, and for good behavior, we gave them stickers. When they had so many stickers, they went to town and chose a toy or something they liked.

In dealing with who could play with whose toys or to avoid the all-out war of your children in who had the right to use a particular toy, we developed a simple technique in distinguishing whose toys were whose—colored paint. Our boys dearly loved their Matchbox cars, trucks, fire engines, and other types of vehicles. One day the boys were having a disagreement about whose car was whose. The car in question was a race car with bright flames painted on the sides and a bright color on the remainder of the long car with a hood that came to a fine point and made a V-shaped appearance. As we walked into the room, we looked at the car as our boys were both shouting, "It is my car!" Kathy and I couldn't decide whose car it was and further contributed to their frustration. We substituted two other race cars and temporarily solved the situation until the next disagreement. Later, we discussed our dilemma on whose car was whose. We came up with the idea of painting a dot on the underside of the car. Dark brown became Joey's color, and light brown was Mark's dot. These colors seemed to appeal to the boys. Before we painted on the dots, we asked the boys to tell us which cars were theirs. If a disagreement came up, we would fairly assign the car to one of the boys.

In the future, whenever a difference of opinion arose about who played with which car, we merely turned the car upside down for them to see the colored dot. After a while, they could turn the car over to see whose car it was.

When the boys were contemplating selling some of their cars, we found the value went down if there was paint on the bottom. The boys solved this factor by keeping all their cars.

Grandma Frederick

Joey and Mark both knew Grandma Frederick well because she lived for many years after my father, Walter, passed on. Grandma had one of the biggest candy supplies known. In fact, she usually had enough candy she could have set up a shop with little problem. Grandma had a practice with all the grandchildren, and it involved candy. Shortly after the children would arrive at Grandma's for the celebration of a major holiday, they would begin asking for candy. About this time, all the moms and dads were in another part of the house catching up on one another's lives.

At this point, Grandma would sit each of the children on the countertop in the kitchen and walk up and down the line with candy. As she would give each of the children a piece of candy, she would say, "Don't tell your mother or father." To my knowledge, none of the grandchildren let the "cat out of the bag." I think they were wise enough to see that they did not want their candy supply drying up.

Snakes in the Riverbank

We lived close to the Portage River, and the old riverbed was immediately across the road from us. It was a common occasion for Joey, Mark, Kathy, and me to take walks in the river basin. On one occasion, we saw a hole in the ground with some mud encircling the hole. The boys asked Kathy and I how the hole got there, what used it, and if they could please see the creature that lived in that hole. Kathy and I were from a rural area, and we had seen many such holes. Although neither of us had ever seen an animal go in or come out of the hole, we were told that snakes lived in this type of hole. When we told the boys about the snakes that probably lived in the hole, they were completely taken up about this story. As they looked around further, they saw some potato peels and other table scraps that had been thrown on the riverbank. Their assumption, which I did not doubt, was that the snakes would eat the potato peels. A short time later, they saw a snake near the hole and were convinced a snake lived in the hole.

That evening and more many evenings to come, the favorite story they wanted to hear at bedtime was about the snake that lived on the river. As time went on, the story about the snake became longer and longer. The version that I best remember is that Aunt Edna, the neighbor who lived by the riverbank, would go out every evening and throw out her table scraps. The snake would watch her throw the table scraps from under a large leaf on the riverbank. The snake would wait until Aunt Edna would go back into the house and only then would they crawl over to the food and eat that which they liked. Night would come, and eventually, the snake would go back to its hole until the next day.

It was on one such evening that there was a very hard rain. The snake heard the rain but was not very concerned about the rain coming into the hole as the hole was located near the top of the riverbank. As the rain came down heavier and accumulated faster, the water was up to the edge of the hole where the snake lived. As water began to make its way into the snake hole, the snake awoke and crawled out of its hole into a river now several feet high. The snake began to crawl fast as it was night, and the snake needed to get somewhere other than the water. Eventually, the snake followed his instinct and found the riverbank where his hole was located, and he climbed onto the wetland made from the storm. The snake found a large plant and crawled under the leaves of the plant to find a dry area to sleep. The snake was very tired from swimming the previous night and finally found a place under a tree to rest out of the rain.

Morning came, and the sun came out bright and clear. As the day wore on, the earth began to dry up, and the water began to recede into the waterline of the river. He inspected the snake hole, only to find that it was very wet from the rain of the previous evening. The snake looked for food but could find very little, so the snake went to bed hungry the second straight night under the large plant with leaves. The second morning, the snake woke and could see that the water was very low in the riverbed. The snake checked his hole and found that most of the water was out of the hole. The snake cleaned out the hole and decided to spend the night in it. As the snake came out of his hole, he could hear someone coming closer to the riverbed, so he raced to cover and waited to see who was coming. As the snake looked up, he recognized that it was the person who lived in the house nearest the snake hole. The lady threw some table scraps on the riverbank and went back to her house. The snake was very hungry and raced over to the table scraps to eat supper. The snake was very tired from cleaning out the hole and decided to go to bed early in the snake hole.

Coon Hunting

When the boys were old enough to hunt, I arranged for them to go raccoon (coon) hunting with a friend of mine. Mark was around ten years old, and Joey was around fourteen years old. Karl had two blue tick bloodhounds that were excellent hunters.

One Saturday night, about nine o'clock in the evening, we met Karl at his home in Portage, Ohio. It was a perfect night for hunting as a light drizzle had wet the ground, making it ideal. We loaded the dogs and went to a woods outside Bowling Green where we had permission to hunt. Nothing happened for the first half hour, and then the dogs began to howl. Karl said that they were on to something. We ran through a woods across a field and into the next woods. The dogs had stopped running and were howling at a stationary point in the woods. We came upon the dogs and shone our powerful flashlights into the tree. There in the top of the tree were the eyes and bodies of two coons. The boys were very excited as was me and Karl.

Karl asked the boys if they wanted to shoot the coon out of the tree. They both did. Both my boys had been trained to shoot a rifle. Karl let Joe aim the gun at the coon, and he shot. The coon fell to the ground, and the dogs killed it. Mark shot next, and the coon also fell out of the tree, and the waiting dogs also killed the second coon. By this time, it was about midnight, and we decided to quit hunting. The boys still talk about that evening.

Eagle Scouts

Both Joey and Mark were fortunate to attain the rank of Eagle Scout from the Boy Scouts of America. My wife and I did much of the planning with three other sets of parents to plan for Mark and the three other Eagle Scouts. In addition to Mark, the Eagle Scouts were Wes, son of

Bruce and Karen Sweeney; Brian, son of Jim and Mrs. Hampshire; and Ed, son of Ed and Pat Hammett. Matt Meyer, the eternal scoutmaster, is always there when needed and in his own unique, easy approach makes sure the ceremony comes together. At the court of awards, a local bagpiper in full garb would lead the new Eagle Scout(s) into the assembly room at the Pemberville Bethlehem Lutheran Church, the sponsoring agency. Listening to the music of the bagpipes was truly an emotional experience as it brought attention to the music and then attention to the new Eagle Scout walking into the room. For a court of awards, the assembled crowd in the fellowship hall is always impressive in terms of size and diversity. The various groups present are fellow Boy Scouts; local and area scout leaders; government leaders, such as Wood County Commissioners; other elected county leaders; state legislators; local community leaders, such as the then mayor of Pemberville, Gussy Oberhaus; and township trustees. Also parents and family of all the scouts, former scout leaders, members of the community, and always several other Eagle Scouts of all ages are present.

Both the programs began with a script of events such as relaying the responsibilities of an Eagle Scout and other meaningful words of wisdom from several sources. The actual presentation of the Eagle Award took place. Next, the festivities rolled into high gear as each of the local, county, state, and national awards recognized the Eagle Scout(s). One by one, each leader presented some memento such as a proclamation from the mayor of Pemberville, a remembrance from the county commissioners, proclamations from the State Senate and House of Representatives, and even congratulations from the Federal Senator and House of Representatives. The awards were then topped off with a meaningful message signed by the president of the United States of America. One remaining activity was the very solemn event of having every Eagle Scout to come to the living circle of joined hands to recite the Scout Oath. It is a spine-chilling experience for me each time I participate in the awards and especially each time I participate in the living circle. The positive actions that may happen as a result of the knowledge and skills gained from being an Eagle Scout are overwhelming. Since only three out of every one hundred Boy Scouts attain the rank of Eagle Scout, young boys have a chance to give much and receive back not just an award but also a philosophy of helping other people by "doing a good deed daily."

Dating

Joey and Mark both dated very nice girls in both high school and college. My father always told me, "If you date a girl, she should be the kind of girl that you can marry." I would have to say that both our sons, in my estimation, did follow this rule. In college, both Mark and Joe were selective in the young ladies they dated, and Tara was one girl in a million that Joe found. Mark remained single his entire life.

I felt fortunate, and I believe Kathy would agree, in knowing the young ladies our sons dated, and we always were able to gain much in our contact with them. The boys always brought the girls home for us to meet. As a result of the young ladies in our young men's lives, we were able to meet some very committed, friendly, and successful parents ranging from teachers to law enforcement officer to financial planner from Joe and grocery store owner to attorney to farmer for Mark. The time we were able to spend with our young men's lady friends and their parents is a very important part of my life. Peggy and Ed Mobley, Tara's parents, have been nothing but pleasant, enjoyable, and open to us, so much so that I feel more than blessed to have their friendship.

Father's Day

I have found that on Father's Day, I am held in high regard by my sons and wife. Father's Day is a special time for family to give Dad a little attention. I have also found that it can be a time for Dad to be in a shock mode because of the many compliments he is to receive. Mark and Joe have always been choosy about the wording of Father's Day cards. They are always honest and vocal about their feelings and are full of positive words in the cards they purchase for me without getting too mushy. Their cards usually reflect that I spend time with them and notice what is happening in their lives and more importantly support them. They often express thanks for my advice and providing a good role model.

On one occasion, Mark paid me a super public compliment. Joe and Mark were both members of the Sigma Phi Epsilon Fraternity at BGSU. Mark nominated me to be a Renaissance brother of his fraternity. This honor allowed me the opportunity to become an honorary member in the fraternity. In his nomination, he cited many inspiring remarks that I didn't think he had ever noticed. For example, he cited how I dropped everything in my life to spend time as his scout leader, baseball coach, and other activities. I was seen as the best father and role model as well as a great man. When I was presented this plaque with the accolades that Mark had given me, I was truly shocked when I heard these words and others being read to the assembly of fraternity brothers and families. After the award, I said to myself I really have to work hard to be worthy of this honor. Now that I was in the fraternity, I felt a little down that I was to miss all those Sigma Phi Epsilon Fraternity parties!

I was equally touched by similar words that were written to me by my wife, Kathy, on Father's Day. Being a good father is very high on my priority list, and I hope it is high on others as well. With the duty of being a father goes the responsibility of carrying through on the many areas of need. I hope I can continue to be a very good father and continue to be and be seen as positive.

PART II

Moving My Workplace from the County to the State Government

CHAPTER 4

Educational Consultant Serving Nineteen Counties in Northwest Ohio

General Duties

While I had enjoyed my past two jobs as physical education and recreation director in Richland and Lucas counties, my educational credentials and desire to work with many counties led me to a position with the state of Ohio. In 1973, I accepted the position as program consultant with the nineteen counties in Northwest Ohio. The position was very encompassing and included several areas I had experience. I was to remain in this position until 1976. I was to accept a new position as district manager in 1975 but was to keep the program consultant position until funds were available for a replacement in 1976.

In this position, I was responsible for approving programs and their state funding for nineteen county boards of mental retardation and developmental disabilities. I did not have direct supervision over employees in these county programs, so it was back to some of my previous experiences of indirectly supervising people. I had found that in indirect supervision, tactfully working with people was a necessary component in being successful. Indirect supervision involves being responsible to see that program objectives are achieved by other people, but the ability to hire and fire is not present. I found that programs and services were usually in good shape, and therefore supervision of people was made easier.

The position of educational consultant was an interesting role. While I was responsible to oversee that the programs conformed to the rules of the state of Ohio Division of Mental Retardation for County Boards of Mental Retardation and Developmental Disabilities, when change was needed, the role of consultant was a bit more challenging. When everything is going well in the county programs, being a consultant is a doable position. When change is needed, I saw my role as a helper with the county rather than a dictator. As a state inspector, being able to provide guidance so that solutions were implemented was essential. The end goal for both sides was that program services and ultimately the persons being served by the program would benefit. I learned real early in working with other people that a positive approach will help more than a more negative one. Fortunately the county board personnel were cooperative people.

Specific Job Responsibilities in the Field

As educational consultant, I was to monitor, evaluate, and consult the mental retardation and developmental disabilities schools and workshops within the nineteen counties in Northwest Ohio. In addition, this was a time for the development of residential homes for this population, and I was to act as a regional consultant in this area. More specifically, I was to programmatically assist group home operators in their residential operations. The position worked with several local state and federal agencies in a variety of program issues. One of the major responsibilities of this position was to perform program evaluations in all classrooms in the northwest district. This would include one hundred classrooms. Likewise, evaluations in all nineteen county workshops were to be conducted, and these workshops numbered approximately twenty workshops. Work programs were usually jobs held in workshops and could be jobs in the community. The evaluations were written reports on all these programs and were submitted to the state department and to the affected superintendent. Additional consultative duties were in the areas of administration, law, personnel, programs, facilities, finances, and management systems. Training programs for the county board staff was both ongoing and periodic.

A state curriculum for moderate mentally retarded persons was to be written by the Ohio Division of Mental Retardation and Developmental Disabilities. I was to be a member of the committee that would write this document. At this time, there was a federal legislation that required each state to develop legislation in concert with the federal legislation on education of school-age students. This federal legislation spurred local training and evaluation of individual educational programs (IEPs) and individual habilitation programs (IHPs). The last area of responsibility was to foster work programs through job placement using major funding and program emphasis. At this time, there were few people with MR/DD (mental retardation and developmental disabilities) working outside the sheltered workshop, and while the market was there, the programs and funding needed to be developed. The job was challenging, and this position was a major step in broadening my work knowledge, skills, and responsibilities.

Central Office

This position was one of the more comfortable ones I held as it allowed me to work in many different counties across many different state departments, and the other employees in this position were the kind of people for the most part who would help you and support you. Both the directors, Dr. Roger Gove and Dr. Norm Nieson, and my immediate superiors, Joe Auberger and Dr. Maxine Mays, were always effective supervisors. While I was to continue living in Northwest Ohio in New Rochester, I was to spend a large amount of time in Columbus collaborating with the other five educational consultants and Columbus-based specialists in the educational and habilitation areas. Habilitation training means that individuals are receiving training in areas they had not ever had training. In addition, I was to work with the in-house architects who drew up plans for the new schools and workshops funded largely by the Division of Mental Retardation and Developmental Disabilities as well as the architects hired by the county board to see the project to completion. Attorneys were available to answer legal questions and give guidance in areas of need. The finance department provided fiscal information plus budgets. The human relations department assisted the employment and related areas. The certification department handled all questions in this area. All county needs were answered through me and usually involved the many central office staff.

Role of the Board and Superintendent

This section was one of the most difficult sections of the entire book to write. One reason it is so difficult to write is that no two boards or superintendents/administrators are alike. The next reason it is difficult to write is that knowing how people think in each of these roles is many times difficult to predict.

There are certain givens that will help us understand this relationship. In working with any county board, it was important that the board and superintendent had roles, knew them, and implemented them fairly. Fairly should mean that any decisions made were for the benefit of the clients being served. The roles of the board and administrator seem similar in private and public boards and organizations. The role of the board as the policy maker and the superintendent as administrator is simply put the essential part of these two positions. It is very clear in the laws for the county board of developmental disabilities that there was a separation of duties between the board and the superintendent. It was also possible that the board members and the superintendent did not follow the letter of the law and allow their positions to overlap. For example, the board members position was to make policies, and while they shouldn't, they may at times also administer staff that the superintendent should be administering. Keeping these two job duties separate is important because the board member or chairperson should not do the job of the superintendent or the superintendent do the board's duties. If the board was making the policies and also administering the program, there would be two direct line bosses. The administrator or the superintendent being one and a board member being the second. In this case, where the board member periodically becomes the administrator, to whom does the staff listen and take direction? Is it the administrator or the board member? Any situation like this places everyone in the organization in confusion. Any organization with a board and an administrator must be careful to do its job and only its job.

Practices in which the superintendent and board do not carry out their respective jobs efficiently will make it impossible to have a good working relationship between the two. Usually, open communications can help solve these misunderstandings. Having administrative rules that the board and staff follow is another must. Rules provide consistency for all employees, the board members, and anyone associated with the organization.

While many boards and superintendents have developed positive relationships, the opposite is also true in that boards may get into administrative duties, not have the entire story, and take actions on this limited information. I decided very early in this management game that if the employment I was in with my board or my employer was developing into an unworkable conclusion, I would look for another job. A bad relationship, for whatever reason, between the administrator and the board or other employer would usually be hard to work out, especially if there was no resolution in sight, and the board or administrator or both were not willing to work out the situation. In this situation, ultimately, the harm to the organization and more importantly the people to be served will usually only grow. My experience with many boards or employers is they are willing to work toward a fair solution. Unfortunately, others are not, and a no-win situation is a common result. Leaving the situation may be the best result yet not the desired result for some of the involved administrators.

Other Experiences as a Consultant for the Department of Mental Retardation

Evaluations in the School

Traveling the nineteen counties of Northwestern Ohio and evaluating and approving the state funds for these programs was a new challenge. The county boards were a group of service providers who worked hard with various organizations, including the state of Ohio, in providing the best services possible to their clients.

There were over one hundred classrooms for people with mental retardation and developmental disabilities who came under the responsibility of the Department of MRDD. On a yearly basis, I was responsible to evaluate each of these classrooms. In Ohio, there was a dual system of education formed when in the early fifties, students had been excluded from public school classes because they functioned low in their skill development. An E-1 card or exclusion card was developed for these students. Once they received this card, they could not attend regular public school classes. Thus, the county board school-age classes were established by several concerned parents, and workshops were established not far behind by the schools.

The evaluation of each room was based on factors related to the Individual Education Plan (IEP). The IEP was mandated in 1974 by federal legislation and had been in use informally for many years before. Essentially, the IEP was developed by a team of competent professionals and parents so that the student was given a plan that allowed them to develop to their maximum capacity. It was an amazing process that brought everyone to a single table, and each parent involved needed to sign their name on the document to be official. While the teacher usually was the coordinator of the plan, psychologists, therapists, administrators, parents, and teacher assistants all had input. This document was the bible used to evaluate the manner in which services were delivered to the students. Specific questions dealing with the more difficult teachings were commonplace in my teacher evaluations. If the IEP wasn't being followed, the service providers were not doing their duties. The over one hundred classrooms in Northwest Ohio were the site of many talented teachers.

Evaluations in the Workshop

There were twenty workshops in the Northwestern Ohio area that I on a yearly basis had the privilege of yearly evaluating. The provisions of services in workshops were also developed on a plan called an Individual Habilitation Plan. The word "habilitation" was to mean learning skills that one never had acquired. Rehabilitation is learning skills that one had learned at one time and now need to relearn. The workshops were organized in many ways. Sometimes there were individuals who would have a difficult time accomplishing any task. These individuals would need to receive training in a task that was available and within their ability levels. Tasks many times in the workshop were assembly type work, packaging materials, or other manual work. At the Richland Newhope Center in Mansfield where I was the acting workshop director, electric meters were disassembled, and the various wires and metals were separated and sold for scrap. These funds were used to pay the workers. Another recycling project that was implemented around this time in another county was to separate aluminum and steel cans. Steel cans were extracted by using a large magnet, and the aluminum cans continued down the conveyor belt to containers, and then they could be sold separately.

Another form of employment that was not very common in the mid-seventies was community employment. People with developmental disabilities were placed in part- or full-time jobs located in the community. Bagging groceries or cleaning offices were some jobs at this time. While this type of employment would be more commonplace in about fifteen years, there were a handful of community jobs at this time.

Program Assistance for Group Homes

The district office in Toledo was where my office was located as a program consultant. The development of group homes or places for people with mental retardation and developmental disabilities to live was being developed by a residential specialist in the district office in conjunction with people from the county boards. The residential specialist would identify potential homes, interview the potential operator, identify potential clients, and help identify funds for the establishment of residential services.

At this phase of my career, I was not responsible for the development of group homes, but I did work in this exciting area with operators on the program plans for people in or going into their homes.

Experiences with the Nineteen County Board of Mental Retardation

Training for the IEP

One of my first assignments as educational consultant was to arrange a training program for administrators and teaching staff in the county boards of mental retardation and developmental disabilities on the IEP. This plan was to be the road map for every special needs child. Federal funds were available for this training, which was to take place the summer of 1975. I began to talk with some of the would-be participants in this training about some potential sites and training. Identifying a training spot that was relaxed, close by, and would provide a fun-type setting for the several days of instruction was an important factor.

After looking at many sites, I chose a place for the over fifty participants. The site was Put-in-Bay, Ohio. This island located off Catawba Island on the southern shore of Lake Erie seemed like the perfect spot. I was excited about the setting as water usually makes an appealing place to be. I took a ride over to the island with Al Deetorie, one of the superintendents, and met with the Miller Boat Line staff to arrange transportation. I then met with the mayor, who also owned the Park Hotel and restaurant accommodations. There was at the time one other downtown motel. We needed both of these two sleeping accommodations and a restaurant to eat breakfast, one for lunch and the other for supper. With the accommodations secured, I double-checked with a Bowling Green University professor, Dr. Blackwell, to conduct the training sessions. The reservations came in surprisingly fast with each of the nineteen counties having around two reservations each. The finances were arranged with the federal government, and I waited anxiously for the day to come. This was a big and important event, so I wanted it to go without a hitch as this would be one of many training sessions I would be coordinating while working for the state of Ohio.

The big day came, and everyone showed up at the specified time to ride the large ferry we had rented to the island. The weather was beautiful and a bit hotter than I was hoping to experience. We reached the island in time for lunch and then began the classes. The classes were held in a room at the Park Hotel. In less than a half hour into the training, I reached my first challenge. The room was rapidly pulling in the heat from outdoors. With no air-conditioning and the room reaching an unbearable temperature, we decided to move the class to a park located directly across from the Park Hotel. The move was one of our best as the class went well, and it was time for supper. We finished up our class for the day, and now it was time to have a little time off. The ping-pong game on a video pong screen had just come out, and everyone was anxious to give it a try. Night life was everywhere on Put-in-Bay, so we roamed the downtown area until it was time to hit the hay. The next few days went well, and before we knew it, the class was completed, and everyone had profited from the great weather, great location, great class, and great people. An evaluation was to be done by the representative who worked with the Federal Department of Education to fund the training. I suggested that I knew how well the sessions had gone, and I could complete the evaluations. That idea did not fly because of a conflict of interest, so the participants proved how well the training project had been conducted.

The last evening we had planned a chicken grilled supper. The food was great, and the drinks were special. The next day, we boarded the ferry and were on our way home. I felt good about all the arrangements as I have yet to see another training session that was done so reasonably and which turned out to be a training next to none. Another positive factor was the enhancement of relationships that had been developed among all the participants. I was to stay in positions with the state of Ohio working with all the participants for over the next ten years. This was to be one of the greatest, if not the greatest training, I had ever coordinated. It was also to be one of the fondest memories of my professional career.

Erie County Evaluation

While I was to conduct many evaluations in the nineteen county areas, there were some memories associated with Erie County or the county seat, Sandusky, that needed to be shared.

Fishing

Visiting Erie County where Cedar Point is located was usually scheduled in the fall for their program evaluation by the Ohio Department of MRDD. During the workday, I would evaluate the Erie County Board of Mental Retardation and Developmental Disabilities, and then I would clock out from work and head toward Lake Erie. I never worried about my work hours as I always put in many hours over the standard forty-hour week.

The fall was perch fishing time, and I was near one of the best fishing spots in Lake Erie, the Huron Pier. I was lucky enough to partake in fishing what many consider the best eating fish in the world. I would bring my fishing rod, my cooler with food and drinks, my tackle box, and my minnow pail. I didn't need a chair as my cooler served as a fine chair. If the weather was tolerable, I would usually catch a few perch, transport them home, and clean them so that Kathy could fix us one of the best meals in the world. This fishing break after work was a very enjoyable time, especially if I caught fish.

The Railroad Ties

On another occasion, I was evaluating the Erie County program, and I had a most unusual time. After the evaluation was completed, I clocked out and headed for the docks in Downtown Huron, Ohio, next to the fishing pier. I had a cousin, Leo Schlotterer, who worked for a company that oversaw the unloading of the giant iron ore ships. On this particular day, I was fortunate enough to scale the structure that was situated above the ships and from that vantage point see the entire operation of unloading the ships. I must admit that I was so high in this structure that I began to get dizzy. It was fascinating to see caterpillars tucked in the structure overlooking the ships and to see how they were lowered into the ship's belly to push together the iron ore that had not been removed by the cranes.

With this experience as a background, the real reason that I had gone to see my cousin surfaced. It was not the see his job site, although this had been fascinating; it was to transport some railroad beams. I was to pick up some railroad ties that had been discarded but still had some life in them. When my parents' cottage was built, they had placed railroad ties next to the water so that a wall of ties held the soil from eroding. We had a truck and proceeded to find some nice ties. The ties were very nice, but unfortunately, they were very long and very heavy. After several attempts, we finally loaded enough ties to repair the wall that had collapsed in several spots. It was a pleasure to visit the cottage and see the great job we had done to restore the wall with the railroad ties.

A School with Unusual Characteristics

My interest in anything that borders on the out of the ordinary is up my alley. A friend of mine who was associated with a school was sharing a story with me about the school building. The building was built near a location where people who had died were stored. It seemed that especially at night, there were many strange sounds that could be heard. Some of these strange yet common sounds were doors slamming, chairs moving, and other peculiar sounds. While nobody was ever seen in the building who originated the sounds, it was an interesting story and one I would have liked to pursue. I had talked with my friend about sleeping in the building, and it was agreed that we would do that someday. Unfortunately, someday never came, and I have not had the opportunity to stay in the building.

Construction Projects

A large part of my position I enjoyed was approving construction projects for the various county boards. My part of the projects was seeing that the proposed construction was meeting the program needs of the future occupants of the schools, workshops, and residential projects. The program approval included many parts of the project. For example, the size and arrangement of the rooms and setup of desks, work centers, and storage location to name a few related the structure of the building to successful programs.

At this time, my major responsibility was in the schools or training centers and the workshops. My role was more minor in the residential construction. As a program consultant between 1973 and 1977, there were eight schools in progress for a total cost of $6,371,893. There were two workshops to be completed at $1,151,537. The total cost of buildings in progress at this time that I was involved was $7,523,430. It was always exciting to see new buildings that hopefully meant more exciting programs. These new buildings would hopefully foster a more positive image of the school and workshop in the community.

Each of these projects usually had a dedication to formally announce to the public that the building was complete, in use, and open for viewing. I was usually invited to say a few words at the ceremony as the state of Ohio had usually granted funds for the construction of the building. I was an official state of Ohio program consultant. This experience allowed me the opportunity to use my public speaking skills. At one of the workshop dedications, I was scheduled to give some of the opening remarks. It was past the time to start the program when the administrator informed me that the main speaker from Columbus had not yet arrived, and they had not been able to contact him to see where in transit he was. She asked me to start the program and talk as long as I could in the hopes that the main speaker might be just a few minutes late.

I quickly wrote down a few comments about the project, the program, the state department, and other related issues concerning county boards. I opened the program with the packed house by welcoming everyone, and then I used my recently compiled list to lengthen my talk. The entire time I was talking, I was watching the main entrance to see if the official from Columbus had arrived. The dedication program was being aired on public television, so I was reaching a crowd much greater than was assembled in the new workshop.

As I was reaching the end of my extended comments, I noticed a distinguished gentleman walking in the front entrance. I was a distance from the man but noticed that he looked a lot like the main speaker. I was at the end of my comments, so I informed the crowd that I thought the main speaker had arrived. As I left the podium, it was easy to see that the man who had just entered was not coming up to the podium. This clearly was not the main speaker from Columbus, and at this time, it did not look as if he was coming. The program moved past the main speaker and into the rest of the program. I had done my best to keep the program going by giving the best off the cuff speech I could. The program went well despite the lack of the main speaker. I have never forgotten the gift of speech that came to me that day so that I could give a speech that I was not well prepared to deliver.

Working with the Ohio Division of Mental Retardation and Developmental Disabilities

Mental Retardation and Mental Illness

I would like to again address a common misunderstanding between the two words, "mental illness" and "mental retardation." They are not the same, although it is possible for a person to possess both conditions at one time.

In a 1975 newspaper article, I came across an article that confused these two conditions. I informed the paper that I wished to clear up these two definitions.

My understanding of mental retardation is that it is a condition in which the person's intelligence does not allow them to attain their full potential in terms of learning and using their learning. Mental illness is a person who usually has normal intellectual abilities but has severe emotional disturbances.

The Boat Ride

One of my first set of meetings in the department was in the summer of 1973 around Vermilion, Ohio. Several items of business were discussed with the other educational consultants, the administration, and the other state program specialists. The chief of the program consultants was Joe Auberger. At the end of the day, we usually ate dinner at one of the local restaurants. On this particular day after the dinner, I asked the group if they would like to take a ride on my brother's pontoon on the Huron River. My brother docked his pontoon at my parents' cottage on the Huron River, and Vermilion is within a few miles of the cottage.

The group thought this would be a nice idea. Since the weather was beautiful, the ride should be very comfortable. We pulled up to my dad's cottage, and I found the keys in the cottage, and off we went. It was a truly beautiful evening, and the temperature was very comfortable with the sun out. We went up the river several miles and then decided to get back before it was dark. On the way back, we began to meet other boats with the same idea we had. When one boat went by us, I didn't think he was going fast enough to create a wake or wave. I was wrong. The front of the pontoon was pretty open, and before I knew it, a large wake or wave came in the boat and hit Joe with great force. After the wave encounter, Joe was wet and very cold in the evening air. Some of the participants in the meeting gave me a hard time about getting my boss onto the river so I could drench him. Joe and I continued our very positive relationship despite the fact that he encountered a wet evening sitting on the front of the pontoon.

Ohio State University

In the summer of 1974, I was enrolled at Ohio State University to take graduate courses in special education. The coursework lasted for several weeks and was taught by the Chief of Program Services, Dr. Maxine Mays. One of the outcomes of this coursework was to be the development of a curriculum for people with moderate mental retardation. Lloyd Harris was the project director and oversaw the writing of this group project.

One of the drawbacks of this long stay away from home was picking my clothing out each day. Since I was color blind, Kathy came up with the idea of numbering all my clothing so that I was able to match the colors. I had numbers on all my shirts, ties, and suits so I was properly color coordinated. If a piece of clothing would go well with more than one pair of pants, it would have more than one number.

The writing of the curriculum took several months, and the product was extremely well written, organized, and should be helpful to teachers and teacher assistants in the state of Ohio in writing and implementing programs for people with moderate mental retardation who attend county board of mental retardation and development disability programs throughout Ohio.

While the curriculum project was to be a success, one other incident associated with the coursework was not. The entire class was composed of around ten people. We would usually eat together at the end of the class day. On one such occasion, we had left and returned to the hotel lobby. One of the female participants returned with the group and went to her room.

As she opened the door, she was greeted by a ransacked room. She had been robbed. Anything of value was taken. She called the police to investigate the robbery. The only way she thought that someone would have known that the room was unoccupied would have been for the perpetrator to have seen her leave her room and the building. Everyone was extra careful in keeping track of their valuables after the robbery.

The Evaluation down South

I was one of six program consultants for the Department of MRDD. Betty Wasserman, a former superintendent, was one of the consultants for whom I had a great deal of respect. She was also a close friend and an extremely knowledgeable person on all programs through the department (MRDD). At times, all the consultants were called in to conduct evaluations of county board. One of the southern counties in Ohio had asked the Department of MRDD for an evaluation.

The other consultants set a date for the evaluation, knowing that I was not free that day and would need to reschedule. The other consultants had completed their evaluations, and it was my turn to travel to coal country to complete a program evaluation using my areas of expertise. After a good night's sleep in the county to be evaluated, I was up early the next morning and found a small restaurant in the country that served breakfast. I ordered bacon, sunny-side eggs, and hash browns. The waitress asked me if I wanted home fries or hash browns. I said the stringy ones. She said, "You want home fries." I explained to the waitress that the home fries and hash browns were reversed up north. She explained that she knew that, and that was why she asked me which I wanted.

I drove up to the front of the school and was met by one of the administrators. As I was being escorted through the program, I noticed the person with me was upset about tape being on the floors since it is hard to clean the floors. I explained my thoughts that if learning was taking place,

I was less concerned about the ease of cleaning the floors. I looked at the rest of the programs and observed some teachers and workshop personnel when they came in to work.

After the evaluation, I explained to the superintendent that I would have my report done in a week after I had explained to him my findings. Leaving the county was interesting as the mountains were like a roller coaster through the beautiful countryside. I was going up one mountain, and when I looked to my left, I saw one of the largest pieces of equipment I had ever seen in my life. As I looked closer at the object, it resembled a strip mining scoop or bucket. It was so large that it could have held at least six cars and maybe more in its scoop. I sat on the hillside with my mouth open for several minutes. I decided I had better continue home and take with we me a large memory of the very large scoop. Leaving is exactly what I did.

Interesting People Whom I Have Met

A frequent opportunity I had while traveling in this position was to talk to strangers who were hitchhiking. I was putting several thousand miles on my private car traveling many lonely miles, especially on the way to Columbus, and I enjoyed talking to people I would meet along the way. The big fear I had was that I would be talking to someone, and they might try to hold me up, or I would say something offensive and be in harm's way. Luckily, neither of these happened. Before approaching strangers, I would look them over closely, look how they were dressed and how they acted. If I felt uncomfortable, I wouldn't talk to them. On occasion, someone would ask me for a ride. I steered clear of females as I didn't want to be accused of any types of actions I didn't or wouldn't think of doing.

If the person looked and sounded good, I would usually talk to them. My wife wasn't keen on me talking to strangers, but as I told her and as I told myself, I wanted to write a book on people I have met. If I talked to someone, I would later write up the information.

I remember one very fascinating man who worked on a shrimp boat. He explained the various jobs on the boat and told me he was a header. I asked him what a header did. He drew a picture and showed the shrimp with a head located at the large end of the shrimp. He demonstrated that he would put his thumbnail at the base of the head of the shrimp, have the shrimp lying on his index finger between the finger and the thumb, and he would cut off the head with his thumbnail. I told him I thought that would make the thumb and index finger sore. He said it only hurt until one was able to form a callus on the thumb and the finger. I never was able to write the book because I didn't have the time to talk to enough people.

Experiences around the Home and Community

A Visit from the Latter Day Saints Church

It was a summer day in June, and I was painting our home in New Rochester, Ohio. In those days, money was tight, and Kathy and I would do many jobs that involved us doing the work and paying ourselves. As I was working on the east side of the house applying the paint to the primed wood, two young well-dressed gentlemen came up to me and offered a copy of one of their religious publications. They struck up a conversation, and I continued my painting while talking to them. It turned into a very informative discussion to me as I listened to the beliefs of the Mormons. I hope it turned into a very informative discussion for the two gentlemen as I explained the Catholic religion. The discussion was well into an hour before they decided they needed to leave. I could have offered them the opportunity to paint, but they were not dressed for the occasion.

As I thought about the discussion I had just experienced, I couldn't help but admire the witnessing for God that they were experiencing. Witnessing for me wasn't usually talking about God directly but was to give by everyday example what I saw as being a good Christian. Several years later, I became involved in a ministry for my church, Blessed John XXIII, to give Catholics not active in the church a chance to renew their commitment to God. It was at that same time I coincidentally read the writings of a very talented and insightful person, Chris Clody. Chris was writing in his e-mail about the redemption of Christ and witnessing of Christ. His words were as follows:

This noble scenario may make a wonderful movie but there is a bigger picture here offered by the sacrifice of Christ for all people. Although He died in our place, He is asking all He loves to allow Him to live on through our lives and a demonstration of our love and gratitude. We actually become part of the Redemption story scripted by God. Suddenly, the mountain of fear before me to tell others about the wonders of Christ become a path that is laid out before me with just enough light for the next step.

Certainly I may feel hesitant to where this path leads, but the light is sufficient for my every step. Remember, like the wedding at Cana, Christ has saved for His friends the best wine for last. Jesus drank the bitter wine of our sin so we may enjoy the sweet wine of our redemption when we join Him at the wedding feast in Heaven. Now that's a movie and a mountain climb all in one!

Let's take the next step.

Love your Neighbor for God so loved the world.

The quotation speaks for itself. I would add that this paragraph is an inspiration to me to continue in taking my next partially lighted step in a public ministry for God. Yes, God's love for us allows us to live and give in this world to others as well as the next.

The Late Night Visitors

It was around 2:00 a.m., and I was sound asleep. Kathy woke me and told me that there were dogs in our backyard trying to kill our pet rabbit. I was up like a flash and quickly put on my pants, my sweatshirt, my boots, and I grabbed my gun and loaded it in record time. As I walked out the side door, I could hear dogs growling and trying to get at our pet rabbit.

I took a shot in the air to try to ward off the dogs. As I stood in my boots in the backyard, I thought, *What will I do if they attack me?* Within a few seconds, I could hear that the dogs had left the rabbit pen and were now in the field behind our house. I thought I saw a dog, so I took a shot at it with my .22 rifle. I heard a dog squeal as if I had hit it. I thought that was a lucky shot.

The dogs left and went toward the cemetery. I checked out the rabbit pen and found that it was in good shape but needed a little repair. I went to bed, and when I awoke the next morning, I had a call from my neighbor Gene Walston. He asked me if a pack of dogs were at our house the previous night. I relayed the story to him and then waited for his response. He told me that the dogs came to his house and killed most of his pets, including a large turkey. As I reflected on the previous evening, I wondered if it would have made a difference to the results of Gene's animals if I had called him. Unfortunately, I wasn't sure exactly where the dogs were going.

The Lost Barbecue Set

Kathy and I had been away on an early Sunday evening and had just pulled into our driveway when we noticed a truck by the barn adjacent to our property. I usually checked out who was on the property, even though it was not my property. As I rounded the corner to the back of the barn, I noticed a familiar person. We talked for a few minutes, and he explained that he was doing some barbecuing and had talked with the owner about using the equipment. It was getting dark, and he needed to get going.

I walked to the front of the barn as he secured the load on his trailer. I watched as he came around the corner of the barn and gave the truck gas to get a good start out of the barnyard. In the driveway that led to the main road, there were a couple of bumps. The trailer caught both bumps, and I saw the entire load go into the air, and as the trailer kept moving, the metal came down and landed not on the trailer, but instead it landed on the ground. The driver continued his trip because he could not see the equipment had fallen off the trailer.

I decided to wait where the grates and side box had landed because the driver would soon notice he had lost his load. About five minutes later, he was back, picked up his load, and better secured the metal. I didn't say anything about the lost load, and he didn't either.

We loaded the metal, and he was off again, hopefully keeping his full load.

Big Brothers of Northwest Ohio

In 1976, I received notification from the Big Brothers of Northwestern Ohio that I had been a Big Brother for five years. As I looked at the award, I could see the two young men whom I had the pleasure of spending time over the past five years. Herb was my first little brother, and when it was the appointed weekend, I would pick up Herb, usually on a Friday night, and take him to our house so we could hang out with each other. We would fish, take hikes, do some shopping, and one time we tried winter camping.

On this particular time, we were camping in the woods with Kathy's Uncle Norb Stang and his boys—Richard, Russell, Leroy, Roger, and Tommy. About 2:30 a.m., it got so cold that it was not safe for us to be out in the elements. We picked up our sleeping bags and beelined it to the house to sleep warmly by the fire.

One of the most memorable occasions with Herb was engineered by Kathy. She would become involved with Herb when appropriate, and at Christmas, decorating cookies was very appropriate for Kathy's involvement. Kathy had made several dozen sugar or cutout cookies. Herb spent time with us a few nights after the cookies were baked, so they were ready to frost. I have never seen anyone enjoy decorating cookies as much as Herb did. He made the gingerbread men dance and had the time of his life putting on the various colored sugars, figurines, and cinnamon drops. Herb used every color and every shape of decoration. By the time the night was over, we had left over on the table and floor enough various toppings for next year!

I was reassigned to another young man who lived about three miles from my house. The second little brother was Kurt. Kurt and I had various projects we enjoyed together. The seasons would dictate some of those activities such as autumn, the time of year to rake leaves. As with Herb, Kurt and I had over two years of wonderful times together. When Kurt's mother, Kay remarried, Kurt could no longer be my little brother.

The importance of my experiences in being a big brother was to surprisingly come together for me several years later. It started when I received a graduation announcement from Kurt, inviting me to his graduation party. I knew I wanted to go to the party, but I was wondering what I would have in common with Kurt after all these years apart. It wasn't going into an unfamiliar situation by myself that concerned me as this type of situation had been a rule rather than an exception for me. My professional career and my private life were built on facing various situations alone. My jobs all required an ability to meet new people and form relationships.

The day of the party, I parked my car at the address on the invitation. I began walking into an unfamiliar setting as Kurt lived in a new town than where he lived when I was his big brother. I walked into the backyard without a hint in my mind about where this was all going. I didn't have a clue that I was about to have one of the most unexpected and rewarding hours of my life. I looked around for Kurt or someone familiar to me.

Within a few seconds, I caught Kurt's eye. He immediately began to walk to me, and I was most impressed by his size. Kurt was many times bigger than when I knew him, and he looked like a football player. Kurt expressed to me how very happy he was that I had come to the party. I could tell by his voice that it wasn't just a social nicety, but he was very happy I was here. I knew he was happy because from that point on until I left, Kurt was by my side. He introduced me to his friends, and of course, I saw his mother. Kurt was very proud that I had been his big brother, and he wasn't the least bit shy telling people. Very quickly, it was evident that at that hour, Kurt and I had gone back in time and were as close, if not closer, than we had ever been. I looked at his high school achievements and saw that he was a standout football player. He was to attend a college on a scholarship, which I believe was in football.

We ate together, talked together, and it was one of the most marvelous experiences in my life. Kurt didn't seem to be very concerned about spending his time with others. As the time went by, Kurt in many ways was telling me how much he had appreciated our time together. I needed to go after about an hour, and I hated to leave such an enjoyable and memorable occasion. I have not seen Kurt since his graduation, but I expect to run into him sometime in the future, and I am looking forward with great anticipation to this time together. Every time I think of this graduation party, it brings tears to my eyes, tears of joy.

St. Thomas More University Parish

We continued our sixth year of attendance at St. Thomas More Catholic Church in Bowling Green. The church existed for students and faculty at BGSU. I had finished my master's degree, and Kathy was working on her bachelor's degree, so we qualified as members. Kathy and I had enjoyed being instructors for the marriage preparation course at the parish. We covered the same faith and different faith sessions. The result was that a marriage can make it with either the same or different faith of the couple. With the same-faith marriage, there is one less challenge to face.

Another happening in May 1976 was that I had been asked by Father Herb to be the chairperson for the Diocese Development Fund. This was a fundraiser for the parishes in Northwest Ohio. The funds were used for many social services, spiritual, and other projects. The funds raised had progressed each year, and with the help of the parish, we were to be successful this year.

Time to Move On

An opening as the district IV manger with the Division of Mental Retardation and Developmental Disabilities, the Department of Mental Health and Mental Retardation for the ten counties in Northwest Ohio came open. It was a management position and involved a great deal of responsibility. I talked with several professional friends and, of course, my wife about the position. The position seemed right, the staff was competent, and I needed to return to management. So another chapter of my life is unfolding.

CHAPTER 5

District Manager and Other Positions

Background

In early 1975, I was appointed to the position of district manager. My prior positions had prepared me for this latest appointment. For example, in 1967, I had started my career in mental retardation and developmental disabilities in Mansfield as the physical education and recreation director. After two years in Mansfield, we left for employment in Toledo in the Lucas County Board of Mental Retardation and Developmental Disabilities in a similar-type position that I had just left. Going to Toledo allowed both me and Kathy to further our education. Another four years passed, and in 1973, I had a chance for advancement with the state Department of MRDD as an educational consultant. In this state position, I was responsible for the development, coordination, funding, monitoring, licensing, and evaluation of community services and programs for the ten counties in Northwestern Ohio. After completing my master's degree from BGSU in 1970, I felt I was ready for this challenge. Some people have chidingly told me at this point in my career that four jobs in six years exemplified well the principle that I could not hold a job.

The many happenings that will be covered in this chapter as in other chapters were firsthand information that I knew well because they were part of my job. The happenings of central office and state, the district office, and the county boards of MRDD was information that on a daily basis, I needed to know and use. Much of the information I was personally involved with providing. The television and newspaper articles often quoted me or others in my office. In dealing with the public relations network, we needed to be honest about the information we made public. If information was privileged, we needed to protect the clients, the communities, the department, and our job. Sometimes it was a tough call, but wherever, possible information was conveyed to the public. We were, in fact, dealing with people's rights or the civil rights of people with mental retardation and developmental disabilities. The issues to be solved were existing, challenging, and required in many cases an attitudinal or monetary change in the provision of services.

District Office
Five Jobs in One
District Manager

Taking over the reins of the district office had its uneasy times. This would be the first time I was responsible as CEO for a large office at twenty-nine years of age. The staff was to grow from eleven to twenty-five people because of federal grants such as CETA and Vista. Major services provided were overseeing and providing public relations and planning with the nine counties in Northwest Ohio. Providing case management services for people in need and instituting a client flow system through a central data bank and process of placement and follow-up required twenty-four-hours-a-day, seven-days-a-week services by my staff. Bottom line was that many services such as lodging and food were essential for all clients, and many did not adequately possess these resources. Working to expand services for the community, including the county boards of mental retardation and development disabilities, was challenging in that some counties had funds to expend on these social services and some did not. Administering the purchase of service funds for residential services as well as development of residential homes were important aspects of the provision of services. The program consultant was responsible for monitoring and evaluating programs with the county boards of mental retardation and developmental disabilities through early intervention, school-age, and adult programs. Licensure of residential facilities was a yearly review and quarterly monitoring. Organizing and providing services in needed areas was constant with the ever-changing directions of the programs. A closer look at these services is important to understand the breath of services to people with mental retardation and developmental disabilities. It is only through close monitoring, consultation, and coordination can the changes with the community and state agencies take place.

Capital Construction

As the district manager and residential consultant, I looked at the capital construction of residential homes from two different viewpoints. As district manager, I looked at all the construction in the entire district, and as residential consultant, I looked at all the projects and all the specifics of the homes. Residential development was at this time exploding as many counties were looking at returning their county residents who had lived in the state institutions back to their home county. Group homes were somewhat common in counties, and many residents were housed in the state institutions run by the state of Ohio. In the ten counties in Northwest Ohio between 1975 and 1979, there were ten residential homes in the process of building or remodeling at a total cost of $4,233,281. This meant that 169 people would have or continue to have their residences. Seeing residents come home to their county of origin or remain in their county of residence and be close to their families and the resources of their county provided positive living circumstances for those involved.

Support services such as maintenance, transportation, and other auxiliary services were needed for all the programs administered by the county board of mental retardation and developmental disabilities. There were five such support service buildings at $129,344.

Overview of Duties

The various tasks of the district office required people with expertise in each of their areas. As in every management position, the easy solutions to challenges do not always come easy. The ability to work with other people and organizations requires that from the top managers down everyone must work together. Boards of organizations work with their executive directors who worked with me, and my people required all of us to be on the same song sheet. Sometimes these song sheets require written agreements; other times they are verbal. The risks that are to be taken in all phases of program provision must be carefully assessed so the clients are the winners. There were several community leaders whose expertise and contacts were essential to success. Specials requests by families for services needed by clients who were either alive or had passed we tried to respect. I was to find early in administration that being nice to everyone was essential. It is essential because it is the right thing to do, and tomorrow they or you may be gone.

Residential Developer

As was just pointed out, residential development was another major component of the district office. Since residential development was an extremely important development at this time and funding was an issue, as was the attitude of the neighborhood, I had the privilege of taking on the responsibilities as the residential developer for one year because of the lack of funds. This position entailed knowing the residential needs in each county, working with the counties to find grants for the twenty new residential facilities in process, and working with the counties to obtain operational funds and the acceptance of people with mental retardation and developmental disabilities in their neighborhood. Monitoring existing homes in terms of the provision of appropriate services was very time-consuming, challenging, and entailed working with communities, advocate groups, and others who had an interest in existing residential homes. Although it was unusual, a few homes were asked to close their doors because of inadequate care. Another major variable to be addressed was zoning for proposed homes. In these times, neighborhoods needed more understanding of people with disabilities. Our next section will review some trying public meetings in which the rights of the developmentally disabled were addressed.

Zoning

The establishment of single-family dwellings was an issue that was addressed in the twelve district offices active in 1977. The issue throughout the state was whether a family home in zoning meant that unrelated people, such as people with MRDD, could live as a family. Another interpretation used in family dwellings is that people living in a family home-zoned area must be related people or family. The result was there are many family home-zoned areas, and if people with MRDD are not considered family under the zoning laws, they cannot legally live in this type of zoning.

In Walbridge, Ohio, in May 1977, a hearing was held to consider whether a group home could be established by the Wood County Board of Mental Retardation and Developmental Disabilities. While the village mayor opposed the establishment of the home, he was also concerned about the passage of a bill that allowed family homes to have up to eight residents. A further concern was that the state could dictate zoning to the local community. Another representative and I gave a presentation on why the group homes should be allowed to be established in opposition to the viewpoints of the city of Walbridge.

The Rossford, Ohio, hearing on a proposed group home was scheduled near the time that the Walbridge meeting was held. Anyone attending this hearing should have vivid memories of these proceedings. The meeting was held at the local Indian Hills Elementary School. A representative of the Wood County Board of Mental Retardation and Developmental Disabilities, representatives of the Rossford community, and I were present. The one rule to be observed was that one question would be asked at a time, the two panelists would answer that question, and then we would move to the next question. As we entered the school, local television camera began to take video. The first question was asked, the second question was asked, and many questions were asked with no chance to answer. The discussion was completely out of hand and was over as soon as it started. The Rossford group home was not established at this time, but the Walbridge home was opened.

It was rare, but it did happen that a home was not providing the proper services. The closing of a home was not pleasant for any of the parties.

Wolf Wolfensberger

One of the well-known developing philosophies of the time was that large institutions should be abandoned or at least downsized in favor of more small homes in the community. In October 1977, I was to spend several days in Delaware, Ohio, attending a workshop by Dr. Wolf Wolfensberger, a well-known expert on residential housing for the mentally retarded and developmentally disabled who advocated this philosophy and many other progressive views. The training was beneficial and provided many up-to-date ideas about residential home size and other related issues.

While the controversy over institutional size was very real, the fact remained that the issues associated with homes for the mentally retarded were real, and changes were beginning to be proposed.

Program Consultant

I came into this position with two jobs, the educational consultant for district 3 out of Lima and district 4 out of Toledo. Since a hiring freeze was statewide, I needed to carry on both these educational consulting positions with my other three new positions associated with the district manager job. We will not duplicate information about the duties of the educational consulting position just described in the previous chapter.

NODC Construction

The fifth major job responsibility and position was to oversee the planning, coordination, and development of the program and twelve buildings for the $8.5 million Northwest Ohio Developmental Center (NODC). These buildings would house 177 residents admitted by the district office into NODC. The plans on the development and refinement of policies and procedures affecting the admissions, discharge, respite care, and other services for NODC was the responsibility of my office. I was the acting superintendent until August 1976 when Ray Anderson was chosen as superintendent by the selection committee.

The Glass

I traveled to other facilities in Ohio to become familiar with various construction and programs. A day before the glass was to be cut for all the buildings at NODC, I was visiting Warrensville Developmental Center in the Cleveland area. As we were walking through the center, the superintendent pointed out to us that all the glass in the buildings was safety glass. A quick check with the other experts accompanying me confirmed my recent fear—all the glass being made the next day for NODC was regular glass. Memories of my previous experiences with regular glass cutting people put a chill down my spine. You never will see a change order executed so fast in your life. The very large glass windows in all the buildings were changed from regular breakable and sharp glass to safety glass. This one experience made the trip worthwhile.

Working Together

I was not interested in being the superintendent of NODC as I enjoyed the district manager position. The establishment of NODC advisory board was to be a necessary group in the start-up and continued operation of the center. Ray and his staff's tireless hours and the time and energy of my staff led to a successful system start-up. The district office processed all the admissions, and the center handled the admissions and programs. The relationship and similar participatory management styles between Ray and me was to lead to some easier solutions in the operation of the new center and the services from the district office.

The Dedication

The dedication of NODC was on October 29, 1976. I had the privilege of welcoming and introducing the speakers. Well-known state and local officials were present. The director of the Department of Mental Health and Mental Retardation, Dr. Timothy Moritz, headed the speakers. Dr. Norman Niesen, commissioner of the Division of the Mental Retardation was next. Ray Anderson followed as the superintendent of the center. Rep. Irma Karmol and Sen. Marigene Valiquette offered their remarks. The Bowsher High School Band provided music, and the staff provided tours. Everything went well until after the program. I was enjoying the success of the program. My four-year-old son was playing on the playground when he fell and cut the bottom of his chin on a piece of wood. It was off to the family doctor for stitches. The doctor did a marvelous job of patching up Joey.

More on the Programs at NODC

The developmental center was to provide transitional programming for people who will usually remain for a few months up to three years. The programming they will receive will be on an individual basis on a twenty-four-hour-each-day basis. The environment will be humane. The short term residential treatment will serve as a transition point for people moving through state mental retardation facilities to community settings.

The Energy to Do All These Jobs

With this background, we can now look at more specifics in my work and my private life. Little did I know upon entering these positions that my energy level would need to grow more than I could possibly imagine. I would need every bit of energy that I naturally possessed, and I was not sure where the additional energy source originated. I had beliefs in God and His ability to give and mine to receive this positive energy and consequently positive deeds or actions. My belief that my twin was a part of my life and mysteriously I would receive energy from my twin for this task seemed real to me. Other people in my life and internal energy were sources of energy that I believe are present, and I am able to identify from others giving me positive interactions and knowledge, and I am able to at times link them to help me spring into action. These forms of energy or help should continue to be observable in my writings.

The downside of energy can be perception by others. Fast motions and quick problem-solving can be uncomfortable for others. I did not hide my enthusiasm, which was often exemplified in my fast actions, until I sensed my actions were making me ineffective with others. In one program evaluation, I was coined "Like a dog chasing a car." When I read this, I knew that I needed to look closer at my actions.

Issues in the District Office

Deinstitutionalization

A major emphasis of the district office was to see that the objectives of deinstitutionalization were adopted. Many of the people with mental retardation and developmental disabilities were living in state facilities called institutions, at home with their parents, or a few were living in community homes. The focus of the MRDD was to move people from the state facilities and into group homes or other appropriate homes in the community. The community is where every person has the right to live. At this time, few homes existed, and the funding for these homes was just developing. The development of group homes and procurement of the funding were the responsibilities of the district office. Institutions could have over one thousand residents, and group homes could typically have four to eight residents. Living in the community allowed residents to use the community resources, such as grocery stores, clothing stores, restaurants, recreation areas, and other stores, which didn't always exist in the large institutions.

Institutions and the Central Services

With the development of the new district office system, money was being stretched as two systems were in place. As one is phased out, the institution, the other is being developed, the community. Thus, not enough money was available for both the institutions and the community homes.

Various systems were being developed so that the transition from one to the other system was able to take place.

In 1976, an example of one such plan that Dr. Robert Carl Jr., superintendent of Columbus State Institute (CSI), and district managers Mary Flanagan, Ray Troyer, and I developed was to take $3.6 million from the CSI budget and use it for the remodeling and construction of residential homes in the twenty-five county catchment area. The population would be reduced from 1,000 at CSI to 250 by July 1979. In 1977, Dr. Carl was to become my boss as an assistant commissioner, allowing more creative ideas to develop.

As we addressed the funding of institutions and community residences, we found we were dealing with a difficult proposition. If monies were required by lawsuits to place more funds into the institution, then where would the monies for community development materialize? Another need was the emergencies of the residential homes in the community, a development we shall see shortly in the case management section.

Another commonly known issue at this time was whether it was right to isolate people with mental retardation in institutions from the rest of society. A ruling in Philadelphia stated that residents in nearby Pennhurst School for the Mentally Retarded violates their Fourteenth Amendment right to equal protection under the law.

In Ohio at Orient Institution, legal action was filed that claimed that the rights of residents to training and education were being violated. By 1982, Orient's population was to go to 350 from 1,000. Little did I know that I would from 1983 to 1985 be on the team that would close the largest institution in Ohio and place individuals in community homes.

On the other side of the fence, residents who were in the institution had the right to leave, but some also felt they had the right to stay. Even if no appropriate living residence was available, they had the right to leave the center. The welfare of the resident was an issue, and as we looked at the community, we would be addressing their rights. Another admission issue was that admission into an institution was more difficult.

Another factor in institutions was if employees were unionized. The ability to strike allows less supervision of residents. This is a scary circumstance. One may ask, is the help in the institutions good help? I have seen it good. I have also heard about the use of drugs and alcohol by workers while working.

In the middle of 1975, legislation went into effect that established the Ohio Legal Rights Services to represent clients who received services from the department. This agency has been critical of the department's actions in improving institution services. While some improvements are cited by legal rights, others such as elective surgery need improvement. In the middle of 1976, Guardian Services were established to provide guardians where needed for residents to obtain needed services such as surgery.

There are many possibilities that will enable the state to take the funds from the institutions and move these funds to the community so they can serve the residents in their home county or communities. Yes, time is required to build facilities, and money is needed to run the residences for the mentally retarded. The availability of funds from the state, federal, or local levies is a constant issue in question.

The Partnership of Local Groups, the County Boards of Mental Retardation and Developmental Disabilities, and the District Office

No partnership was perfect, yet the development of some type of system was essential between the district office and county boards of MRDD. The district office with its planning, coordination, development, and placement of residents into residential facilities and other services needed capital and operating funds. County board service was at the apex in the development of a successful system. There were many challenges in working through this process. The success rested on the partnership between the state the county and the other local providers.

Within each county were several service delivery systems in which organizations and even families were the providers of residential services. In a report by Jeanne Lippert from the district 4 office in December 1978, there were twelve residential homes in process for 248 people, and several letters of intent had been submitted for hundreds of community residential beds from state residential funding.

The results from these partnerships produced many success stories that allowed people from institutions/developmental centers and the community to live in or remain in a typical neighborhood. The acceptance by other neighbors has in most cases been very positive. The ability to hold jobs, shop at the local stores, sleep in their own room, have family meals, and yes, even take vacations is the result of many working toward a common goal—normal living.

Case Management

Case management is the central social worker who oversees the planning of services for people with mental retardation and developmental disabilities and works with the family and other community agencies. Many times, the beginning of service is to assess the needs of the individual and then plan and provide information and referral on services. An underlying principle is to protect the rights of the person being served.

It is essential to develop and use a plan so that services can be identified, coordinated, accessed, monitored, and provided. The provision of direct services out of the district office is often given by other agencies, not the district office. The provision of services may be in a number of areas such as a comprehensive evaluation, residential, health/medical, professional services, behavioral, counseling, and the legal area of guardianship, trusteeship, and protectorship. Emergency or crisis services and respite care are often services needed now. The accessing of state and federal funds is essential to accessing services. The case management services or social worker services while not a contract service in the district office would be in the near future.

Being a big part of the overall management of a person's life in terms of their daily needs and services could be a challenge. The direction of the plan required research and available resources. Being a case manager was a pleasure in a position of serving the rights of this population.

There were many cases in which the use of case management did not seem to be present. One case that many would say case management planning was questionable was in the rights of a baby in Washington, D.C. National attention was given several years ago to the case of a Down syndrome or mongoloid baby at the Johns Hopkins University Hospital in Baltimore, Maryland. The baby had an intestinal blockage that prohibited digestion. For fifteen days, the parents did not allow the doctors to operate. The baby starved to death. This was not the only case like this I was familiar with. There are many cases where human beings die because of their life condition, and case management may not be a part of this process.

Another unforgettable case that helps us understand the variables of case management was out of my office. There was a man who had lived forty-seven years in an institution. Recent legislation gave residents certain rights to leave institutions. Therefore, in 1978, he was living in the Toledo area. He had stolen a cab in Chicago and had lived in several group homes and under viaducts near highways. The weather was getting cold, so outside living was becoming dangerous. Twice in a short period, I was called to pick up this resident. The police in Woodville, Ohio, called me as the district manager and head of the office very early on a weekday morning to locate assistance in transporting this person to his dwelling. I decided to go to Woodville and transport the person to his group home.

When I picked up this person, the officer told me he had hitched a ride on the turnpike and had emptied the mailboxes from the turnpike to

Woodville. The mail was returned, and I transported the person to his boarding home. A few days later, I received a call from the Libbey Glass Company in Rossford telling me this same person had no place to live and needed a ride to his home. I again decided to pick up this person early in the morning. He was returned to his home. I received an experience that helped me better understand the role of my case managers. While this person had lived in many group homes and other residences, he would decide that day to leave his present dwelling, which he was legally able to do. Although we made available different placements and programs, he didn't like them. He left the city because he didn't agree with the options available to him.

Other Issues on Rights of the Mentally Retarded

One very successful progressive city zoning ordinance was passed through the city of Toledo, with the cooperation of the Old West End Association and the district 4 office. It was the first such zoning ordinance for the mentally retarded in the state of Ohio. This zoning allowed group homes to be established so that they could exist in a fair manner for all people involved.

In a case that came through the district office in September 1976, a lady was planning to move to Honolulu with her two mentally retarded sons. She was told that she and her sons couldn't stay in that state. We informed her of the family's right to move and stay.

Another rights issue for people with mental retardation and developmental disabilities was to vote. Laws did not exist at this time that restricted a person's ability to vote because of being mentally retarded and developmentally disabled.

A related issue in deinstitutionalization was the issue of community placement being better than the institutional setting. Individual examples have gone both ways on this issue, and a person being in the least restrictive setting is an important consideration. The placement needs to be right for the resident.

The placement of residents is a paramount issue. If a resident is to be released from an institution and the institution is in county A but the county of residence is from county B, why should county A pay for a resident who came from another county such as county B? One argument used is that the state takes money from the institution as it is no longer spending money on this person who is leaving the institution. Therefore, county A isn't spending its money on another county's resident. The other argument is that the county of residence is the first place for a person to try their community placement.

Edward S. and Edward B.

In March 1975, I had been in the office early when one of my employees informed me that Edward S.'s mother had visited the group home and claimed that the person she was told was her son was not her son. She was to claim in a lawsuit that her son died on October 22, 1972, and the nursing home had concealed this fact from her. She first learned of the death of her son on April 1973 when she visited the home. A lawsuit was filed by the mother of Edward S. in March 1975.

The other involved resident was Edward B. When interviewed about the burial, Edward B.'s father was certain that he had buried his own son. Both the Edwards were placed in the same nursing home in Toledo from Apple Creek Center located by Apple Creek, Ohio. While the paperwork confirmed that the dead child was Edward B. and that Edwards S. was alive in the nursing home, my office conducted a coordinated investigation with Apple Creek and central office to look into the questions on the identity of these two residents.

All the available paperwork was examined, and the direct care worker from Apple Creek familiar with the case traveled to Toledo to view the remaining resident. The results of the investigation were handed over to the court, who settled the case with the involved people. I never knew the actual settlement because the case was between the involved parties. I also was instructed not to release any of the information from the investigation as the investigation was conducted to settle a private lawsuit.

Several years later, I was at the state convention for the Ohio Association of County Boards of Mental Retardation and Developmental Disabilities (OACBMRDD) when my contact person from Apple Creek in charge of their investigation in this case approached me. He asked me if I had heard the latest on the Edward S. and Edward B. lawsuit. I said that I had not heard anything, and I had not talked to anyone about the case other than people such as himself who had been involved in the investigation. He told me that it was all over the news in Cleveland as the case had been made public, and the person buried on October 22, 1972, was Edward S., not Edward B. The family of Edward S. was going to exhume the body and place it in the proper burial plot. Shortly after that, a member from Edward S.'s family contacted me and invited me to the exhuming of the body and the reburial.

I was flattered to be invited to the events, but my time commitments were tight. As much as I would have liked to have met the family and pay my respects to Edward S., I could not free myself for the day. I did receive a copy of the proceedings and through this media was able to be a part of the happenings. I was, after the story was made public, finally able to talk about the true facts of this case.

The case was to say the least very unusual. While this case was very involved and time-consuming in its unfolding, the fact that the correct bodies were finally linked with the correct families made a gratifying conclusion.

Group Homes in Wood County

In January 1976, the Wood County Board of Mental Retardation submitted an application to the State Department of Mental Retardation for three homes to house twenty-four people. One home was for ambulatory residents, and two were for nonambulatory. These were the first of several homes the Wood County Board would open.

The project was proceeding as planned until it was brought forth that the location of the homes would be across the road from Wood Lane School. The other possibility for this land was that a jail may be located on the same eighty-acre site as the group homes. The point my office and central office made on the construction of the building on this proposed site was that the residential flavor must be present for state funds to be granted.

After much discussion and the donation of land in Portage, it was decided to move the location of the homes to have a residential-type setting. This was a good example of a building project being turned around so that residents would have the opportunity to have an acceptable living environment. The homes opened around December 21, 1978.

District Managers' Meetings

The district managers had an association called the District Manager's Association for the Division of Mental Retardation and Developmental Disabilities. There were periodic meetings usually in Columbus to receive updates on where the division was headed and to receive information on happenings in other parts of the state and from other departments. In an election in 1976, I was elected as a member of the executive committee. In 1977, I was elected to be the chairperson of the association.

As the chairperson, from time to time, I would meet with other district managers to discuss important issues of the day. I remember around this time I was meeting with four other district mangers in Mansfield. As we were going into Creamer's Restaurant, I opened the door for one of the district managers, who also happened to be a woman. As I opened the door, the woman told me, "I am perfectly capable of opening the door for myself." I was a little stunned by the remarks, and without thinking, I let go of the door, and it hit her. I tried to stop the door from hitting her. I was too late. Although it might have looked like I was intentionally trying to hit the lady with the door, that was not the case.

My adventures to and from Columbus had been many over the forty-one years I had been employed. One that I was not to forget happened in 1978. I was returning from Columbus on Route 23 and came to the Carey exit. I had the choice of continuing on Route 23 through Carey and Fostoria. In Fostoria, I caught Route 199 home; this was the scenic route. The other option was to pick up Route 15 to Findlay and take Interstate 75 to Route 6 and home, the route that avoided small town driving and was highway driving the entire route.

Since the time and mileage difference is negligible, I chose the scenic route. Going through Carey gave me the opportunity to get out of the car and rest on the two-hour trip.

I had traveled through Carey and was in Fostoria approaching a curve where 23 took a right turn at a stoplight and then went down and up hill to turn to the left and continued through Fostoria until I caught Route 199. As I began pulling up to the stop sign, I was slowing down because I rarely hit a green light, and I was going to turn. Out of the corner of my eye, I saw something moving between two houses on my right. I began applying my brakes a bit more, and I saw two boys coming from between the two houses close to the road. I slammed on my brakes and watched one bicycler go in front of my car and the other behind my car. I had just missed both of the boys whom I imagine were maybe ten years old. I sat in the highway for a few minutes motionless, thanking God and others who had just spared me a terrible accident and the potential of hurting and possibly killing two young boys. I was shaken and confused. I cautiously proceeded home and watched every building for another biker. Every time I passed those two homes, I watched for the bikers. The homes were eventually demolished, but I still watch for the bikers coming out of the two vacant lots.

Traveling Slower

With the establishment of NODC, a car was made available to me. I was traveling to Columbus for staff meetings on a regular basis and was constantly traveling to facilities in the ten counties in Northwestern Ohio. The car I used was an old state highway patrol car. The Plymouth was capable of traveling at a very high rate of speed, but of course, I watched my speed as it would have been a very poor example on my part to be caught for speeding.

There was one occasion I had a problem with speeding. I had been in Columbus for the entire weekend coordinating the meals for the Ohio Special Olympics. We would prepare and serve meals to all the participants and coaches, and noon meals included the volunteers. Around five thousand people were given food at the lunch meals and over two thousand at each of the other meals.

When I went to work on Monday morning with very little sleep over the weekend, I probably was not at my peak. I had pulled out onto Route 199 on a curve, and I wanted to make sure that any car that was coming around the corner after me didn't hit me. I built up the speed on my car very rapidly. As I reached the peak speed of around sixty-five or so, I saw a highway patrol car coming from the other direction. I looked at my speedometer, and I was close to being OK on the speed limit. Well, the patrolman turned around, and I had a ticket in a very short period. This was not a good way to start my Monday morning. A few days later, I was in Columbus in the central office, and the fiscal officer told me he had gotten a notice about a speeding ticket on the state car I drove. I told him the story, and I also told him it wouldn't happen again. It wasn't bad enough I had to pay for the ticket, but now I was wondering if the entire central office was going to know. I was lucky that the fiscal officer, Dick, was the only one to know about the ticket. At least I got something positive out of this ticket—a good story.

Children Services

One of the more challenging group homes we dealt with was the residential care unit located on the grounds of the Lucas County Children Services Center on River Road in Toledo. The residential care unit was for people with severe mental retardation and had over twenty but less than sixty residents. Upon taking over the district manager position, I was approached by the new director to visit the facility. I went on a visit of the facility and during the process was introduced to the unit director. The director informed me that the funding was tight. That was not good news to me as I had few available beds to house the individuals. Together, we worked hard to come up with alternate funding. A number of changes took place, and within a short period, we had solved the funding problem and my need to come up with alternate placements. It was a change in services that was able to accomplish all the factors that needed to be addressed and preserved the relationships between my office and the Lucas County Children Services. A well-fostered relationship between the two organizations was essential to the success of this project.

Abolish the District Offices

This abolishment was to be one of the most trying times of my life. I had worked to have the proper educational and professional credentials, was about to finish my Ph.D., and an office I had worked day and night to be successful was going to be abolished. This job was my dream job, the one that I enjoyed greatly. While my employees were promised other jobs, I wasn't sure it would happen. I had no idea where my future was going.

Though I had planned the change the best I could, work began at least by the end of 1977 to replace the twelve district offices with six regional centers. The commissioner of mental retardation was not pleased with the district offices giving services to newly released residents from institutions. The discussions on the future of the district office were difficult and hard to face, especially when the district offices were doing well considering the circumstances under which they were operating.

The proposed change took its toll on the office. Personally, my health underwent many negative changes in terms of my sleep and metabolism. With treatment, I lost little time on the job. Dealing with losing my office and my staff was made more difficult as the reasons for the closure made little sense.

Family

An Honor

When one least suspects it, some very positive happenings can come your way. That is what happened in May 1976 when I was named with two other Pemberville men to be Outstanding Young Men of America in their 1976 edition. The award is sponsored by the Jaycees and a number of other men's civic and service organizations across the nation. There were nine thousand men listed from America for their public service, achievements, and civic leadership. The criteria for selection include a person's voluntary service to the community, professional leadership, academic achievement, business advancement, cultural accomplishments, and civic and political participation. The award mentioned, in part, "In every community, there are young men who work diligently to make their cities as well as their country better places in which to live. These men having distinguished themselves in one or more fields of endeavor, are recognized for their achievements."

It was a nice touch, and since I believe in the recognitions of others for deeds well done and have tried to give these recognitions, I accepted the award as I hoped other people accept my praise for a job well done.

Mark Is Born

The birth of our second son, Mark, was a bit easier than our first son, Joe. The reason was simple, we had been through it once. There is no joy greater than observing life. This time around, I was in the delivery room and experienced firsthand seeing the entire birth. We did not know if we were going to have a boy or a girl. As this baby was coming into the world, I gained an immense amount of respect for Kathy. The obstetrician said, "The shoulders are too big to be a girl." He was right, we had a boy.

Elvis Comes Again

It was April 23, 1977, when we had a second opportunity to see Elvis and one that would allow us to be much closer to the performer. As Elvis took the stage, it was easy to see that he had put on weight from the last performance we had seen two years ago. While it was exciting seeing "the King," the first concert was that, the first, and it held a special place in our lives. The music was great, and Elvis put on a great show. The greatness of Elvis was to soon be somewhat diminished as his death was just around the corner, and the facts on his drugs usage and lack of wanting to go on stage were made known. Despite these facts, he was still a great performer, and it was a pleasure seeing him on stage.

Grandma Long Passes

Kathy's grandmother passed away in the middle of a winter storm. She had been ill for some time, and her time had come to be with God. Her friendly ways with others and kind smile would be missed. On the day of the funeral, the winter snow storm continued to linger. Kathy and I had decided that it would be best to take our two boys to my sister Mary Lu, who lived near the Bismark Church, St. Sebastian, where the funeral was to be observed. The boys were young, and the church would probably be cold with the subzero temperatures.

Since the storm was in full force, Kathy went to the church with her mother, father, and grandfather as I may be delayed in delivering the boys. As I started down Old Military Road toward my sister's house, the snow was becoming deeper and blowing at a pace so fast it was near or at a whiteout. As I continued down the deserted road in my Dodge station wagon, I felt an impulse to jam on my brakes and did. I quickly checked the boys and opened the door to see why I had stopped. I saw a pile of snow on the hood. I backed up the car and saw that the grill of my car was embedded in the snowdrift. A few inches more and I would probably have been stuck in the drift. If I had been stuck, the alternative of carrying my sons in the snowstorm in the whiteout would have been a pretty impossible situation. I had no way of finding help as cell phones were not common.

I somehow turned the car around and headed for the only safe alternative left; I took my sons to the church. I found a spot in the choir on the mezzanine where I could watch them and the funeral at the same time. I have often wondered why I put the brakes on just before I was to hit that large drift. Could it have been my twin protecting the three of us, or was it God or both?

Kenny Rogers

One of my favorite songs that taught me many lessons in administration was the "Gambler." The singer of that song, Kenny Rogers, was to be in Tiffin, Ohio, at the Ritz Theater on November 23, 1978. Tiffin is about forty-five minutes from our house. We obtained tickets for an evening performance. When Kenny came out to do his show, I was mystified with the selection because I was familiar with about every song he sang. Hearing the "Gambler" was a great treat as I love the song, love the melody, love the words, and loved singing it with Kenny.

Wise and Careful Use of Time

I have found that I learn many times by making mistakes, and sometimes the mistakes happen more than one time. Many times if I had taken a bit more time and thought what I was doing, I would have saved time. Here are a few of the simple examples of how I could have been more careful and saved time:

1. I was taking the potatoes to the basement. I didn't turn on the lights because I thought I could see where the potatoes were to be stored. I couldn't see when I reached the basement, so I had to go upstairs to turn on the light. I need to take time to turn on the light.

2. I was taking out the trash. When I returned to the garage, I noticed a bag of biodegradable vegetables that was to be disposed. I had to make a second trip. I need to take time to look the first time.

3. When I came down the steps after dressing, I saw my money clip on the kitchen table. I wanted to comb my hair first and forgot to pick up my money clip. I need to do a task when I first think of doing it, lest I forget to do it.

4. We have a bowl by the back door that holds keys. Often, I forget to put the keys in the bowl when I come into the house. When I am ready to go someplace, the keys are not in the bowl, and they may be upstairs, in the front closet, or some other place but the bowl. The keys go in the bowl when I come home.

5. I was to have the oil in the car changed. I had laid a tire by the car for my trailer to have the leak repaired. I was having my oil changed, but the tire was not in the car. The tire should have been placed in the car, not beside it.

6. I was going to the post office to mail two letters. I mailed one and missed the other. I went to the wallpaper store and picked up the paint but forgot the paintbrush. I went to the grocery store to pick up some Jell-O. I thought I knew the color of Jell-O and was confused with the flavor options. I called my wife to save the day. When there are several tasks to be accomplished, my wife has taught me to make notes on a piece of paper of what is to be done, the order they are to be done, and the specific directions to accomplish these goals. My note should have read: (1) Mail two letters, (2) Pick up the paint and paintbrush, (3) Pick up two Jell-O lemon artificial flavor 13 oz. gelatin dessert.

Friends

The Myers

Jim and Diane were very close friends of ours when they lived in New Rochester. Jim worked at the lime plant in Woodville and was the type of guy who was ready to go all the time. There were many projects that Jim and I undertook. Jim was more the brains in the projects, but I could handle the essential tools such as the hammer. One of Jim's major projects was gutting his upstairs, and one of mine was redoing the kitchen. Redoing the kitchen meant that we needed to put in a new window over the sink and installing a new Formica drainboard, installing a back plate, and other time-consuming tasks. Jim and I had stayed up all night getting everything ready for the tear out and putting in the window. In the early morning, taking out the old sink and the countertop was the agenda. We were at the point of ripping out part of the drainboard when Kathy came down the steps as pregnant as ever and proceeded to the bathroom to begin her morning ritual of morning sickness. As Kathy proceeded to toss her cookies, Jim said, "What is that?" I explained that Kathy was pregnant, and she got morning sickness. Morning sickness was not something Jim was close to, nor did he want to be close to it. His wife, Diane, never had morning sickness, and Jim wanted to keep it away from her, and particularly, he wanted to keep it away from him. The project was finished, and very soon after this project, Jim and Diane with their children Josh and Jamie moved to Midland, Michigan. I hope their move had nothing to do with the kitchen project.

Fishing

Jim Myers was an avid fisherman. He owned his own boat and enjoyed a good day of sun and fishing. I remember one occasion that we went fishing on Lake Erie. The walleye were biting well, and there was no time like the present to go fishing. Jim asked me to go fishing, and he warned me that it was supposed to be rough. The day was overcast, but we were on our way. A fisherman's creed goes something like this: "A good day of fishing is always a better day than anyplace else."

We weren't out on the lake too long when a bad storm came up. I have a very weak stomach, and it doesn't take me long to get seasick. On this day, it took less time than usual. We had no fish, and if we would have caught one fish, we would have called it a good day. I began to vomit as I fished in the storm. Jim had covered much of the boat, and there was room for only him and me. As I vomited, I thought I felt something on my pole. I reeled in the line, and I saw a nice walleye, which Jim netted. Jim was also fishing, and I could see that he really wanted to catch a fish. Who wants to be out fished by a sick fisherman? I put the line back in the water as the boat continued to roll and pushed Jim and me from side to side. I had my lure in the water and tried to adjust the depth as best I could. I continued to vomit and felt like the world was coming to an end. Jim was really fishing hard and trying to catch a fish. I thought I had another fish on my line. I didn't tell Jim because I wanted to make sure I got the fish in before I told him. Jim was on to me and said, "Do you have another fish?" I said, "I think so." Sure enough, I pulled the line in, and another beautiful fish came in. Jim netted it and began to fish hard again. I don't remember how many more fish I caught, but I do remember that Jim fishing off his own boat caught none, and I had a really good day fishing. I don't know if Jim and I went fishing on his boat after that excursion, but I sure did enjoy the fish I caught, even if I was sick. I sure did miss Jim and Diane when they moved to Michigan.

Blizzard of 1978

January 1978 was the most easily remembered blizzard of my life. We woke up in the early morning to a howling snowstorm that had already deposited ice on the power lines, causing them to collapse in many areas and leave the people with no electricity. Electricity meant heat, and we and many others had none. Very early in the morning, we knew we had to leave the house, but where to go, we were not sure. Our neighbor Sue Welty had a wood-burning fireplace, and after checking, we found we were invited to stay with her. We were to make one trip to Sue's with all the belongings we needed and could carry. As Kathy, the two boys, and I left the house, the wind and snow made it impossible to see. We were only going a few hundred feet, so we pushed on with each of us carrying a boy and clothing.

The further we went, the more confused we became about the location of Sue's house. While it is just across the street, we were beginning to get lost. Just as the fear of getting lost was the greatest, a slight drop in the speed of the wind allowed us to see Sue's house. We hurried to the driveway and eventually were ushered into the house. Sue had two children, Carol, our babysitter, and James, a friend of our sons. The next two days at Sue's were to seem like weeks, but they were for the duration of two days.

After heat, meals had been one of our biggest concerns as we had no place to cook except the fireplace. Since there were no accommodations for cooking in the fireplace, the next-door neighbor, Edna, was our best bet. As we made plans with Edna for meals, we discovered that her gas supply was very low as the gasman hadn't filled her up as promised the previous weekend. With the gas supply nearly empty, we were fortunate that Edna was able to live in her kitchen and do the necessary cooking with a very small supply of gas. The way it worked was that Edna would prepare the meals at a set time, and I would walk sideways between the drifts of Sue's house and the garage of Edna's until I reached her side door.

We had brought all the diapers we had for our second son, Mark, who was a little over a year old. We were down to the last diaper as diarrhea had set in. One of the neighbors was able to make it to the house where we were staying. When we were asked if we needed anything, we said, "Diapers." Our prayers were answered.

Another neighbor came to check on us and relayed the story about one of the older neighbor ladies. As the storm had set in, catching many people off guard, one concern was for an elderly lady who lived by herself at one of the entrances to New Rochester. A number of the men in town went to her house as soon as there was a break in the blizzard. They knocked on the doors and windows and could not rouse the older lady. In desperation, they broke the back door window and went into the house. They found the lady in bed with layer after layer of blankets. At first, she was afraid and fought off the men who were trying to save her. Finally, they convinced her to allow them to carry her in the blankets to one of the neighbors who had heat.

Another task that the men of the town carried out was to drain out the water pipes and to pour antifreeze into the plumbing in those houses without heat. To be safe, we drained out the hot water heater as we were afraid it would freeze. We were also concerned that water from the water heater would freeze the drain pipe, so at my house, we used my five-gallon carboys to carry out the hot water. On one occasion, I was emptying the carboy when the hot glass came in contact with the cold snow. The carboy shattered into many pieces.

That evening, our boys and Kathy slept where the fireplace was located, and the rest slept wherever there was a bed. I remember my room was colder than I could remember a campout being at Camp Alaska. During the day, I remember Carol going up to her room on the second floor and sewing on a blanket or some type of a material for her future husband, Jim.

After fifty hours of living in Sue's house, the electric came on. We moved back into our house. One of the first items I noticed was our frozen tropical fish tank. The fish were frozen in the solid block of ice. Another remembrance we had was at night, we heard the sound of a large piece of machinery. As we looked out our east side window, we saw lights high in the air and a machine that was clearing the road, both sides in one sweep. We were not sure where this monster, the likes of which I had never seen, was coming from, but we were glad our road was being cleared.

When we were close to the walls, the coldness they had absorbed was easily felt by our bodies. It took several hours to replace the cold air and replace it with the warm. As I went to bed that night, I was tired as I had not slept decently for two nights. I hit the pillow and was out until three o'clock. I decided to check the house and see that everything was functioning properly. The water pump and heater were fine. I checked the furnace, and it was working fine. When I checked the front room, I instantly noticed the smell of something burning. Fear was my first reaction as I wasn't sure people to man the fire engines were available. I inspected everything in the room and found that the burning smell was coming from a blanket that we had used near the fireplace at Sue's. I was back to sleep in a short order.

The Monkey

Hoz was one of my college friends. Every once in a while, when we would least suspect him, Hoz would visit us. This time when Hoz came to town, he brought with him a friend, a cloth monkey puppet. Hoz had worked with this monkey so it could make about any motion possible. It actually made one feel like there was a real person in this puppet.

The evening of his visit, we decided to go to town with some of our friends. We found a nightclub to have a few drinks. As we walked into the bar, Hoz decided to go up on the stage with the singer who was performing. Within a few minutes, it was the "Hoz and the Monkey Show." The Hoz show came to a close, and he and the monkey came down to our table, and we enjoyed a few drinks. The monkey didn't have a drink because he was still giving a show to the other patrons.

Community

New Rochester

Speed Limit

New Rochester was a small neighborhood with many children. On June 18, 1974, Kathy Frederick obtained the signature of twenty-one residents in New Rochester and forwarded it to the Wood County engineer, Max L. Rothschild. On April 29, 1975, the Wood County commissioners approved a speed reduction on North River Road in New Rochester. The state of Ohio Department of Transportation received approval to reduce the speed limit in New Rochester, and it was accomplished. It is rewarding to see democracy in action.

New Rochester Ditch

When we moved into New Rochester, there was water that had gathered on the south side of North River Road. The water was there because several years before, the basin of the old Portage River was moved from close to North River Road to a new location farther south, forming a new Portage River basin. This created an old river basin that still retained water, and it was not able to flow into the newly created river. One of the results was that there was a problem with mosquitoes breeding in the old river basin.

On November 28, 1978, eight residents of New Rochester sent out a letter announcing that after one and a half years of searching for a solution to the stagnant water in New Rochester, a solution had been found. A community meeting was held, and $75 was asked from each landlord and property owner who drained into this area. Later, because of the fact that a bulldozer could not be used but a digger would be used, the fee was raised $25. Ditches from east to west of New Rochester were completed and leveled.

There were several agencies contacted to assist in this project. The adjutant general verified that the property in question was private land, and they could not undertake the project. A work program through Wood County was contacted, and this group removed several trees that were in the old river basin. The majority of the ditching was done by Alton and Rodney Beeker. The ditches created are periodically cleaned by the citizens of New Rochester so that the water can continue to drain. This project exemplifies what can be accomplished when several concerned citizens come together for a common cause.

St. Thomas More Parish

We were members of St. Thomas More Parish for over thirty years. The continuation as extraordinary ministers has always been a privilege for Kathy and me. As chairperson of the maintenance committee, seeing the needs of the physical facilities addressed has been a fulfilling duty with the number and diversity of the buildings. Being part of a close and friendly parish helps one's purpose in life to have meaning.

Ohio Special Olympics

Basketball

While my career path had changed into administration, I still was able to keep my involvement in Special Olympics. The state basketball tournament in April 1976 provided me with the opportunity to use my referee skills. It is rewarding to see teams evenly matched play well after many hours of practice. Knowing that I was in on the ground floor of the Special Olympics is a very positive feeling.

Ohio Special Olympics Summer Games

For the number of years the Summer Games have existed, I have had the privilege of being part of the festivities. The meals committee has been my special interest and responsibility. Serving over five thousand people in about a forty-five-minute period is rewarding. The summer of 1976 was a close call with one of the volunteers' children. We were in the hot tub near the pool at the Holiday Inn when suddenly, Ronda lost her hold on the side and went under in the four-foot-deep enclosure. Luckily, I saw her go under and was able to pull her out with very little effort. The poor child was coughing and gasping for air for a while. I was happy I was near and lucky enough to catch her with the first try of my hands.

Boy Scouts

Around 1977, I was able to attend a campout at Camp Courageous. Camp Courageous is a camp in Lucas County for people with developmental disabilities, but the Boy Scouts were using it for a campout. The turnout was pretty good as it involved several other troops. One of the activities was an obstacle course and racing through some concrete tiles, which requires the scouts to lower their heads enough to clear the tiles as they went into them. Unfortunately, one of our scouts, Jimmy, didn't lower his head enough and cut his scalp. He received medical help, and as usual, the camp went on with new activities. I have been amazed throughout my Boy Scout experiences the amount of time that leaders give to their scouts. I have heard and believe that it is the responsibility of every Boy Scout to give back to scouting the time that their leaders have given to them.

CHAPTER 6

Northwest Ohio Developmental Center

The district office had been one of my dream jobs, and now twelve district offices had throughout the state been combined into six regional offices. I had been told by the commissioner of developmental disabilities that to advance to the regional commissioner office, it was necessary for me to become superintendent of a developmental center. I was familiar with the programs at both the Tiffin Developmental Center and NODC as my office was involved with placement in both these centers. I knew NODC located at 1101 South Detroit Avenue, which served the ten counties located in Northwest Ohio, well as I was involved in the building of the center as well as the opening and placement of consumers into the center. With my district manager position eliminated, NODC superintendent vacant position seemed like the best available job alternative in my career plans in Northwest Ohio. I interviewed for the position with some other very competent applicants, and after the scores were tallied, I was the top contender. I was offered the position and accepted the offer. The challenges to be faced were to be more than I imagined, and the elements of success were always balanced by the possibility of defeat. This job was to be one of the greatest rides in my career as the opportunity unfolded for many to move from state facilities to community-based facilities and delivery systems.

Lawsuit

My father instilled in his children the importance of hard work. If we were not successful at a task, the analysis would ultimately look at the simple fact whether we slacked off or we gave it all we had and then some. If that is the case, I should have been successful at NODC because the greater part of my experiences in this position and others was work, not smelling the roses. While NODC had good services, there was a lawsuit that had been filed against NODC before I took over the helm of the ship. The lawsuit stated that the individuals were not receiving the services they had a right to expect. This lawsuit complicated people's opinion about NODC services as the filing of a lawsuit can bring doubts into people's minds, where, without the lawsuit, a much more positive opinion existed. In this case, it made it very difficult for me to expect understanding from parents and staff since the lawsuit was in place, and questions about NODC's services had been tainted by the simple filing of the lawsuit. When staffing patterns came to the forefront, the staffing at NODC was as good as, if not better than, other facilities. While the patterns that existed when I came into the position were not as good as they had been when the facility opened, more criticism built as reductions were in the wings.

Since a lawsuit was filed, the logic was definitely present that something was wrong at the center. This logic isn't consistent with the laws that say that you are innocent until proven guilty. At the same time that I came in as superintendent, I was informed by central office that NODC was at one of the highest funding levels in the state of Ohio for a developmental center. I was informed by my boss that I needed to cut $1 million out of my $6 million budget. The first meeting I had with staff members and parents, I was informed that staffing was low, and another $1 million in additional funding was needed. Much work went into showing staff and parents that the present staffing ratios that were seen as light in personnel were in essence highly equipped with more employees than any other developmental center. The staff and I were to spend many hours working to have the fiscal situation addressed as well as to have the "right to treatment lawsuit" dismissed.

Worked Hard to Have the Right to Treatment Lawsuit Dismissed
The General Overview

A right to treatment lawsuit was originally filed in May 1979 on behalf of people with mental retardation and developmental disabilities saying that the people in NODC do have a right to be treated according to state and federal laws. The lawsuit is saying that the treatment is not happening as it should be, and the lawsuit is asking the courts to intervene to see that the treatment is being provided. At this time, this type of lawsuit was very common.

As the staff and I began to look at areas of change to give better service, there were several areas we gave attention.

Two Systems to One

As I took office, one area caught my eyes as needing change. I foresaw the need to have a one-unit system with one supervisor for the entire center of 170 residents rather than the two supervisors and two systems, one for each of the two units, or approximately 85 residents for each unit director. Problems with two sets of rules with two supervisors and employees going from one set of rules to another did not sit well with the consistent delivery of services. I was still under a freeze of funds at that time. I developed a proposal that would go to the one-unit system and would have one cottage supervisor instead of two unit systems. The one supervisor would be responsible for the direct management of all the units. The system was implemented with few hitches, and it has worked successfully for years.

In instituting this new one system, several procedural areas needed better definition. All duties of all staff, especially the direct care, needed to be defined so that there were no questions about the who, what, where, and why of our operations. When two systems became one, there were those areas that were done in one manner and now had changes to deal with on a daily basis. The input and implementation of the various staff was so successful that a state recognition of the procedures was given to myself and the center. The awards stated that the estimated annual savings for the procedures to standardize operations was worth $49,500. It was one of the highest savings of the eleven awards given. I was not eligible for a state cash award as I was a manager. One of the procedures covered "corrective actions." Corrective actions could mean dealing with positive or negative employee action and involved twenty different steps or action steps. An emphasis on letters of commendation by the managers reversed the number of letters of commendation and suspensions, removals, and reductions. Seeing more letters of commendation than suspensions, removals, or reductions was reinforcing for the managers at NODC.

With the roughly $1 million (actually $780,000) loss of funds and a new management system being developed that ensured a manager in each of the cottages at all time, the proposal generated the restoration of $50,000 to our budget to pay for these needed supervisors. The relationships with parents were improved because there was a supervisor to go to and a supervisor to meet and attend public functions with parents, families, and others. Residents' needs were more closely listened to/observed and, wherever possible, met. Another management innovation was a staff advisory committee that worked with concerns of the staff to overcome obstacles.

A Procedure Pay Off

One of the essential procedures dealing with residents was called the unusual incidents report. Why was it important? Many incidents happen to residents, and unless these incidents are documented immediately, useful and needed information can be lost.

One of the mothers of a resident came to my office wanting to know why their daughter had a broken leg. We had recently implemented a procedure following our new procedure guideline. I asked that any "unusual incident report" on this resident be brought to my office immediately. I looked at the various reports and found an instance where this resident had tripped on the curb and fallen a few days earlier. On the report, it showed exactly where she had hit the same leg that was now being assessed as broken. I showed the mother the report and how at the time it was a scrape and had turned into a break. The mother was satisfied with the report, and I was satisfied that the system had worked. This was one less injury that would be discussed as part of our services under the "Federal Right to Treatment Lawsuit."

An Eating Program in Cottage 601

One of the populations that required time to see that they were properly nutritioned was our very low-functioning population in Cottage 601. With the roughly $1 million cut in funds in which staff was cut from 288 to 243, we were forced to be resourceful in many of our care programs. We immediately began a staff volunteer program in which people would give of their time from mainly the administrative area to help residents eat. It was a program that matched people's available time with the needs of the residents. I personally found the program rewarding as it gave me the time to work directly with the residents and have a grounded knowledge of the residents' and staffs' needs and abilities.

Food Service

In 1980, a new system of food service was being developed. It made it possible to have food prepared on site. Residents were very happy with the arrangement. However, the contracted cooks were unhappy with their work conditions. In late 1980, a union vote was held, and union results were announced around eleven o'clock in the morning. The noon meal was to be the last from the contract group. At around two in the afternoon, the food contract company announced it was withdrawing their services immediately. We had three hours to obtain supper for 177 residents. It was a struggle, but it was completed as the Medicare Survey was to take place.

Nursing

The availability of nurses was an ongoing problem while I served as superintendent. Agencies somehow had a process where they could procure nurses for employment easier than we could. At NODC, the pay was lower than the contract agencies paid. This caused budget problems as it increased the amount of pay for the nursing line item. When we could not find a nurse to work, we called the contract nurse agency, and they sent us a nurse.

In the break room at NODC, nurses would find out that the contract nurses were making more money than they were. This would not help the situation, and it was possible to have nurses jump ship from NODC to the contract nurses. Contract nurses did not always work the same shift with the same residents, so continuity of services could be a problem. We were finally able to offer employment that better suited the needs of nurses and reduced the contract nurses to a minimum. Contract nurses served in positions where continuity of care was less of an issue. A big problem requiring big solutions.

Internal Self-Policing, Thirteen Investigations

When one talks of self-policing, NODC had always been a top participant. We once had an unusual death caused by a malrotated bowel. The bowel twisted, and the blood supply had no place to go but to burst. There were thirteen investigations into this death being prompted as I remember largely by the "federal right to treatment lawsuit." Seeing that we and our contract physicians had done all we could to give services or to improve our services was a goal. Many medical physicians, including coroners, were some of the medical personnel involved in these thirteen separate investigations. Nothing was found of substance in these investigations. This case was one of many that helped us exit that lawsuit.

With the federal right to treatment lawsuit finally dismissed, consumers and staff had been through a lot. We now had several groups admitting that good services were being offered at the center. We knew that good services had been present, but we all had to do a lot of convincing. These sections were a few of the innovative ways that staff worked to dismiss the lawsuit.

Staying at NODC

I had been invited out to dinner by an acquaintance of mine. As the evening meal proceeded, it became clear that the person I was having dinner with was a person who wished to occupy my position. While there was another position open, I was more interested in staying in my NODC superintendent position and expressed that fact. My acquaintance brought up many issues at NODC that needed attention. Yes, there were many areas that needed attention, but they all must be done in due time. It was at a meeting of the county superintendents a few days later when it was announced that I was taking a position in the regional office. The regional office had been my goal but not now and not in the position being offered.

I was shocked that my job move was announced without my involvement. That evening, I received a call from Dr. Rudy, the director of the department and a truly good administrator. He asked me if I was interested in switching to the position in the regional office. I said I wasn't. Dr. Rudy said it was settled I stay at NODC. I have seen in more than one incident that when people try to railroad something through the system, they may not be in a strategic position to represent their viewpoints. The world is not always fair, but we need to be ready to deal with any situation that arises.

Medicare Survey

A major funding mechanism for NODC was through what is termed an Intermediate Care Facility for the Mentally Retarded. There are pages and pages of standards that must be met. The judgment of the surveyors was the determining factor if we were to pass or not pass a particular standard. If a deficiency was found that was either serious enough or was a repeat citation, steps up to and including decertification could transpire. Decertification meant that one would lose federal funds, which could be the majority of one's funding. Shortly before Christmas of 1980, there was a survey.

The results of the survey determined that there were some concerning deficiencies. The four major deficiencies I remember were a fuzz ball in one of the cottage entrances, a physical therapist who was to start in January but was not on site as of December, green beans were one to two degrees cooler than the required temperature, and the fourth had to do with posting a food menu in the cottage.

NODC had the opportunity to explain why it should not be cited by the department of public welfare for these deficiencies in a state administrative hearing. The hearing was scheduled and conducted after the survey results were received. The administrative staff and myself all testified in Columbus why we should not be cited. On the trip back from Columbus, all the administrative staff and myself were more than convinced the hearing had gone well. This was not to be the case.

Between Christmas and New Year of 1980, we received a notice that the deficiencies from the original survey had been upheld and that the decertification and loss of funds was to take place. The Northwest Ohio advisory board, my professional board, voted to obtain legal counsel to defend NODC in the accusations from the department of public welfare and the department of health. In meeting with attorney Richard Walinski in preparation for the parents' lawsuit to keep funds flowing to the center, we conducted a computer research on the past successful ways that there had been in overturning a decertification. This was the first computer search I had been a part of in my life. In a few minutes, the computer responded that one such violation of the law on the part of the state department was that the action of decertification had been taken without giving proper notice to the residents. This reason was to be used to stop the decertification by Judge Don Young. Judge Young granted a temporary order blocking state officials from terminating or reducing payments for the education, care, and treatment provided to recipients at NODC. As an aside, Judge Don Young was the Huron County probate judge who took my driver's license away from me for one month as I entered college. I had maintained that the stoplight was caution, not red, when I went through it.

A hearing was set on the preliminary injunction that was conducted on February 6, 1981, in U.S. District Court in Cleveland before Judge Ann Aldrich. This was not the star performance that I had looked forward to in my life, but I was to be on the stand for the vast majority of the trial justifying why myself and my administration should continue to receive funds and in the end given a chance through a resurvey to keep the funds flowing. My boards, Attorney Walinski, my superiors in the Department of Mental Retardation, and certainly my administrative staff at NODC were all supportive of me in an essential, strong, and appreciated manner.

The outcome of this district court hearing was that there was to be another survey of NODC. A specialist, Rick, was hired to work in my office to help fine-tune all the compliances for all the standards, and a survey was conducted by the state. This move allowed me to continue managing the facility while Rick fine-tuned anything that needed attention. Everyone connected with the center was concerned about this survey, and there could not have been a finer team effort because NODC was as near perfect as possible in this survey.

I learned from this experience that laughing is important in life. I also learned I wish I could have and would have laughed more. Unfortunately, near the end of this experience, my father was to die of brain cancer, and I was taking exams for my Ph.D. degree as well as trying to settle on a topic for my dissertation.

The result of the grueling survey was that we did pass, and the facility continued to offer excellent services and be reimbursed.

Other Happenings

A Marriage and a Kidnapping

An event occurred that I had never in my wildest dreams thought would happen to me. The date was June 6, 1980. My son Joey was the ring bearer for my neighbor girl Carol Welty and her husband-to-be, Jim Biddle, from Williamsburg, Pennsylvania. We were at the reception dinner at Kaufman's Restaurant in Downtown Bowling Green. I received a call from the *Toledo Blade* near the end of the dinner, asking me as the superintendent of NODC for a statement on the young boy under my care who had been found in the Maumee River. I did not yet have information on this event but promised the *Blade* that I would get back to them in fifteen minutes. My heart sank. What had happened, and why hadn't I been contacted?

I called my program director and explained the call from the newspaper. I was told the eleven-year-old young boy was playing outside the cottage after supper. He was under supervision and was playing in a grassy area surrounded by asphalt. He would not walk on asphalt. He was seen a few hours later by staff at a festival north of the facility. He was found crying on the shore of the Maumee River by a passing boat. The young boy didn't cross the street and couldn't talk.

The young boy would not run off and was being supervised from inside the cottage. An unauthorized person must have taken him off the grounds. He was found unharmed. That evening, I met with the parents and explained what had happened. To obtain more information, it was attempted to procure a federal agency such as the FBI. The only evidence we had was another resident who saw what happened, but this resident was without speech. No new information was obtained after this point, and the supervision procedure was changed in the cottage.

During the afternoon before the wedding, we were having a party in our yard with many of the people associated with the wedding. A tradition in rural Pennsylvania of stealing the bride was to take place in Ohio. Several of Jim's friends invaded our yard and stole Carol. It was a well-planned event! The wedding proceeded that day after the stolen bride was returned, and that evening, I spent most of my time at the reception talking to the media about the kidnapping.

A Fundraiser

When funds are tight, fundraising is one way to raise a few dollars for the residents. A member of my staff was working with an establishment to raise some funds for the residents of NODC. On the day of the fundraiser, a raffle was to be one of the means of raising cash. The raffle was held, and the winning number was drawn. The prize was given to the winner, and my employee inquired about the nature of the prize. The answer to the question was marijuana.

My employee came back with the $500 and informed me that the prize was marijuana. I knew as did my employee that we needed to return the money. I informed my boss of the issue, just in case it became an bigger issue. In the public's eye, there could be criticism for this issue coming up. Some people thought the issue should have been solved before it happened. We had many uses for that prize money. The only use we had with this money was to do what was right, and that was to keep on the good side of the law.

Another Lawsuit

The last year of my tenure at NODC, I was sitting in the human relations supervisor's office when I looked out the window toward the main highway, Detroit Avenue. As I looked out the window, I saw one of our vans hit two cars on Detroit Avenue. I looked further, and one of our residents was leaving the wrecked van. I recognized the resident and began to run out to the van as I was concerned that the resident might be hit while walking on this main highway. I was not the only person who heard the crash as the resident was under the care of a staff member before I was able to access the wreck. I found out that our resident had gone into the maintenance building, taken the key, started the van, and ran the van down the NODC boulevard into the car on Detroit Avenue.

I was at the scene for a few minutes when Steve, the chief of operations, informed me the wrecker was coming to tow the van. I asked Steve how long it would take for the wrecker to arrive on site, and he said a few minutes. I asked him to call the wrecker again and get the wrecker here now. I was concerned about the van being in the street and possibly causing more accidents. I was also concerned that live coverage by the media wouldn't do anyone at the center any good. With the new timeline of "right now" established, the wrecker came and picked up the car and left the site about one minute before the TV media was there, ready to shoot film. Changes were made immediately on the safe storage of vehicle keys.

The New Truck

My company car had to go in the shop for an oil change, and I borrowed the maintenance truck at NODC. This truck had an extended cab and a nice size storage bed. I had been working late, and it was dark as I started home. I was about a mile from my house when I saw to my right something running toward the new truck. I saw one deer, and then two, and finally three coming from the west toward the side of the truck. I applied my brakes thinking the deer would pass in front of the truck. One of them did pass in front of the truck, and I barely missed it. The other two hit the side of the truck so hard I was going down the road sideways. I worked to bring the truck under control and came to a stop. I got out, put on the hazard lights, and checked to see if the deer were injured. On had a leg injury. I called the Wood County Sheriff's Department to report the accident. It took a while for the deputy to arrive, and just before he came, the deer took off running.

The maintenance department was not happy about the dents in the truck, and I got the feeling that they really didn't want me to cause any more damage to their truck. I didn't either.

Passing of a District Office Employee

It was about this time when one of my faithful employees, Jean, from the district office had died. We had been on vacation and learned of the death the day we came home. The information we had said that the funeral was to be the next day. We changed clothes and immediately went to the Deck-Hanneman Funeral Home in Bowling Green. Our eldest son, Joey, knew the deceased well. We had gone to her house on business many times, and Joey enjoyed the birds that Jean's mother fed.

As we walked into the room, we saw the sign-in sheet was for George. We knew we had the wrong person, but by now, we were too far in the room to leave, and there were many smiles from the friends and relatives of this young family who had come to pay their respects. Kathy and I briefly talked, and all we could think of was that Joey was going to say "This is not Jean" when he was viewing the casket, especially since we had prepared him for Jean. As we were walking up to the casket, I whispered in Joey's ear, "Please be quiet. This is not Jean." At the same time, Kathy and I were trying to think what we would say to the family if they said, "How did you know George?" Luckily, Joey said nothing nor did the family, so we gracefully left the room. The funeral director was at the entrance, so I asked, "When is Jean going to be shown?" He responded, "Tomorrow evening." We were at the funeral home the following evening feeling much more relaxed with our visit, and Joey did talk to Jean's family.

My Health

During my employment at NODC, headaches were becoming more frequent and severe. Aspirin was a frequent friend of mine and would give me the relief that I sought. Unbeknownst to me, while my headaches were usually controlled by aspirin, the aspirin was damaging my stomach. It was the morning of Labor Day in 1980 that a great physical change was to take place in my body. For about a year and half, I had been dealing with many pressures in my job. Almost a year to the day earlier, I had received a card from two of my employees complimenting me on how well I had held up under internal and external pressures in my job. They had predicted that I wouldn't be smiling a year from then as I had been at that point.

On that morning before Labor Day, I become unbearably sick at four thirty in the morning. At that time, I began to vomit. The substance that came out of my mouth did not have the consistency of food. I turned on the light in the bathroom and looked into the toilet bowl to see a substance that even I could identify. It was blood. My heart sank because I was afraid that this might be my end of life. I faintly remember passing out twice in the process of calling Kathy for assistance. Kathy found a sitter for our children in a matter of seconds. I was feeling a little better, so she transported me to the hospital. I had a blood pressure of sixty over forty when they examined me in the ER. I was told I needed to stand up as part of my admission. I protested and told them I would go into shock if I tried to stand up. As I stood up, I went into shock, and they forgot this test.

My twin and God must have been with me because I lived. I received a blood transfusion to restore the blood I lost. According to the physician, I had a weak stomach lining probably caused by the aspirin that I took for my headaches. When I had vomited, there was a flap in my stomach lining that opened up and allowed blood to come into my stomach. Even before I had been diagnosed and treatment had started, the flap had returned to its original spot, and the bleeding had stopped. This event caused me to take a close look at my health and my life. I was out of work for a short period and became very careful about substances I put into my mouth. As fate would have it, my dream job was to open in a few months.

Another Job Opening

I was to interview and obtain the job I desired, the regional commissioner job. As part of my responsibility, I was to be responsible for both NODC and the Tiffin Developmental Center. Tiffin had been known as a sound mental health center and now a stable developmental center for the mentally retarded.

The years at NODC had been full of challenges. The staff members, other service providers, residents, parents, families, and community had grown to support me and the center.

I must recognize the most important other person in my life, the one I fall in love with each day of my life, my lovely wife, Kathy. She was always there to support me and share with me this very important part of my life. As I recognize Kathy, I would also like to recognize the other significant persons of NODC employment, past and present. They supported me, and they have given more than I will ever know.

I read an unknown quote that best summaries my experiences at NODC and some of my experiences yet to come. It went like this: "As we sail through life, don't avoid rough waters, sail on because calm waters won't make a skillful sailor."

Best of luck in the future, and thank you for the pleasure of working with all of you.

Family Happening

Swimming Pool

It was at this time that we decided to buy an aboveground round swimming pool and place it in a location near the back of our garage. The water had always been the number 1 area of recreation for me my entire life. I had a two-foot pool when I was young, swam in and managed the Willard City Pool, boated and fished at the conservation league and Lake Erie, scuba dived in high school, and the family had a cottage on the Huron River, which leads to Lake Erie. Let's get back to the pool in our backyard. We were to not only buy the twenty-six-foot pool and install it with the help of our neighbors; we also built a deck so that there was an entrance and exit into the pool. The pool provided many hours of fun for both Mark and Joe, who were three and six at the time we installed the pool, but many of the neighbors were able to take advantage of the pool on very hot days. Michelle Lopez comes to mind as one of the frequent swimmers. The swimmers liked a particular game and played it continuously. The game was called Marco Polo. The way the game worked is that the swimmer who had their eyes closed and was chasing the other swimmers would say Marco, and all the rest of the swimmers to be caught would say Polo. When the person "it" or the chaser would catch another player, the person caught was "it" or Marco. If a person were to leave the pool while playing the game, they were reminded of the rules and how they must be followed if they wished to play in the pool.

There were safety rules that Kathy and I had put on paper and that we went over with all swimmers. As long as swimmers followed the rules, they could swim. If they did not follow the rules, they were out of the pool. I don't remember any trouble with safety after we had posted and explained these rules.

One difficulty we had one summer was bumblebees in the backyard near the old chicken coup that was close to the pool. I remember coming home from work one day, and all the swimmers were concerned because there were big bumblebees around the pool. I investigated the ground around the pool and quickly discovered where the bumblebees were living. Unfortunately, they discovered me as I discovered them, and the attack on me was in progress. This bumblebee had some similarities to another bee stinging story. Several years previous, I had been working on the farm mowing around the pond. I cut the head off the bumblebee nest, and several were in my hair, in my face, and in my shirt. Every time I tried to take my T-shirt off, they would sting me harder. I ran a quarter of a mile to my sister and brother-in-law's house, and he removed the T-shirt with the bumblebees still alive in the shirt. My brother-in-law asked me why I didn't jump in the pool and drown the bees. I thought he had a good idea.

Let us go back to the pool. The story about the bumblebees around the pool was heating up as they were now upset by my presence near their hive in the ground. As the bumblebees were close to me around the pool, they were beginning to sting me. I remembered my previous experience mowing the pond at the farm. With the bees in close pursuit, I ran over to the pool and flipped my body into the pool fully dressed. When I came up in the water, there were no bumblebees around. I had learned a lesson well on the farm and saved myself from several beestings next to the pool.

Missy

Since our first year of marriage, we had been blessed with a black miniature French poodle. The dog had been named Mistress Juliet de Glenwood. Glenwood was the name of the street that we lived on in Mansfield when we obtained Missy at the urging of our close friends Butch and Phyllis Rothschild. We had no children, and a dog was a good substitute at the time.

Missy was around thirteen years old on September 24, 1980. Her ability to climb stairs and control her bodily functions was going downhill. Joey was nine, and Mark was three. They loved Missy as did Kathy and I. We were pretty certain what was going to happen at the vets, but we needed the vet to examine her. Dr. Jones handled the matter as best he could, but bottom line was that Missy had lived a long life, and her health was failing, and there was only one option. The injection was quick, and Missy had little, if any, pain. The funeral was very sad, and the entire family had their final goodbye. It was a hard lesson for everyone, and we were never to replace Missy.

Joe's Broken Arm

A family party was under way in the summer of 1980. We had a treehouse in the front lawn that my father had built for the boys. Joe was in the treehouse and was coming down the ladder. One of his shoelaces had come loose, and as he descended the ladder, the loose lace caught in the ladder. He tried to put his shoe down to the next rung of the ladder, but instead, he lost his footing and fell down the ladder and hit his arm on the way down. He came to the house holding his arm and saying it hurt.

Kathy and I were off to the Toledo Hospital. One of the doctors tried to set it, but it wouldn't go into place. We were informed that the orthopedic doctor would be scheduled for surgery the following morning.

Joey was given medication for the pain. It was decided that I would stay with Joey that night in his room and be there for the surgery in the morning. Kathy went home to finish the party and be with Mark. All evening and night, I kept thinking that Joey must be in pain. Morning did not come any too soon. The doctor came in the room, looked at the X-rays, and said let's go. The operation was a success, and Joey was fitted with a cast just in time to go on vacation.

Neighbors

Halloween Party

Many of the holidays were celebrated with our good neighbors in and around New Rochester. One of the favorite holidays was that of Halloween. Gene Walston owned the big barn next to our house, and Gene liked a good party. We would have different people in the neighborhood to volunteer to arrange food, games, music, decoration, and a hayride. The food would be a mixture of sandwiches, side dishes, drinks, and other specialty items. The games would be for best, scariest, prettiest, and many others. Apple bobbing was always a favorite game. The music was constant all evening with someone's portable music player and speakers. The decorations were traditional paper witches, cats, pumpkins, and ghosts. The weather in November isn't always warm, so Gene would set up his large space heaters so that the barn was warm.

The big attraction of the evening was to get on one of Gene's wagons and go to Pemberville. The ride would usually take us to a bar called the Animal Shelter, where we would overtake the bar by numbers and talk with the other patrons. After the trip to the bar, we would huddle together and try to keep warn on the trip home. One could never forget such an eventful evening with the cross section of neighbors around New Rochester.

Mark's Third Birthday

Many news articles that were missed in large newspapers were captured in the small-town newspapers. The *Pemberville Leader* was during this time a paper that we did not miss reading. In 1979, there was a report on Mark's birthday party by columnist Mrs. Leila Sanders. There were seven friends and his brother, Joey, at the party. The big deal at the party was no other than cake and ice cream. I bet the cake was made by his mother.

Phil Donahue Television Show

It was around 1980 that Phil Donahue brought his show to the Masonic Auditorium in Toledo. Six area women, including my wife, attended the show. I had forgotten this event happened until I read an old newspaper article in the *Pemberville Leader*. This makes me wonder how many events we forget in our lives such as Christmas caroling, New Year's Eve parties, and simple Sunday afternoon visits to neighbors, friends, or relatives.

Hungarian Night

When we attended St. Thomas University Parish in Bowling Green, we had the good fortune of knowing several of the parishioners. One of the parishioners was a native of Toledo and invited Kathy and me and other members of the parish to his Hungarian night party. Frank seemed to know most of the people at the affair, and we had a great time dancing, eating, and socializing. I was not that familiar with Hungarian food until that evening's experience. It would be nice to see Frank again and go to the festival with him. Unfortunately, Frank was transferred with his job many years ago, and like so many people in our lives, we rarely, if ever, see them once they move.

Toboggan Riding

Kathy and I were invited to go tobogganing with some of our friends. I was a snow sledder when I was a kid and enjoyed it. We went to a rather large hill in Perrysburg at Fort Meigs park. There were around six people who were going to go down the hill on one toboggan. Each person sat down on the toboggan and wrapped their legs over the person's legs ahead of them. I ended up being last on the toboggan and barely got my feet and hands in place as we started down the hill. I found out fast that there were two dips at the top of this hill. As we hit the first dip, the toboggan went ten feet in the air. As I looked down, I saw that I was in midair with the toboggan about six feet below me. I also saw that the pad on the toboggan was not on the toboggan where it was to be but was to the side. As I hit the toboggan, I felt the wood rib hit my butt. It caused an excruciating pain like my tailbone had been broken. We hit the next dip at the top of the hill, and once again, I came down on the wood of the toboggan and not the pad. I rode the toboggan down with the rest of the group, and when I reached the bottom of the hill, I could not get up.

I had hurt my posterior very bad, and it was numb. The group loaded me on the toboggan and pulled me back to the car. I debated going to the hospital, but I was able to walk to the car once I was near it. While I could walk, there were several positions I could not occupy without much pain. I went to a meeting in Lima a few days later and discovered shortly into the trip that I could not ride in the car comfortably. I did, but it was painful. In my office at NODC, I sat on a heating pad all day for several weeks until my lower back felt better. I have not been back to Fort Meigs to go tobogganing since this experience and seriously doubt if I ever go back!

Luminaries

One event not forgotten in New Rochester and the area is the Christmas tradition of lighting the way for the Lord. Since 1980, approximately five hundred lights are placed on the side of the roads for Christmas Eve. The candles burn into the early morning and light the two streets of New Rochester, the St. Paul's Church, and the front of the cemetery on Zeppernick Road. All the arrangements are made by the New Rochester and area citizens. It is a sight to behold.

CHAPTER 7

Regional Commissioner

The experiences at NODC had been challenging and helpful in my future years as a manager. When Walter Solarz decided to leave the regional commissioner position, I knew where I wanted to go. I had worked for Walt less than ten years ago and knew he would help me in my adjustment period. This position had been one of my dream jobs. There had been talk that the regional office could be done away with, but since most other state department systems had regional or district offices, it didn't make sense to do away with the regional offices. I was excited about the position, knew many of the major service providers, and therefore, I was anxious to obtain and guide the region II office in its growth.

The Role of the Regional Office

The role of the district office and the regional office had many similarities. Two of the big differences were that the regional office served a larger geographic area and also was responsible for NODC and the Tiffin Developmental Center.

The regional II office was located in Toledo as part of the Ohio Department of MRDD. The office coordinated and monitored services for people with mental retardation and developmental disabilities for the nineteen counties in Northwest Ohio. One of the major functions of the office was to bring together a comprehensive regional plan composed of information contributed from each of the counties. By law, the county board of mental retardation was responsible to provide or contract for services for the MRDD population. Residential services had been provided by the state of Ohio in institutions, and then the focus changed to developmental centers so that residents were prepared to live in the community. The trend of living in one's home county had been ongoing for several years. The regional plan addressed needs, goals, objectives, and resources needed to obtain these goals and objectives as well as a definition of the present service delivery system. The region II plan was combined into a state plan for the Department of MRDD. Residential planning was the area of big program growth and was therefore a large part of this regional and state plan.

The Region II Advisory Council

It was an exciting time to be involved in the program changes, especially in the residential area. Along with these exciting times were many challenges on how the needs of the MRDD population were going to be met. For example, if a residential home was needed in the county, where were the funds going to be found? Another question was who was going to provide these services? The county board or a contract agency. The region II advisory council provided direction to the region II staff and the region. This council was a wide-range representation from community residential facilities, county boards, Association for Retarded Citizens, workshops, developmental centers, Ohio Private Residential Association, and area universities. Their guidance was invaluable in helping to answer these questions and others such as expansion in multiple areas. A new residential placement in the area meant the need for a new workshop or community job placement with the other expenses that go with living in the community.

The region II advisory board had committees in the public relations, planning, finance, residential, and program. These committees addressed issues pertinent to funding, eligibility for services, residential development, planning, objectives, media communications, and many other issues.

Residential Development and Implementation, Funding, Monitoring, Licensure, and Evaluation

At this time, there were ninety-one licensed community residential facilities often funded by the Department of MRDD, serving over 650 residents and eight intermediate care facilities for the mentally retarded (ICF/MR), largely funded by the federal government, serving over 300 people, plus two developmental centers under the direct control of the region II office. Tiffin Developmental Center had 220 residents, and NODC had 170 residents, with a mix of private, state, and federal funding. These facilities enabled the intake and placement staff of the regional office to identify appropriate placements in the community on a twenty-four-hour period. The calls for residential placements came at all times of the day and night, so the twenty-four-hour on call was accurate.

At this time, most of the nineteen counties had some type of residential home. The law required the provision of the most appropriate, least restrictive environment, and that type of placement might not be available in each county, so available placement might be required in another county in the state. With the advantage of serving all nineteen counties as well as contacts with the other five regions and the developmental centers, a placement was needed to be identified within a short period. The developmental center closest to the county of residence would become the last option.

The placement of a person from one county into another was not always an easy matter. A new person placed into a county different from where they were previously living was an additional expenditure in day programming for the new county. The solution to funding issues was not always an easy matter.

In each regional office, there was a residential development specialist who searched for potential home operators, discussed the available funding and license requirements, and identified with the case managers the client(s) who were eligible and available for placement into the particular home.

Another essential section that was housed in the region II office provided expertise for the over ninety homes. The license specialists and monitors did initial an annual review and quarterly monitor of the homes licensed by the Department of MRDD.

Fiscal Department

In region II during this time, there were $8.5 million of purchase of service funds within the nineteen county area. During fiscal years 1983, 1984, and 1985, it was projected that $14 million of purchase of service would be converted to federal Medicaid funds. This would convert to several million-dollar savings to the state. Only through close monitoring, consultation, and coordination would these conversions take place. The region II office would be involved with these changes to ensure the use of purchase of services in other residential development.

Monitoring and Evaluation of Educational and Workshop Programs

Housed within the region II office were program consultants. These consultants were responsible for ensuring that the rules and regulations of the MRDD as well as other state and federal regulations are met. The consultants ensure the flow of educational and transportation state funds to the county boards. As a result of the flow of information from the state to the county, the program consultants provide new ideas in the program delivery system.

Case Management

At this time, the regional offices provided the case management services to all people living within the state-funded and ICF/MR Medicaid–funded homes. It was recommended that the case management within the regional office be contracted with the county boards of MRDD while a small core of case managers in the regional office managed these contracts. In a survey counting all moderate, severe, and profound people with mental retardation in the nineteen counties served by the region II office, it was recommended that on a 1:300 ratio, at least twenty-seven case managers and case manager supervisors were needed. The role of case management was to be a major discussion area as systems changed in the next few years, one I would be having a different and major role in very soon.

In-Service

Because of the ever-changing state and federal legislation and the need for in-services in administration, program, fiscal, and legal area, a staff development and training task force consisting of twenty-five members met monthly to assess and plan regional programs. The task force had representation from a variety of area educational programs, resource organizations, and providers of MRDD services. A few of the training sessions were on such topics as human sexuality, Title XX, guardianship, client programming, and other state and federal funding.

More on the Role of Regional Commissioner

Media

When anything of importance happened at the regional office, the media was somehow notified, and the results were reported in the paper. Dealing with the media was an ongoing task requiring much time and expertise to properly present the facts.

Winter Traveling

Going to and from Columbus provided me with many interesting travel experiences. I will share one instance involving a trip to a meeting in Tiffin. After the meeting, I was to travel to Columbus for another meeting. I do not remember the purpose of either meeting, but I do remember the trip from Tiffin to Columbus.

It was winter, and there had been an ice storm the night before. Shortly after I had left Tiffin, I approached a hill in the road. As I slowed down, the car turned sideways, and before I could react, I found myself on the right side of the road in the front yard of a house. A mailbox was on my left side, and the home was on my right. I had probably ten feet of clearance on each side of the car. I also noted that the ice was breaking, and there was snow beneath the ice. Since I didn't know how deep the snow was and was afraid of getting stuck in the snow and the path ahead of me was clear, I did not try to stop the car.

I successfully passed several more houses on the right and mailboxes and newspaper holders on the left. I was looking for lawn ornaments in my path and also a break from the mail and newspaper boxes on my right. Like a miracle, I saw an opening that led to the road and did not have mail and paper boxes in my path. I looked for any traffic on the road and turned my wheel to the left and gave it a little gas so my rear end would help me turn left. The car turned left and started up a slight incline. As I began to reach the road, I turned to the right again, gave it a little gas, and I was on the road. I stabilized the car by straightening the steering wheel. I slowed down to a crawl and regained my composure. As I reviewed my experience in the front yard of several residents living on this road, I immediately realized I was very lucky to have come through this incident without a scratch on me or my car. I felt that a force higher than me aided in helping me manage this circumstance.

To Mount Vernon Developmental Center

At this time, there was a hearing on one of the residential homes in my area. I had enlisted the help of other superintendents to conduct the hearing. On the way down to Mount Vernon, I had a huge gas attack. I looked for a gas station so I could relieve the pressure. I found a restroom and was going to make it until I found the restroom door was locked. I didn't make it safely to the restroom but was able to contain the runny bowel movement in my underwear. I threw away the underwear and was able to clean myself up. I arrived at the hearing on time, and this is the first public statement on how I made it to the hearing in a presentable manner.

Lawsuit

A lawsuit was filed against the MRDD as a resident had obtained the keys to the van at NODC and drove it into another vehicle. The lawsuit was settled as were other lawsuits.

Capital Construction

From the time I began working for the state of Ohio, I was involved in building or renovating several residential homes, workshops, and schools. A total of nine schools, thirteen residential homes, and three workshops bringing several million dollars to Northwest Ohio was obtained. Another state project costing $8.2 million resulted in NODC, which served counties in Northwest Ohio.

Regional Office to Be Abolished

Richard Celeste was elected governor of Ohio on November 3, 1982. Abolishing the regional office was now a reality. On February 22, 1983, I was asked to submit a letter of resignation. I submitted my resignation and was fortunate to obtain another job in the department.

Several months earlier, I began to have a chemical imbalance in my body. I received help and was back on the job within two weeks.

Unusual Happenings

A Clip

Our family had invited my mother to go with us to see my brother Walt and his family in the early 1980s. We had spent a week and were on our way home. We began our trip home in our Plymouth station wagon, and while in the central part of Kentucky, I noticed the car was losing power.

I told everyone that there was something wrong with the car, and I was pulling off to the side of the road. As I said those words, I noticed an exit was coming up. We made it to the top of the exit ramp, and I saw a truck stop to my right, so I luckily coasted in. It wasn't a filling station but a place specifically set up to serve truck drivers. I asked the manager if he had a mechanic on duty because my car stopped running. The manager told me they had a mechanic, but he usually worked on trucks. The mechanic came out and began working on the car.

We took the two boys into the truck stop to get out of the sun and see if there was some way to occupy them. There were truckers everywhere trying to buy fuel, trying to shave, trying to take a shower, or trying to eat. The drivers looked at us kind of funny because we really didn't fit into this setting. The longer we waited, the more uncomfortable my mother became with the situation. The mechanic discovered that it looked like the alternator was the culprit, and he needed to take it off and send it to another shop to be checked out. That pretty well killed my idea of getting out of the truck stop quickly. I walked into the truck stop to give them the good news and was met with a screen of smoke. This wasn't the best place for Kathy, my mom, or the kids.

About an hour and a half later, the alternator was installed. After much tinkering with the motor, the car did start. We paid a bill around $200, and we were on our way. We were not well on our way because we didn't have the $200 and had to put the bill on our plastic card. We ended up really paying the bill another day. I did have a bit of trouble starting the car when we arrived home. I took the car to my mechanic in West Millgrove, Ohio, and he began to work on the car. After looking it over for a short period, he said, "Here is your problem." One of the wires running to the alternator had a clip on it, and this clip was loose and would short out the motor when it was in a certain position. When the truck stop in Kentucky removed and reattached the alternator, it changed the position of this clip, and this position enabled the alternator to successfully connect. The new clip cost was 79¢.

Family

Annual Campout

In the early eighties, a practice was started at our home that lasted about twenty years. That was our annual family campout for the family from the Theodore and Loretta Long family. Albert, Paul, Ruth, and Grace were the sons and daughters who attended as did several of their offspring.

This get-together got started one summer when we needed a new roof on our older garage, and the family said they would do it! We set the date, and the rest is history.

Each family would bring salads, vegetables, desserts, and about anything good to eat. The meat was bought at Frobose, the local butcher shop, and the cost was split according to the number in attendance. As can be imagined, people were not called to eat more than once, and you can bet that the food disappeared shortly after the prayer was said.

This campout was filled with all kinds of fun. Everyone visited the Stony Ridge, Ohio, festival and flea market, along with numerous garage sales along the way. The weather was always hot, making our pool a favorite spot. The kids loved making ice cream, which was enjoyed with delicious pies and cakes at supper. Mass was often celebrated in our backyard by a priest who was also a friend.

The highlight of the campout other than the food was the scavenger hunt and the campfire. The scavenger hunt consisted of the children dividing up into teams and scouring the neighborhood looking for a list of hard-to-find objects. A political pin, bird's egg, frog, dried corsage, cherry pit, pony or horsehair, pheasant feather, and brown egg were not something every household possessed, while a button, wheat penny, sugar cookies, spiderweb, cricket, red button, hairpin, and a matchbook were more easily obtained. Most of the forty-eight items listed were found by one or more teams. The motivation and excitement of the event was at a very high pitch, especially when one considered that most of the children were present and involved in the hunt. A converted old trophy was the coveted prize for the winning team.

The campfire was well attended; in fact, everyone attended. As the darkness came to full fruition, it was time for the anticipated ritual of four small children picking up adults in the 250-pound category. The mysterious lift was done methodologically and seriously to preserve the spell involved in the levitation of the chosen adult. The procedure first involved each of the four children placing their hands in a rotating manner on top of the adult in a chair without touching others' hands. This went on until all eight hands were on top of the sitting adult. As the last hand was placed on top of the other seven hands, everyone present maintained their silence as the climax was about to take place. Each of the children then placed their joined hands with their index fingers pointed straight out. The two children in back of the adult placed their index fingers under the armpit while the two front children placed their fingers under the adult's knees. As silence reigned supreme, all would lift together, and somehow the 250-pound adult would raise up at least a foot or more into the air. If everything happened as planned, the spell would last until the lift was completed. If anything went wrong such as a touching hand or a spoken word, the spell was broken, and the lift would not take place. I have seen the lift happen several times, and am still in awe that anything like this was possible.

More food like campfire pies or smores, along with great stories, was also a highlight of the campfire.

Uncle Paul always told us that you cannot get drunk on cold whiskey. For years, that was the saying, and I think everybody half-believed it. Since the campouts stopped, Paul has passed. Whenever I see any of Kathy's male relatives, they are still singing the song that "You can't get drunk on cold whiskey."

These times were always special, and they will always be memories not to be forgotten.

New Year's Eve

For years, a favorite activity of our family and Larry and Diane Schaffwer's family was sharing New Year's Eve. For years, we would journey to Norwalk, and the two families would start the evening with a delicious dinner. Larry and Di had four lovely daughters—Amy, Carrie, Lori, and Katie. Usually, there was snow on the ground, so all the kids would bundle up, get their sleds or snow disks, and travel to the hills around Larry and Di's home. There were at least two good sledding hills. The first hill was outside the kitchen window and started at the top of a steep hill and ended on the driveway. Since the driveway next to the kitchen window was shoveled, the decent from the hill would stop before the sleds came close to the house.

The other hill was behind their house and led into a valley. The kids would laugh, roll in the snow, and become white snowmen within minutes of hitting the back door. Speaking of snowmen, the snow-packed snowmen would dot the background landscape. It was our boys and their four girls. While the kids were outside sledding, the adults would be inside catching up on their lives.

Since Larry and I both had jobs in management, we had much in common. Di and Kathy were first cousins and had spent portions of their entire lives sharing the past and the present and projecting the future. Di worked in a salon for years and had a wide knowledge of not only the business but also the culture of the Norwalk area. Kathy's work experience as a teacher provided her with a wealth of knowledge. Di and Kathy were never short on subjects to have conversation.

As the evening grew closer to midnight, the excitement of six children and the four adults fueled the activities of the party. Sometimes other mutual friends or relatives would stop and enjoy the comradery of the party. The celebrating reached a peak with the advent of midnight. The party was not as expensive as going out to a formal affair. The memories of a party of good food and drink and most notably being with one's relatives made the evening a priceless affair of memories.

Since my family stayed overnight, the party went on until they left on New Year's Day. "All good things come to an end," and the good part about the end is that we all have our memories.

Florida and Disney World

In 1983, my mother, niece Denise from North Carolina, Mark, Joe, Kathy, and I were on our way to Disney World. My mother had insisted that we take her car to our first stop in North Carolina, and it naturally followed that after we visited relatives, we picked up Denise, and we were in no other position than to take her car to Disney World as that was the only car available.

Arriving at Disney World was an unparalleled excitement with all the cars, people, and colorful rides and characters. We were at the gates each morning when they opened because we found that if we were early, we could be first on the rides that were the most popular. The castle was one of the first sights we observed, and walking through the castle was a big treat. The rides were well constructed, attractive, and safe. The teacup rides tended to give some of us the chance to have butterflies produced in our stomach or to almost become sick.

In the afternoon was the most beautiful parade we had ever seen, the "Parade of Lights." In this parade, there were many lit-up, float-like attractions. The Beautiful Princess was a young lady sitting over fifteen feet in height surrounded by a beautiful gown and many white lights. At one of the refreshment areas, we thought we saw our neighbors Jackie and Jim, the mayor of New Rochester. As we moved closer, we discovered that it was, in fact, our neighbors. They were as surprised to see us as we were surprised to see them.

The three-day pass was over, and we made our way through the parking lot. As we came closer to the car, we could see that all good things come to an end. The driver's mirror had been vandalized, and it lay lifeless on the wires that controlled the direction of the mirror. We decided that we had a great time and that the broken mirror wasn't going to be allowed to "rain on our picnic."

As we traveled home, we noticed some beautiful wildflowers called status growing in the median of the highway. My mother really wanted me to stop and pick a bouquet, and I really didn't want to get in trouble with the law for illegally parking and illegally being in the median strip. Before I could decide what to do, we had passed the patches of flowers. As I reflect back, I wish I had taken the chance of picking the flowers. My mother rarely wanted anything, and those flowers were the exception.

Locked Out of the Car

On a family outing in 1982, I was becoming upset with my two sons' behavior. I stopped the car and went around the car to give the boys some verbal instructions on how they should act in the car. As I tried to open the back door, I found that one of the boys, I believe Joe, had locked the door, so I couldn't get into the car. Kathy was in the front seat, so things cooled off, and I decided to give the boys a second chance before I gave them any instructions on behaving.

Wine

An Unfortunate Event with My Wine

One evening I was cleaning one of my five-gallon glass wine carboys. My niece Denise from North Carolina was in the wine cellar with me watching me clean the bottle. Denise was in Ohio because she had gone to

Disney World and was staying with us to complete her vacation. As I was shaking my five-gallon container, I moved too close to the water outlet, and the glass came in contact with the metal. I heard a crack and looked down to see that the carboy had split at the neck, and the larger bottom section of glass was headed for my wrist. I looked up, probably because I did not want to see the glass hit my flesh.

For a brief moment as I looked up from the container, my hand felt like it had lost feeling. Fearing the worst that my hand had been cut off, I looked down. To my surprise, my hand was still attached to my arm. As I expected, there was a large amount of blood around my wrist. I knew from my Boy Scout training that I needed to grab the wrist to stop the bleeding, and if a tendon had been cut, this action could possibly stop the tendon from becoming severed and snapping up the arm like a rubber band.

Kathy cleaned up the wrist as best she could, and we were off to the hospital. At the hospital, we were to find out that I needed several stitches, and neither my artery nor the tendon had been severed. Both were missed by a fraction of a second. I was happy that the cut had not been as severe as it could have been. I was especially happy that my hand was still attached to my arm. An exciting evening was had by all, mostly at my expense.

Another Unfortunate Event with My Wine

By now, it may seem that wine making is a dangerous hobby. The real danger in wine making for me was the glass. The glass containers do at times seem to jump at each other, as is the case with the next story. In my wine cellar, I have a long countertop that can hold about ten carboys of five-gallon wine jugs. With the ten containers on the countertop, there is still enough room to move the jugs so that I can perform different tests to measure the specific gravity of the wine. When the specific gravity is very low, that indicates that the sugar has become alcohol. Another test is the taste test to determine if the wine is palatable.

On this evening, I needed to move one of the glass jars to the front of the countertop so that I could both taste the wine and test the specific gravity. As I pulled the glass jar forward, it hit something on the countertop, probably some dried sticky fermenting wine.

I was pulling the jug forward, and it was not moving. This caused me to pull a little harder on the jug. As the carboy then jerked forward, it went to the side a bit. That bit was enough to cause the container to jump into the closest other carboy. When glass hits glass, it usually breaks. In this case, there were two five-gallon containers filled with wine.

One glass container broke, and five gallons of wine almost instantly covered the countertop and the base of the other nine carboys. Within a few seconds, the wine and broken glass was on the concrete floor of the basement wine cellar.

What a mess! Where does one start in cleaning up five gallons of sugary, half-fermented wine with pieces of glass distributed on the countertop and on the basement floor? This is not to mention the frustration that one is experiencing because of the loss of a jug and the contents. A loss of at least $50.

I found the largest concentrations of wine on the countertop and pushed it on the floor. I then swept the wine to the drain, making sure that the glass didn't go into the drain. I then swept up the glass on the countertop and the floor. Any remaining wine was then swept into the drain. At this point, the countertop and the floor were extremely sticky, so we washed them down several times with clean hot water.

Believe it or not, there were a few positives in this mess. Luckily, my wife was able to help me clean up the mess. The other positive was that only one carboy broke, so I only had half the problem to clean up. The other positive in this story is that I did not break the instrument I was using to conduct some of the tests, my glass hydrometer. The last positive in connection with my wine was I received first and second at the Wood County fair wine making competition.

CHAPTER 8

Impact Grants Coordinator

The regional offices throughout the state of Ohio had been abolished. While there was nothing I knew I had done to affect the office's elimination, I was still without a job. A new wave of closing state facilities and having residents placed in the community was a Ohio reality. While residents had been placed in the past into the community, there were more challenging residents who were now to be placed. Since my credentials were very strong in the area of programs for the mentally retarded and I had worked with many of the superintendents of county boards of mental retardation and developmental disabilities, I was offered the job of impact grants coordinator. The job was to place residents, primarily from Orient Developmental Center south of Columbus, into day programs preferably in their home counties. While the placement of people into a county required food, clothing, and a home to live in, the provision of rehabilitation or habilitation services was essential. My job was to specifically work with the county boards to use existing placements, help find new facilities or placements, and see that program funds flowed to these newly placed residents and their counties of origin.

At this time, Orient was for sure being converted into a prison; there was also talk of other developmental centers such as Apple Creek being converted into a prison. The other happening at this time was developing group homes in the community. Several communities were opposed to group homes in their neighborhood. One reason was that property values would decrease. Property values did not decrease.

One interesting factor was whether the community be involved in the development of the group home, or since it might be seen as a right of the mentally retarded to live in the community, they could be established without asking for special permission.

Another criticism is that people were moved too fast out of the institutions to community homes without proper staff training. The original date to close Orient was December 1983. Because of court actions, the last resident moved out on April 12, 1984.

As people moved into the community, there were accusations of not enough monitoring of the new community residents from developmental centers by case managers who did the monitoring.

Friends and Neighbors

Gene's Interests

Our neighbor Gene Walston had a knack for the unusual. This unusual trait was in many different areas and in many appealing ways. Gene was not any different from you or me; he just had many different experiences that also made him a very unusual and likable person. For example, he collected many different items such as drinking glasses, porcelain ladies, flat wall hangings, metal cows, you name it. New antiques were not unusual in his home. When traveling down the road, seeing and visiting an antique store was not unusual. What was unusual was for Gene to go into an antique shop and to buy nothing. As computers and eBay became popular, Gene found that he didn't have to leave his home to purchase his collectibles, which were many. One item he collected on the Internet was three-inch wall hangings of animals, flowers, and birds. The bird plaques were especially interesting because Gene had always had an interest in birds. Gene always figured if one was good, then two or three would be better.

Another collection was Gene's mouse, rat, and bird traps. His traps were usually not simple and involved a mouse going into several holes until eventually it was caught in one chamber. If Gene had one trap, he would surely have a dozen. When he was a boy, he would use round cages made of wire mesh to catch and band various hawks. The trap was most interesting in how it worked. Gene would tell us the story of how he would find a field mouse and put it in the cage to attract the hawk. On the top of the trap, he would place many round looped knots made of nylon line so that when hawks tried to catch the mouse, the trap would catch the hawk by entangling his claws. Whenever the hawk would fly away, the knots would tighten around the hawk's feet, and this would enable Gene to tag the bird and release it. Gene would also tell us the stories about how he would participate in the annual bird counts, usually conducted in the springtime. When Gene would recall past counts, he would remember the year, the bird, and the count. He would also remember anything unusual about the hunt such as people and their attributes.

One of Gene's somewhat recent undertakings was to plant twenty-six acres of asparagus, which was said to be the largest field of asparagus in Ohio. I remember one day in 1984 going out to the barn to see something unusual. The unusual site was that the entire main corridor of the barn was filed with these roots that all came from the middle of the plant and flared out to the outside of the plant. Gene told me they were asparagus and that they would produce for about twenty-five years. While the first few years of production was not great, after that, Gene's unusual venture was to pay off handsomely as he would work very hard to keep up with the demand.

Gene's experiment with the asparagus would provide many people with a very delicious vegetable. The asparagus plants were to outlive Gene and produced for about twenty-five years.

Snowmobiling

We did not have a snowmobile, but Gene and brother-in-law Fred Eldred did have snowmobiles. In 1984, there was a deep snow perfect for snowmobiling. The boys, Kathy, and I took off for Willard to use Fred's snowmobile. We switched drivers with Mark, Joey, and me. One time I was driving, Mark was in the second seat, and Joey was last. As we were going over the drifts, all was well until I hit a drift, pushing me back, and Joey came forward, so Mark was hit from both the front and back. We stopped to give Mark a chance to catch his breath.

We went to the other side of the road and ran the snowmobile on the frozen creek that was a few feet wide. The water wasn't frozen solid, so the ice was breaking behind us. We gave the snowmobile more gas to avoid getting stuck in the water. It didn't work; one of the front blades got stuck in a tree root. We got off the snowmobile to push it backward and then pushed it off the river. Our feet were wet, and so were our pants.

We were about a half mile from the road, and the snowmobile wouldn't start. There we were with three people very cold and a snowmobile not starting. Luckily, we had some starting fluid with us, so we sprayed it into the carburetor. It worked, and we were on our way home to dry out. I wondered what I would have done next if the snowmobile hadn't started. We were too far from the house to walk, and we were freezing with wet boots and pants.

Celebrating My Doctorate

I was approaching my fortieth birthday and had finished my requirements for the Ph.D.. We celebrated with a Mass at St. Thomas More Parish. The Mass was a thank-you to the several people involved in helping me reach this goal. We had a luncheon to top off the memorable day.

Scholarship

A few months after I had left the impact grants coordinator position, I was informed that a scholarship had been named in my honor. The scholarship was to be given to an Eastwood student, the school district I lived in.

CHAPTER 9

Chief of State Case Management

With so many residents being moved from state developmental centers to their counties of origin and with existing residents of various facilities such as group homes having many needs, the staff person responsible to see that the plans for the provision of all services was the case management specialist. Every county had at least one and larger counties several case managers to overlook the long-term and short-term everyday needs of people with mental retardation and developmental disabilities. One afternoon in early January, Director Johnston called me into her office and informed me that I would be responsible for 184 employees in each of the counties in the state of Ohio. Some case managers were employed directly on the state payroll, and others were employed by the counties. Regardless of employment, I was to provide the direction and rules for this statewide system. One of my major goals was to see that all the responsibility for managing the case managers switched to the counties.

I held a meeting of all case managers early in my tender. There were over one hundred case managers, and I held the meeting in Columbus to outline how case management was to shift from the state to the county. The shift took place after much work by myself and others.

Shortly thereafter, at three o'clock one afternoon, I was informed that the administrative rule for case management was to be presented to the governor the next day. I had started on the rule, but it was not complete. I arose around three in the morning the next day and went into the central office in Downtown Columbus to finish the rule. The guard at the office was not going to allow me in the building until I told him I was completing a report for the governor. I finished the rule, and it was retyped and sent to the governor that day.

I was to live full time in Columbus.

Case Management Services

A Few Cases

Each day had many various happenings in Ohio, and many times I had to direct case managers on how to handle the cases as the buck stopped with me. The following are a few of those cases that me and my staff had to directly deal with.

Water Burn

In one northwestern county, a mentally retarded adult was taking a bath. The water temperature was scalding, and the aide placed the person into the water. The individual was burned and later died of complications.

Man Stabbed Lady

I was walking to work one early morning crossing the Veterans Bridge in Columbus when I received a call on my phone that a case manager in the county of residence was entering a courtroom where a mentally retarded man was being charged with attempted murder. The case manager asked me what she should do. I said to ask for a new date so we could prepare a defense case. The continuance was granted.

The background information was that the young man had previously received a check for social security. He had met a young lady who was friendly with him, and he gave her his check. The girl he stabbed reminded him of the lady who had taken his check.

Young Girl in Chair Choked Herself to Death

I was reviewing an unusual incident that had been sent to the state. All major unusual incidents in the entire state had to be reported to my office in Columbus. A girl was in a chair and had slipped down, causing her to choke on one of the straps that held her in the chair. I called in one of my assistants and told her to call this home and have the resident placed in another safer chair. As I was giving instructions to my assistant, another assistant came in and said the same girl had slipped again and had chocked to death.

Three Brothers and Sister

I remember one call that came in where there were three adults with developmental disabilities living in a house with their elderly mother. How elderly was the mother? Very elderly and very sick. She was in need of an operation and had no resources to take care of the three offspring. My caseworkers had evaluations done immediately, and as quick, homes were found for the three adults so that the mother could have her operation. Successfully handling this type of situation is why social services exist.

Exit Report

Later in the year, I was to leave this position so I could take a position closer to home. I was to prepare a large notebook on all the areas that needed attention in my area of responsibility. A large document was prepared that contained many areas that were in process. One of these areas was not followed up on by an assigned attorney, and she lost her job as a result of her inactions.

Other Happenings

Winter Traveling

Earlier we reviewed an experience in Tiffin where I lost control of my car in the front yard of several residences. This story is another somewhat similar incident that happened to me when I was the chief of case management for the Department of MRDD for the state of Ohio. On this day, which was a few years after the incident around Tiffin, I was traveling on Interstate 71 from Columbus to Dayton. There was a special residential project in which several people from the state developmental centers had come back to Dayton to receive training so they could live in the community. I was to meet the managers of this residential facility. I had left Columbus very early in the morning so I could travel to Dayton, to do my business, and to return to my Columbus office. I was living in Columbus at that time while my wife and sons were living in New Rochester.

As I set out down the interstate, I noted that the weather was very frigid and damp. I had gone about halfway to Dayton when I approached an overpass bridge. I was going the speed limit that would have been around sixty-five miles per hour. I traveled under the overpass only to find out that as I came out the other side, the car was traveling at almost a right angle to the road. I looked out the window and saw the road sideways under my car door. Immediately, I sat straight up in my seat and slowly turned the wheel to the right so that the car would begin to come out of the partial spin. The car responded by pulling the rear of the car to the left. The rear of the car came back to the straight position, but it immediately went to the right again, and I was about three quarters of the way sideways with the rear of the car now to my right side. I turned the wheel slowly to the left, and eventually after several movements of the rear end to the right and then the left, I had the car under control. For several days after this experience, I slowed down at overhead road bridges just to be sure the pavement was not icy. Once again, I received some help from God as it was more than luck and good driving that got me out of that jam.

This incident proved consistent with the experiences I was to know in this job. A ride with turns and twists and quick stop and goes would be the norm. This job was to be extremely rewarding because meeting challenges with a staff who shared their ability to do their best when the best was needed proved to be the standard.

Jet Lure Contest

About this time, there was a fishing contest sponsored by Jet Lure, Ohio's oldest walleye lure, for three prizes ranging from $300 to $100. It was for the three largest walleyes caught and reported in Lake Erie caught on this lure. I was fishing with my eldest son, Joe, and I believe Mark might have been with us. On a Sunday afternoon, we were fishing out of Meyer's Beach near Vermilion. The beach was owned by Kathy's uncle, Bernard Meyer. As we trolled for walleye, I had one of the lemon yellow Jet Lures called a Perch Scale on my rod. I felt a tug and knew I had a big fish on the line. I pulled the fish alongside the boat, and my Joe netted it. We took it to Parson's Marina in Vermilion, and it weighed six pounds three ounces with a length of twenty-six and a half inches long. I took third prize of $100.

PART III

A Second and Third Chance with the County and Bowling Green State University (BGSU)

CHAPTER 10

Wood County Director of Day Services
and Director of Special Projects

At this time in my career, I was ready to leave the state system and obtain a job where I could live with my family and work nearby. Working in Columbus as the director of case management for Ohio had been a more than challenging position with responsibilities in each of the eighty-eight counties in Ohio. I had located various superintendent jobs around the state and was originally planning to apply for them. When I talked over my options with my wife and two boys, I found that they had ideas different from mine. The major difference between their plans and mine was that they all three wished to stay in Wood County. My wife, Kathy, had lived in Wood County for fifteen years and really preferred to stay in the area. My son, Joe, was in close reach of high school and was not fond of leaving the area as was my youngest son, Mark. Each of them had their friends and didn't wish to leave the area.

I, on the other hand, did not have a job possibility close to our present home and needed to find a job elsewhere. I had for the past several years been in CEO-type positions that were responsible for many employees and the services to many consumers. I had the experience, and I had my Ph.D. in educational administration and supervision. Working with other people, I have been told, is a major strength of mine. I was in the middle of making a very difficult decision. What seemed best for me was to move, though my family didn't necessarily agree with me. I spent many hours trying to come up with a decision that everyone would be happy. I used any energy that I could muster from my twin, my God, my reserve energy source, and then I went back and tried to find more energy. In the meantime, I had my position in Columbus and could buy some time until other options might develop. At the time, I was ready to apply for positions not close to our present location.

I really didn't know what to do but to pray. It worked; finally, I heard that there was to be a position created in Wood County called the assistant superintendent/director of day services position. I have for years known many employees from the Wood County board. In several of my former jobs with the state of Ohio, I had grown to know the administration and several employees who were none other than top-notch professionals. They say that you can tell the organization by its leader. I have already talked about Ray Anderson and his wife, Betty. Ray's leadership lasted until 1976 when he became the superintendent of NODC. Ray was succeeded by Douglas McVey, who had been a longtime business associate of mine by working with me and others to start the Ohio Athletic Association for the Mentally Retarded in the early 1970s, which became the Ohio Special Olympics. Doug and his wife, Ann, had been acquaintances of ours for years, and the position had many pluses.

Since I first worked in Richland and Lucas counties, a lapse of twelve years had taken place. While working for MRDD, I was working with, at times, the same population, the funding, and the manner of delivering service was different. The state was more monitoring of services and in at least one job; the superintendent of NODC, the emphasis was on a particular population rather than all populations in my area of responsibility. Since the service and delivery of service was changing, a look at these areas from the year 1985 seems warranted.

The job holder was responsible for many facets of the program's operations. In addition to being responsible for the superintendent in his absence, it was responsible for over one hundred employees in the following departments: the Wood Lane School under the supervision of Caroline Dene, the Wood Lane Adult Services with Dr. John Roberts at the helm, Community Employment Services (CES) conducted by Bill Clifford, Special Olympics led by Mary Sehmann, community resources with Liz Sheets, food services headed by Sonja Hammer, transportation with Linda Donley, and maintenance and grounds managed by Mark Carpenter.

I applied and was chosen for the position. While this position was to be one of the most challenging of my career, it was to be done with a group of truly professional people. A few of the many activities that were to take place in the next ten years are the following:

Several reorganizations, new programs, or buildings construction took place at this time and within the responsibility of this position. The start-up of a shuttle system to take people to their jobs in the community was established. A system to plan, monitor, or report on all new major capital construction and the remodeling of the existing buildings was developed through the director of maintenance and grounds department head. He had the characteristics of being a genius with anything that moved, a skill greatly needed with the twenty vehicles and twenty buildings needing his department's skills. Two major buildings, the mobile work crew/ transportation building, and the Nichols Therapy Pool were constructed. We worked with Wood County to establish a fuel center that provided gasoline at a reduced rate through a bidding process and dispersed the fuel via a PIN number. My secretary, Michelle Solether, was responsible for the billing of fuel for all county agencies using the fuel station.

Many changes were undertaken as needed to reorganize personnel or job duties in the school, adult services, and psychology and volunteer departments. Some people were hired, and some people went to other positions. A system-wide safety committee and programs in environmental programs such as asbestos, fire, and radon testing were implemented. Special Olympics went to seventeen sports while public relations and system-wide evaluation process of employees was updated.

In the policy, procedure, and forms, system changes were made by the various department heads, and the overall organization of the system was pulled together by a graduate student from BGSU, John Liebeck. It is amazing how a project can become much easier to accomplish with a fresh look by an outside person, in this case, a student. Several new policies/procedures such as fair labor standards, use of facilities, personnel areas such as overtime, assault and battery pay, rescheduled time, waiting list, safety programs, and other departmental updating were accomplished.

I would like to go into a little more detail in the changes taking place in various departments so that an update from 1973 in county boards of mental retardation and developmental disabilities over the past twelve years is understood as well as an understanding of where fifteen years of my professional career are being spent.

Wood Lane School

At this time, there were few states that had a system of education similar to the Wood County Board. It should be further pointed out that the county board system provided school-age training and education because before 1975, there were no legal mandates to provide education and training to the mentally retarded and developmentally disabled population. There would not have been training and education programs on a statewide basis for school-age persons in this category had it not been for the county boards.

At this time, articles had appeared in local papers in May 1986 on meetings taking place in Fulton County, a county two counties away from Wood, about transferring the students ages six to twenty-one to public schools and participating as much as possible in the public school activities. Federal legislation titled Public Law 94-142 first said in 1975 that handicapped students had a right to free public education in the most appropriate and least restrictive setting. For some time, there had been talk about segregated schools such as Wood Lane being incorporated within the regular public school settings. At this time, Wood County had been looking at the possibility of the transfer of classes and decided to hold a public forum and invite parents and other interested parties to this forum. This was a major policy change that was being discussed. As the person responsible for day services, I was working very close with the superintendent, Doug McVey, and principal, Rob Spence, to see that the forum accomplished the goal of giving a direction to where and how classes were to be provided to the school-age population being served by Wood County. While the results of the meeting could not be predicted, the presentation was an area under our control.

At the forum, several pieces of data were presented to the many parents and others present. Discussions took place on the pros and cons of what was termed mainstreaming or allowing handicapped people to be in public school classrooms, not segregated settings. Also presented were the segregated settings, such as Wood Lane School, in which the educational advantage to students can give a better chance for a total educational system. To be truthful, there are advantages to both systems, and that is why the forum was assembled. At the end of the forum, the conclusion reached by the parents was very clear. They wanted their children to be students at Wood Lane and felt that was the least restrictive, most appropriate alternative. Wood Lane School was to continue to house the classes, and the educational and training opportunities would allow the students to have the best possible education.

In 1985, some of the preschool classes were located in a few of the public schools. This arrangement was practiced since it would allow individuals with a disability to be in the same school of students without a disability. On one occasion, a preschool teacher noticed that there were bruises on one of her students' legs. The teacher reported this as is required by state law. The investigator from the Department of Job and Family Services made a home visit to the mother's home that same day, asking about the bruises. The mother said that there were no bruises on the child's leg when he went to school that morning. The prosecuting attorney recommended that the teacher take a lie detector test so that the investigation could move forward. The investigation of a parent had now turned into an investigation of a teacher following state rules. The teacher had the lie detector test and passed it, thus allowing the rest of the investigation to take place. The circumstances of a teacher having to prove her innocence made sense from one viewpoint, but from another, it seemed unfair to the teacher.

Another of the education/training programs was the early intervention program. Here individual services were given from birth to preschool age or three years of age. These services were linked with local hospitals so that services began at birth.

Community Employment Services

A few years prior to my arrival at Wood Lane, the CES Advisory Board had been formed. Several plans had been developed by Bill Clifford and his staff. In 1985, the goal of placing ten people into community placement per year had been established. In the history of job placements at Wood Lane, there had only been a handful of people placed in community jobs. The goal of CES is to make sure each job in the community is completed that day. If a person placed by CES is ill, they will see the job is accomplished. CES has many other services needed to make employment a possibility, and transportation to and from work is essential. One of these services was a transportation system. This transportation system complete with drivers and vehicles was established at this time so that workers from CES continued to be successful. In the year 2008, there are over one hundred people working in the community as a result of CES's efforts. Working in the community is one of the very important goals of community living. Living in the community is another goal that we have already addressed.

Funding Initiatives

Several buying cooperatives were instituted or upgraded to save the Wood County Board of Mental Retardation and Developmental Disabilities over $20,000. These purchases were for food items, maintenance supplies, and office supplies.

There was a need at this time to replace the roofs on the Wood Lane School and the Wood Lane Industries building, and we had no money. From 1986 to 1989, we worked to replace the roofs and the parking lots through the use of House Bill 264. This was an energy bill that public schools and county boards of MRDD were also able to use to borrow funds, if there could be shown a monetary savings on energy as a result of these capital projects.

Since there were few delays on this project, the roofs were being installed in the winter months. In fact, I can remember myself and other maintenance people working their Christmas vacation in December 1988. Having a maintenance director with a wide knowledge of maintenance issues such as roofing and parking lot installation was essential to this project. We also used Poggemeyer Design Group to develop all the needed drawings and specs to make us eligible for the funding of this project. Bruce Schermbeck also spent many days over the Christmas break with Wood Lane staff and the applicators of the roofing.

I also remember wondering how we were going to be able to pay the first draft on the construction bills as it was brought to light that there was a question about Wood County Board of MRDD being able to directly borrow the monies for this project. The attorney who was taking care of the legal papers for the loan had died, and the legal work needed to be completed before the bills that were in my hand could be paid. It was done, and I was glad to see that Doug McVey, superintendent; the Mid-Am Bank; and Ray Fischer of the Wood County Prosecutor's Office had the energy to help me calmly get the job done while working with all those contractors, the bank, and the attorney who were waiting for their money. In our case, the monies were borrowed through Otsego School with the cooperation of Larry Busdecker, superintendent, and the Otsego Board of Education. We are the only county board to my knowledge that has been able to use the borrowing mechanism through HB 264.

The Growth of Programs

There had been growth in many area of services in the county board of MRDD. The most exciting experience was that the growth of programs in Wood County made us one of the pacesetters in the entire state. The growth began with this board, and at that time, the superintendent, Doug McVey, orchestrated the institution and development of needed programs through his competent directors and the many other competent employees of the program. The following are some of the program that made huge differences in the lives of students, workers, residences, parents, and families. Through their financial support and volunteerism, the community was involved in positive change. It was a gratifying positive social change with which to be involved. Here are some of these programs.

Early Intervention, Preschool, and School-Age Education

Training the developmentally disabled from birth through preschool and school age has provided many challenges to parents, teachers, and students. Some counties in Ohio have opted to transfer their school-age students to the school district of residents. The parents of developmentally disabled Wood Lane students were asked where they wished their children to be educated, and the answer received was at Wood Lane. The classes have remained at Wood Lane from the 1950s into the 2000s, and I have heard of no plans on the horizon to change this arrangement.

Individual programs from birth to the end of school age have provided programming in four major areas: the physical, the psychological, the social, and the educational. Parents must be involved in the programs of their children by law. The exciting part of these programs is the parents have been happy about the growth of their babies, children, and young adults. The programs are working to the benefit of the recipients of the services.

CES

CES was begun in early 1985, a few years later was approaching the one hundred mark for people with developmental disabilities being placed in gainful employment in the community. The jobs varied from working in fast-food restaurants, cleaning the eating area, cleaning the stores in Uhlman's Department Store, and bagging groceries in Kroger. Some of the jobs created were within the Wood County system. These jobs included cleaning jobs within the several service buildings and at times the creation of separate agencies such as Laser Cartridge Express, which was filling ink jets for anyone in the community. This agencies received many awards because of the hard work of the staff and the many talented workers.

Wood Lane Industries

The Wood Lane Industries continues to provide employment in sheltered workshops by obtaining jobs from local industries, business, and the community. Assembly jobs involving doing advertising, assembly, and other jobs are in the community. The success of these jobs began with finding, quoting prices, and obtaining jobs by the staff and quality work by the people with mental retardation and developmental disabilities. This program remains very successful today and, in fact, at times gives work to other county programs.

Special Olympics

By leaps and bounds, the participation of people with developmental disabilities has grown as has the number of sports. The sports offered in Wood County in the year 2012 has grown to twelve. A look at one of these sports on a regional basis saw bowling grow from 90 bowlers from nine counties in 1979 at a tournament in Fremont, Ohio, to 175 bowlers in 2010 at the Varsity Lanes Bowling Center in Bowling Green and 30 professional bowlers paired with the Special Olympics bowlers. The manager of Varsity Lanes, Jay Young, was responsible for combining Special Olympics bowling with a professional bowlers tournament called Special Olympics Pro-Am. This was a creative approach to bowling for both Special Olympians and professional bowlers. Varsity Lanes then hosted weekly 100 local athletes for weekly Special Olympics bowling.

Another creative approach to Special Olympics programming happened in about 1990. At that time, there were 140 Special Olympians at Wood Lane. There were several other people eligible to participate in Special Olympics in the many school districts in Wood County. A proposal was made to combine all the resources of the county and use Wood Lane's resources to coordinate the entire Wood County Special Olympics. While there were a few concerns about the combination of all these groups, they were short-lived. In the end, 450 Special Olympians under one roof helped the program grow beyond expectations.

Special Olympics needs to raise money to keep the program afloat since all its funds do not come from the Wood County Board of MRDD. Its biggest fund raiser was to become the Prime Rib and Crab. A moneymaker that lasted a few years was their golf outing. It was held at the Forrest Creason Golf Course at BGSU. I am not a golfer, but I have on occasion done some golfing with my sons and in some tournaments for some of the special charities I am involved. Since I was responsible for this program, I thought it best for me to enter the field.

I had a special philosophy and preparation for these tournaments. My philosophy was to look good at the first tee. This was the first and only hole that many people would see me hit the ball. My technique for being successful was very simple. I bought a practice tee set used to improve people's swings. It had a metal screw-type stake in the ground and a long nylon cord attached to a golf ball. When the ball was hit, it only went about twenty feet and stopped. I would start a month before the tournament to daily hit this ball straight and hard. As a result of this practice, I was usually able to at least connect with the ball and convince people I was somewhat of a golfer!

The day of the tournament came, and I mentally had been preparing myself for the first swing. After the first swing, only three other people would see my golf, and they were good friends, so they wouldn't tell anybody how well I would play. It was my foursome's turn to tee off. I was second to approach the ball, and there were a number of people to witness my shot. I placed the ball on the tee, stepped back, smiled, took a deep breath, and swung at the ball. I sliced the ball a bit to the right, but it went a fair distance. I called that drive a great success.

Residential Services

While there were many residential homes in the community in the 1990s, there are now many more homes with people living in these homes. Greg Bair has overseen the development of these homes, pretty much from the beginning. Homes are available for all ranges of abilities. If one is very dependent on others for his or her care, there is usually a home available.

My Managerial Philosophy

Proposing an ever-changing complete philosophy on any topic is difficult. The purpose of this section is to give an idea about how I tried to grow and offer the chance for people to be happy and successful managers at work and at home. Since management and supervision are a central part of our professional and private lives, the importance of these skills cannot be overemphasized. As one advances in one's profession or private life, how one conducts business becomes even more important because of the pitfall of daily living. In relationships with spouse, significant others, or one's children in our private lives or in our profession, it will surely involve working with fellow employees, a boss, and at higher levels of management dealing with boards. In all these cases, one must manage themselves, a not-so-easy undertaking.

In this section, some ideas and philosophies will be presented. While the conclusion may not be as specific and prescriptive as one would prefer, the brief exercise will address some specifics.

The constant variable now more than ever is doing the "right thing." In our private lives or at work, doing the "right thing" for your employee and organization depends on the interpretation of the one who is the focus of one's communication. If I am communicating with six different employees or family members, I could be faced with having six different judgments or opinions on what is the "right thing." Therefore, it is not unusual to have a scattering of opinions presented with each being defended as a solid way of getting to the "right thing."

While positive comments have been presented to me on my private and professional life, I would like to deal with some examples of what people conveyed to me as not doing the "right thing." If we are doing the "right thing," we already know how to act. If we are not doing the "right thing" by several people's standards, how do we handle this situation without being negative? Leading us to the "right thing" is the goal of this section. This section will provide a method of dealing with other people's opinions of the "right thing" as all of us must broadly deal with this variable.

Being a very active person has led people to certain judgments that have been communicated to me that this trait is at times seen as negative. We all have judgments applied to us that we see as either positive or negative. For example, you may be seen as too slow in your response to act either at home or in your place of employment. You may be seen as a person who stays with the status quo, or you don't make changes in your life or work fast enough to suit other people.

My input from others is similar too but at the other continuum of the preceding sentences. Some people have told me that I act too fast at work and at home; at times, I make decisions too fast before I have all the facts, and some were uncomfortable with my changes at work in terms of the table of organization or of job duties for employees. At home, I may also initiate change too fast.

At this time, I would like you to develop some characteristics you see in yourself at home and at work that guide you in doing the "right thing" with others. Please write down the different ideas. This exercise gives you some idea of your management philosophy.

My "right thing" in summary is the following: my response to the ideas presented by others is, I would say that I do work as quickly as is needed, and part of my responsibility is to see that people are in tune with me. I must say that I have tried to listen and comprehend what is told me. Interrupting others is to be avoided. I also try to adjust my rate of work as it affects others.

My further responses are as follows: In regard to the point of making decisions too fast, if agreement is not something that happens, I believe after the decision is made, continually try to understand other people's viewpoints. I expect employees to continually try to understand my decisions and my issues. I have fears when employees or family have radically different ideas on the direction of the organization or the home setting because a team may not be present, and the success of the organization or home becomes harder to achieve. All employees may need to compromise somewhat to form that team. As long as employees are able to operate within the organizational structure of work, we are on our way. A fact to remember is that the president at work or mother and father at home are the only positions that see all that is happening in the organization or home. These head people are responsible to use this information to the advantage of the organization or home, which, in either case, includes the employees or the members of the home. Making a decision is something that involves my employees at work or my family at home. Sometimes decisions must be made on partial information, and that should be communicated. Conveying my decisions or actions taken to involve everyone is essential.

One of my philosophies is if I can use the idea of an employee or family member rather than my idea, use the one from the employee or family member. This system will certainly do nothing but good for employee and family. The goal is important, and how to reach the goal is secondary. A manager who places his way of reaching the goal as number 1 may be saying, "I am strong if I have my way." The truth of the matter is a manager with strong and successful practices allows others into his world of management.

In all the above, what is it that people can give me to guide my behavior? What can I give my employee and family members to help them be a better employee or better family member? Before reading the rest of the paragraph, please look at what you put down as your management philosophy. It is time so see what I propose as some of my management theory. First, we wish to have a good life. This good life will be based on selfless rather than selfish behavior. Giving your employee or your family member the opportunity to be a part of decisions, change, and other factors that go into living is essential. This gift of giving to others the opportunity to be a part of something that will affect their lives is one of the greatest gifts one can give another. The answers as to what guides your management theory are the same two values from my mother and father—enjoy life, and give or receive from others.

One caution must be given, and that is all the ideas from employees or family cannot always be used. While the process does not always offer a chance for others to get what they give as a solution, it is based on principles that offer growth and, when possible, compromise. Growth is essential to progress.

The Board

It would be impossible to talk about the positive factors I experienced at the Wood County Board of MRDD in my fifteen-year stay without talking about the people who guided the program. My experiences of thirty-nine years in the field made me a believer that the Wood County Board was truly made of the "right thing." The board encouraged staff to develop plans for and to implement state of the art programs. Employees were respected for their accomplishments, and the board allowed the superintendent to do his work without interference but with proper guidance.

The board composition appointed by the Wood County commissioners and the probate judge were excellent choices and allowed them to proudly serve. Working with this board was a true pleasure. Boards must know their job, which is to create policy and hire the superintendent and other major employees. The superintendent is hired to manage the program. These two functions must be respected and followed to be successful.

One of the board members was the local editor of the *Sentinel-Tribune*. I was to become close friends with Dave Miller and worked on many different situations with him. He was one of the people who interviewed me for the job in Wood County. Unfortunately, Dave had problems with his heart, and from time to time, he needed special hospitalization and care of his heart. Dave was involved in more community organizations than I knew existed. As editor, he had to take many positions on local issues and candidates and, as a result, was not always popular. He did his job and took what came with making sometimes unpopular decisions. I had a great deal of respect for Dave. We worked with others to establish the Black Swamp Humanitarian Awards, which is functioning to this date having given out over 450 awards for humanitarian deeds. Dave lost his battle with his heart ailments and died somewhat unexpectedly at a younger than average age.

My Private Life

The Different Blouse

Wherever I worked, it was always important to know people on the job and off the job as well. When I was invited by one of the employees in the adult-related programs to spend an evening with him and his wife, Kathy and I thought it would be a nice idea. On the assigned evening, we approached the house we had as the address and were greeted by my associate and his wife.

We had some enjoyable conversation, and since the two couples did not know each other well, we had some interesting conversation about our lives. Later, we played some cards. Our favorite cards are euchre, and their favorite was the same. A light supper of sandwiches and snacks followed with another drink. The evening came to an end, and we relayed our appreciation for an enjoyable evening.

As soon as the doors were closed on the car, Kathy asked me, "What did you think of her blouse?" I responded that "It was a nice light color." "No, I am not talking about the color. I am talking about it being see-through." I looked at Kathy and said, "Really?" Kathy's response was "You mean you didn't notice the kind of blouse it was?" I said, "I must have not noticed it." That was the first and maybe the last blouse that I did not see through.

Test for AIDS

In my previous job, I had a brush with a serious condition that caused bleeding in my stomach. I was given a transfusion to replace the lost blood. Several years later while in this position, I heard an announcement that anyone who had a transfusion between 1980 and 1985 should have their blood tested as the blood had not been tested during that time for the HIV virus. I made arrangements to receive the HIV blood test.

Before taking the test, several happenings relative to the HIV virus began to take place. When I was in a waiting room and picked up a magazine, articles on the effects of HIV on the body would jump out at me. Television programs on the negative effects of HIV and other infections with similar symptoms as AIDS would present themselves to me. I even had some physical symptoms indicative of the HIV virus. When I called to receive the results on the HIV test on the appointed Monday morning, I was told by the nurse the results could not be given. My first thought was that I probably must receive the results from the doctor as it was bad news. That same afternoon, I did call back as instructed and received the results. The way they stated the initial results led me to believe that I had HIV. After a long conversation, I was told in language I understood that I did not have AIDS.

A short time later, I was talking with a nurse friend of mine, and she informed me it might have been better to have the results reported in such a way that it could not be traced to my records. In any case, I was glad that set of tests was over, and I did not have the HIV virus. I had hopes that this was the end of these tests.

Family and Friends

The Broken Leg

Our neighbor Gene Walston was the type of guy who would give you the shirt off his back and then ask if there was anything else you needed. Gene was one of four sons and one daughter of Oliver and Grace Walston, neighbors of ours. Jim dealt in hardware, Dick was a preacher, Denny was a photographer and criminal justice specialist, and Tekla was a nutritionist. The whole family was exceptional in that they were very concerned about others and were extremely friendly. The first story centers on a broken leg and Gene's admirable trait of trying to be of service to his fellow man.

When farming is your business, it is not unusual to have accidents. One of Gene's workers was pounding tomato stakes into the ground, and the pole broke. The sharp point of the stake went into the foot of the worker. Gene made sure medical help was available.

Another story I heard about Gene and his giving to others involved a fellow farmer's worker. It seems the worker was picking tomatoes, and after each basket was full, the basket was thrown into the bed of the truck, and after the hamper was empty, a token was put into the bottom of the basket, and both were thrown down to the worker. On this occasion, the basket with the token was thrown down to the worker, and when the basket came down to the worker, the token flew out of the hamper, and the person who deserved the token followed it into the path the truck was using. The worker reached for the token, and somehow his foot slid into the path of the truck, and his foot was run over by the truck. The worker suffered a broken leg in many different places and was in need of a place to stay since he couldn't travel back to Texas.

Gene was approached to have the injured worker stay at one of his houses as he had heat in the building, and there was no other option available to the worker so late in the season. A few days later, an inspector came from the appropriate government unit, and he asked Gene for his license to operate the home. Gene explained that the license had not yet come from the state department, and he had paid his money at the beginning of the season, and the responsible state department would give him no answer as to where the license was in the approval process. Gene explained the reason for having this one worker in his dwelling and offered the proof that he had paid for the license. The inspector said that he wasn't authorized to accept a license in process, and he would have to fine Gene. Unfortunately, being kind to others can at times get one into trouble that they otherwise would have been able to avoid.

Money Needed for the Workers

It was on another occasion that Gene Walston came to Kathy and me with a problem. He had a family of workers who were coming from Texas to Gene's farm to work in the fields harvesting the crops. The family had gotten as far as New Haven, Ohio, and they had run out of money. In times past, when money was needed by workers, Gene had merely wired them money. Wiring was not an option in this case, and unless Gene could get them money fast, they were in no position to eat or travel, and the weather was very hot where they were with little shade. Gene knew that we were from the Willard area, which was a few miles from New Haven.

His question was "Do you know anyone who lives in the New Haven area and would be able and willing to give this couple money so they can make it here to work for me?" Immediately, Kathy and I began to think of people we knew who lived in New Haven. We were drawing a blank until we expanded our thoughts a few miles from New Haven. We told Gene that our good friends Butch and Phyllis Rothschild lived just a few miles from New Haven, and they would be in a position to give them money so they could finish their trip to Gene's farm. Gene's face lit up like a Christmas tree. Like so many of our friends and family, almost everyone who has set foot on our property had also had the privilege of meeting Gene. In fact, it was not uncommon for visitors to ask about Gene. Gene was the type of person you never forgot once you met him. Butch and Phyllis knew Gene, and Gene was elated he knew Butch and Phyllis.

We gave Gene Butch and Phyllis's number. Within minutes, he had made contact with them, and the business arrangements were smoothly arranged. Gene felt indebted to Butch and Phyllis for years to come, and as nice as Gene always treated everyone, after the Rothschilds' generosity, he treated them even better. While Gene could have personally traveled to New Haven to take care of the situation, this gave him an additional couple of hours to keep his complicated and active farm business in order. Gene obviously appreciated the help he received from our friends from back home.

The Underground Railroad

When we first moved into our home at 5570 North River Road, we heard from more than one person stories about the hotel that stood at the corner of New Rochester Road and North River Road. The hotel stood on the north side of North River Road. We could look out our home's east window from the dining room and see the plot of land where the Myers Hotel once stood. One of the stories we had heard was that the Myers Hotel was a house of ill repute. The second was that slaves would stay hidden in the hotel, which was a part of the underground railroad. The housing of the fugitive slaves was said to take place in a secret inside room. One of the stories was that the secret holding room was in the second floor of the hotel. The fear that the slaves had as they made their way north to Canada was to be caught by slave catchers and be shipped back to the place from where they had come.

The Myers Hotel was located in the field directly off the New Rochester Road. Today a walk from the New Rochester Road north of the former wood bridge and the steel bridge location into the field will yield many pieces of broken pottery that according to the stories of neighbors came from the Myers Hotel. All that is left of the steel bridge today, which replaced the wood bridge location, is two cement supports from the steel bridge.

Straight Ahead

Another story took place on the pontoon in North Carolina, and I was not on that cruise. It seems my brother Walt organized a men's night out with his sons and son-in-law. His two sons, Trace and Pete, and son-in-law, Tommy, were out having a good time doing the things that men do together. As the evening went on, a fog began to develop, so there was a point man stationed in the front of the pontoon to look for any possible obstruction.

Walt was driving until he reached a very uncomfortable situation with the fog coming in very, very heavy. At this point, Walt took over as the point man and asked Tommy to drive the pontoon, and Trace and Pete would keep Tommy company. It looked as if the fog was lifting a little, and Walt yelled back directions to Tommy. Trace and Pete saw Tommy make a funny face, and they asked what the matter was. Tommy said, "Walt just told me, 'Go straight ahead, you little bastard.'" Trace and Pete began uncontrollable laughs, and when they were done, they said, "Tommy, my dad said go straight ahead a little faster."

Kathy's Fortieth Birthday Party

I had decided that Kathy should have a surprise party for her fortieth birthday. I rented the auditorium at St. Thomas Moore parish in Bowling Green. I invited guests, planned the food, and began planning the entertainment, a "This Is Your Life" review of Kathy's life.

The date was set for June 18, 1987. Everything was set, and most people had returned their slip, telling what they were going to say behind the curtain as Kathy tried to guess who was the next unknown friend or relative. There were well over one hundred guests.

Kathy was going out to dinner with a few friends, and they were to stop by church so she could drop off something. As she entered the auditorium, it was dark, and I turned on the lights and said, "This is your life, Kathy Frederick." We started out with her parents, went through her family and friends and then my family, and finally, our present friends and family. The boys came in just before the meal and were the last people to be introduced. Just as our boys were finished, a storm came and knocked out the electricity. We opened the doors and had enough light to serve the warm meal. Halfway through the dinner, the electricity came back on, and the evening progressed as planned.

It was a great event, and I don't believe I could ever do it again!

The Hearse

It was a sunny day in late 1988 that I had gone outside to take the tin cans out to the garage for further recycling. As I looked across the road to our neighbor Sue's house, I noticed a large black station wagon. I took a better look at the station wagon. A closer look at the vehicle made my heart jump. It was a hearse, not a station wagon, that came into our neighbor's driveway. I ran to the house and told Kathy about the hearse. She walked out the back door, looked at Sue's driveway, and told me it was a friend of Sue's hearse. It was a relief finding out that Sue was in her house alive instead on the hearse dead.

Baseball and Our Family and Friends

Baseball Vacations

Both my sons were big-time collectors of baseball cards. This fact can easily be proven with a trip to their closet and a look at their impressive collection of boxes of baseball cards. A few football cards were also in the mix. A few times a week, the three of us, my sons and I, would journey to Maumee to gaze at the packs and boxes of baseball cards at the Pitcher's Mound baseball card store. The Pitcher's Mound was located next to the old movie theater on the main drag of Maumee. Several brands of name-brand cards were available. Topps was the most popular with Donruss and Fleer also being popular brands.

Occasionally, Kathy would ride with us so she would be able to at least understand the nonstop conversations at home on baseball cards. Having enough money to purchase a box of baseball cards composed of thirty-six packs of cards was like being a millionaire to my sons. Saving an unopened box as a future investment just didn't happen. After owning a box of cards for a few days, the joy and excitement of opening all the packs in the box was just too much of a pleasure to deny one. In addition, the fact was always present that there was always a chance that a card worth a few hundred dollars could be, but never was, in the box. I had but one baseball card, and that was for my Cleveland Indians outfielder who warmed up by shifting his bat behind his head to his back so that he could go through his stretch. Yes, it was Rocky Colavito, my childhood idol and great sportsman of the 1950s.

Baseball card shops were not limited to the northwestern part of Ohio. When relatives or friends were to be visited, all of them knew that baseball card shops were a must activity for our boys. There were baseball card shops near Williamsburg, Pennsylvania, when we visited Jim and Carol Biddle and family. Carol was our former babysitter and my former wine bottler. In Philadelphia, there were several baseball card shops near Walt and Judy Frederick and the kids. In Atlanta, near Bob and Barb Frederick and family, there were cards. Mike and Marge Frederick and the girls lived in Cleveland with many card shops available. Names such as the Batter's Box and the Home Run were found in many cities.

The real purpose of baseball cards was not the cards, but it was for whom the card represented. The representation of the card was of big-time Major League Baseball players. There was one pretty sure place to see these heroes, and that was at their work site, the baseball field.

The location of baseball fields greatly influenced our yearly family discussion on "Where will we go this year for vacation?" The result was to visit relatives in Atlanta and also see the Braves, visit more relatives in Philadelphia and enjoy the Phillies, travel to Cleveland and watch the Indians, and enjoy the Cincinnati Reds and Detroit Tigers. One of the most memorable experiences was Comisky Park and Wrigley Field to cheer on the White Sox and the Cubs, respectively.

It was at Wrigley Field where we were to be exposed to the ivy walls of center field and the "Bleacher Creatures" who so openly supported their Chicago Cubs. Obtaining tickets to the game was a process that started early in the year. By the time I had secured these golden tickets, the game had been nearly sold out, and I thought I was early in obtaining tickets. As we walked to the ball field after luckily finding a close parking spot, I picked up the tickets, and we found our way to center field. From the time we sat down until the time we left the stadium, there was nothing but noise. The Cubs were playing Minnesota.

There was a center fielder named Brett Butler, soon to have a name change to "Butt Head." "Butt Head" as many of his faithful anti-fans called him was the target of a barrage of words from the time he walked into center field until the time he left. He was also badmouthed from the time he came into the on deck circle until he left the field. "Butt Head" could do no right. If "Butt Head" spit on the grass, the crowd would scold him for spitting on the grass. If "Butt Head" tried to make a play on the ball, the "Bleacher Creatures" produced such noise that the possibility of concentrating on the ball was about 2 percent. If "Butt Head" stomped his shoes on the ground, he received a severe scolding for ruining the grass. "Butt Head" made the mistake of looking into the center field crowd and immediately was told that it was not his business to look at the center field fans.

The anti-Butler actions reached its height as a chorus of voices sang to "Butt Head." The word was easy because the first line was sung to an A below middle C. Then a second group immediately sang "Butt Head" using middle C. The third part of the course was an E above middle C. The final note used was an F above middle C. As the fourth part of the chorus came in, the volume on the singing was turned up to very, very loud. It would not have surprised me if fans' voice boxes from the chorus were to be lost and would pepper center field. Kathy and I were a bit afraid of being in center field because we had heard about young ladies exposing parts of their torso in the heat of the game. We were hoping for a home run from the opposing team so the tradition of throwing the ball back on the field could be achieved.

The crowd sitting in front of us was to give us one more treat as policemen came down to our section and escorted a whole row of younger men and women out of their seats and out of that section of center field. The remaining group of fans in this section began to speculate on why the whole row had been extricated from their position. The real fear was that with all the commotion going on about "Butt Head," had that group been innocently blamed and further were we next. About twenty minutes later, two people came back to their seats in front of where we were sitting. The big question posed to the two returning fans was "Why were all of you taken out, and why were two allowed to return?" The answer was quick and to the point. The other people in the row were using drugs, and the two convinced the agents that they were not users. I always wondered how those two could so quickly convince the authorities that they had not been using drugs, but it was back to the excitement of "Butt Head" entering center field and getting ready to spit on the Wrigley Field grass. The day was one to never forget!

The Picture of the Baseball Player

My son Mark was dearly in love with baseball memorabilia. His favorite memorabilia was baseball cards, but every once in a while, something else would come along. He was ready to go after these pieces of history, as long as it was something he wanted and also if it was not expensive, hopefully free. That is exactly what Mark thought he was onto. How was it that Mark was going to come up with this free picture of one of his Major League players? All Mark needed to do was to call in on this 900 number, and eventually after many calls, his wish would be answered. Mark thought the 900 line was free like the 800 numbers, so he would call and not be charged for a call while he was able to obtain his picture.

When we received our telephone bill, it was clear that someone had made over $20 worth of long distance calls to a 900 phone number. We asked Joe if he knew anything about a 900 phone number. He pleaded innocence on knowing anything on calling and being billed for the call.

Our next stop was Mark. We asked if he had made any calls to a 900 number. He was extremely pleased with his free baseball picture that was coming in the mail, so he said yes, he had called the 900 number but that it didn't cost any money. The 900 calls were just like an 800 number call, free. We showed him the bill to the tune of over $20, and he was very concerned. He did not have $20, nor did he have any plans to earn that kind of money. Well, he didn't have any plans to earn $20 before he found out about the phone calls, which were charged to Mom and Dad. The bill had to be paid, and Mark could not pay it. Mark learned the lesson to beware of something that is billed as being free usually isn't. Mark was determined that he had called his last 900 number.

The picture of Dave Winfield came a week later. Mark was very pleased the picture came and that it was a beautiful piece of memorabilia. Mark would have been happier if he hadn't looked close at the signature of the ballplayer. Mark's picture had the signature that would have been beautiful if someone had not smeared the first and last name.

Baseball Heroes, Yes or No

On September 20, 1988, I wrote a letter to a syndicated columnist, Mike Royko. I had read some of his columns and felt he was the type of person who called a spade a spade in the world of sports. The reason for my letter was that I had been to a baseball game in which the Boston Red Sox was the visiting team. It is the custom for autograph seekers to stand behind a roped-off area after the game where players walk from the stadium to board the bus. There is usually a long walk from the locker room to the bus that the player must walk. It is at this point that people seeking autographs will entice the players to sign the program, a hat, a piece of paper, a baseball card of the player, or another valued possession. As the players came out this evening, some began to sign, some waved, and a few looked straight ahead and wouldn't even acknowledge that fans were present, let alone sign and autograph. One of the nonsigners was on the bus, and he had just opened his window. A fan decided that it was his/her turn to bring up some information about this player's private life. This infuriated the player, and while he couldn't spend time outside the bus to sign, he did choose to take time to make negative statements to the fan.

In my letter to Mr. Royko, I expressed my opinion that baseball players are heroes and that heroes have some responsibility to at least acknowledge their fans somehow if they are not willing to sign their name a few times.

What does a wave cost, as Tiger Woods and his fellow golfers continually acknowledge their fans?

It was not until 2009 that I heard the rest of the story. I was in Columbus having dinner with a college friend and my two sons when the topic of signing autographs became the topic of discussion. I relayed the story of certain athletes not signing autographs. John, a security director for many PGA tournaments, relayed some stories to us about professional golfers signing autographs and coming close to injuries. John relayed to us that one time, he was working security, and Tiger Woods was signing his name for the crowd. As the signing progressed, people became more focused about obtaining a signature. As Tiger was ready to move, he noticed that his foot was not moving with the rest of his body. A man in the crowd had stepped on Tiger's foot. Luckily, he was not hurt, but the fact remains that spectators wanting autographs do not always treat the sports figures as kind as they need to be treated. The signing of autographs should not be met by the athlete with the potential of bodily injury.

Mark's Unfortunate Experience in Eastwood Junior High School

Mark was in seventh grade in 1989 while our eldest son, Joe, was a junior in Eastwood High School. It was a Friday night, and Joe was dressing to go to a high school football game. Mark, also known as the social being of the family, announced somewhat sheepishly that he wasn't going to the game. While that was his choice, Kathy and I suspected something negative.

After much probing, we found out that one of the students at Eastwood was making threats against Mark. We decided that our best bet at solving this problem, which by now was keeping Mark from attending anything but his classes, was to talk to the principal, Ms. Sue Wynn. This strategy turned out to be the best possible solution and one of the few available.

Ms. Wynn was an in-control person. This trait was essential for running a junior high school. We talked to Sue about the problem, and she went out on the limb and told us that the problem would be solved. We hoped that she was right. In short order, the problem was solved, and Mark was comfortable in attending all his school functions.

It was thirty years later when I was having a conversation with Sue and I learned the true story of how Mark's fears were solved. Sue relayed to me that she believed in bringing together students to eliminate the "wedge" that existed among them. It made sense to me, it worked, and it took some intestinal fortitude to carry through such a plan. Thank you, Sue, for being you!

The lesson of people influencing others has been more predominant than I ever imagined. The first lesson of this incident was to have my son and another classmate face the issue with the help of the principal. After the meeting took place between the two boys and the principal, a positive solution transpired. Twenty-three years after this incident, I asked my son Mark to review what was written for accuracy and his approval. As I was tying on another chapter late one evening, Mark came into my study and said, "Dad, what you have is accurate, but there was more to this story." I asked, "What more was there?" He said, "My classmate that was involved in this incident became a friend of mine." I said, "Thanks for telling me, Mark. I will finish the story."

BB Gun

In the early spring of the year, it was common for the Portage River to thaw and cause the water to overflow the riverbank and flood the lowlands next to the river. One place this would happen was across the road from our house. In 1990, this is exactly what happened. Since the neighborhood boys were not able to get close to the water as it was ice, the spring offered the first chance to explore the riverbank when the ice had moved out of the river. New Rochester was blessed with neighborhood children from one end of the village limits to the other on both North River Road and New Rochester Road.

On this particular day, our son Mark and one of the neighbor boys from the other end of town, Nick Coe, decided that they should explore the overflowed river across from our house. Mark had some boots to use in his wading, and Nick decided that I would not mind if he used my waders. The plan was set that they would take their BB guns with them in case there were any wild animals, and they needed to protect themselves. They were walking along the water's edge, and slowly, they began to walk into the water a little further as they proceeded down the temporary riverbank.

The excitement reach a high point when Nick stepped in a low spot in the water, and his waders filled with water. As he was rapidly going to the bottom of the hole, he yelled to Mark to help him. Mark was within a few feet of Nick and in a little over a foot of water. Nick took the only item that he had handy, his gun, and extended it to Mark so he could pull him out of the water. Mark grabbed the barrel end of the gun and began pulling Nick out of the water. As Mark pulled the gun, a shot ran out. A BB flew past Mark's right ear and missed it by a fraction of an inch. The next part of the face that was missed by less than an inch was Mark's eye. Evidently, when Mark pulled on the barrel, Nick must have had his finger on the trigger, and the gun discharged. Mark said to Nick, "You almost shot me." Nick's response was "I almost drown."

Nick was safe, and so was Mark. The two left the new river and came back to Mark's house to begin the drying-out process. Nick lay on his back and put the waders in the air to get out the water. While much of the water left the waders, his feet would not come out as a suction had been formed in the bottom of the waders. Nick thought that they should cut off the waders, but Mark thought not. If they cut up the waders, Mark reasoned that would tell me that Nick had used the waders, and neither of the boys wanted to face me with cut-up waders. Much time and energy was put into pulling off the waders, drying them out, and putting them away before I came home. I was not to find out about this event until twenty-two years later at a bachelor party for another former neighbor, Scott Danielson.

The Wet Canoe Trip

Activities with my sons were always a treat for me. I knew that they would grow up, and I was certain it would be fast. On this particular occasion in the spring of 1990, I had promised my son Mark, and his friend Mike Lentz to go on a canoe trip. It was the springtime, and the water was high and fast. It was a Saturday morning, and we had planned on an early start. I knew the person who lived at the point we wanted to put in the canoe. We arrived around seven o'clock in the morning, ready to go with our life preservers on, our lunch, and a few other incidentals. We quietly walked around the house, picked up the canoe, and put it into the Middle Branch of the Portage River. The sun was barely out, the temperature was fifty-five or sixty degrees, and we were ready for an adventure. An adventure was exactly what we were going to experience.

As we rounded the first corner of the river, we noticed some squirrels playing on the bank. A little further and we were coming to the bridge that went under Kohring Road. We heard a loud noise to our left. As we looked to our right, we saw the riverbank, and as we straightened ourselves up and looked beyond the bank, we had a huge awakening. The sound was coming from what looked like one hundred large geese, not Canada geese, that were walking, not running toward the river. We quickly put two and two together and surmised that we were the targets because we were directly in their line of fire, no one else was around, and clearly this was their space. It was flee or deal with the consequences of the beaks of these very large birds. We paddled and paddled and paddled faster than fast. The geese were gaining on us, and just as they were coming into striking distance, we reached the curve in the river and were out of their territory. We had a battle plan if the geese caught us, and it wasn't to leave the canoe.

As we paddled down the river, we began to see more wildlife. We saw a raccoon, a rabbit, and a wood duck. The current was flowing fast as we reached the halfway mark. There was heavy traffic ahead such as fallen trees, branches, and leaves. As I looked ahead, I saw a large tree covering one-half of the river and debris covering the other half. In the middle of the river, there was a small opening that I thought we could squeeze through. The water was running very fast as there was no place for it to go except the small opening in the middle of the river. I figured I was the adult, and I should be able to get us out of this jam. I estimated the depth of the river was close to over our heads, if not deeper. I shouted for everyone to look up, and we were going to go through the opening in the middle of the tree. Saying all this took me about three seconds, and then we were face-to-face with the tree. Since the water was running very fast, the paddles were becoming worthless. I saw a branch and thought that was our trip to freedom. I grabbed the branch so I could pull us to the side of the tree and ultimately through the open hole in the middle of the fallen tree.

My plan couldn't have been faultier than it was. As I grabbed the tree branch, the current pushed the canoe into the tree, and with me holding the branch to guide us through the opening, I instead had capsized the canoe into the very cold Portage River. As I went into the water rapidly, I tried looking around where the other two were because the river was very powerful and cold. I saw Mike swimming toward shore, and I thought it best for me to get out of the swift current before I had an experience such as being caught on the bottom and having the current push me under the water. I quickly looked for and called for Mark. I approached land and did not see Mark. I was alarmed. The options for Mark were not the greatest. I then heard Mark asking Mike and me, "Why did you get wet?" I looked up, and there was Mark standing on the big tree that was blocking one-half of the river. I asked Mark, "How did you manage to get on the tree?" He replied, "I saw the tree coming, and I didn't want to get wet, so I jumped so I wouldn't get wet." Mike and I looked at Mark, and then we looked at each other. We both must have been thinking, *I wish I was dry instead of looking like a river rat.*

The conclusion at this point was simple, Mark was dry, Mike and I were not, and both of us were freezing cold with no towels, no dry clothes or shoes, and we weren't sure where anything was in the river but the canoe. We pulled the canoe to shore, loaded up the supplies we could find, and looked for and found another opening through the big tree. As we drifted by Mark, he quickly jumped into the canoe. As we started down the river past the fallen tree, we found the other two life preservers; our lunch, which was still pretty dry; and some of the other equipment we had brought. We lost very little, and other than a few scratches, we were happy to be on our way to Pemberville to meet up with our dockage point and our car that we had dropped off last night. The sun came out, the temperature was rising, and all three of us were to have an adventure that we were unfortunately never to forget.

Marine Science Class to the Florida Keys in 1991 and 1996

My first two trips to the Florida Keys as an adult volunteer bring back many memories of Eastwood students and their talented teachers. Terry McKibben, Mike Godfrey, Teri Hansen, and other volunteers did a great job of making the trips a great success. On both trips, we started early in the day and drove all day and all night before reaching the Keys in the afternoon the following day. My driving partner on the 1991 trip was Pat Ruck. In the wee hours of the morning, it was my turn to take over the driving, but I was very happy that Pat drove a few hours more as I was not ready to drive. The extra sleep allowed me to safely complete my nighttime driving.

On the first trip, we used a former dolphin training camp with a conch research facility and the sleeping accommodations next door as our base camp. On the second trip, we stayed at Pigeon Key, Florida, one of several islands in the Florida Keys where the roads and bridges were being built so travelers had a reliable passageway through the keys. Pigeon Key was the island where some of the constructions crews were lodged. A not-for-profit agency now runs the island and allowed us to use the facilities as a base camp operation for a reasonable fee.

On the first trip, everything was new to me. On the evening of the first night at the former dolphin training center, my son Joe and a few of his friends were on the dock trying to find some marine life. The class had been studying marine life for months, and they were anxious to see firsthand the many species they were familiar with in the wild. Their trusty net was used to scoop up something they saw on the bottom. Turns out a spiny lobster was their catch. Since lobster was not in season, they wisely elected to release the lobster faster than they caught it.

The next several days on both trips were to be spent diving on the various reefs of the coast of Florida. On my first dive in 1991, the reefs were beautiful but shouldn't be touched by humans. Touching the coral can cause it to discolor or die. The result is that marine life will suffer without the live coral. The sights were amazing as we snorkeled in the ocean and inspected the coral. The variety of fish and other organisms was indescribable. I saw big and little fish that looked like neon signs. Even with my inherited color blindness, I saw many colors. The colors I saw were many I could identify and others either I couldn't identify or were unfamiliar to me. The shapes and sizes of the fish ran a spectrum of familiarity to first-time knowledge. The first-year diving was more unfamiliar than the 1996 experience. I fell in love with the many types of fish and had little fear of anything I saw.

On the 1991 dives, there was a school of barracuda fish. I was snorkeling with my partner, and I noticed that one of the barracuda came close to me.

I saw a gold substance in the fish's mouth. As the three- to four-foot fish came very close to me, I saw that the gold item was a hook with fishing line attached. As the school of barracuda left us, I looked down on the bottom of the ocean and saw an even larger barracuda. I became a bit uneasy about what looked like a six-foot fish. I carefully watched the fish as its mouth moved back and forth as if it was chewing on something. The only substance I saw to eat was the coral. I moved a bit closer to the barracuda to see what I could see. The closer I moved, the more uncomfortable I felt. We moved on to smaller fish.

It was on the 1991 trip that I decided to make my primary goal of finding as many moray eels as possible. I was able to find three species of eels that year. Spotting eels is difficult because they are nocturnal, and we were diving during the day. One of the three eels I observed was near a deserted island a short distance from one of the Key Islands. The group used canoes or kayaks to paddle out to this deserted island. While hiking on the island, we observed remnants of the former inhabitants such as clay pots and plants. After the land tour of the island, we decided that we needed to explore the reefs on the east side of the island.

A few minutes after we headed north of the landing dock, a large half-round rock with the round section of the rock facing up, covered with brain coral, was spotted. Also seen was a green moray eel partially covered by the large rock. The eel came out a distance and retreated the same distance under the rock. This was a definite Kodak moment. One of the snorkelers, Nate, decided that he really needed to capture one of the best, if not the best, underwater pictures of the trip. He aimed his underwater camera at the eel and descended directly upon it. He was so caught up in the moment that he forgot that the image in his camera was actually about two to three feet farther away than the actual distance of the eel. I looked around, and his fellow divers were screaming at our picture taker, moving their hands in the water, signaling that the diver should move back from the eel. The picture taker continued to move toward the eel, setting up for the big shot.

Everyone forgot that they were not to be heard or seen as the picture was the only concern of the photographer. I had visions of an attack by the eel on the picture taker on a mission. Much to everyone's surprise, the picture was taken, and the smiling photographer jetted to the surface. To this day, I can still picture the brain coral in the round rock, the moray eel, and the diver/photographer who was going to be attacked by the moray eel. It didn't happen, but the memory is still there.

The trip to Key West was always the last big hoorah of the trip. It meant we could travel in our vans to Key West; visit the shops, the capsule marking the farthest point south in the United States; eat pizza; and see the sunset, ships, and the many performers doing the dog, knife, and escape acts. After the big show on the dock, anxiety rose high, for all knew it was time for the awards ceremony. The awards were always given after the meal, and each student and volunteer received many. In fact, I saved my six 1996 awards. My awards were for Problem Solver Award, I Did It! Award, Pack Rat Award, Thinking on Your Feet Award, and Safe Driver Certificate. My Pack Rat Award was for saving four (or more) months newspapers to read during every free second of my vacation time. The leaders had a continuous commitment to documenting these awards. The humorous and accurate awards were done in partial jest, and there were many that everyone had forgotten or wanted to forget. To this date, I have a hard time understanding how these leaders came up with all these ingenious awards.

After several days of snorkeling and seeing God's beautiful marine biology creatures, we packed up our belongings and proceeded back to Pemberville. There is one last story of the 1996 trip that must be reported. During this trip, we were traveling at night to our destination. We had citizen band radios or CBs in all the vans. Periodically, we checked in with one another to make sure we knew where we were traveling and to have some interesting conversation. At one point, a trucker who was on our channel entered in the conversation. He sounded like a male, and we thought it would be interesting to have some outside chatter. Talking on the CB helped everyone pass time and know other CBers. As we traveled along and exchanged stories on the CB, it hit me that now was the time to tell everyone about my cousin David's poem on the nonsense talk of life. I had memorized this ditty when I was very young, was very proud of my cousin's poem, and was going to knock the socks off anyone who was listening. While I had previously introduced this poem, I felt it appropriate to repeat these words. Here is the poem that I delivered to the trucker, other truckers monitoring the channel, and the marine biology group:

David's Poem

Ladies and gentlemen,
hobos and tramps,
cross-eyed mosquitoes and
bull-legged ants.
I am here to address you,
not to undress you,
I am here to tell you of a subject I know nothing about.

Christopher Cucumber sailed down the Mississ-slopy River with
the Declaration of Indigestion in one hand and
the Star-Speckled Banana in the other.

There shall be a meeting in the men's hall for women only.
There shall be no fee,
pay at the door,
pull up a chair, and sit on the floor.

After a long silence, the trucker came back on the air and directed his comments to me that the person who had written and said that poem was a very intelligent person. I had the impression that he had never heard anything like this and was pretty much speechless. His speechlessness did not last long as a new topic of discussion took center stage on the CB.

The return trips from both 1991 and 1996 to Ohio went smooth, and all the participants seemed to have fond memories of their eventful learning experiences in marine biology. As a reminder of the trips, T-shirts were printed and distributed to those participants who ordered them. I was surprised to see that the back of the marine biology shirt for 1996 had printed "Save This Minute Mystery." Number 12 was titled Frederick's *Ode to the Truckers*. My cousin David would have been very proud to have his poem given this type of recognition.

Mark's Deer

Mark had always been a good marksman and a good hunter. I remember the first deer that Mark shot in this area because I was with him. Mark would have me go on a set route to drive the deer, and he would be in a strategic spot if I kicked one up. On this particular day, Mark was in his deer stand located on the east side of the Walston woods. I had kicked up a buck deer, and it was running along the west side of the woods. Mark took a long aim at the deer and hit it on the run. It was an impossible shot, but he made it. He was, of course, very proud of his hit, and so was I. Mark gutted the deer, and I brought back my trailer so we could take it to town and register the deer.

Mark had the deer head mounted, and it is still hanging in his room. Unfortunately, Mark passed in 2016 and is with us in spirit.

Williamsburg, 1993

Kathy and I decided to spend some time around Williamsburg, Pennsylvania, with some friends of ours, Jim and Carol Biddle. We had stayed at their house and enjoyed the beautiful scenery and the nature, including a beautiful stream that ran through their property. It was in this stream that an unusual happening occurred either before or after this trip. Jamie Welty, Carol's brother, was with us on this occasion and was fishing in the stream. We could see him from the front porch of Carol and Jim's house. We saw Jamie try to pole vault the stream. He only made it halfway as he didn't have enough momentum. He simply fell backward into the water, still holding onto the pole. We all had a good laugh at Jamie's expense.

On another trip in 1993, Kathy and I had finished our two- or three-day visit in Williamsburg, Virginia. We decided to take off in the last afternoon and go through Washington, D.C., on our way home. This was the long way home. We reached Washington, D.C., around ten o'clock. It was dark, and we pulled into what we thought was our motel. We found out that we didn't have reservations, and our motel was farther along. The motel we were at had no vacancy. We somehow got lost as the numbers on the road didn't correspond to the directions we had. It was now about eleven thirty in the evening, and we were running out of gas. I had the phone number of the motel, but we didn't have a portable phone. We pulled off the main road, looking for a gas station, another motel, or a telephone. We were in the middle of the city in a rundown neighborhood. We did find a phone booth. I parked the car and told Kathy to lock the door. I went to the phone and called the motel where we had reservations. With new directions, we proceeded toward the motel. The gas gauge was showing empty, and it was now after midnight. We pulled off the highway and did finally find our motel. Everything was dark except for the motel sign.

After a good night's sleep, we woke up and found that a gas station was next to the motel but was closed the night before when we arrived. It had been a very scary and confusing night, but we filled up with gas and were on our way home.

Home Tour

On December 12–14, 1993, we were scheduled to be on the home tour sponsored by the Pemberville Library. We began preparing for the tour a year before it was to take place. We repainted several rooms, and we patched the ceiling crack in the kitchen and repainted it. We bought several new items to decorate the interior and exterior of the house. We asked our son Mark and his friend Kevin Madaras to dress up as Santa and Mrs. Claus and welcome the guests. Since I made homemade wine, we set up a wine demonstration in the garage and gave out free samples of our wine. There were around 190 visitors through our house that weekend. We had several friends throughout the house to act as guides. Our large two-story farmhouse looked great.

There was only one little problem with the tour that weekend. Since we were one of four homes the visitors were to tour and the groups were divided up into four separate groups, we had the whole event backed up. Nobody wanted to leave the wine tasting room. Everything did eventually work out, and that was the first and last public tour we gave of our home. It was really a lot of fun for a good cause.

Where Is the Wine?

Making wine has been an established hobby for me since 1972. I have made around 150 gallons of wine a year, even though I could make more legally. I legally cannot sell wine since I do not have a license. Kathy and I have a large giveaway wine project on an ongoing basis since we cannot possibly drink all the wine I make. I have been known to give people enough champagne or wine for the toast at a wedding, or I have given other people enough that they can have a party.

At times, providing the wine can lead to very unusual circumstances. The first such event was at Kristy's wedding, my sister Ann's daughter, in 1999 at the Norwalk Armory. I was sitting in a crowd enjoying my conversation, food, and drink. The band stopped playing, and I saw Ann coming in my direction, and I also noted that her eyes were on me. She came directly over to me, and I could sense that it was more than Ann who was now looking at me as Ann told me, "We are ready for the wine." I said, "When are you ready?" She said, "Now." I said, "Did I tell you I would bring the wine for the toast?" She said, "Yes." I think I mumbled out loud, "I didn't remember saying I would bring the wine." I got up as if to be going out to get the wine, but in my head, I was trying to think of the closest wine store. I remembered there was one a short distance and began to go to my car thinking that they would just have to wait for me. On my way out of the hall, I remembered that I had brought some wine for my first cousin George Schlotterer and given it to him earlier. I quickly found George and told him the circumstances and assured him that I would bring him wine the next time I saw him. We rushed to the car and rushed back in to face a wedding party that was overdue for a toast. Everyone loved the wine, and everyone was happy with everything else about the wedding. I was very glad that God had given me a brain that could think under pressure.

The second unusual circumstance was at the champagne brunch of Carol and Ron Carpenter's daughter. Carol and Ron have been close friends of ours for years. Ronda, their only daughter, was to marry, and I had volunteered to have a champagne brunch at the wedding shower for about twenty people. I decided to bring enough strawberry champagne for the entire group, and when it was time to make up the punch, I decided that I would taste the champagne first. I tasted the champagne and found that it had outlived its life span and was sour. Luckily, I had brought with me as a backup some Asti Spumante. I tasted the Asti before pouring it into the punch. It was superb. The party went on with only the servers knowing that there had been a change in the menu.

Cancer

Kathy had for some time been seeing a dermatologist for cancer surgery. Her physician had concerns about her complexion because she has a type of pigment that frequently paired with skin cancer. For some time, she would go to the dermatologist, and it was not usual for various unusual spots to be identified, removed, and frozen. On one occasion in the late 1990s, she came home with the news that she needed to have skin surgery to remove some basal cell cancer. The surgery was involved, but she came out of it in good shape.

As a result of Kathy's experience, it was decided that I should visit a skin physician. I made the arrangements and started my periodic visits. At first, I had a few suspicious spots, and they were removed. No cancer was found. The next time, I had a suspicious-looking mole the doctor identified as pre-melanoma. I asked what pre-melanoma was, and the doctor explained among other facts it could be deadly. This quickly got my attention. After he explained what pre-melanoma was, I researched the topic on the Internet. The test I had run on me would have an influence on my future. Death was one of the real possibilities if I had it. My Monday appointment confirmed that I had pre-melanoma. The doctor had tried to contact me over the weekend because he wanted me to know the result of the test and figured the faster the process of treatment, the better. I was very nervous going to the doctor's office for my follow-up treatment. I was seeing the worst possible results, and they were not good. The doctor explained that it was pre-melanoma, but they thought it had not spread beyond the area he had just removed from my leg. This was neither the first nor probably the last time that a medical situation had threatened my life. The removal of the affected area on my leg revealed that they had been successful in ridding me off the pre-melanoma. I have not had any serious skin disorder since the pre-melanoma, nor has my wife since her basal cell.

Joe's Rock Painting

Joe and Mark were in the same fraternity at BGSU, the Sigma Phi Epsilon. Mark nominated me as an honorary member of the fraternity, and I was accepted as a member. When Joe and Mark were looking for a college, they informed Kathy and me that they liked BGSU, but they wanted the college life, not more homelife with us in constant communication. Kathy told them that they could live a few miles from us at BGSU, and we would not be calling or visiting them unless it was their desire. Both thought that made sense and was a good deal. Joe was a few years ahead of Mark and provided us with good training in preparation for some of Mark's activities.

One of the most memorable events that Joe provided us with started with a phone call. It was the wee hours of the morning, and Kathy and I were sound asleep. The important phrase is "were sound asleep." The phone rang, and both Kathy and I were instantly wide awake. Our first thought as parents was *Is everything OK?* Joe was on the other end of the line and wanted to know what we were doing. I told him we were thinking about sleeping.

Joe got right to the point. He said, "Dad, do you still have all those old large paintbrushes that you used to paint the house?" I assured them that I had them and knew exactly where they were. Joe told me he would be home in a few minutes because the fraternity had no paintbrushes and couldn't buy any as the stores were closed. Not wanting to get too deeply into my son's business, I asked if five brushes were enough to accomplish their task. He assured me that the paintbrushes were going to paint the big rock on campus, and he needed to leave for the brushes now.

Joe came to pick up the brushes within minutes. I asked him if there was a great risk of getting in trouble painting the rock. Joe informed me that all the Greek organizations paint the rock, and it was his fraternity's turn. I must admit Kathy and I were a bit worried about this painting expedition, but Joe got in no trouble painting the rock. I felt much better seeing the positive looks of the painted rock the next day. I even felt a little proud having contributed to the success of the task.

Spain

It was spring of 1997, and Mark was attending BGSU, majoring in criminal justice. I received a phone call around suppertime from Mark, who was explaining to me a recent discovery of his about fulfilling his Spanish language requirement in a very short period.

I asked how that might be accomplished, and he informed me that he "could fulfill his language requirement by taking classes in Spain." I asked how that could be done, and he filled me in on a sister university of BGSU named the University of Acola near Madrid, Spain. I asked when the next chance to go to Spain was, and he said, "Soon." I asked him what the deadline was to register for this coursework. He informed me it was "tonight." My wife and I were at the university within an hour, and Mark was registered for the course with little time to spare.

While in Spain, Mark had many good educational experiences, and on weekends, the class traveled to many points of interests in Spain. We found out after he came home that on his first evening in Spain, he got lost. His Spanish was not that good as he had only one day of college classes under his belt, and his high school Spanish, which was taken a few years prior, hadn't made him fluent. Luckily, he found a taxi and was able to give enough directions to reach the safety of the home where he was living.

Another adventure he experienced was in relation to an assassination of a political figure in Northern Spain. One of the very popular politicians was murdered in Spain while Mark was there. As Mark was taking the train to Madrid, he was following a group of people who were talking in detail about the murder. Mark decided to follow this group from a distance.

The running of the bulls was taking place at the time he was in Spain. He called us one evening and asked me if we thought he should go with his class that weekend or go to the running of the bulls in Pamplona, Spain. I quickly researched the event on the Internet and found that many garages were converted to bars and that it was not safe to sleep under a tree as one might be urinated on by one of the party people. It was, however, a once-in-a-lifetime event. It was a difficult call for me, and I told Mark to go to the running of the bull with another friend. Kathy thought he should go with his class. Mark went with his class.

Mark returned safe and sound to the United States from his trip and to this day still has many stories about his adventures in Spain. Probably some of these adventures that Kathy and I would be better off not hearing.

The College Student Boarders

In a few short years, we had the opportunity to share our home with three college girls, all who were attending BGSU and who were either direct relatives or friends of relatives. Our house is a century home and had three large bedrooms, with at least one being unoccupied. There was a fourth bedroom, but that had been converted to needed closet space. We did not hesitate to open our home to each of these boarders as college and family have been very high priorities in our lives. Each of these three boarders offered us views that supplemented the existing ideas we had from our two boys on what it is like to be a college student. All three of these girls added something unique to our home mainly because they were girls, and we had lived with boys in our home. We always thought this was a positive venture as it gave us a chance to keep up with the younger set.

Cassandra from the West

The first boarder in the early 1990s was Cassandra from California. Cassandra's mother, Roseann, was my first cousin, and throughout our early years, our two families were very close as relatives and as Catholics.

My mother and Roseann's father were sister and brother. Cassandra was a big help around the house and had a special relationship with both our boys. Mark, in particular, was always plotting ways in which he could throw a scare into Cassandra. It was no secret that scaring Cassandra was not a difficult task. The result of the scare was predictable; Cassandra would express her fright with a scream that was heard anywhere in the house.

I remember one evening when Cassandra was leaving for the dorm, she had packed most of her belongings in the trunk of the car. It was very dark, so the stage was perfect for a scare. Mark crawled into the trunk with Cassandra's belongings and pulled down the trunk lid so it was almost closed but not latched. Cassandra was now bringing down the last load to place it in the trunk, and Mark was ready for the big scare. As Cassandra opened the trunk to deposit the last few articles, Mark remained perfectly still, somewhat hidden among Cassandra's possessions. As Cassandra opened the trunk lid and looked into the trunk to see where she was going to put the clothes, she finally saw Mark, just looking at her. Cassandra was startled I thought she was going to jump out of her skin. She gave out a scream that any screamer would be very proud of.

On another occasion, I was placed in an unusual situation. Cassandra and a friend of hers were pulling into our driveway. I was in the middle of a project trying to find a nest of yellow jackets that had been threatening to sting members of the family. As Cassandra came in the driveway with her friend, the yellow jackets discovered me, and at least one of them flew up my pants leg. From previous experiences, I knew I was in danger of taking a sting from this wasp, and I knew that it would be very unpleasant. I immediately stripped off my pants and was in a compromising situation with my pants off and my underwear exposed.

As quickly as possible, I jetted to hide behind the garage, only to find that I could go nowhere without someone's assistance. Fortunately, my wife delivered a pair of pants, and I had the opportunity to explain to Cassandra and her friend my embarrassment. The yellow jacket had given me a not appreciated gift of a stinger, and Cassandra and her friend had given me understanding.

Amy from Norwalk

The next boarder was Amy, a daughter of Kathy's first cousin Diane. Diane and Kathy were always best buds, and for years, Diane and Larry would invite us to spend New Year's Eve at their house usually with the children sledding on a hill beside their house and the four adults enjoying the peace and quiet as well as the feelings of being relatives and friends.

When Amy called and asked if she could spend a semester with us, we told her yes as we still had Joe's vacant bedroom since he was off to college and enjoying life in the Sigma Phi Epsilon fraternity house at BGSU.

Amy was in her senior year and working to complete her methods for her teaching certification. Amy had the ability to look at life with a calm face. So Amy's time with us was spent studying, helping around the house, sleeping, and attending classes. We enjoyed her company during the week as on the weekend, she was off to other activities.

Abby from Cleveland

The third boarder was Abby. Abby's mother, Chris, was the sister of my sister-in-law Marge. Chris and her husband, Vaughn, as well as Mike and Marge, were from the Cleveland area. Abby only stayed with us a few weeks as there were some complications with the room arrangements at BGSU. Had Abby been staying with us for a longer period, we would have been exposed more to the musical education as a vocalist.

St. Sebastian

Kathy's home church was St. Sebastian. Bismarck was originally a German Catholic farm community where St. Sebastian Church and school were located. The only buildings in Bismarck were a church, a small school, and two houses, one used by the priest and the other used by the nuns. The church sat in the middle of a large cemetery. The school had closed in 1960s as a new school was built a few miles down the road. The nuns stayed a few years in their house until they no longer taught in the public school. The church was shut down because of the lack of priests in the late 1990s. What ultimately happened is that there was no need for the buildings by the Catholic Church, so it was decided to sell the school, the nuns' house, and the priests' house. These three buildings were located side by side on one side of the road with the church and cemetery on the other side of the road.

The closing of St. Sebastian Church in 1996 was an action that was not lightly taken by the members of St. Sebastian parish. When the church was closed, all the movable items were taken out and stored by the Toledo Diocese. The diocese owned the church, and the bishop is the administrator of the diocese. After the closing of the church, no one was allowed in the church. While there were prayer services in the church parking lot, Mass was to never be said again in St. Sebastian Church. By the way, this was the church that Kathy and I were married in.

The sale of the three buildings, excluding the church, was set. A former student at the church, Ralph Phillips, a businessman from Shelby, Ohio, purchased the property and announced that he wished to renovate the homes, rent them, and use the proceeds to fix up the school. He wished the school to be a senior center and community center. The contents of the building were also part of the purchase. This included silverware, pots and pans, and dishware. The school was also in need of repair as it had sat vacant for several years.

Until the closing of the school, it had been used for serving food at the parish festival. The parish festival had also ended. The renovation of the school and nuns' house was undertaken, and monies were sought from former parishioners and others. The basement of the school had been remodeled, and some progress was evident in the classrooms upstairs.

It was announced that a celebration was to be held on August 30, 2009. All the former students of the school and other parishioners were invited for chicken noodle soup, chicken and turkey sandwiches, assorted side dishes, and the famous pies made by women of the former church. It was an event to behold as people returned to their roots after many years of absence. After the meal, a meeting was held, and a silent and verbal auction was held to raise funds for the renovation projects. The event was a huge undertaking with Ralph, Deb Bumb and Joanne Schaffer, and others heading up the various committees.

While the events of the day were well planned and over two hundred people attended, there was that underlying feeling that things would never be the same, though many wished they would. The three buildings under renovation were taking shape, but the use of the church as in former days was not to be. Not being a member of the parish, I could not experience the feelings of loss that were present. People losing their place of worship and needing to become a member of another parish was, is, and will always be a great change to adjust to.

Boy Scouts

The Sand Dunes

In the middle of these dunes near Oregon, Ohio, where no other living being had been seen, some scouts could have been observed playing capture the flag in their underwear.

Shortly after the start of game 3, out of nowhere, two young couples were seen approaching the playing field area. Most of the scouts immediately hid behind the dunes and put on their clothes, well, at least their shorts. One scout had been a distance from the discovery of the four walkers and had not taken the liberty of turning around to see the oncoming human beings. The leaders and the scouts were telling this lone scout that there were some young women and men walking toward them in the sand behind them. The lone scout with only his underwear on wasn't looking behind him to see the couples because he was sure that everyone was trying to pull one over on him, and he was not going to be taken in by this scam.

It had been clear throughout the day that the scouts were the only people in the dunes. Our lone scout with only his underwear on must have figured that the odds were ninety-nine to one that his fellow scouts were trying to put on over on him and one to ninety-nine that there were other human beings in these dunes located miles from civilization. The chanting continued with the scouts yelling to the lone scout that the walkers were coming closer. The lone scout was saying, "You are not getting me to look. Who do you think I am? Someone who was born yesterday?" This went on for a good ten minutes as the two couples were off in the distance when they were first seen. As the couples came closer, the chanting became louder. The couple now was on a course that would place them about thirty feet from the lone scout. As the couples began to pass the lone scout, they appeared too embarrassed to look. The lone scout, on the other hand, saw the two couples passing by his side and finally looked at them and finally took off to the dune, where his clothes were hidden. The lone scout was by nature very white in skin appearance. The lone scout after this experience was more the color of embarrassed red.

Camp Berry 1986

For many years, our Boy Scout Troop 344 of Pemberville had gone to Camp Berry near Findlay for summer camp. Camp Berry had many programs and offered merit badges for most of the program areas. A merit badge means the scout has become proficient in an area such as swimming and has thus mastered the required skill areas to earn the swimming merit badge. It was not unusual for a scout to receive several merit badges at Camp Berry in one week when during the school year, it could take several months to earn one merit badge. When my eldest son, Joe, attended Camp Berry, he received swimming and lifesaving merit badge. As a result of these merit badge experiences, Joe was in a position to use his knowledge. This opportunity took place at the Middle Bass Island public swim beach later that same summer on July 20, 1987.

I was standing on shore, and my wife and two sons were independently swimming at the public beach. I looked out at the swimming area and saw a young boy around six and a girl around ten years old carrying her brother into deeper waters. As they went out further, they both were unaware that there was a drop-off in the swimming area from three feet to nine feet. As they reached this area, I yelled to the children to stop. They continued to go into the drop-off area, and both disappeared under the water. Shortly thereafter, the girl came up and swam to safety, but the boy didn't. I quickly looked around and saw my son around ten feet from where the boy went down. I shouted to my son to get the boy and could see my son diving under the water. For several seconds, there was no movement in the water near the site of the incident. Other people were now in the area looking for the boy, and the beach was in an uproar as the swimmers learned that someone was under the water. The clear sound of the ten-year-old sister crying was heard, and the mother of the boy was frantic. A few seconds later, I saw a small body come out of the water near the site of the mishap, and then I saw Joe's hands around the young boy's body. It looked like a small whale followed by a big whale shooting out of the water. There was a lady close by who immediately took the small boy to his parents. I went over to talk to the parents, but within minutes, they left the beach with their children. As soon as the near tragedy took place, it was over, and the noise level returned to its previous high level.

A year later, I went to Camp Berry as a leader, and after breakfast one morning, they asked for stories about scouts who had used their skills. I began to tell the story about Joe using the skills acquired at Camp Berry. As I began the story, the dining hall almost instantly went quiet. As I talked about the boy going under the water, there was not one sound to be heard from the several hundred scouts until I finished the story and received a standing ovation. I thanked the counselors for their excellent instruction and Camp Berry for their programs. Joe was nominated for a National Medal for meritorious service from the Boy Scouts of America. His mother and I attended the dinner in which he was given his award in January 1988.

As a Boy Scout leader and participant in family campouts, I always enjoyed the role of storyteller. The reinforcing part of my storytelling experiences was that people were attentive to my stories. For years, I had the desire to write about my unique life.

Yes, all our lives are unique, shaped by the wonderful people in our lives. These same people have given me the opportunity to experience an enjoyable moment or two and often to learn a valuable life lesson. The combination of writer and storyteller was an attractive dual role to me.

Scouts to Florida 1999

Matt Meyer has been the scoutmaster for several years of Boy Scout Troop 344. His assistant scoutmasters are Terry McKibben, the marine biology teacher at Eastwood High School, and others. I was asked at the last minute to go to Florida with the boys as another leader was not able to go. I thought about it for two minutes and said I was glad to go.

Snorkeling is only second to scuba diving in the Keys. There are several spots to dive; Lou Key, Sombrero, and Indian Island are some of the most notable. In diving, one must be careful not to step on the coral as it can cause pieces to break off and eventually die. The corals are not fast in regenerating, and anything done to harm the coral is a threat to the wildlife that it supports. We had many experiences in which we saw unusual nature life. One stingray at the bottom of the ocean floor buried itself in the sand. When it rose, it was ten to fifteen feet in length and width. Barracuda, sergeant majors, groupers, angelfish, moray eels (my special interest), sea turtles, parrotfish, puffers, and spiny lobsters are just a few of the sea creatures.

On one dive, I was to experience the most unusual sea creatures I had ever seen. I was diving with Matt when he pointed to three fishlike creatures. One on the bottom was swimming in a fast circle and looked like a giant nerve shark. Above the shark were two three feet in diameter roundfish that looked like sunfish. They were also swimming in a round formation, keeping above the shark. The three were gone faster than they came.

Later in the week, we went to the Dry Tortugas Island. The prison island located south of the Keys was the prison that Dr. Mudd served his sentence for fixing John Wilkes Booth's broken leg. As we snorkeled around the island, I became engulfed in several thousand small fish, the size of minnows. For about fifteen seconds, it was as if I was part of the school that had literally taken over a five to ten feet wide and several feet deep section of the ocean.

Yearly Weekend Travels with Our Friends and Relatives

Larry and Carol Moore

We had known Larry and Carol since our early years in the Toledo Jaycees in the late 1960s. Larry and I were on the board of the Jaycees, and we learned a lot about leadership. When the Jaycees sponsored the Special Olympics program in Lucas County where Toledo is located, we met a number of people, Jaycees, and their wives, who were caring, energetic people. When I left Lucas County to work for the Department of Mental Retardation, we hooked up with Carol and Larry because they were residents of Pemberville, our mailing address. In 1995, the two couples decided to go on a weekend excursion or weekend outing to Saugatuck, Michigan, and we were somewhere once a year. The responsibility to plan a weekend rotated each year after that point. Since near the beginning, the planning group had kept the destination a secret until the arrival point was reached. Here is the start of our weekend trips, which will be continued into other chapters.

1995, Saugatuck, Michigan

As the four of us talked about a weekend excursion, the Moores proposed traveling to Saugatuck, Michigan. This lumber town and port was known for being an art colony and place where tourists came for arts and crafts. The unusual stores, scenery, and Saugatuck Dunes State Park were all attractive to the four new travelers. Having a vacation close to Lake Michigan and the Kalamazoo River made the setting even more inviting.

Our Friday afternoon ride up to Saugatuck on a pleasant fall day helped set the stage for our first joint outing. As we approached the city, we were amazed at the number of people walking in the downtown area. This is truly a tourist town, and it appeared there were lots to do in the evening. We found a pleasant restaurant to eat and enjoyed the gathering room at the bed-and-breakfast.

The weather was a bit cold as we took a ride around the outlying areas on Saturday morning. We stopped at a garage sale, more to see what garage sales are in Michigan than to buy anything. An oak toilet seat was one potential purchase at the garage sale. The downtown area was becoming colder and wetter as we began the circuit of shops. Art was a definite factor in the type of merchandise available. I found a few nesting dolls to add to my existing collection of around fifty dolls. Looking was more the game than buying in the art-type shops.

The evening included eating and walking downtown. On Sunday, we drove to the sand dunes at the Saugatuck Dunes State Park. The morning was windy, cold, and included sand. As we looked over a sandy area, we noticed a large print that could have been a bear's. We walked with caution and brevity after the sighting of the print. A pleasant ride back in the rain brought up the discussion of returning to Saugatuck someday in the future. We shall see!

1996, Southern Ohio

In keeping the record straight, Fredericktown is not connected to my heritage. The person who owned the bed-and-breakfast and horse farm was a person who originally lived in Pemberville, left, and became a teacher. She had a farmhouse she lived in, and we stayed in a new structure that contained the two-floor bed-and-breakfast. The countryside was rolling and beautiful. We were told that the couple who had rented the lower accommodation were getting married that very Friday, and they would be coming in late to their room that night. We concluded that the newlyweds were on their honeymoon, and we probably would not see much of them. We were right on both counts.

On Saturday morning, we had breakfast in the farmhouse and then proceeded to the barn where we were going to pick out our horse for the ride that day. Carol and I picked out nice but ordinary horses. Kathy picked out a Tennessee Walking Horse. It is said that one can ride a Tennessee Walking Horse and drink a glass of wine at the same time without spilling a drop. The walking horse has a gait so smooth that there is hardly any trot or bounce. Kathy was to agree with this statement. Larry, on the other hand, is a bit larger than either Kathy, Carol, or me. The person in charge gave Larry the choice of riding a draft horse by the name of Justin. Larry was agreeable to this plan. We had a wonderful ride in the country for hours, and we had no accidents. This was fine with me because horses and I have not always been good friends.

The rest of the weekend was spent walking in nature. At some point, we did say hello to the honeymooners for a very short passing encounter. We were not going to spoil the honeymoon, even though it would have been nice to at least have a short conversation. This conversation was not to be.

1997, Lebanon, Ohio

Lebanon, Ohio, is a small town in Southwest Ohio. I know of at least three well-known sites associated with Lebanon: antique shops, the headquarters for a large elder care living center called Otterbein Homes, and the site for Otterbein Lebanon Homes. Larry and I were to ultimately become members of the Otterbein Portage Valley Homes Board in Pemberville. Kathy and I had previously visited many of the antique shops in Lebanon and nearby Waynesville. Our goal on this Friday was to be at the Golden Lamb Restaurant and Hotel.

Our usual check-in time to the hotel is the late afternoon or evening since we travel in the afternoon to arrive at our destination. This afternoon was no exception. What was an exception was that the two rooms we had reserved in the Golden Lamb were very different, and a decision needed to be made who was to sleep in which room. The first room was the Ulysses S. Grant Room. The bed was elevated and had huge corner posts on each corner. Elaborate curtains surrounded the bed. The other room was a large room with a bed and nothing elaborate. We flipped a coin to see who would get which room, and Kathy and I won the Ulysses S. Grant room.

The Golden Lamb is famous for the fact that there have been eleven United States presidents who have stayed there.

We all seemed happy enough, so we went out to dinner for the evening. When we returned, it was late, so we all decided to go to bed. Larry and Carol went to their room located to the left of our room. I was about to fall asleep when I heard noises like children playing. I was able to eventually get to sleep and thought little about the noises.

At breakfast the next morning, Larry asked me first thing if I had heard any noises the night before. I said I had heard some sounds that sounded like children playing. Larry explained to me that there was a little girl next door to them or two doors down from our room in which a little girl was up most of the night running around in her parents' room. Larry relayed to me that he had gone down to the front desk when the sound got too unbearable and reported the incident. Shortly after two o'clock in the morning, the manager came to the noisy room and told the occupants they needed to keep the noise down as people were trying to sleep. A time after that, the little girl did quiet down.

As we were checking out on Saturday night, I watched as Larry received his bill, and there was no charge. Larry asked about the charge and was told that his stay was free for the one night as they had been disturbed by the young girl. I told them we had been disturbed minimally by the little girl, and we received a percentage off our room bill.

The next day, we decided to visit the shops in Lebanon and the antique shops in Waynesville as there were numerous shops to browse. That evening, we ate at the Golden Lamb Restaurant. I had my favorite meal, lamb and mint jelly, and despite our best try, we were not able to spot the little girl from the night before.

On Saturday night, we stayed in a small cottage in Lebanon. There was a room downstairs to sleep and a small loft to sleep upstairs. Kathy and I thought it best we stayed upstairs. We did not hear any small children playing all night in an adjacent room. To this date, it is a big joke that

Larry and Carol slept in the wrong room at the Golden Lamb and missed a night's sleep while on vacation.

1998, Centerville, Indiana

Centerville, Indiana, is located near Dayton, Ohio, and was the hometown of Carol and Larry, our traveling partners. This meant that they had planned this year's outing, and this was the high school where they both had graduated. This was also the setting from which their romance had incubated. The first night, we had checked into our bed-and-breakfast, eaten, and went to Carol's mother's home. As we walked in, Larry affectionately said, "How is the old bat doing tonight?" I looked at Kathy and she at me. Larry explained that he had always called Carol's mother the "old bat," and it had always stuck with her. We had a nice visit and decided it was time to go back to the bed-and-breakfast. The bed-and-breakfast was filled with a number of antiques. The bed-and-breakfast was also home to a cat that had claimed the entire house, including the dining room table.

The next morning, we toured Centerville and a few of its shops. We saw the Centerville High School and the other civic buildings and ended up meeting relatives of Carol at a neighborhood restaurant. Carol's mother and her brother Richard were the other family members. Carol's father and both of Larry's parents were deceased. The evening was an enjoyable mixture of food, drink, and discussion. Now Kathy and I knew what Carol and Larry's Centerville was when they talked about their hometown.

1999, Columbus, Ohio

Kathy and I looked far and wide to find an appropriate setting for our 1999 weekend with Larry and Carol. Since we had visited Columbus at least one long weekend a year since 1973, we knew our way around the city.

One of our favorite sections of town was German Village located south of Downtown Columbus. So we found two bed-and-breakfasts, one for us and one for our friends. Unfortunately, we could not find two rooms in one bed-and-breakfast, so we found two that were located close to each other.

A supper in one of the local bars was followed by a walk around German Village. The next day was Saturday morning, and we decided to visit one of the bakeries. They had a great assortment of goodies, and we chose a great assortment to eat. The rest of the morning we spent in antique shops. There are several shops, and the assortment of antiques offered a great variety. In the afternoon, we took a trip to our son and daughter-in-law, Joe and Tara, for a visit to their apartment near Westerville. It was then off to Easton Mall, to one of my and Kathy's favorite malls.

More antiquing in German Village completed the afternoon. Suppertime was fast approaching, so we had decided on Schmidt's Sausage Haus and Restaurant and all their famous sausages. We had reservations, and this ensured that we had great seats in a very busy restaurant. After supper, it was time to visit the chocolate shop with all its varieties of delicious candies. The Loft was the final store of the evening. The Loft is a large house, and it is divided into several rooms, each for a particular type of book. Traveling from one room to the next gives one the opportunity to become lost with little effort. This has to be the largest and most diverse bookstore in Columbus. If they do not have a book in stock, they will find it.

The next day was Sunday and our day to travel home. Powell, Ohio, is known for its antique and specialty shops, so we made a stop to visit a few. Kathy found a small chest of drawers in one of the shops. We measured the trunk space available, and it fit. It was a good purchase for the right amount of money. Everyone seemed to have a good time on our trip to the state capital of Ohio.

2000, Piqua

Piqua, Ohio, is located north of Dayton off I-75. When we arrived on Friday afternoon, there was a rather large car show in progress. There were also many pumpkins for sale. The downtown area had a grain mill and a theater showing a cowboy movie.

2001, Ashtabula County

Ashtabula County is located in the northeastern part of Ohio. When we arrived at our bed-and-breakfast, we discovered our weekend dwelling was a large converted barn. The barn offered many spacious rooms and a great view of the many acres of grape vineyards behind the barn. The sight of vineyards was literally as far as the eye could see. That Friday evening, we picked a vintage restaurant for our dinner. The meal was excellent, and the waitress offered us a tour of their underground railroad in the basement of the restaurant. I had for years wanted to visit an underground railroad station that aided slaves in traveling from the South to the North. We promptly finished our dessert and were on our way to the basement. The tunnel was large enough for a person to walk in while bending down. As I remember, the tunnel went under the road and into the cemetery across the road. It was a memorable and most unusual event.

The next two days, we were to acquaint ourselves with around ten different covered bridges. All the bridges were made of sturdy wood and impressive architecture. They were of varying size with a common characteristic of appearing large. The other feature of Ashtabula County is wine. We visited a wine cellar and tested the fruits of the winemaker. Kathy had chosen a worthy destination for our weekend. We traveled with Larry and Carol for twenty years.

Getting to Know George and Betty Schlotterer

George Schlotterer is my first cousin and also a very close friend. I am near George's age, and our parents were close and raised all the children in a similar manner based on the Catholic religion and being charitable and giving to other people. The four of us—George, Betty, Kathy, and I—had talked about getting together for a weekend for some time. Since our marriages, we had visited each other for a few hours but not for a weekend. In the early part of 2000, we made plans to get together. We had so much fun that we also decided to do it in 2001. Each of the weekends up to the present will be addressed in the appropriate chapter. One of the rules was that each year, the activity and responsibility to plan the weekend would alternate. The other rule was that the planning couple would not reveal the destination and activities until the day of the event. Our travels will continue into the future chapters.

2000, Waynesville

The first year activity was George and Betty's responsibility, so we traveled to Centerville, Ohio, to see our cousins. The next year's location chosen was Waynesville. Waynesville is known for its many antique stores, and all four of us tremendously enjoyed this activity. While there were many beautiful shops in Waynesville, we did not buy anything special. A few items for a few dollars was the end product of our adventure. At the end of the weekend, we talked about doing this get-together each year. Since Betty and George had planned this year's activity, it was up to Joe and Kathy to plan the next year's activity, and Betty and George would travel north to Pemberville.

2001, New Rochester

The second year in the early part of 2001, George and Betty came to our house in New Rochester and brought us some gifts. Luckily for us, Kathy had bought a few gifts for them. Friday night was eating and talking. On Saturday, we introduced George and Betty to Pemberville. The first stop was the well-known Beeker's General Store. Candy was the big purchase for all of us as the penny candy we knew well was being sold at a much higher price. While the fabrics and different types of men's and women's clothing were available, we continued our interest in the candy. After all, the candy section was at least twenty feet long. The next stop was Riverview Antique Shop. The antique shop is located downtown in an old store next to the Union Bank Company. Three floors of well-displayed and varied antiques were everywhere in the well-stocked store. The next stop was the recently remodeled Pemberville Opera House located a short distance from downtown and at that time was in the same building as the police department. The opera house was pristine because of the remodeling project and is well kept. The house is used for plays, displays, musicals, meetings, and more. We then went to the railroad depot in Pemberville.

That evening, we had a treat for supper. Our neighbor Terry Hoepf was a cook on a fishing boat in the Bering Strait in Alaska. Terry had connections to buy seafood from the Bering Strait, and one of those seafood items was giant crab. The crab legs were around three feet long, and they were in some spots over two inches in diameter. The crab was a hit, and Betty and George were amazed at the size of the legs. The next day was Sunday, and we wanted to show our guests the country. The most interesting part of our drive was viewing the asparagus patch of Gene Walston. At one time, Gene had the largest field of asparagus in the state at around twenty-six acres. As we looked over the field, I showed them the asparagus picker. The picker is a wide piece of steel close to the ground with five stations to pick asparagus. The middle position controls the speed and direction of the picker. There are footrests at each of the five spots, so the picker's feet can be spread so that the asparagus comes between their legs, and it can be snapped off and deposited in a plastic box. After the asparagus is picked, washed, sorted, and placed in trays or boxes, it is ready for the refrigerator prior to being sold. Other landmarks such as the tombstone in Fish Cemetery in the shape of a tree trunk with broken-off arms is always interesting and sad because of the relationship of the mother and the children. The tombstone was discussed in more detail in chapter 9. After more coverage of the countryside, George and Betty headed home with the knowledge that they would host us in 2002 in Centerville.

CHAPTER 11

The Doctoral Degree and Teaching at BGSU

Completing the Doctor of Philosophy Degree (Ph.D.)

To be a professor and teach on your own right, it is necessary in the departments I was to be teaching—educational administration and supervision and special education—to have a Ph.D.. In 1984, I had been granted the doctor of philosophy from the Department of Educational Administration and Supervision at BGSU. Dr. Bill Reynolds was my advisor. In 1970, I began my work on my Ph.D.. In 1974, I completed my specialist degree in educational administration. The specialist degree is a degree earned after the master's degree and before the Ph.D.. The major purpose I had in obtaining the specialist degree was to protect the many courses I had already taken for the Ph.D.. If I didn't receive the specialist degree, all the courses I had taken between 1970 and 1974 might have to be taken again as the courses were not protected. The specialist degree protected the courses so they would count for the Ph.D. even if the timelines on the courses were not met. There were reasons other than coursework at that time why I could not complete my Ph.D.. At that time, there was a requirement for a doctoral student to take a foreign language. I saw no reason for taking a foreign language. I would have also needed to quit working and go to school full time as a graduate student. I could not give up my job as I was supporting a family, and once one gives up a job, what assurance do they have that they will be able to obtain that job or another job?

With the specialist degree, I had my courses protected and hoped that there would be a change in both these areas so that I could finish the Ph.D.. Within a few years, I found that the requirement that a Ph.D. student would need to go to classes full time wasn't still in place and didn't bother me. The requirement that I would need to give up my job was dropped. Likewise, the requirement that I was to take a language still stood, but computer science was now one of the options. Computer science was a language that was to be useful to me the rest of my life.

While taking one, two, or three classes, I needed to find time to attend class and also find time to read the coursework and prepare for the required papers and examinations. Later in the process, I would need to write my dissertation and accomplish all the other course-related jobs. All this work meant one thing to me. I could use evenings and Saturday morning to attend class. With my job, I spent a great deal of time with evening meetings and doing my reading and paperwork. There was little time for my prep work and writing the dissertation except to take the time out of my normal sleeping hours. So that was how it was. I needed to restrict the time with my outside organizations, try to spend time with my family, and take the time I needed to do my classwork and dissertation out of my sleep hours. Many hours from 1970 to 1984 were spent studying instead of sleeping. This pattern of not sleeping and working instead was a pattern that carried over to other parts of my life. When I would have something on my mind, usually in the middle of the night, I would get up and either write notes to myself so I didn't lose my train of thought or complete a draft document on the areas that had robbed me of sleep. I can remember in college I would wake up, have a paper or test on my mind, and decide that I might as well get some work done. I probably would not sleep well after waking up, and probably I would forget the inspiration that had awoken me.

The coursework was for the most part very interesting. Unfortunately for me, the courses were centered on public school administration, not county boards of mental retardation and developmental disabilities. This meant that to apply the principles of my classwork to my profession, I needed to learn the public school information and then apply them to public school and then to MRDD programs. For example, in the course on school plant planning, I would need to learn about schools, curriculum, administration, sports, and other areas a public school superintendent would need to know as well as the construction and use of buildings and grounds. Then I would need to apply the knowledge learned about buildings and grounds for special education programs. Additional information must be learned on special education programs such as case management, volunteers, Special Olympics, workshops, and group homes. Plant planning for maintenance in twenty-five smaller facility settings and for an adapted swimming pool is not something always a part of the public school plant.

As time grew closer to the dissertation and I was completing my courses, there were qualifying tests that must be taken and passed. I had taken my qualifying tests and had the approval of all the people on my committee except one person from another department. I talked to my advisor, and we decided that I should work with this one committee member in obtaining an approval of my writing style. After one year of writing a paper of involved research, I handed the final copy to the committee member who was working with me on my writing style. I found out that the committee member had been promoted and was no longer on my committee. His replacement had no problems with my writing style. So I now had a complete committee composed of Dr. Bill Reynolds, my advisor; Dr. Ramona Cormier; Dr. Fred Pigge; and Dr. Robert Blackwell, and they all passed me on my written exams. In fact, all my committee members spent an inordinate amount of time helping me attain my Ph.D.. I am forever indebted to these generous educators for all the time and energy they gave me in this quest for knowledge. I will never know where I found the energy to complete the Ph.D.. There was never a doubt in my mind about finishing the degree as I had this abundance of energy. There was always a doubt about where I would find the time. This was definitely a time I found extra energy when needed, and I feel much of the energy came from my twin. The energy was present to work when I was extremely tired. The ability to stay up or get up in the middle of the night was present. The ability to accomplish my full-time work when my body was tired was also present.

Graduation

The formal final touch to completing the Ph.D. was the graduation ceremony. I had all the copies of the dissertation made for my relatives and BGSU. All the registrations for graduation were made, and unlike the specialist degree, I was as they say going to walk or be present for the formal awarding of the degree. The sad part for me was that my father was not present for the awarding of the degree. He had worked very hard to support me and make it possible for me to have the opportunity to earn four degrees. I thought of him often on my graduation day as I remembered my acknowledgment to him in my dissertation. My words were written as follows:

To my deceased father, Walter E. Frederick I, the person most responsible for my pursuit of higher education and especially the Doctor of Philosophy degree, I wish this dissertation to be in his memory.

I remember there were twelve doctoral candidates on that day, May 12, 1984. Three were from the Department of Educational Administration and Supervision. While I did not know the other two candidates, I knew well the other two advisors and former instructors of mine, Dr. William York and Dr. Neil Pohlmann. In a few years, I was to teach a graduate course with Dr. York in human relations to superintendents of county boards of MRDD. Dr. Pohlmann had always been a favorite of mine, especially for his course in school law. Of course, my advisor, Dr. Bill Reynolds, had stuck by me through thick and thin, helping me choose a topic on more than one occasion and supporting me through the entire process of the dissertation, which included writing the four chapters and assembling the bibliography and appendices. This, of course, included setting me up with the statistics wizards.

We must not forget that there were qualifying tests that needed to be prepared for prior to the dissertation, both of which were several hours long. One story I would like to share was during one of these written exams. I had shut off my pager because I needed to concentrate on my several hour-long tests. At exactly the time I was taking the test, a story was released on some funding difficulty at NODC, where I was the superintendent. Since I did not answer the page, the story went to print, and my name was paired with the negative phrase "unavailable for comment." I often wondered how people would react to this statement if they knew I was taking a test for my Ph.D., and that was why I wasn't available. I looked like I was avoiding the press, and no statement could have been further from the truth, but that was how it came out.

The twelve doctoral students and their advisors had the best seats in the house. As my name was called, I felt like the eyes of everyone at Doyt Perry Stadium with several thousand people were all watching me. As my life always goes, something will always rain on my parade. That day, there was no rain, but the wind was blowing across that flat football field. My mind was trying to figure out what to do with my mortar board that wouldn't stay on my head as my name was called. I did the only thing I could do, and that was to tuck my hat under my arm. As I stood facing the crowd and my advisor and another official placed the hood over my head, I felt it was really worth it. My father had always said, "People can take away lots of things from you, but they cannot take away your educational degrees." As the cap was placed over my head, I thought, in my work, there were many good times and there were many experiences where I had been unfairly treated, and at times, I would not even know why. I guess that is administration.

However, today was my day, and I was being given what I had earned, the highest scholarly degree in the land, the doctor of philosophy degree given for outstanding knowledge and outstanding research. All this is based on years and years of study and effort. Instead of attending all the family weddings and other recreation events, I gave of my time to the study and research needed to accomplish the Ph.D.. The part that was so very difficult were the many nights I slept only three or four hours so that the rest would be spent on my education. In later years, I was talking to my sons, and I was reminded by at least one of them that he always thought that I never slept because whenever he got up in the middle of the night, I was always awake reading or writing. I always hoped that I was not neglecting my wife, Kathy, and my sons Joe and Mark.

As I began to leave the platform, I was to have the first of two surprises. As I passed the board of trustees, I could see someone leaving their chair and coming toward me. I looked up, and Shad Hanna, a prominent local attorney and the vice president of the board, had come over to congratulate me. Shad was a longtime acquaintance, and his wife, Sharon, and three children attended our church, St. Thomas More. I left the platform, watched the rest of the ceremony, and greeted my family and friends after the service. My mother was especially happy because she was the one who watched the money, and she was very involved in shaping my life and the lives of my five brothers and sisters. She was also happy that my father was present in spirit seeing all the time money and energy that they had put into all their children and today seeing me attain the highest degree in education that exists. Although I never asked her, I bet she was thinking of my twin and how he/she was with me today and throughout my life. Mothers never forget the children who were born and those the unborn. For Mom and for me, my twin was a bittersweet experience.

I was talking to all my friends and relatives who had made the trip when I heard someone congratulate me on my accomplishment. I turned around, and there was Bob Thorton, a prominent attorney from my hometown, Willard. Bob expressed his sincere congratulations to me for accomplishing such a great task. He informed me that his son Andrew had received his bachelor of science in business administration. I was honored that Bob had made the long journey down the football bleachers to see me. Bob was a member of my hometown church in Willard, St. Francis Xavier, when I worked in Jump's clothing over the Christmas break. He, or brother Kenny, also an attorney, and other businessmen came in to talk and see what was happening. I also knew Bob because his daughter Becky and my youngest brother, Bob, dated in high school.

The Mass

God has always been the central theme of all my actions. To properly celebrate God's gifts to humanity, the Mass was instituted. The Mass is the celebration of Jesus Christ dying on the cross and thus giving of Himself so all human beings have the opportunity of accessing eternal salvation. After his death, Christ rose up and started his new life. The theme of the Mass and the party that followed was "One of the nicest things that one can do in life is to be of help to others." It was expressed to all present that their help, especially to Joe, is being celebrated with a "thank you" for being a "special part of our lives." "Our special prayer was that we can all grow more deeply in our relationship with God, each of those present and with each other." These statements were signed by Kathy, Mark, Joe II, and me.

The ceremony was a most beautiful one starting with the entrance. Representatives of my family, including Fred Eldred, Tom Herner, Mike Frederick, and my family, bore candles in the opening parade. Also bearing candles were representatives of Kathy's family, Agnes Clayton and Dave Long. There were two readings presented by Kathy's brother, Dave Long, and my mother, Marion Frederick. I gave a brief homily of thanksgiving and thanks to all present. Joe II and Mark were the ushers and carried up the gifts. The prayer of St. Francis was recited during the communion as this prayer was a favorite of my father, Walter E. Frederick I. Pat and Nancy Fitzgerald, our close friends, were the lay distributors of the communion.

The Mass could not have been possible had it not been for Fr. Mike Tremmel, our pastor and friend. Musicians John Husbands and Ken Phillips made it possible for the music to fill the air. The program was made possible by Kathy Snyder. A wonderful program and dinner followed.

How to Deal with This Title of Doctor

Immediately after I was awarded my doctor degree, I was faced with the decision of when to use the title. I have never been the type of person to see myself as better than other people. Although I had earned the right to use the title, at times, there seemed to be some awkwardness in its use. For example, if I fill out a check in an office, the person receiving the check frequently asks what type of a doctor I am, such as a general practitioner. When I tell them I have a Ph.D. in educational administration and supervision, I usually get a blank stare.

What I have resolved myself to do is that if other people are using their titles, then I will use mine. I wish to respect other people and have others respect me.

Use of My Educational Experience in My Work

Over the years, I have developed a list of twenty-six management principles that guide my actions. I had always been open with my employees about this list by distributing it and also talking about it. I would like to present this list at this time so that the reader is aware of these principles that have guided my actions in either a paid or unpaid position. The reader may better understand my actions if they know some of the rules I have put into practice. The rules may require some thought, but they are all pretty self-explanatory.

Rules of Management

by

Joseph B. Frederick

1. Don't get your honey where you get your money.
2. Many people will not act until they are shown by example.
3. Don't give surprises unless it is someone's birthday.
4. Don't make promises that you can't keep.
5. Have reasons for your actions.
6. Do whatever you do in a way that can be defended in court.
7. Always get input.
8. Public relations are the name of the game.
9. Be sincere in your role.
10. Don't exploit or be exploited.
11. One can't manage unless one has people to manage.
12. Choose your fights.
13. Don't blow your cool.
14. Direct contact is best.
15. Don't promise flowers but do as Churchill did and promise blood, sweat, and tears.

16. Money does not make staff; people do.
17. Most decisions are not final.
18. Your voice is one of the greatest controls that you possess.
19. Twenty people will have twenty different attitudes. Your job is to get the job done using all twenty.
20. A good manager has all people singing off the same song sheet.
21. Always follow up.
22. Always express yourself tactfully and ask. Don't TELL people.
23. If you don't know the answer, try to find it.
24. Don't answer a question unless you know the answer. Find the answer and get it to the asker.
25. You may win the battle but lose the war.
26. If there ain't no pain, there ain't no gain.

Teaching at BGSU

For approximately ten years in the late 1980s and early 1990s, I had the pleasure of teaching at BGSU in the department of special education and the department of educational administration and supervision. In those years, I usually taught one night a week for two to three hours. I taught such courses as introduction to special needs persons, mental retardation, employment of the handicapped, and human resources. While I was reimbursed for teaching, the reimbursement was not significant. Adjunct professors are paid according to a contract and therefore do not have status as an employee of the university. In the beginning years of teaching, there were around twelve students. As time moved on, the small classroom was converted into a huge lecture hall, and seventy-five-plus students with no graduate assistant was the norm. Each of these students was paying several hundred dollars for each course in which they were enrolled. Since the adjunct professor would be receiving a few thousand dollars per course, significant money was to be made by the university. With my Ph.D., I was able to teach on my own credentials.

The goal of students is to attend classes, study, take the tests, and pass the course with high grades. The manner in which each of these goals is met by the student varies according to the individual student.

Zipper

I was late to my first class because I was not able to find a parking spot. Since it was the first class, I asked the students to fill out a form that had identifying information that I could use if I needed to contact them. I decided to take a trip to the little boys' room as they were filling out the form. As I finished my business, I pulled up on my zipper. The zipper did not come up, so I figured I must have caught something in it. I soon learned that I was wrong, the zipper was not caught, and I had a broken zipper in the beginning of my first class. I overlapped my pants as best I could to hide the opening in my pants. As I went back to the classroom, I passed the special education office, and I took the chance that I might be able to find a safety pin. No luck.

I walked into the classroom sideways and with my back to the students, and I sat down in my chair, trying to hide my open zipper by sitting at a side angle but not a conspicuous side angle. The class went on, and we soon took a break, but I never moved from my chair. I made it through without anyone noticing my defective zipper. The result of this story will be that every former student of mine who reads this account will wonder if they were present when this event happened.

Consistency of the Classroom

When I taught at the college level, I would try hard to keep positive relations with my students. I figured if they were not treated right, they would not learn. One of my class sessions challenged my belief. I had given the class an assignment to complete in groups. The assignment was not difficult. As I asked each group to report its findings, one group reported it had not gotten to the assignment as they had talked about raising strawberries, a topic not related to the assignment. I looked at the group and said, "Next time, let's try harder to talk about the assignment." Out of nowhere, I heard a student from another group say, "Well." I assumed she wasn't in agreement with my simple comment to the group about completing its assignment. As class ended, I asked the student who said, "Well," to please see me after class. I waited until all the students were out of the class, and I asked her why she had said, "Well." She said she thought I hadn't treated the students fairly. I informed her that I felt I had been more than fair.

Before the next class, I talked to the department head of the special education department, and he asked me what had transpired the previous class as a student had said that things were getting out of control in the class. I explained what had happened. The moral of the story is that one student feels I am not controlling the class and another thinks I am overcontrolling the class. I drew the conclusion that sometimes you just cannot win even when you are trying your best.

State Board of Education

One of the principles I taught at BGSU was the employment of the handicapped class was that of generalization. I had learned the principles from a colleague of mine, Dr. Ernie Pancsofar. The generalization principle works this way. If a person learns a skill in one example, then they can use or apply those principles in another similar setting to be able to master that task. For example, buying a candy bar in a machine may be offered for sale in fifteen different types of machines. If we were to break down the skills in obtaining a candy bar for the fifteen machines, we could find that if one learns, say, five different selected machines, one would be able to obtain a candy bar from all fifteen machines. There may be five different machines that if learned how to operate to obtain a candy bar would allow the person to operate all fifteen candy bar machines.

An example of how two types of machines work will now be explained. Machine 1 may be very simple and allows the person to put in the money and press a button with a picture of a Snickers candy bar on the selection bar. Machine 2 may require the customer to put in the money, identify the Snickers candy bar in the display case, and find a code of A-16, which is needed to obtain the bar. The customer would then deposit the money and press the "A" button and the "16" button to obtain the candy bar. Since we have explored the operation of two types of machines, there are three other types of machines to learn how to obtain candy bars. If a person learned the five different machines, they would be able to operate all fifteen machines and obtain a Snickers bar. The generalization principle held that if one learns, in this case, five machines, they will be able to operate all fifteen machines and obtain a Snickers bar. This principle applies to using washing machines, dryers, radios, televisions, telephones, microwaves, refrigerators, ranges, car and house locks, and many other types of daily used items and changing tires on cars.

How do these principles relate to a student? A student came up to me in one of my classes and asked me if I knew that one of my former students was to give a presentation to the State Board of Education on the principles of generalization. I said that I was not aware of this fact. They went on to tell me that the student had given a presentation to the board, and they were very interested in the philosophy, application, and results. The student informed me that the board wanted to know who had taught the student this system of learning. The presenting student replied Dr. Frederick from BGSU. An interesting lesson was in this experience. One doesn't always know the influence of one's actions.

Studs Terkel

Another topic always included in my employment of the handicapped course was a video by Studs Terkel on *Working*. Studs was a writer who traveled the United States and interviewed people in different jobs. He would then write up the interviews, and he published his writings in a large book titled *Working*, which I viewed as the premier writings on people and occupations. Students hopefully gained a wide awareness of various occupations as well as understanding the people in each occupation. When they were involved with teaching at any level, they at least had an introduction to various occupations and people in those occupations. It was always interesting for me to see the manner in which Studs presented these wonderful people in these diverse occupations.

A Tragedy

Over the course of my ten years of teaching at the university, I had probably taught over 750 students. On September 7, 1996, a resident of Mourning Dove Lane in Bowling Green was stabbed to death. The resident was a former student of mine and worked for the same program I worked, the Wood County Board of Mental Retardation. Police Officer Alan Carsey was awarded a Service to Others Black Swamp Humanitarian Award for catching the murderer on his bike. At the awards ceremony, the girl's mother presented the policeman with one of the stuffed animal toys left at the girl's grave. I know this to be true; I am the chairperson of the Black Swamp Humanitarian Awards Committee.

Columbus Teacher

My eldest son, Joe, and I had entered a fast-food restaurant to pick up a meal for our families. As we were ordering, I noticed a young lady sitting with a man. She seemed to be looking at me as if she recognized me. After ordering, I walked over to the young lady and asked her how she was doing. She said, "Fine," as she continued to look at me. She finally said, "Are you Dr. Frederick from Bowling Green State University?" I said that I was. She reminded me that she had me for a special education class a few years earlier and was now teaching in the Columbus school system. I asked her if she had used the information from my class in her teaching, and she assured me she had. Our order was ready, and we parted. It always amazes me that one can renew acquaintances many miles from home.

Our Friends, the Baileys

A professional associate of mine as the superintendent of Perrysburg Schools, BGSU professor, and a fellow member of the Black Swamp Humanitarian Awards Committee, Dr. Joe Bailey, had passed away the end of March 2008. Kathy and I attended the viewing. At the viewing, his wife, Carol, was receiving guests. Since we had not seen Carol for years, we explained who we were, and she immediately said to me, "The professor who helped me with special education." She also remembered us bringing asparagus to her from the largest asparagus field in Ohio. She reminded us how much Joe and she thought of Kathy and me. I told Carol how "Joe had always been my model in positively working with other people because he was the master." As we left the Witzler-Shank Funeral Home, I was reminded how Joe had paid me a positive compliment at a Black Swamp Humanitarian Awards Committee meeting. As we were wrapping up the meeting, Joe Bailey looked at me and said, "Joe, you run the most efficient meeting of anyone I have known." Yes, Joe was a great model.

Joe was buried the same day I wrote this section of this book. "Goodbye, Joe!"

Final Exam

One semester I was administering the final exam, and a student told me she had a disability and needed to take the exam by herself. I told her I had not been informed of this fact by the disability counselor and had made no arrangements. I checked the next classroom, and there was no exam being given. I told the female student that she could take the exam in the next room, and she should contact me if she needed help and return the exam when she was finished.

I had a large class and devoted my attention to monitoring the exam with the room full of students. At the end of the exam, I had collected all the exam papers and remembered the student in the next room. I walked into the room and found it empty. I went to the special education office to see if she had placed the exam in my mailbox. Somehow I received the exam. I was not sure how to handle the situation and scored the exam. The student had received an F on the exam. I gave all the final grades and never did find out why the student had left the classroom.

CHAPTER 12

Henry County Board of Developmental Disabilities

After thirty-five years of public service, most of which was in the area of developmental disabilities, I decided to formally retire through the state's public employee retirement system. At the same time, I had procured a position as the superintendent of the Henry County Board of Developmental Disabilities, also known as Hope Services. I accepted this position because I was not ready to stop working at fifty-seven years of age, and I enjoyed the challenge of a superintendent or CEO position. Also, there is a financial advantage to this move.

I was aware that the position with the Henry County Board as with any county board at that time was to be challenging. I expected that this job would be like any other position I had held, if things were to go any way, it would be the hard way. I also knew that a big key to success in my tenure would be a positive relationship with the board, the staff, the consumers and their families, and the community. The changes coming down the line would require a board and staff to think of others and act as a team. If I was receiving energy from God and my twin, it would be needed because the economics alone would be one of the most taxing, if not the most taxing, undertakings in the job.

Why was the fiscal part of the job to be so difficult? The budget was very tight. At this time, the funding base of Medicaid for the residential program was being substituted for the existing funding base. This meant that continual change in terms of expenses and income would be constantly varying with what the federal government would allow. Other changes on programs, staff, and community perception would produce more challenges than the board, staff, or I could imagine. Much of the change just happened and cannot be explained on a rational basis because that is the way change is in government, federal in this case, and it cannot easily be predicted. It has been said that the product of government is many times like the process of making sausage. What the input into the sausage looks like and what the end product looks like are two different-looking items.

The Start

As I seriously looked at this position, I reviewed important variables I would face, including how I would need to interact with the board. A look at some of the basic management and board guidelines will be given.

Board and CEO Duties

The cardinal rules of the board that hires the CEO or superintendent is to set the directions or develop policies to operate facilities, programs, and services as the board is concerned with the overall direction of the organization. The cardinal rule of the CEO is being responsible for the day-to-day administration or management of the organization and to carry out the workings of the board and direction. If these cardinal rules are observed, the many hours spent by the CEO with the board (usually the board chair) can be successful for both parties.

The board and CEO must work together. Like a good marriage, the board and CEO relationship is based on good communication. The communications of speaking and listening is a two-way funnel—board to CEO and CEO to board. Boards and CEOs must be concerned about what is best for the organization or company. It has been my experience that doing things my way or in a self-centered matter leads to trouble for both parties. Open communication with the board, administration, employees, consumers, and the general public is essential with consumers' concerns being paramount.

Management Philosophy

Over the years, there have been certain management philosophies that have been useful to me, and I would like to briefly discuss them. One management philosophy I have used for years is that I work to be respected, not necessarily liked. Being respected is essential; being liked isn't always possible. This is especially true when I needed to cut funds, usually an unpopular decision. The board, available funds, law, personnel issues, and good practices are variables that force the CEO to face the issues.

Another principle of management philosophy that has been helpful is that employees report to the CEO, not the board. As a manager, it is important to address the employee by listening, talking slowly, and understanding the employee. Management involves great risk, and being successful is not as easy as one would prefer.

It is impossible to implement all of one's priorities. Ordering the priorities with others' input is important. In ordering one's priorities or any other decision, "Be cool and don't blow your cool." Mending fences is harder than building them.

Most decisions are not final. Always keep open to the possibility of change while choosing a path to follow. In making a decision, remember that everything you do must be able to be defended in court. Watch television and see how people get in trouble when they don't follow the law.

A simple fact that I used throughout my profession is that if someone had a particular way of solving a problem, which is not my idea but one that would work, why not try to use it? What is there to lose? The difficult part of using others' ideas may be that the money to implement the idea is not available, and it also happens that what one party wishes to see implemented may be the exact opposite of the needs of other persons to be served. It has been my experience that not having money to spend on needed projects is the least accepted by others and the most upsetting reason to others for not implementing an action. Working through the various options with others may produce results that are satisfying, and this is gratifying. One needs to be as tactful as possible in implementing decisions that are not to the liking of others.

A CEO must remember that the board is the one boss. Unresolved issues between a board and CEO must be solved, or the CEO, not the board, usually may not be staying around. The CEO must know the other associated influences you must deal with on any basis.

Let us now look at the issues facing the Henry County Board of Developmental Disabilities, the consumers and family, the staff, and the community.

Fiscal

Philosophy on Spending Funds

Henry County has its county seat in Napoleon, Ohio. The county is a farm-based community, and local taxes for the county board of mental retardation and developmental disabilities are based on property taxes, farm acreage being a major source of revenue for these taxes. While the community is willing to pay for services that they see are needed, convincing the county voters what is needed can be challenging. Rarely have the tax levies for mental retardation and developmental disabilities been voted down. Approximately half the taxes must be voted on periodically, and thus every few years' time, energy goes into campaigning for existing taxes. The last time that new levies had been passed when I came to Henry County was more than ten years previous. The other factor in spending funds on services by staff within the program was that if services were needed, a way should be found of obtaining those services. Here lies the bind of spending funds where needed by the staff and making sure that only those needed programs are funded. The definition of need varies from taxpayer to the provider of services.

Budgets

The budgets in many government agencies are a system-wide budget. That was the case in 2001 when I became superintendent. For accountability of funds to take place, a departmental budget is needed. To have departments that are well structured, it is important to have stable departments and stable organizations. As we will see with any organization that is going through fiscal change, as were all county boards in the state, with the shift of Medicaid funds and with a change in who is providing services. One of these changes was from county boards providing residential services to contracting for residential services. Many organizational and personnel changes were still taking place when I became superintendent. While the departmental budget was a priority and would be developed by the time I left Henry County, the ability to develop the budget while the organization was still developing its role was difficult. Another factor that was present with the organization was that all services were not provided in one spot. The buildings occupied by the board were a rented building in Napoleon where staff literally lived in more than proximity to one another and a school building in the country and plans for a newly remodeled building in Napoleon. The rented facility could have been sold at any time, and the staff would have needed to have another building to have offices if the new building was not complete. All these change factors with extremely tight projected budgets helped make the mix of an organization on the move challenging.

A look at the 2002 budget can best capture the fiscal situation. The budget for Hope Services was over $6 million. The budget for 2002, the first full year that I was to be in Henry County, turned out to have $20,000 excess funds for the fiscal year 2002. There were operating dollars for the first few months of 2003 with additional tax funds from the new fall levy of 2002. This is essentially no funds for any type of emergency. The only response I had for staff when they needed anything new was there are not available funds. This does not win friends or influence people.

Some projections in 2005 for the next five to six years showed that the cumulative fund balance for 2010 would be around $4 million. This was due to a loss in revenue from legislation, which is to decrease property tax; losses in Medicaid revenues; and losses in tax equity (funds we were receiving because we had low tax equality with other counties) and housing grants. An increase in expenditures for salary raises, employee benefits, waiver match for supported living/residential services, maintenance contracts and supplies, and other expenditures contributed to these shortfalls. From these examples, it can easily be seen that the ability to have funds to operate is more than a major concern. Both the increase in revenue and the cuts in expenditure would be needed in adjustments to the budget for the future. So what else has been new in the fiscal world? Unfortunately, the constant change in funds created constant change in everyone's temperament.

At this time, the board came up with fiscal guidelines for 2006 and 2007. The plan called for balanced budgets by increasing revenues and decreasing expenditures. All vacant positions required superintendent and board action. There were other stipulations, but without this type of plan in the face of budgetary challenges an organization is not doing its job.

These variables were painful and uncomfortable for staff and the board but necessary.

In managing a budget that is tenuous at best, the obligation I always tried to observe is being fair with others. My managers and my board must be fair if they were always concerned about being ethical to others. It was a constant and is a constant struggle for all. In the end, each of us will answer to our God on how well we handled our services/profit.

Corrective Action Based on Employee Evaluation

For an organization to be successful, each employee must be successful. This means that every employee must know where they are going, how they are going to reach their goals, and how the judgment of this process will take place FAIRLY. Where the employee is going is called their goals and objectives and is based largely on the employee's job duties as documented in the employee evaluation.

Another facet of employee behavior is rewards and corrective factors. Employees who are meeting their job description and their performance goals should be reinforced. If employees are not meeting the goals of their job description, then it is the responsibility of the supervisor and the employee to follow up in an effective manner to deal with the strengths and weaknesses of the employee. The processes we are talking about are not just the supervisor's responsibility but also the employee's. If I were to identify a management and employee weakness, it would be for both the supervisor and the employee to effectively deal with those strengths and weaknesses. Having to face tough employee issues is an area that must be pushed by all supervisors and employees so that the goals of the organization are met.

Let us look closer at employee corrective action that includes both recognition and discipline. There are several horror stories on both sides of the fence when dealing with employee discipline. A friend of mine once told me that he was in the process of disciplining an employee and found it necessary to terminate this person, who was well-known in the community. Because he terminated this popular person, the board terminated him as the CEO. So my friend lost his job because he did his job but, in this case for him, the wrong person. On the other hand, I have seen it more common to not deal with employees' behavior. Harm can come to fellow employees because the rules were not being upheld. Client care suffered because employees were not carrying through on their direct care services with clients. To be very truthful on this important area, I know that to develop goals and objectives was much harder than to simply complete a checklist on employees. Also, getting into the nitty-gritty of employees behavior can result in innocently entering a bees nest. This can result in difficult communications with employees who may feel that approaching certain areas of behavior is unwarranted, unfair, or unnecessary. Trying to deal with changing employee behavior is often difficult and is a necessary part of a supervisor's job. We must remember that in client-related services, actions must be very swift so that nothing negative happens to the client.

My past management experience will tell us that dealing with these sensitive areas, the employee evaluations and the rest of the corrective action process, was of very high priority for myself and my supervisors in Henry County and every other place of employment. I do not think that I have been as successful in any job as I wished when it comes to employee evaluation and corrective action largely because it is an area that can be loaded with land mines from the board, administrator, employee, their families, other employees, and client's viewpoint. None of the following programs will be successful unless the organization's services to the students, clients, or residents are the best possible. Therefore, none of the services can be monitored unless everyone has a song sheet and a method to judge the effectiveness of the songs. In this case, the song sheets are the job description and the evaluation, goals, and objectives. Simply stated, employee evaluation and corrective action is not always popular for the ones most involved—supervisors, employees, or at times the board's viewpoint.

Since the county employees are under the civil service system, one needs to observe a system of corrective action and discipline protective of the public employee. Private sector employees can carry out their corrective action swiftly and observe the rules of their company. Private companies go by company rules and not the rules of the entire civil service system. The only check on the management system could possibly be the private board, not the courts, of the civil service system is protective of its employees and wants to be so there is no possibility of its employees being disciplined without due process. This means that another element is present, that of progressive discipline. If an employee has committed an infraction, unless it was a grave deed, termination will not usually take place on the first infraction. A reprimand, verbal or written, may be the first step. In the private workplace, the same infraction may be seen as strongly against company policy, and suspension or termination may result on the first occurrence.

The civil service system allows a hearing if there has been a reprimand of three or more days. If at the hearing, doubt about the action is present, the reprimand could be overturned, and the administrator goes back to the drawing board on the corrective actions for this employee. I for one would not want to go back to a civil service hearing after the employee I tried to discipline before had a successful overturn at the previous hearing.

Does this mean one doesn't go through the corrective process that can result in discipline, including termination? Absolutely not; the balancing act of successfully going through the process has some pitfalls, but the job of the manager is to be a manager and do the pleasant and the unpleasant.

It would seem that knowledge of the civil service system would be good for the CEO and boards of the private sector board. This could aid them in better making their decisions and in the treatment of their employees, if that is a concern.

The CEO of a public agency is responsible to monitor and follow through on their discipline hearings. It is a board's responsibility to set policy on this area. While the CEO may apprise the board of his corrective action, the CEO is responsible to administer the corrective action programs.

In the private and public arena, there can be only one boss who manages the ship, and that is the CEO. The board must set the overall policies for the direction for the organization. Bad things get worse, and good things get better when these rules are followed. The employee's professional life is at stake. The employee's private life is also at stake. A decision by an employer has been blamed for their death at the hands of a distraught fired employee.

Programs

The Henry County Board of Mental Retardation and Developmental Disabilities served 400–550 people, depending on which people were included. The services offered were some of the best I have ever seen in Ohio. The programs were from birth and before until death. The programs offered from birth to six years of age were the responsibility of Sherri DeWyer. The first program to be offered could start when a couple knew it was going to have a developmentally delayed child or even earlier with genetic counseling to help couples decide if they wish to take the chance of having a developmentally delayed child. Once the baby was born, services could be given immediately through the hospital and at home. Services would be to help the parent adjust to a special child, to be able to assess progress, and other daily living skills such as feeding. Until the age of three, individuals would be eligible for early intervention, and at the age of three, a preschool at Hope School becomes an option. The preschool, while administered by Hope Services at Hope School, is operated jointly by the four school districts, the Four County Educational Services Center, and Hope School. The four school districts are Otsego, Napoleon, Patrick Henry, and Liberty Center. All these school-based centers met monthly to discuss programs and finances for the approximately one hundred students in this program.

Ancillary services are occupational therapy, physical therapy, speech and hearing therapy, and physical education. The saying with early childhood programs is you pay now or you pay later. In other words, if you put money in early childhood programs so children can take care of personal needs, learn job-related skills such as attending to task, fine and gross motor skills, you will not pay as much later. If you pay later, you will have adults trying to learn skills of getting along with others and job skills, and the cost will be greater as skills not learned when one is young will need to be performed by someone other than the person who didn't learn when they were young. One of the fiscal implications with the preschool program was that voters needed to see funds spent on the preschool program. Since the school age programs had gone back to the local school years before, the public needed to see funds going for some children's program from the Hope budget.

The next phase of the programs is school-age programs. While the actual school program had moved back to each of the school districts or the educational school center, Hope Services continues to offer case management, Special Olympics, and other recreational programs.

Adult programs include a choice of employment programs called supported employment in the community or employment at a sheltered workshop in Stryker, Ohio, called Quadco. A senior program that offers a wide variety of recreational and educational programs is available at the Hope Services Building in Napoleon. Habilitation programs are offered by private contract, and one habilitation program is offered by Hope Services in fourteen homes owned by the Henry Association for Retarded Citizens (HARC). The habilitation programs include daily living skills such as living in a community setting with other people or by oneself. Several of the people who attended Quadco were given a chance to have adult programs in Henry County. Hundreds of thousands of dollars were saved as a result of providing programs locally rather than traveling to another county. Jack Boyd oversaw the many developments and savings realized through this department and did it despite the death of his brother and mother.

Other services such as case management services, which is the glue that keeps all the other systems together and oversees the Individual Program Plan to qualify for Medicaid funding, were directed by Sandy Karmol. There were three case managers when I arrived on the scene in 2001. When I left in 2006, there were eight case managers. This increase represents setting goals and achieving them. The increase in case managers was not an accident; it was deliberate and needed to access federal Medicaid funds.

HARC also sponsors the recreation program for qualifying people and includes summer camp, bowling, parties, and other outings.

Special Olympics are offered to all qualifying school age and adults in the county. Basketball, softball, swimming, and track and field are a few of the sports offered.

One of the programs that affected all other programs in terms of support was the maintenance department. Bill Wicks had been head of the department at Hope School, and another person was head of the maintenance department in Napoleon. After the Napoleon department head left, Bill was made head of the department. Before I left, a comprehensive work order system was developed in which every person who placed a short-term or long-term maintenance request was notified that the request was received, the status of the request in terms of it being done or not, and the timelines and priority. More work orders were processed faster and with fewer employees.

One of the first board in-services done was the relationship of the board and staff. It outlines how the board, superintendent, and staff interacted. If the board were to try to manage the staff directly, there would be no need for the superintendent. More time and energy by boards and superintendents will help establish relationships that will foster longer and more productive mutual beneficial activities. I know superintendents and boards who would have been better off in the long run to not worry about power struggles and vendettas and spend time on working for better relationships within their respective roles.

Some outside counsel was always available from Rick Edmonds, superintendent of the Defiance County Board of Mental Retardation and Developmental Disabilities, and Paul Oehrtman, CEO at Filling Homes.

Staff

The staff professional who work with children and adults in the area of habilitation or training have certification requirements that they must meet. Habilitation is accomplishing new skills that had not been learned before, while rehabilitation is accomplishing skills that had been present before.

All staff receive various training on trying to be updated in changes in their areas of responsibilities.

Over one hundred employees were scattered over several locations, so another constant emphasis was on being a part of the team when one was not located in the same building, not performing the same duties, and doing so in an atmosphere of change and fiscal uncertainty. The major emphasis I employed was that the board sets down the policies; the superintendent, not the board, administers the programs; and each staff member is responsible for their area of responsibility. If they have questions, they go to their supervisor for guidance.

Several different adjustments were made with the staff over my employment. The ongoing change was making sure that every employee had enough responsibilities, was as happy as could be with their tasks, and was treated by me and other staff as fairly as possible. Because of the change that had taken place in the organization, there were times that certain staff could have tried harder to work with other people. A special consultant was brought in to work with the staff, and this had some positive developments. Another goal in the table of organization was to make sure that responsibilities were clear for all areas. The maintenance director was made responsible for all maintenance, not just maintenance in the school. The human relations person was responsible for all human relations functions. The fiscal department was responsible for all fiscal and payroll issues. The case management supervisor was made to be a permanent rather than interim appointment.

Government in Henry County

Most of the various officials in Henry County were viewed as very positive government employees. A few years after I was in the county, things began to change. Somehow the county began to see the elements of defensive actions, and with these actions, people tend to go after others. Supportive actions tended to lose their emphasis. One of the department heads was accused of stealing prescription drugs, and he resigned shortly after this incident. An auditor department director was accused of not completing the proper transfers of public funds, and she resigned. A county commissioner was accused of following a young girl in Toledo, and he ultimately resigned. The last very public means of raising funds through the county sales tax became a very heated public issue. The county commissioners had raised the county tax because of the need for taxes to keep present services intact. After they raised the tax, a vote by the Henry County voters repealed the taxes. The tax was put on the ballot as the lone tax issue, and it passed with much work coming from the citizens of Henry County. Hope Services was considering a tax levy but decided not to go on the levy with the move toward having only the county sales tax on the ballot. Working in an atmosphere of personnel uncertainty in terms of employment is not a positive environment. Legal advice is always at a premium and helps keep one out of trouble and the court. The Henry County prosecutor, John "Jay" Hanna, gave needed guidance and helpful information on more occasions than I can remember.

The Henry County Community

Henry County Community Organizations

There are several strong community organizations that make the county very strong. The United Way of Henry County has one of the strongest directors of any agency. Tom Mack runs a very successful campaign and uses every person in the county who will give time to become a part of the fundraising efforts. Fundraising is not only a pledge from each of the citizens but also involves many small campaigns to raise funds such as the chicken dinner. The funds are publicly raised and are publicly spent.

The radio station WNDH is another very successful organization. From the station manager through the broadcaster and the office staff, everyone in the county has the opportunity to know what is going on and the confidence that the broadcasts are accurate. The radio station press release was my first item of business after a board meeting. I was fortunate there were few changes that had to be made on the press releases. In addition, whenever there was a special new program or finances, the radio station was always ready to report at a moment's notice.

The newspaper serving Napoleon was the *Northwest Signal*. This paper was a very special way of notifying the public of news.

Another Henry County community organizations that served the community well was the school boards. John Wilhelm of the Four County Educational Services Center worked long and hard privately and publicly to better the Hope School program. The four school districts are Otsego (James Reiter), Napoleon (Dave Watson), Patrick Henry (Sue Miko), and Liberty Center (Jack Loudin) Schools. Each of the school organizations had to deal with several challenges from operating dollars to new and renovated buildings, changing curriculum, public relations, and student deaths many times from car accidents. Having worked so closely with each of the superintendents, especially on the property and income taxes, has caused me to gain an enormous amount of respect. One of the common ties that each of the school districts shared was athletics. Many of the schools had rivalries with one another or other school districts, and the public supported their teams in a winning or not-so-winning season.

I have great respect for all the county agencies. To name one would not be fair. Each time I had a need for Hope Services on programs for our child or adult population, the department heads and their employees were always supportive. Many times, discussion was needed as we were in a great deal of flux since our funding base was changing from local to federal funds. This produced almost daily program questions usually based on funds. This forced an extremely close working relationship between my office and the fiscal department. Constant predictions and forecasts on funds were essential.

I would have to say that Hope Services also was a much respected organization in the community. When I was in public, people would often relay to me that one of their relatives or friends' son or daughter had attended or was attending Hope Services.

While most of the time relations were professional, I can remember one time that a community agency came to the board meeting. While the board meeting is open to the public, I had an agreement with this particular person that if I went to his board or he came to my board, we would notify the person ahead of time and tell what was going to be proposed. This community agency came to the meeting and proposed a very outlandish need for dollars that were not available. I was tempted to go to his board and expose his unfair request.

Henry County Transportation System

The Henry County transportation system was just beginning when I joined Hope Services. Mike Saneholtz was the first director and was in that position when I left. The purpose of the Henry County Transportation System was to provide transportation to citizens in need of transportation. While some people paid privately for the services, the vast majority of people were paid for through other organizations that they qualified for services. People needing transportation were people who do not have transportation or access to transportation. Services provided by the system grew by leaps and bounds. It was always positive to hear about individuals who would not have their dialysis, would not have been able to shop for groceries or go to their medical appointments, and who could not attend recreational activities without the transportation system. Denying services when funds were tight was always a hard decision. The Henry County Department of Job and Family Services and Hope Services were the two largest contract agencies. Connie Schuette from Job and Family Services, Rita Franz from the Henry County Commissioner's office, Robin Small from the Senior Center, and Jack Boyd and I from Hope Services were the original board members. Let us look at some of the experiences that happened in Henry County or happened to my life in general.

A Strange Night

Even the nicest communities have strange happenings. I will never forget one evening in 2003 when I was leaving a HARC meeting in Napoleon. It was rather late in the evening, after nine thirty. HARC meetings were noted to go late as HARC was responsible for many facilities and programs important to Hope Services. I had checked the coffeepot, checked all the doors, and shut off my computer. It was an extremely dark night, and I was particularly careful to look around the outside of the building as I left. One could never tell if someone was lurking around the building as some of our vehicles parked behind the building had been vandalized, and some strange, loud, unauthorized parties had been reported. We were looking into having a video camera installed by the police to see if we could capture some of these activities, but they seemed to have stopped.

As I drove away from the building and turned onto the roads that led me to Route 6, I had this weird sense that I needed to go slower than usual and pay close attention to the road. It was like my twin was saying watch it. I had gone about ten car lengths when I saw something out of the corner of my eye. There was a young boy about six years old walking onto the road in front of my car. I slammed on the brakes, and the boy looked straight at me and turned and walked into the front yard of a home that was situated near the back of the property. I turned the car toward the house, jumped out of the door, and saw an adult telling the boy to come to their car. I watched the boy get in the car. I felt lucky that I was able to stop fast, and each time I went by that area in Napoleon, I remember the night that I received help from some force in helping me be careful in my driving.

Where Is the Computer?

The original writing of this section was lost by a computer glitch, the type of glitch that I feared could wipe out a whole chapter. As I checked the document, I found the glitch included this section and the entire chapter. My backup contained the chapter before I had updated this new section. Funny how this section is on a computer, and this section was lost through a computer.

The OACBMRDD held periodic training sessions, usually in the centrally located city of Columbus. The purpose of the training sessions had been for federal funding programs in Medicare. While the Medicare system did provide funds, the knowledge of what those funds would be and the changing circumstances surrounding how the funds would flow were in constant flux. The uncertainty of this program mandated that the person I needed to deal with on a continuous basis was my fiscal person. While I drew heavily on my six directors, I was forced to expect more and faster from the fiscal department. The availability of funds and the projections on spending monies rested on her shoulders. When monies are tight, the decisions on spending cannot be made until the amount of money available is known. When information is sketchy at best on the amount of funds available, the spending patterns are scaled down. Money that is not available cannot be spent. These facts make for an unpopular superintendent, and those close to the fiscal department can be seen as guilty by association.

I was at such a conference with the OACBMRDD at the Hilton located in the Easton Town Center in New Albany, Ohio, on the northeast side of Columbus. I was trying to do as I had asked my managers to do, and that was to save money any way possible. I did not stay at the Hilton but obtained free room from my son Joe, who lived near the New Albany area. The Hilton is a beautiful hotel. It has parking around much of the building and a large guarded parking lot by the conference center. I usually parked in the large guarded lot because it was close, and I felt more secure with a guard present.

At the end of the first day, I had pulled together all my papers, and I thought I would spend some time on my laptop computer answering e-mail and working on some projects, probably related to the fiscal area. The first year I was in my position, funds were tight, so tight that on a $6 million budget, I had $20,000 in the black or positive. With a start like that, fiscal was growing to be very important and required an enormous amount of time. I had no explanation to give to my board if I allowed more spending than I had the money to spend. Yes, fiscal was always in the forefront. As I walked out to my car, I saw that the sun was shining, and it was a beautiful day. I walked a short distance to my Toyota Four Runner. As I went around to the driver's side, I noticed that there was glass on the blacktop. I put my papers on the passenger's seat. As I opened the door behind my seat, I noticed that the sun was shining brightly through the rear window behind the passenger's seat. A quick look on the rear floor produced more of the red-colored glass. I looked up and saw the rear window had been broken. Why would that have happened? My computer was on the floor behind the passenger seat, covered by my overcoat.

I quickly went around the car, opened the door, and saw no computer under my coat. I made a call to the police. When they arrived, I gained information that there were many break-ins to vehicles in the area. I found my fiscal director, Cheryl, and she called the insurance company and assured me that the stolen laptop had no access to our confidential documents. That was a relief. The hotel taped up the broken window with some vinyl covering and duct tape. After the glass was cleaned out of the back seat by the hotel, I went to my son's in a very depressed mood. I felt violated by the person who had taken my laptop computer. The car did not feel right. I had bought the vehicle new when I started this job, and even though I had put over 175,000 miles on the car, mostly work related, I had never had any serious damage to it. The laptop was for my use, and now I had lost the ability to even answer my e-mail. I was not feeling very positive about the person who had caused me all this trouble. I guess they needed money to eat.

Vacations

We have always taken vacations, some short and some longer. It was not until my good friend Pat invited Kathy and me to a trip overseas to Ireland that we seriously considered a trip across the ocean. For those of you who have traveled to faraway lands, this section on vacations should bring back memories. Although the countries visited will vary in geography, people, food, and entertainment, the mystique of traveling is always with us. For those who have not yet or may not ever travel long distances, these sections will give you some new excitement, and it may prompt you to travel more.

Anyone with good health can travel. Once the plunge is taken, it is easier to repeat with another trip.

Ireland Trip

From August 11 to 21, 2001, Kathy and I flew from Detroit, Michigan, to Dublin, Ireland, to be Irish for at least ten days of our lives. We left the WBGU TV station in Bowling Green on Sunday, with Pat Fitzgerald and Pat Koehler as our faithful tour guides and coordinators of this memorable trip. Credit should be given to the station for not only the arrangement and carrying out of the trip but also for the video, *Ireland 2001 August 11–21*, copyright 2003 by P&P Productions. This video helped give the travelers the ability to remember the many happenings we experienced on the trip and also helped me structure the following pages into a more organized and inclusive retelling of the trip to Ireland.

August 12, Sunday

We arrived in Dublin on August 12 and met our Irish guide and bus driver, Bobby. Bobby was to be responsible for getting us to our destinations and making the trip a memorable occasion. No time was wasted as the first day we visited the Power Court Garden. The power was there in looks, smell, and overall appeal. A large pond, beautiful flowers, and a downpour of rain combined for an interesting start. The rain only made the experience more appealing.

A trip to Ballykissangel in a quaint village called Avoca, County Wicklow, helped all the tourists into the mood to shop and, more importantly, drink at our first of many water holes, Fitzgerald Pub. The pub had the same last name as one of our guides. That evening, it was back to the Brooks Hotel for dinner and other festivities. After the meal, our guides had arranged an activity to break the ice with one another, sharing a blessing. For example, one blessing was the happiest day of the past will be the saddest day of the future. We were also to begin our knowledge of limericks as Harry, one of our fellow travelers, recited one of his more conservative limericks.

August 13, Monday

We toured Dublin and were amazed at all the old buildings, statues, and cities. As we passed one of the banks with large columns, the Dublin guide told us how during an uprising in 1603, a skirmish took place around the bank, and several bullet holes were still visible in the columns from the fight. The next stop was an old prison called Kilmainham Gaol. Cells were located on many different levels. Some were very high off the main court, some were a few feet up, and we realized that none of us wanted to be on the first floor as it was solitary confinement. Each of the prisoners' names was seen over the cell door. I couldn't leave the prison fast enough.

Later, we visited the oldest college with the largest research library in Ireland, Trinity College. We saw the famous manuscript probably produced in a monastery called the Book of Kells. As we looked at the original manuscript, we could see that it was beautiful and was told it contained the four gospels. A famous street, Grafton, lies between Trinity College and St. Stephen's Green. Grafton is the home of smart shopping areas with many fashionable shops.

August 14, Tuesday

On Tuesday, we left Dublin, and about an hour after we had left, I discovered I had left my passport in my pillow at the hotel. The security of sleeping on my valuables had worked for several years while traveling with my many jobs. Bobby used his contacts, and within a few minutes, they had sent my passport to our next hotel. It is not good to travel without a passport. My safe practice of putting my valuables in the pillow I slept on while traveling had just been proven to be unsafe.

August 14 was a Tuesday. An excellent breakfast was experienced by all in the hotel. We were traveling through the countryside when Bobby relayed to us that he had a special treat for us. We stopped on a hill at the base of an old church. Bobby announced that this was St. Patrick's first church, and it was not as good as it used to be, but it was safe. The church had no roof. I climbed to the second floor, realizing I was in the section where the bell and steeple used to exist. The walls around the base of the tower were partially there with little in the middle of the floor. One could slowly walk around the outside of the tower, but with the wind blowing, it was important to hang on to the walls. As I passed from one corner of the tower to another, I felt I was accomplishing a great task. As I looked over the outside wall, I felt wind, a strong wind, against my body. My safe trip around the perimeter of the tower base now turned into the game of "How do I get down?" I quickly walked around the perimeter and, despite the wind, made it to the safety of the steps.

On one of the winding roads near the ocean, we saw several sheep free-ranging. They were on the hills, beside the road, and at times on the road. In the evening after dinner, it was time for our favorite activity, the pub. This pub was in the Abbey Hotel and featured a guitar player, an accordion player, and a sporadic drummer. The unique part of this band was that they had a spoon player. One of our fellow travelers, Marion, decided that the spoons were her calling, and before the night was over, she was playing the spoons with the band and played like a professional. I don't believe I mentioned that in Ireland, the beverage of choice is a dark beer called Guinness.

That evening was the live entertainment at the Burlington Cabaret. We had dinner reservations at the theater, good food, great wine, and excellent entertainment. Our group from Ohio was recognized by the announcer in this very large hall. There were dancers, singers, and musicians. The dancers were mostly females, and they all had the traditional bright Irish dress. Each of the ladies had long hair. The very young blond-haired female dancer sported curls and wore a smile on and off stage and was a hit with the crowd. The dancing was fast, and the legs and feet were always moving in all directions. My legs were tired after watching the first few minutes of dancing. There were a few male dancers. A comedian, Noel Ginnity, performed and kept the audience laughing. There were several sets of dancers and singers to keep the show going at a very fast pace. Everyone seemed to enjoy the show.

True to tradition, it was time to visit a new pub, and that we did. Each of the pubs had its own musical talent, their unique interior, and their constantly thirst-quenching brew.

August 15, Wednesday

We took a trip through County Donegal and some of the town shops. Donegal is a beautiful country setting. At the top of one of the hills, we encountered the Grianan of Aileach. This was a round-shaped fortress of stone. The stones are arranged so that there are four different levels with the top level offering a beautiful view of the country. Five counties can be seen from this strategically located stone vantage point.

Peat was a sight we saw throughout our travels. On this day, we were to see the bogs that contained the peat. The peat is harvested with a rectangular-shaped shovel. The optimal size of a piece of peat is dug out and laid to dry. The peat bogs are very wet, and the peat is a soft variety of a coal type of material. Dried peat seemed to be a fairly common form of fuel.

In the afternoon, we had the treat of stopping at the Tabhairne Leo (Leo's Pub). Leo is the father of Enya, a very successful singer in

Ireland. The walls of the pub were lined with Enya's records that had sold abundantly in Ireland. That evening, we relaxed at a familiar type of setting, another pub. A guitar player and accordion player gave support to the many patrons consuming beer. While whiskey is another type of drink, I did not see many people drinking whiskey, but I am sure it happened more than I observed.

August 16, Thursday

We started our day at one of the local clothing shops that had its own weavers. The looms are very large, and it was good to see the craft of handweaving alive. When I was a young boy, there was a weaver who was related to a friend of mine. I enjoyed watching him weave as I enjoyed watching the weavers in Ireland. The weaver from youth was blind and had taken up the skill to make a living. My mother bought most, if not all, her rugs from this weaver. As I began to leave the shop, I noticed a wool sports jacket that I purchased and continue to wear in colder weather.

In the late morning, we arrived at a village that preserved living as it had been known in years of the past. There was a small shop that pastries and drinks were available. Scones, which are a small type of pastry, had grown to be one of my wife's favorite treats and took center stage as a well-enjoyed food item.

Donegal Bay and Killybegs offered the sight of large ships lined up for our viewing pleasure. They were large oceangoing ships. There were small attractive shops that offered us the chance to shop and eat our lunch.

It was on to the Belleek Group that specialized in China pottery and Irish porcelain products. The painting of articles such as plates and other ceramic pieces was hand done masterfully by the talented employees. The factory is very large. The other factory known for its crystal was Waterford. We had time for only one tour, so Waterford was not a choice.

A well-known poet was from Ireland. That person would be W. B. Yeats. Born on June 13, 1865, Yeats died on January 28, 1939. A well-known and well-respected poet, we had the privilege of visiting his grave.

August 17, Friday

The end of the week was upon us as we left Slago Park Hotel. As we were on our way to our next site, we noticed that there were trailers parked along the road. Bobby explained to us that the people living in those trailers were called tinkers. Tinkers were known to travel the countryside and obtain work by fixing items such as pots and pans. The phrase of not giving a tinker's damn came from these tinkers. The estimate was that there are twenty thousand people who were tinkers or Irish Gypsies.

We reached our destination and were introduced to the Croagh/Patrick Pilgrimage. The pilgrimage was a long walk to the top of a mountain on rocks, many of them sharp. A fall on the sharp rocks enabled one to cut up their legs, hands, arms, and other body parts. Kathy and I decided not to take the trip, and judging from the damages incurred by some pilgrims, we had made the right choice not to scale the mountain. Our stay in the pub at the base of the mountain made a much better pilgrimage than the climb that could have endangered our flesh.

August 18, Saturday

This Saturday provided a relaxing ride in the country. The fields were covered with rocks. These rocks were gathered by the landowner and placed strategically so that enclosures were made that could keep the sheep and other animals within the confines of the rock fences. As we traveled the countryside, we saw the opposite side of the stone fences called free-ranging. Throughout our travels, we saw cows and sheep crossing our path and lying beside the open road. At about this time, we had a Mother Nature treat. We encountered a beautiful waterfall beside the road.

A stop into a shop that made the drums used in many of the pub bands provided interesting entertainment. One of the people in our group had the opportunity to show off her skills as a drum player.

August 19, Sunday

We started out the day with a trip to Ailwee Cave. As the story goes, a young boy was out exploring the woods when he happened upon a cave of great length. Eventually, bears were found in the cave, and it is now shared with people having an interest in both. We toured the entire cave and saw not one bear.

The next point of interest was a rocky field in the hills. The person who owns the field of rock stood at the entrance gate and allowed people to give a monetary reimbursement for the right to enter his most interesting field. The rocks were arranged in many different patterns. Some had two flat rocks with a large one sitting on top like a table. Before the beginning of each day, the story is that spirits rearranged the rocks so they were always different. There was interest among some of my fellow travelers to hide and see how the rocks were changed. A number of interesting pictures were taken at this site.

The expedition in the field of rock aroused our interest in Mother Nature. Our next spot was to expose us to sights beyond our expectations and give us a look at what a "Wonder of the World" could be. The Cliffs of Moher are located next to the ocean. It was hard to see from one end of the cliffs to the other end as the space between was expansive. Walking next to the edge of the several hundred feet deep cliffs caused me great fear, which was intensified greatly with no fence around the edge. At the same time, the beauty of the sites was calming. The pure nature of the sights challenged my ability to know immortality in terms of strangely somehow having some control over the nature in front of me.

As I looked at the bottom of the cliffs next to the ocean, I could not help but wonder how many people may have been overcome by the trance of the cliffs and lost control of their balance. A look behind me revealed a small castle tower. I saw people standing in the top of the tower and walked closer to the unusual structure. As I entered the tower, I saw many souvenirs of quality. We had been asked by a friend to find a pen with liquid in the stem and some type of moving object for her son's pen collection. They sold exactly what we wanted, and we found it with only a few days of searching remaining. We took one last look at a sight we probably would not see again. The trip was worth just seeing the cliffs.

As we meandered to our next destination, another castle was seen across a golf course with no trees, lots of grass, and several rocks. Since we had several fellow travelers, they decided to play a few holes. I went to the clubhouse and searched for some golf balls from this Irish golf course. I found some and knew they would make great Christmas presents.

The evening was to be another unforgettable experience. We were to travel to a castle called Knappogue Castle from the fifteenth century located in County Clare. There, we participated in a royal meal starting with mead, proceeding through supper, and finishing with dessert. As we entered the castle, we were greeted like royalty. There were many different rooms and alcoves that housed fiddlers, guitarists, and singers. All the while we were at the castle, we would be entertained by many talented musicians. The castle was mammoth, the food and meal scrumptious, and the entertainment superb. The company was outstanding and the entire evening captivating. We drank our soup from a bowl, no spoons please, and banners added a touch of medieval atmosphere. The dancing was of the medieval period as were the dress and talk of the many performers. The mead drink was quite tasty, and I needed more than one, thank you.

There was still time to wander to one of the local pubs after we returned from the castle. The guitar, banjo, and hollow wood block keeping the beat with the drumsticks were waiting for us. Our group tried not to miss a thing in Ireland as it may be our last trip. At one point, a local kicked off her shoes and did what I judged as an Irish jig. There was not a rule in Ireland about smoking in public buildings. The rule seemed to be the opposite of where the USA was going as everyone smoked as much as possible anywhere one wished. On the wall in the pub was a newspaper article from May 6 and 13, 1916. The title was "Rebellion" in Ireland Sinn Féin. War stories, songs, and talks were common in Ireland as was the division between Northern and Southern Ireland. It was back to the hotel for a good night's sleep.

August 20, Monday

The week started out with a trip to Craggaunowen Village, a very primitive village where fires and smoke filled the atmosphere. We also saw one of their large boats used for travels outside protected areas.

I had heard of Durty Nellies or Dirty Nelly's restaurant. This establishment was noted for its tasty beer and delightful food. Everyone enjoyed the restaurant and vowed to come back, knowing that the circumstances of our travel would probably never allow our vow to be fulfilled. A trip to Bunratty Castle was next, and our evening meal followed. After supper, my wife recited a limerick that she had composed. As she introduced the limerick, I knew I would not be spared any embarrassment. Her limerick went like this:

There once was a man named Joe.
Who somehow had lost his dough.
It came his way the very next day,
And on his trip he did go.

The story of me leaving my passport and money in my pillow at one of the early hotels was to be a topic of conversation, like forever.

It was on to another pub after our supper and Kathy's limerick. We met in the lobby and enjoyed the rest of the evening with banjo, fiddle, and keyboard music and a drink of one's liking in a pub of our choice.

August 21, Tuesday

Our day to depart had come. It was time to leave our newfound home, Ireland, and return to the U.S. of A. As we departed our hotel, I checked to make sure I had my passport and money. The passport was the same as when we arrived, but I had lost a considerable amount of money somewhere in Ireland. We arrived in Shannon Airport and checked all our baggage and tickets. As I looked over at a corner of the airport, I noticed a great deal of activity. Upon further checking, I found that there was a duty-free shop that sold, of all things, Irish whiskey. Rather than turn in my Irish money for U.S. currency, I looked over the display of spirits. I was about to have one of the unanticipated pleasures in my life. The lady in the shop was giving out free shots.

Sunday morning may not be the best time to sip free whiskey, but I reasoned I would never get another chance like this in my life. I was grinning from ear to ear and had to pinch myself to see if this was really happening. In the United States, it would seem like some type of illegal and sinful activity to drink whiskey in a public retail store. Needless to say, I had my way with a few of the bottles, and knowing I had my fill, I invited some of my fellow passengers to partake of something they would never have a chance to experience again. Not only would they be drinking in the spirits shop, but they would also be doing it free.

I bought the maximum amount of spirits at the best possible price. We entered the plane. As I looked around at all the people from my group boarding with me, a strange thought controlled my brain. This was to be my last trip with all these wonderful people. It was a sad moment, but I did have one item to keep me going—I had my memories, and I hoped I would never lose them.

Our River Cruise in Germany

The second European vacation was taken a little over a year later. It was a river cruise down the Rhine, Main, and Danube rivers from Amsterdam to Austria. Pat Fitzgerald was the manager of WBGSU-TV in Bowling Green. Pat and Pat Koehler are the two who arrange tours all over the world for patrons of the station. Pat and his wife, Nancy, and two daughters have been friends of ours for over thirty-five years. Credit must go to WBGU-TV for the production of the *European River Cruise 2002*, produced by WBGU-PBS, copyright 2006. Kathy and I, along with other close friends of thirty-five years, Ron and Carol Carpenter, were making the trip with other friends from the area.

The Start

We boarded the bus on October 19, 2002, in Bowling Green. We instantly noticed other associates of ours, Father Tom, a Roman Catholic priest, and Harry, a prominent area attorney. Approximately fifteen other people were on board; some of them we knew from our Ireland trip, other were acquaintances, and others were to be new friends. We left for the international airport in Detroit.

Overview of the Cruise

The cruise trip in Germany was on a large luxury cruiser owned by Viking Cruise. The services on board were impeccable, and the management and help did their best to help you in any way possible. The ship held over 120 passengers. There was a lower deck for sleeping, a middle deck for sleeping, and the galley and an upper deck for cabins and the lobby and recreation area. The big advantage of a river cruise is that one never had to change their sleeping quarters. If one wished, they could stay on ship all day and night and enjoy the sights.

As we cruised down the three rivers, there were markers periodically. Each passenger had a guide with each of the number markings and names of various castles, cities, vineyards, or other important landmarks. To proceed up and down the rivers, a series of locks are in place. The water displacement is a few feet to a height of eighty-one feet. The rivers are a highway on water. Large ships and small boats are constantly on the river. I remember seeing a captain at the helm of a large ship with his wife and child by his side. On board the barge was a car and playground equipment for their child. This family must have lived on their commercial boat.

October 20, Sunday

We arrived very late in the evening and took our luggage to the MS *Viking Europe*. After a boat ride on the canal passing the Anne Frank House, it was decided that we could go to the red light district. As we headed for the district, my wife informed me that she didn't bring her umbrella, and it was raining very hard. I told her I would try to duck into a shop and buy her an umbrella. I didn't want to lose the group. In fact, I was terrified to think that I could be lost in Amsterdam, in the red-light district. I had euros because we had converted some of our money into euros at a Toledo bank. I saw a shop and ran in, found an umbrella, and paid for it. I luckily caught up with the group, thank God, and gave Kathy her new umbrella. Kathy opened the umbrella and strolled down the street.

I had seen a special on one of the national news programs on the red-light district. Their cameras had shot several discrete scenes of the "Ladies of the Night" at their place of business. Their places of business consist of a large window, a door, and a private area where she did her business.

As I walked by a ladies' place of business, the proprietor was in the open-window area. I thought this would make a good shot. As I photographed the lady, she disappeared instantly. I put my camera away and noticed the same lady I had just shot coming out of a side entrance yelling at the top of her voice, "I am going to kill you!"

It didn't take me long to figure that she was talking about me, and she was very unhappy about me taking her picture. I received an inspiration of wisdom at this time because I quickly faded into thin air and promised to never take this type of picture again. The crews I saw on television must have done something that I had not done. This was the second time that I had been near a red-light district in my life. The first, as you may remember, was in Washington, D.C. In this first incident, I was almost beat up, and in the second, I was threatened with death.

October 21, Monday

A drive through the lovely country brought us to the living open-air museum "Zanse Schans." Large windmills are still in existence and in use near Amsterdam. We visited one and saw the large grinding wheel turn and grind a substance that produces a grain oil. As we walked in the city, we noticed bicycles parked everywhere. This form of transportation is very popular and very useful with the rising price of gasoline.

Next, it was on to Rijksmuseum. This museum is large by any standard and the home of many artists' works. I was familiar with some of Rembrandt's paintings and was astounded how close I could be to them. As I stood within a hand's length of one of his paintings, I was surprised that I could have touched it.

October 22, Tuesday

After breakfast, it was time to look at some of the sights from the moving ship. We noticed a sign that said Remagen. Immediately, my wife, Kathy, informed us that this was the bridge blown up in World War II. Her uncle Harvey Meyer was one of the last Americans to safely go across the bridge. Uncle Harvey was to come home after the perils of war and be killed shortly thereafter in an automobile accident.

After breakfast, it was time for a tour of the galley. The chef informed us that for this ship, there were nine hundred pieces of dishware and cups used daily. There didn't seem to be a lot of room to work, especially for the pastry chef. The cooks do get all the work done and very handily, so there must be enough room.

Koblenz was one of the next cities we were to dock. At Koblenz, there is a majestic statue of Kaiser Wilhelm I made out of metal, maybe bronze, on a horse greeting anyone who comes to the city. The size of the statue was large by any standard. In the city, there was an ornate fountain of men rowing in a boat. As we left the city, we encountered the most beautiful part of the romantic Rhine. It was not long before we heard the voice of Loreley, trying to entice sailors into her port. Unfortunately, the experience that the sailors who listened to her would have been a wrecked ship, not what they expected.

October 23, Wednesday

Our next destination was the quaint town of Rüdesheim. The Mechanical Music Museum proved to be a most interesting different form of music. A player piano of great size provided familiar music to us. The piano is similar to, but larger than, the one we had in our home. Several cylinder phonographs were present and playing. A most unusual mechanical player with several violins played simultaneously and provided excellent music on a mechanism I never did understand. Lunch on the ship with German food, good entertainment of music and singing, and the ever-present beer for drink.

Frankfort is a beautiful old German city where most of its buildings were destroyed during World War II. Frankfurt treated us to tours of many buildings and various shops. The visit allowed us to match the name with the real city. With all this walking, we became very thirsty, so a stop at the pub and entertainment was in order.

Aschaffenburger Handbell Ensemble provided entertainment that evening. Later, we passed through a lock, which was by now a common occurrence since we were to experience sixty-six of these locks.

October 24, Thursday

As we approached Miltenberg, it was apparent that this was the city dominated by a castle bearing the same name as the city built in 1210. We docked at Miltenberg, the location of an old brewery. In our tour of the town, we learned of the accusations of witches and being locked up in cages and at times being burned. The trials as we were told were not always the fairest.

It was on to Wertheim to observe the glassblower and to buy some Christmas gifts for family and others. Later in the day, the chefs showed how to make apple strudel, and the passengers displayed their skill of consuming it.

October 25, Friday

Wurzburg is situated on the banks of the Main River, providing us with the outside and inside view of one of the most magnificent palaces on the tour. A priest held the title of prince-bishop and, with the money he collected, lived in this castle. Everything about it was large and exquisite. The artwork included many famous mural fresco paintings.

Rothenburg was the next stop. We visited a large church with statues fixed to flat surfaces. Beautiful windows adorned the high walls up to the ceiling. This medieval town displays flowers of beautiful colors. We observed a clock in the front of a building, and at least on the hour, figures would move and mark the time.

A special display of pastries was served after supper, and sparklers provided the introduction. Entertainment that evening was medieval music with a singer playing the dulcimer.

October 26, Saturday

We started the day on ship with a party at ten fifteen in the morning enjoying beer, pretzels, and strudels. Later, we visited the town of Bamberg. As we visited another large cathedral, we continued to wonder how the workers could have built these wonders.

The evening entertainment featured a yodeler/guitarist and an accordionist playing traditional Bavarian folklore music. The infamous chicken dance was played to the delight of the crowd. It seemed that about everyone was a good chicken dancer. We had to appreciate the different countries and the culture. Some of the passengers indulged themselves in a game of euchre. The women accused the men of looking at their cards, so the art of holding the cards next to one's bosom to restrict any peeking was enacted.

October 27, Sunday

Nuremberg is the second largest city in Bavaria and provided us with a look at Adolf Hitler and the Nazi Party. Of all the landmarks that was the most impressive, it was in Nuremberg, and the parade field used by the German army under the leadership of the Fuhrer, Adolf Hitler. As we departed from the bus at the parade field, the remains of the coliseum-type seats spread as far as the eye could see. The parading of the German army for the citizens was an all-day event for the entire family. The guide showed us pictures of the parade field and the accompanying seats as well as the small platform that Adolf Hitler used to review the troops. I was astounded by the fact that the guide was describing the parade field and its activities as anything associated with Hitler was rarely spoken of in today's Germany.

As we passed the building where the Nuremberg trials were held, we could see the window for Courtroom 600, where twenty-one of twenty-four Nazis were tried for war crimes.

In the square, we were once again treated to a clock tower with moving characters. In this case, not only was there a bell ringer, but also seven women entered from the right side of the central king figure. As they passed the central figure, they turned toward the king and then exited on the left side. It was an experience to be remembered.

That day, we entered the Danube River and approached one of the deepest locks that was close to eighty feet high. Being the bottom of this lock aroused an uneasy feeling. I had been told that the sixty-six locks took thirty-two years to build. It was on this day that we reached the highest point of our trip and crossed the European watershed.

October 28, Monday

In the morning while taking a boat ride through the Danube Gorge, we saw on the hill Liberation Hall, which was built in memory of the liberators of Germany. These liberators from Germany helped preserve Europe from the Napoleonic oppression. As we approached the round structure from the river, we enjoyed the majestic view of this large circular building with a cone-shaped copper roof. The construction of the building was finished in 1845 by King Ludwig I of Bavaria. The interior was a display of pillars and angels of stone and other architectural features.

While going to the abbey of Weltenburg, we had the pleasure of riding on a beautiful open boat and the opportunity to consume an excellent beer made by the monks. I was able to bring back a six-pack of what I considered the best beer I had ever drank. This was a highlight of my day! We visited the origination of Weltenburg beer as well as the Benedictine chapel. The chapel was adorned with murals, pictures, stone, and beauty beyond description.

It was on to Regensburg where we toured and stayed overnight.

October 29, Tuesday

We visited St. Stephen Cathedral in Passau for a concert from the world's largest church organ. A tour of Passau was on the agenda for the afternoon. We learned that Passau is "the Town of the Three Rivers" and has a two-thousand-year-old history.

In the evening, we had a special Austrian dinner. After the dinner, the crew always performs a talent show toward the end of the cruise for the passengers. Tonight was the night. There was dancing and singing and making sure that whatever was done would be entertaining for the passengers. Even the captain was in the show, and everyone couldn't help but wonder who was running the ship. The show was successful in starting the process of drawing the cruise to a close.

October 30, Wednesday

Walhalla is located near Regensburg. This is a memorial to Germans who have made a large contribution to Germany. The crown prince Ludwig of the Kingdom of Bavaria started this massive project. Inductees include politicians, sovereigns, scientists, and artists of the German tongue. The outside of the building consists of huge pillars; the inside is ornate and honoring the famous people of Germany. There are several busts and commemorative plaques. Close to two hundred people are honored in this museum. A few of the well-known people recognized are King Ludwig I, Albert Einstein, Martin Luther, Ludwig van Beethoven, and Wolfgang Amadeus Mozart. I asked where Adolf Hitler's bust was and was informed it was in the basement.

In the afternoon a short stop was made in Straubing for a tour. There were many quaint shops in the area, and my wife sought and bought a necklace in one of the stores.

A low railroad bridge was in the path of our ship, and the river was flooded; it was questioned as to the ability of the ship to go under the bridge. Everyone disembarked and watched the crew try to take the ship under the bridge. As the passengers watched, the captain turned the ship around and guided the ship under the bridge backward. Several measures such as taking on more fuel to lower the ship were taken. As the vessel approached the bridge, it did not look like it was going to pass safely under the bridge. Slowly, the *Viking Europe* began to go under the bridge with what looked like a clearance of one inch. The ship inched its way under the bridge as I hoped no wave would develop. It did make it under the bridge, and we were able to go aboard and sleep in our room that evening.

October 31, Thursday

A tour of the Benedictine Abbey of Melk was first on the agenda this day. We were informed that the monastery was destroyed and rebuilt many times in the past. Seeing the abbey from the river was a most impressive sight. Seeing the inside of this beautiful building's statues, the gold, the painting of the Holy Family, the ceiling scenes, and the inside of the dome left me speechless. The talent displayed in the interior of this church surpassed any I had experienced.

The next stop was Vienna. The shops were attractive, creative, and eye-catching. One shop had animated activities in the window, and it was well worth the time I invested. I was captivated and didn't want to leave the window. There was a gold figure in the square, and I wondered if it was a statue or a human being. I stood close to the statue and couldn't decide. Finally, it moved, and I knew it was truly human. The Vienna Opera's design left me in awe.

That evening was a concert in classical music of Mozart and Strauss. It was performed in historical costumes together with ballet dancers and singers. Some of the music was familiar; all of it was very good. The champagne at the break was a nice touch. Opera is a most appealing, entertaining, and beautiful experience. I wish the program could have lasted longer.

November 1, Friday

It was time to head for home. I was anxious to get back to work as the Henry County Board of Developmental Disabilities had a new levy of 1.9 mills on the ballot on November 4. I had worked very hard on the levy before the trip and hoped that I had worked hard enough for the passage of the additional needed funds before taking the vacation. If the levy passed, it would be twelve years since we had a new levy.

While leaving the boat, I reflected on the fact that I was leaving one of the greatest vacations I had ever experienced. I have said many times since the cruise that I would go back to the German river cruise in a minute. But there are other considerations. First, there are other places to go. Second, there are other people to meet. As we started home, it was evident that we would never forget our friend, Germany.

Idaho with Jackie and Carlos in 2003

This was the third big vacation that Kathy and I took while I worked in Henry County. My son Joe; his pregnant wife, Tara; and my brother Walt and his wife, Judy, from North Carolina went along. This trip was to Sand Point, Idaho, to visit Walt and Judy's daughter and son-in-law, Jackie and Carlos Suarez. We were to visit a number of sites in the area, including Glacier National Park, which incidentally was having large forest fires at the time.

Our adventure to Sandy Point began with an airplane trip out of Columbus. Kathy, Joe, Tara, and I were all safely in our seats. The plane was loaded and ready to go on time when the pilot came on the PA system and announced a sensor was not working on one of the wings. I leaned over to my wife and said there would be a delay, and we would miss our connecting flight in St. Paul, Minnesota. Missing the connecting flight was bad enough, but we were to meet Walt and Judy in St. Paul so that Kathy and I, Joe and Tara, and Walt and Judy could all land together in Boise so that we could go to Jackie and Carlos together.

Within two minutes, a maintenance man came aboard the plane with a screwdriver in his hand. At that time, Tara called our attention to dirt and mold on the plane's wall. We assumed the plane had been taken out of mothballs. With the amount of mold, the mothballs had not been very successful. It was not long before the pilot informed us that we would be taxiing back to the terminal, and another good plane was being brought to the terminal. The pilot informed us that we should be under way soon. I told Kathy we were going to be late and miss our hookup in St. Paul. All the passengers left the plane and were instructed to stay in the area. I told Kathy the other plane would not be here for an hour. Unfortunately, I was right.

The new plane and new pilot took off for St. Paul, and we were hours behind our hookup. Upon arrival at St. Paul, we had to find a new connecting plane to Helena. Well, you guessed it, the next flight was hours and hours away, and we could be spending our first twenty-four hours in the airport instead of with our relatives. We found a plane to Portland, which would leave St. Paul in a few hours. From Portland, we would take a puddle jumper to Spokane. We could arrive around suppertime, get a car, and be at Carlos and Jackie's for a late supper. That is if everything went OK. It did go OK. The only problem we had was that Tara needed to have something to eat, and the only food we could find in our connecting flight at Portsmouth was a candy bar. We arrived on schedule at Spokane and rented a car. We could have been out of there with the car, but there are about five thousand insurance packages that one must choose. I made it pretty simple by calling my insurance agent on the cellphone, Lindsey Insurance, in Willard. I asked him what coverage I had and what I needed. We now had everything but our luggage, which was in Columbus to St. Paul. They said they would deliver the luggage to our residence of choice.

We arrived at Carlos and Jackie's and had a wonderful meal. Both Jackie and Carlos are excellent cooks, but since Carlos takes a great interest in cooking, he is the iron chef. We got to bed late, and just as we were settling in for a nice sleep, someone was knocking at the front door. It was three thirty in the morning. It was also our luggage.

For the next few days, we went to Glacier National Park. There were several streams, beautiful flowers, and animals. We also saw airplanes with large cables attached to their fuselages that were carrying vessels containing water. This water was used to fight the forest fires in the park. We were to go up the West Sun Trail, but because of the fire, we needed to use another approach. As we reached Logan Pass, we noticed glaciers, a tourist center, and several goats and sheep. Carlos, Joe, and I needed to use the men's facilities. As we were minding our own business, I heard a loud explosion and saw glass flying all over the restroom. I had just finished my job, so I zipped up for safety and walked around the corner to see a ram with large horns looking at the window he had just smashed. As quick as he came, he left, and as quick as the ram had left, the maintenance man was there with a broom and a dust mop.

That evening, we stayed at the largest structure I had ever seen in the wild made out of wood. It was called the Prince of Wales Lodge, and it was located in Canada. As we were about to approach the lodge, I saw several cars along the side of the road. We pulled over both cars, went over to the edge of the road, and looked down in the valley. There in the valley were three herds of elk. I didn't count, but there were hundreds upon hundreds of them. After checking in, we all went to supper in the lodge. The center of the lodge houses the restaurant and in this area are massive poles made from the native trees. The food and services were very good. We consumed several bottles of wine, except Tara.

The next morning, we left bright and early after a hearty breakfast to find bear. We didn't go far before we saw people along the side of the road. We pulled over our two cars and walked over to this berry patch with the rest of the tourists. It didn't take too long to see a black bear in the thicket eating berries. To my surprise, there were several children going very close to the bear. Their parents were nearby, but if the bear had gone after the children, I do not think the parents would have been much protection. We went on further and saw a grizzly bear. By now, it was time to go to a nearby bison and animal preserve. One must be in their car, and there were several bison, antelope, and other animals that I am not sure what their breed was. Within this beautiful country, there was one very large buffalo. This buffalo was either three or four times the size of the other buffalo. We pulled up close to this buffalo.

That afternoon, it was time to begin leaving Canada. As we were traveling through Canada, we noticed several steers along the side of the road with no fences. This reminded Kathy and me of our trip to Ireland where sheep run loose. Carlos informed us that the steer were free rangers and that we as drivers were responsible to see that we did not hit them. As we left Canada, there is a checkout point. I was in the first car, and the immigration officer asked us what we did in Canada and if we were all born in the USA. We said yes. We pulled ahead and started to go slow, waiting for the second car to clear. We waited and waited and waited. Finally, the second car pulled up beside us. We rolled down our window, and they rolled down their window. We asked what happened at the checkout point. Carlos said they asked if anyone was born outside the USA, and since he was born in Cuba, he said yes. Well, one thing led to another, and Carlos had a real thorough background check done on him. He must have passed because he was with us and not being detained back at the border. This was no big deal for Carlos!

The next day, Carlos had promised us a boat ride on the lake by his house. This lake was several miles long. So after an inspiring service Sunday morning at the Creek Church, we jumped on a boat for a day of sun. Carlos took us to an island that had a large rope hanging from a tree, and we swung over the water and let go of the rope. The big highlight of the trip turned out to be a large crack or crevice, that was into the side of the rock fascia. The crack was so large that our boat went into the crack, and the hole inside was large enough and deep enough for the boat. Carlos affectionately named the crack "Uncle Joe's Crack" in memory of my amazement at the beauty and size of the crack. Since then, the crack has been known to have another meaning.

Our Journey to Romantic France

Kathy and I had talked for years about visiting a country that by most standards was the most desirable to spend one's money and time. The country we decided to visit was France. The capital of France, Paris, with the Eiffel Tower, the picturesque area of Provence, and the ever-intriguing French Riviera were but a few of the attractions that called us to this section of Europe. And so the adventure began on November 4, 2004, on Northwest Airlines flight 50 at nine thirty in the evening.

November 5, Friday

Our flight and arrival in Paris went without a hitch. We arrived after a fourteen-hour flight in the "City of Lights." After settling in our rooms, we had some free time. Little sleep was something I observed on the flight over, and the direction we were given was not to sleep during the day as our sleep that evening would not be enjoyable. I walked around somewhat like a mummy with the knowledge I would sleep well that evening—and I did.

I had dreamed of seeing the Louvre firsthand, and the first stop had to be the *Mona Lisa*. Leonardo da Vinci was one of the most famous persons of all time in the arts and the sciences. As I walked into the area where *Mona Lisa* was displayed, I looked around the room several times to see the painting. There was no large painting in the room. I noticed a very small painting in the far side of the room with many people looking at it. The painting was covered with a clear protective covering. I made my way closer and saw that it was a small-scale painting of the *Mona Lisa*. I asked someone where the real *Mona Lisa* was being displayed. They responded that I was looking at the real painting. I was shocked; that was not what I expected, but it was what I had been given. The size was 23.18 inches wide by 35.18 inches high.

We left the *Mona Lisa* as it was time to see two of the statues being displayed, the Winged Victory and Venus de Milo. After having seen these well-known pieces, we saw more statues, pictures, and murals. The number of pieces of artwork in the Louvre is overpowering and unbelievable.

That evening, we traveled above the skyline of Paris and ate dinner in the Eiffel Tower at around two hundred feet above the ground. An excellent dinner with the French drink of wine completed the meal. Pictures next to and of the Eiffel Tower provided us with a memento of the evening. The evening was complete with a cruise on the Seine River.

November 6, Saturday

The Cathedral of Notre-Dame de Paris is an exceptionally large and interesting building. One of the more famous parts of the cathedral, other than the name, is the flying buttresses or supports that are seen at the rear of the church. These large supports allow high ceilings to exist without taxing the safety of the building. Upon entering, large rose structures made of stained glass are visible. The rose-shaped widows are very large and usually appear high on the side of the building. The organ, one of the largest in the world, has several thousand pipes. Four bells are present.

Confessions are available all day in a cathedral that has many statues, many columns, and many pieces of art. A particularly interesting group of carvings depicts the several times that the risen Christ appeared. To appreciate the many significant displays in the cathedral, a personal visit would be helpful and overpowering.

The Arc de Triomphe is one of the most famous monuments. It honors those who died in the French Revolution and Napoleonic wars. The French victories are listed as well as the involved generals. Beneath its vault lies the tomb of the unknown soldier from World War I. It is an easily recognized monument.

Another of the most famous monuments came from the World's Fair in 1889. Taking pictures of the Eiffel Tower can be accomplished from about any vantage point. At night, it is rewarding to see the lights periodically flickering.

The Orsay Museum was next on the afternoon agenda. The building housing the museum is an old railroad station. As I walked through the building, I saw many famous paintings of Picasso, Matisse, Manet, and Monet.

I also saw a picture familiar to my childhood. My mother and father had a copy of a famous painting. It was the prayer we were told happened at noon, and the painting was named *The Angelus* or the *Paita Angelus*.

A French painter named Jean-François Millet was the originator of the painting. The 6:00 a.m. and 6:00 p.m. were the other times the Angelus was traditionally recited. The farming couple portrayed in the painting were praying to our Lord and His Blessed Mother. The Angelus portrait and prayers remind us of the angel Gabriel announcing to Mary that she is to be the Mother of our Lord Jesus Christ. The Hail Mary prayer is the conversation between Mary and Gabriel.

That evening, we had supper in a second-story restaurant. I had heard of escargot or cooked land snails as an appetizer in France. There, they were in front of me on the dinner table, waiting for me to pick them up with a snail holder and small fork to pull them out of the shell. They were fantastic as was the meal. An accordion player provided the music for the evening and treated us to a few courses of the chicken dance. I, of course, with many of the other travelers, showed off our ability to move our hands, our arms, and our lower body, proving Americans are great chicken dancers.

November 7, Sunday

Versailles was to be the most memorable trip of my life. The aristocracy has for years been part of the French history, and Louis XIV's Palace of Versailles are words common to many. Maria Theresa of Austria was his first wife, giving him six children. A visit through this palace must be received by a knowledgeable guide so that the many interesting details are exposed.

Versailles was magnificent. Inside are decorated rooms with murals, statues, and large chandeliers. Outside, there are many gardens, fountains, statues, and buildings. It was large and became the main home of the king. Although the court did go to other castles, Versailles was considered the main one. Food was prepared in a location separate from dining area.

Because of the distance between these two areas, the food may be cold and had to be warmed before serving the king.

There are a few other interesting stories about Versailles shared by the guide. The consummation of the marriage and the birthing of the heirs to the throne were documented by the other aristocrats. This was made easy since these events took place on a raised bed with a viewing area of chairs. The bedroom was also the place where the king's rising and retiring were a public happening. Since there was no plumbing, the human waste was thrown outside and created undesirable smells and an unsanitary sewage situation.

The afternoon was an eventful time as we saw the *Water Lilies* of Claude Monet. His home and gardens are located in Giverny. Another group of well-known artists was to be ours that evening at the Paradis Latin Cabaret. The music, dancing, and beauty of the costumes were overpowering, not to mention the sit-down dinner featuring my favorite dish of salmon.

November 8, Monday

We boarded a very fast train to the countryside. We stopped at Avignon to hear the story of the six popes who did not reign in Rome but did in Avignon, France. Pope Clement V was the first pope to move the papal court from Rome. From the early to the late 1300, this move took place. Our day ended in Aix-en-Provence, and we readied ourselves for the next few days.

November 9, Tuesday

In the market, we enjoyed many shops and particularly enjoyed the open-air flower shops. Artists are plentiful in this area. We visited Cezanne's workshop, which was exactly the way he had left the shop when he left this world. A visit to Santons Fouque provided us with the opportunity to see and buy from a great collection of different clay models. Three generations of Fouques have created more than 1,800 different models.

November 10, Wednesday

Another day in Aix-en-Provence provides us with the freedom to sightsee several small towns in Provence. Arles and Saint-Rémy-de-Provence are two of these inviting towns.

Arles has a well-preserved Roman arena and a Saturday market that attracts many farmers from the surrounding area. Vincent van Gogh painted his famous *Starry Night* in Saint-Rémy-de-Provence and added to this town's fame. The town is picturesque and pretty. Fine wines and excellent cuisine is characteristic of France, and this evening was no exception.

November 11, Thursday

A cruise to Saint-Tropez is a popular area enjoyed by movie stars and artists. It was said that Bridget Bardot lived in Saint-Tropez. It was then off to Cannes and then to Nice, the capital of the Riviera.

November 12, Friday

In Nice, we saw outside shops of about anything. There were flowers, herbs, spices, mushrooms, candies, fruits, and fish.

Today we saw the famous Monte Carlo Casino located in Monaco as we were still on the famous French Riviera. While the Monte Carlo was a most impressive Casino, we visited the adjacent small casino. It was interesting to see the expensive cars driven by the patrons as they were parked in front of the casino and placed on display. The French Riviera was not what I had expected. The beach on the French Riviera is natural rock, not sand. This made it a little hard to walk on the beach.

The Cathedral of Monaco is where Princess Grace is buried. While alive, Princess Grace started a foundation in her name. The foundation started by assisting local craftsman and women through a handicraft shop in Monte Carlo. It expanded to students in dance, music, theater, and cinema in the Monte Carlo area and then the arts in the United States. The sick children, medical research, children's hospitals, and an Irish library were added.

November 13, Saturday

This was the day for perfume. My first visit to a shop associated with perfume making was to be special. The entire process was explained as was the equipment that had been used in making perfume. The most memorable fact to me was that the perfume is sampled by a person called the nose. The sampling is done by the human nose, and there are few people able to carry out this task. This was a good spot to buy Christmas presents, and what we bought was well received.

That evening, we went to a very popular restaurant near Nice. It was located in the mountains, and when we walked in, we could see that the restaurant had a fireplace in the middle with three legs of lamb hanging next to the fire. Somehow the legs would rotate so that they would evenly roast. As we drank our wine, we could watch the lamb cook. The lamb was excellent, and the entire meal was one of the most memorable I have experienced.

November 14, Sunday

We departed from Nice at 6:30 a.m. on Northwest flight 1260. The flight was long, but our memories helped us enjoy the trip. This was a trip that we would consider in the future.

George and Betty

Part I

During the time frame from 2002 until 2006, the four of us, Betty and George Schlotterer and Kathy and I, continued our yearly weekend excursion to various interesting spots, mostly in Ohio. George is my first cousin. The results of these five years provided new experiences and helped continue the development of strong positive relationships. These adventures will now be presented.

2002 Trip

Since we alternate each year the couple responsible for planning the trip, it was our turn to visit George and Betty in Centerville, and they had planned the trip. Friday night was talk and go out to dinner night. The restaurant was always something new. On Saturday morning, we were ready to go early. After a great home-cooked breakfast, we were on our way. Since we knew not where we were going, we watched for any indication that would tell us where we were headed.

We went south on I-75 and looked off in the distance to see all these giant jungle animals. We were informed that we were at our destination. Jungle Jim is located on six and a half acres of land. The store has all types of foods beautifully displayed. They have 150,000 different international items from seventy-five countries. Many countries are displayed in their own area. There was a gift shop with a wide array of special items. A Penny Wise cooking class gives the participants a chance to learn how to cook special meals at home instead of going out, the more expensive route. Jungle Jim has one of the largest display collections of wine in the world. Approximately fifty thousand shoppers known as "foodies" visit Jungle Jim each day. The founder of the store in 1974 was "Jungle" Jim Bonaminio.

Time was getting away from us, so we took off for another spot in the area. The area we were to discover was Lebanon, Ohio. The destination was one of the oldest and well-known restaurants named the Golden Lamb. As usual, I have lamb whenever it is on the menu, and I am always hungry for this tasty morsel. After lunch, we visited the gift shop in the basement of the restaurant and hotel.

We arrived in Centerville for Catholic services and for a homemade supper by Betty and George. The evening was topped on with catching up on our family and friends. The annual small gift exchange took place each year on Saturday evening. We arrived home Sunday late afternoon in time to get ready for another workweek.

2003 Trip

George and Betty arrived on Friday night, and the traditional go out to eat supper was observed. Our friends Carol and Larry Moore own and run a small restaurant in Pemberville called the Forks. Two branches of the Portage River, the South and Middle Branch, come together in Pemberville. The restaurant we ate at that evening is appropriately named the Forks Restaurant. I almost always order the broasted chicken as I have not found a better-tasting broasted chicken. The evening was filled with talk about our worlds.

It was a great home-cooked breakfast on Saturday, and then we were off to see the sights of Pemberville. George, Kathy, and I had many railroaders in our families. Our friend Dale and Karen own a railroad station or depot, and we were scheduled to make a visit. It is furnished like it should be, a train station. The furnishings are at the height of the passenger train era. The ticket window, the waiting area, and the boarding area are full of memorabilia. While Kathy and I had visited the train station before, it had been a while.

It was on to Beeker's General Store, one of the few general stores in existence. One of the big draws at Beeker's is the candy counter. Several feet of all types of candy are displayed and available for purchase. The way it works for kids is that they come in to buy candy, and the first order of business is to obtain a small sack to hold all the candy they wish to purchase. After all the decisions are made on what candy to buy, they take their valuable cargo to the cash register table. The clerk will pour out the candy and tally the amount of money due. If the child has money, they will pay; if the child has no money, they will look to their parents or grandparents to pay the bill.

The village of Pemberville is very conscious of its heritage. In addition to the general store, one of the older houses in town is the Furry House. Behind the Furry House is a fully equipped schoolhouse. These two buildings are used for many community events such as Halloween, when everything is decorated for the season. Another of the well-known historical places is the Pemberville Opera House located over the village council chambers and the former home of the Village Police. The opera house is accessed by stairs to the second floor. The opera house was originally built in 1891. In June and July 1998, the Pemberville Opera House Restoration Committee began the restoration. The scraping of the ceiling revealed an eighteen-foot fresco. This fresco was restored as were the rest of the ceiling and walls. New electricity and two new furnaces were just a few of the projects. On October 23, 1999, during the autumn fest, the opera house was opened to the general public. Activities in the opera house include, but are not limited to, plays, performance of singing groups, silent movies, and other community activities. It is a sight to behold.

After Mass at Blessed John XXIII, it was time to go home for a family meal. My brother Mike and his wife, Marg, came to our house to surprise Betty and George. It was a true surprise. One of Kathy's wonderful meals topped off the supper hour, and the rest of the evening was used for discussion. Everyone left in the early afternoon on Sunday after a full breakfast and light lunch.

2004 Trip

It was down to Centerville for our yearly outing with George and Betty Schlotterer. Friday was the usual eat out and family discussion. On Saturday, we were informed that we were going to the Cincinnati Museum to see the showing of St. Peter and the Vatican. We had heard of the show and were delighted to have the opportunity to attend the exhibit. Since we are all Catholics, the display went deep to our roots, and we saw many items we had only heard about when we were younger. The mock-up of the Sistine Chapel ceiling helped us appreciate the paintings of Michelangelo. The several paintings, clothes, and staff crucifix used by Pope Paul II were interesting. Upon leaving the exhibit, I was surprised to see Dr. Mike and his family. Mike is a dentist and member of my board.

After the exhibit, we spent some time at H of Brauhaus, a German bar. The waitresses and band members were all dressed in full German regalia. The atmosphere was truly German, and the food and drinks followed suit. We then traveled into Covington, Kentucky, for Mass at St. Mary Cathedral and Basilica. One of Betty's home-cooked meals began the evening. Conversation that evening and a big breakfast the next morning signaled our departure back to New Rochester.

2005 Trip

Betty and George paid a visit to us beginning on a Friday in February 2005. A Friday evening meal at a local restaurant and time with one another completed the day. On Saturday, we motored to Whitehouse,

Ohio. Betty's aunt is a nun, Sister Mary Marilyn, and lives in Whitehouse. After the visit, it was time for lunch, so we went to Waterville to one of our favorite old-time restaurants, the Coral Restaurant. The atmosphere is fifties or sixties, and they have one of the best-tasting hamburgers that exists. In addition to their sodas, they have a wide variety of milkshakes made in the old-fashioned metal canisters. It makes me hungry thinking about it. The prices are also very reasonable. There is an antique shop on the corner that is always good for a few minutes to remember the past and relax. We didn't buy anything, but we enjoyed the days gone by.

It was off to near Bowling Green to see Snook's Dream Cars. On the way, we took time to see the giant wind turbines that provide electricity to several homes in Northwest Ohio. A co-op of several cities led by the city of Bowling Green helps preserve our natural resources by using wind power. Shortly thereafter, we arrived at our destination of vintage preserved cars. Mr. Snook decided to display his many cars in a building especially built for his cars. The cars are all completely restored, and the thirty or so vehicles on display range from racing cars to a Cadillac. There is even a garage to service all the vehicles. It is a trip back in time and one cannot help but appreciate all the time, energy, and money invested in these cars.

By now, it was time to attend Mass, and we decided to go big. The Rosary Cathedral in Toledo is a beautiful structure inside and out and is the building used for official ceremonies of the Toledo Diocese of the Catholic Church.

A supper meal by Kathy and a relaxing evening set the stage for an early breakfast and Betty and George's trip back to Centerville on Sunday.

2006 Trip

It was the Fredericks' turn to travel to Centerville, to visit George and Betty Schlotterer. Friday night was the traditional "go to a new restaurant" evening. On Saturday morning, we began our travel toward Dayton. Since

Kathy and I did not know our destination, we looked for any sign help to determine where we might be going for the day. We began to notice that signs were being displayed for the Wright Patterson Air Force Base. As we pulled in a parking lot, we noticed a very large building and signs that said "Wright Patterson Air Force Base."

The last time I was at this base was when I was in Boy Scouts. About all I remembered about the base was the barracks and playing ping-pong. I remember very little about the airplanes. This trip was to be different. We were to see more planes today than we would see in our entire life. As we entered the building, we saw a sign to the left that advertised a side trip to see Air Force One planes. Knowing what I know about making reservations, I knew we had to at least make the reservations if we even thought we wanted to go. We could always not go. If we waited till later to sign up, our chances would be small to none. As we looked to our left, there was a gift shop. A quick trip through the shop made it evident that there was about anything having to do with airplanes for purchase. There were small planes, larger planes, and just about anything I could think that related to airplanes.

We went with the crowd and soon found ourselves in a very large building where airplanes were on the ground, suspended a few feet off the ground, and high off the ground. The planes were large, small, colorful, or not so colorful. Some were somewhat familiar and others I had never seen. While several of the planes were very interesting, I found the large transport planes in which the bottom of the airplane opened up to load personnel, equipment, and supplies were large beyond description. Vehicles could drive up the ramp made by the open bottom of the plane. A second plane that I found interesting was the Wild Weasel, which was to find enemy antiaircraft guns and surface to air missiles, seek them out by radar, and destroy them with missiles. The reason this plane was interesting to me, other than its looks, is that my cousin Ron was one of the few instructors for the Wild Weasel. There were so few instructors for this plane that he was not able to go into combat since he was needed to be an instructor.

After touring what seemed like endless exhibits of airplanes, it was time to finish the afternoon with a tour of Air Force One. I was not sure what to expect other than the past presidents flew in these planes. A bus took us a distance to the hangar that housed Air Force Ones. As I walked into the hangar, I was overtaken by the number of planes, all having the Air Force One insignia, except for one plane that was for the presidents' wives. The planes were for presidents, which went back to at least Franklin Roosevelt. While viewing the inside of the various planes, it was interesting to see which presidents used which planes. The conference rooms were interesting to me as I thought of the many discussions and decisions that were made in these rooms.

By far the most interesting and emotional room was standing on the spot that Vice Pres. Lyndon Johnson took the oath of office after Pres. John Kennedy had been assassinated. Posted was the famous picture of Lyndon Johnson standing next to Jackie Kennedy on his left and Lady Bird Johnson on his right. Jackie's wool suit was stained with the blood of her husband. When I stood in the spot that President Johnson stood, I could see to my left the place where a section of Air Force One had been removed so that the casket of John F. Kennedy could travel instead of below in the cargo area.

Larry and Carol

Part II

2002, Michigan City, Indiana

We arrived in Michigan City near dark. Kathy and I were completely unaware where we were going as we did not pick the destination this year, and it seemed we just kept on traveling west of Ohio. Michigan City is located on the southern end of Lake Michigan. Since it is on the water, it is a beautiful location. The bed-and-breakfast was a Victorian home with beautiful paneled walls. One of the walls we found had a secret or false panel. We learned to open the panel after being instructed by the owners. On Saturday, we visited some of the area antique shops. One of the unusual features of some stores is that they are multi-floored. That means the antiques went up and on forever with so many large floors to cover.

A wine shop was inviting, and after dinner that evening in an old brick wall restaurant on Lake Michigan, we took a walk on the pier. The view from the pier was beautiful, but the weather began to turn cold. After a talk with the owners of the home, we turned in so we were ready for the next day. Our final day was a trip to the sand dunes. The dunes were tall and picturesque. We had enjoyed Indiana, which can be a feat for Ohioans.

2003, Willard

Of all the trips we were to take with Larry and Carol, this was the one we were most familiar and comfortable with, our hometown of Willard. It had been five years since we had visited Carol and Larry's hometown of Centerville, Indiana, and now we were in the Willard area, ready to share the stories of our youth. We found a bed-and-breakfast; rather, Kathy found a bed-and-breakfast in Norwalk. Norwalk is about fifteen minutes from Willard, and Norwalk is the county seat of Huron County, the county where Willard is located. Both these towns are located in the northcentral part of Ohio. Friday night found us checking into a large bed-and-breakfast located on West Main Street in Norwalk named the Georgian Manor. The home was large and beautiful. Kathy shared that when her mother was younger, the housekeeper at this very home was a relative, and her mother would occasionally visit her. The owners seemed interested in hearing the story about Kathy's mother and invited her to visit sometime in the future.

A popular restaurant, Berry's, was the site of our Friday evening meal. After dinner, looking around the house occupied the rest of the evening.

Saturday was a busy day. The local antiques shops in Downtown Norwalk are always fun to frequent as their stock has a turnover, and their items are interesting to view. We headed to Bellevue to visit the Railroad Museum. In the museum, we saw several engines, cars, and cabooses. There was a passenger train as well as a wreck-clearing train. Larry enjoyed the museum, and as a former railroad employee, he knew much about the railroad. In the afternoon, we drove past the former hospital in Norwalk where Kathy was born and stopped by the Sorrowful Mother Shrine near rural Bellevue. We drove by St. Sebastian Church in Bismarck, where Kathy and I were married in an ice and snow storm. I have not heard, nor will I ever hear, the end of getting married in January. We stopped by Kathy's home to see her mother. Kathy's mother has a positive disposition that any son-in-law would be proud to claim. It was on to Willard to see the downtown area. Jump's store is a clothing store located downtown, and I worked there every Christmas vacation through my college years. I probably was hired at Jump's since that was where my brother Walt worked before my appearance on the scene. I have many good memories of working at Jump's and also living in Willard as was documented in previous chapters. We drove by my original home at 519 Clark Street and my parents' new home on 534 Butte Ave. The St. Francis Xavier Church and Willard High School were whistle stops as was Kathy's brother Dave and sister-in-law Diane's house. Since Larry was a railroader, we drove by the Willard railroad yards. We didn't stop at many spots in Willard because we did not have the time, and Kathy and I had learned that new people moved in, and we rarely recognized people that we may have known in the past.

We found a nice steak house Saturday night for supper and finished our tour in Milan, Ohio. On Sunday, we saw the Thomas Edison birthplace and the Thomas Edison Shop downtown, which sells and repairs old phonographs and related accessories. We enjoyed showing Larry and Carol a part of our lives to which they had not been exposed.

2004, Amish Country

The trip to Amish Country was a surprise from Larry and Carol but one that always offered us something new about the Amish religion, people, and culture. Kathy's mother and father liked the area so much that one time my father-in-law stated, "If I ever come up missing, all you have to do to find me is look in Amish country."

We arrived in Millersburg, Ohio, county seat of Holmes County on Friday afternoon and found our way to the Millersburg Hotel. Our morning began early, and we searched the countryside for Amish men, women, and children at work in the field or at home. While finding Amish people may be possible, taking pictures is not something allowed by their religion. Cheese is big in Holmes County, and the first stop was the Heini's Cheese Chalet. "The History of Cheese" is a large painted mural depicting the history of cheese and ending with a billboard of the ten-ton wheel of cheddar cheese that was shown and made at Heini's. The big cheese was destroyed when the refrigeration was accidentally cut off in the 1990s. A long corridor allows guests to see the cheese making process behind glass. The cheese was available for purchase in their gift shop.

The next stop was another cheese factory, Guggisberg. I remember this shop best for its baby Swiss cheese and also because I had a hard time spelling the name of the cheese. During the time of day in which cheese is being made, one can see from the gift shop the large stainless steel vats full of cow's milk and mechanized paddles running up and down the vats to help make the famous Swiss cheese. After a pass through the gift shop, it was on to another venture. Lunch was, of course, at the Der Dutchman in Walnut Creek. This lunch is always a treat as they have many prize entrées, and if you are not full, there is the opportunity to have a homemade pie. I am on the lookout for lemon meringue, cherry, or pumpkin with whipped cream.

We noticed a sign for Yoder's Amish Home tours beside the road. We decided to take the tour of the home, barn, and an Amish school. We learned much about the Amish culture at all three sites. In the barn, Kathy was talking with an Amish man about nails to hang up our horseshoes, one from her childhood and one from our present farmhouse. The Amish man said he would send the right size horseshoe nails to us. He did a few weeks later, and we installed our horseshoes on the entrance to our pergola in the backyard.

The next morning, we found a few antique stores in the area. Our ride home through Amish Country proved a delight just as our time in Amish country.

2005, Chillicothe, Ohio

We had always had an interest in the Chillicothe area. When I was a child, we had gone to this area to see the Serpent Mound but had not been successful in locating the mound. Kathy had researched the area and found a nice bed-and-breakfast and some other interesting events in the area. We arrived on Friday night and were immediately impressed with the bed-and-breakfast. The collections of the lady who co-owned the building were most impressive. Everywhere one looked, there was a collection, and I might add complete collections of the various items. There were toys, dolls, dishes, and anything imaginable. We were taken back with the number of collections being displayed in the home. We ate supper and wanted to get an early start in the morning. The next morning, we visited the impressive Hopewell Indian Mounds, and I decided it had been worth the wait. The culture was active from 200 BC until AD 500.

After walking the ground at the mounds, we worked our way back to the bed-and-breakfast. We met the other co-owner of the home who was a former school superintendent. He was getting ready to go fishing for catfish. Fishing on the river is an enjoyable pastime in this area. We ate dinner, and then we were off to a show. Tecumseh is an outdoor play in the area, and we had tickets for this very night. The play was very exciting. Seeing Indians ride into the center of the play area was pretty exciting. Knowing that Tecumseh was defending his sacred homelands in the late 1700s gave the play a special meaning. The weekend was a trip back in time and one that gave all of us a different perspective on life.

2006, Dearborn, Michigan

Our trip that Larry and Carol planned was close to home, the Detroit area. As we pulled into Greektown, an area close to Detroit and Dearborn, we could see that something was happening. It was the playoffs in hockey and baseball. All the TV stations were displaying the Red Wings and Tigers games. We ate our meal and took off for our bed-and-breakfast. The bed-and-breakfast was a nice homey setting. There was a nice game area in the cellar, and we took advantage of the various games.

The next morning, we were off to the Henry Ford Museum. This museum is a large museum and covers transportation and many other areas, including early home furnishings. Many cars are displayed as well as trains and associated vehicles. It took us a whole day to go through the various displays. After supper, we enjoyed the games in the cellar of the bed-and-breakfast. Sunday was our day to go home, and on our way, we met Darrin, Larry and Carol's son, and their daughter-in-law, Lisa, who live around Detroit. After a pleasant lunch, we were off to Pemberville.

Family

Mark, Joe, and Bryan Go Fishing

Fishing is a sport that the entire family enjoyed. After my son Joe was married, Mark was still living at home, and we would hit the river frequently in search of the "big ones." Mark had discovered a secret fishing spot on the Portage River, and periodically, we would go fishing at this hole. Interestingly enough, we caught many fish, but we didn't always catch large fish. If large fish were to be caught, I would usually be the one to catch them.

On this particular evening in the summer of 2003, Mark; a friend of Mark, Bryan; and I decided to go fishing. We started early in the evening so that we would have more time to fish. As we arrived at our fishing hole, we all began to catch a few fish. The suggestion was made to go down river to see if there was any better fishing. As we waded down river in our old tennis shoes, we discovered that the fishing wasn't much better.

We decided to go just a little more downstream since the sun would start to set within the hour. I was using the same reel as everyone else, a spinning reel, but my rod was a bit longer than the other two. We were all using synthetic grubs and a few other lures. I cast my lure toward the left bank, and almost immediately, I felt a fish on the line. Since big fish are more of a rarity than small fish, I knew that I had a "big one" on the line. I fought the fish for about fifteen minutes. During that time, the fish would run with the lure, and then I would begin to bring him in toward me. He would run and jump, and I would reel in as fast as I could without breaking the line. When the fish was close enough to get a good view, everyone was amazed at the size of the bass. I did finally maneuver the fish next to me and put my thumb into the lower jaw of the fish and thus temporarily immobilized my "big one." Luckily, we had a camera with us, so we took several shots of the fish.

Everyone, including myself, was impressed with the size of the fish. I knew it was no fish story because I had the picture to prove my story and two witnesses. As usual, we released the fish so another fisherman could enjoy the big catch.

The Broken Leg

Kathy broke her leg in November 2006, just a month before I was to retire. I wondered if this was the beginning of but more negative happenings in my retirement. It happened as Kathy was going down the back three steps and thought there were only two steps. Her sister, mother, and sister-in-law were coming that day to go shopping. She decided to do the obvious, go shopping. That evening, she asked me to take her to the emergency room. She has her priorities together. The ER doctor confirmed what Kathy already knew, that she had a broken leg. The first X-ray with the specialist showed the break had aligned beautifully. He wanted to take another X-ray a week later, and this time the bone was now off-center, and surgery was in order. Six screws and a plate later and Kathy was on a slow road to recovery.

Remodeling the Upstairs

Kathy's broken leg coincided with the start of a remodeling project upstairs in our home. Much of the remodeling was planned to be either a redecorating or repainting job. We had been picking our colors; rather, Kathy had been picking out pastel colors for our entire upstairs. As we looked at all the walls and ceilings, we noticed that they all looked good except for a ceiling in Mark's room. The wall had a bulge in it, so we thought we should tear out a small section so that we could fix it.

Terry, our neighbor, was to do the painting. We had a meeting of the involved parties, and Terry, Kathy, and I cautiously began to tear down the bulging plaster. As we pulled out a small section, we saw that we needed to pull out another small section of the plaster. We ended up with an opening over five by four feet in our ceiling. As we looked closer at the open area, it became evident that the wood was charred many years ago. Our guess was that someone in the past was either smoking in the room or had a candle burning in the room, and it caused a fire that damaged the original plaster and the slats of wood.

It was very uncomfortable for us to know that a fire had been started in one of our bedrooms before it was our bedroom. It didn't look like there had been any more damage than we could see, so we made plans to have the ceiling and wall replastered and painted.

Neighbors

The Neighborhood Gang

For years, we have gotten together with neighbors to celebrate birthdays and holidays. The practice started in the early eighties when we moved into the neighborhood and included Edna Restemyer; Sue Welty and her daughter, Carol, and son, Jamie; and our family, Kathy, Mark, Joe, and me. At times, other neighbors were involved in the gatherings, but gradually, the group shrunk to only a few people as death and moves reduced the group's numbers to just few people. In the nineties, a group was revived with Gene and Ellen Walston, Pat and Ed Hammett, and Terry and Lori Hoepf. All these neighbors lived in proximity to us. When the parties were for Kathy or me, at times, Sue Welty, Larry and Carol Moore, and Dave and Judy Miller were present. If the party was for Ed or Pat Hammett, Gene and Wes Long were usually present. If the party was for Terry or Lori Hoepf, Tim Hoepf and Terry's parents, Ray and Mick Hoepf, usually attended. The occupation of the various partygoers, at that time, was quite diverse. Gene was a farmer and elected township trustee, while Ellen was a legal secretary. I worked as an administrator in programs for people with developmental disabilities, and Kathy was a special education teacher in Washington Local Schools. Ed was an administrator for the Environmental Protection Agency or EPA, and Pat was a teacher at Penta County Joint Vocational Center. Terry was a cook on a fishing boat in the Alaskan Barrier Reef, while Lori was involved with the floral business. Sue Welty was a retired teacher, while Larry and Carol managed the Forks restaurant in Pemberville, the Village Laundromat, a recycling center, and several rental properties. Dave Miller is editor of the local paper, the *Sentinel-Tribune*, and Judy worked in the retail business. Gene and Wes Long were teachers in the Eastwood and Toledo School systems, respectively. Tim is in food management at BGSU, Mick is a retired nurse, and Ray a retired retail manager.

These parties were lots of fun, and usually birthday cards and small presents were given to the birthday girl or boy. The birthday cards were of a funny nature, and there was always unspoken competition to see who could come up with the wittiest of cards. The presents could be a bottle of wine, something homemade, but almost always of a meaningful nature to the person who was the object of attention. For example, a sheep-related gift for "Big Ed" Hammett, "the shepherd" or a wine-related gift for myself, "the winemaker," were most appropriate. Lori is an accomplished knitter, so her gifts could be a scarf or gloves handmade, while Ellen and Gene would bring asparagus for all during the season as they at one time had the largest field of asparagus in the state.

Gene Fights His Illness

Around the end of 2002, Gene visited his doctor. The doctor did a test on Gene's lungs. A few months later, Gene called the doctor's office to see how his lung test had turned out. The office informed him that they had sent out a notice to him, asking him to make an appointment to discuss the tests. Gene never received the notice. When Gene went for his results, he found he had lung cancer. Gene went through the process of chemotherapy and radiation at the Cleveland Clinic. The doctors wanted to operate on his lungs and remove the cancer. The operation was very hard on Gene. It wasn't too long, and my good friend Gene was gone. Gene was one of those people who knew everybody and loved everyone. He was active and an officer in many associations such as the Soybean Association and the Pemberville Elevator. Gene was a Freedom Township trustee for several terms. There is not now a Gene Walston or will there ever be one. This fact is a loss to the world.

The Coon Visitor

The date for this particular party was in the summer of 2003. We were at the Walston farm and were eating supper in the garden. Many times, we would have a light meal with soup, salad, and pie; we usually started with a drink and hors d'oeuvres. The party started in the early evening about six thirty. Because of daylight saving time, the light extended longer into the evening hours, and the sun was still brightly shining. I sat down to enjoy my meal and also to enjoy the fact that the location of the Walston farm was at the top of one of the few hills in Wood County. There were no mosquitoes that evening as was common at many of the other farms and houses in that area, so the view was not spoiled.

As I began to eat my salad, I looked down the hill toward the road and noticed in the field to the east an animal walking across the field. Because of the fact that it was daylight and also of the fact that there were few wild animals, I closely watched the animal cover a path that was straight in line with our little dinner party. As the animal reached the road, which was about one hundred yards from our location, I brought the animal's attention to the rest of the party. The consensus of the group was that a coon was coming directly toward us. Since coons are nocturnal animals, usually awake at night, the chance was very high that something could be wrong with the coon, such as rabies. Sick animals are not common, but I have periodically come across them as I lived most of my life in the country. I was familiar with animals in this condition, and they were not an animal with which you wanted to have close contact. In case the animal has rabies and it was to bite you, there had always been a series of painful shots that one must undergo if they wish to avoid the consequences of rabies. By now, the coon was coming in close enough to see that human beings were present, yet it was still traveling in a straight path toward us. When the coon was over halfway up the lawn, I and the rest of the party wisely decided it was time to go into the house and have something to drink. We waited inside the house for a few minutes and decided to go outside and check on the coon. The coon disappeared, and everyone was happy to see that we did not have the pleasure of seeing the coon again that evening. Some problems work themselves out while others do not. We got lucky.

Neighbors and Their Short Visits

Living in a neighborhood where the neighbors are such a delight is so much better than having to deal with someone who orders you off their property and you didn't even know you were on their property. The following is an example of a friendly and interesting neighbor.

One early evening, Kathy Ninke, a neighbor, was rolling past our house on her covered golf cart. She saw Kathy and me walking around the house, and she pulled into our driveway. We walked over and asked her how she was doing as well as her husband, Jack, and her son, Dean. Everyone was doing well, and we told her everyone was doing pretty well in our family. I asked Kathy, "Where are you going next?" She responded, "I am going up to the cemetery. I hope I don't stay there."

Leaving Henry County

After forty-one years in the field of developmental disabilities, I began to evaluate if it was important for me to continue working. In a few months, my contract was up, and a decision on my employment would need to be made. I had served the five years I had promised myself to give to this job. There were several factors weighing on my mind. One factor that had recently arose was the change in residential funding by the federal government and the associated difficulty of projecting finances. The unpredictable funding was making its contribution to factors such as employee and board satisfaction.

From the beginning of my education and experience as an administrator, there had been some cardinal rules that governed my conduct and that of the board. I had observed times in my career where these rules were not always followed, and when they were not followed, it caused grief for both parties. The first rule is that the administration of the program was the responsibility of the superintendent or CEO. The approval of budgets and finances and setting policy was the board's responsibility. There can be only one boss in either of these capacities. These rules are simple, but they are not always easy to follow. After serving Henry County for five years through many trying fiscal times and challenging personnel times, I was questioning how much longer I wished to carry on these duties. I was beginning to feel uncomfortable with the way I was seeing the future of the program developing. Beliefs that I had about the future of certain aspects of the program were being challenged. My job was getting to the point where it just wasn't fun anymore.

On the other hand, many of the Henry County-based organizations and staff, like other counties I have worked in, were very professional in their actions, and I had enjoyed these relationships. The time was right to face my decision. The question was, should I face it today or in a few days? I decided to face the decision today and avoid uneasiness tomorrow. A considerable amount of energy was given to me by God and probably my twin in facing what was to be the last three months of my employment in Henry County.

Leaving

When the job is not as much fun, it is time to consider moving on. Five challenging years caused me to look closely at where I wanted to go with my time and life. This book had been weighing on me heavily because there was so much to do and, yes, so little time. I felt the Henry County program was in many ways better than when I came, and in others, there was still much work to be done. I had promised myself to stay four to five years, and this was my fifth year. I and many others had done what we could to improve the program, and that is all that one can be expected to accomplish. In times of severe change, it is many times much more work than one anticipated or had time to accomplish. That was the case in Henry County, and I knew it was time to move on to the next challenge. The past must be the past because to try and relive it often is to cheat the present and future out of valuable time and attention.

Honors

Leaving my professional career as an administrator seemed like a good time to review the various times I had been in the right place with the right people to see positive happenings. While my name was placed on many awards, I knew that other people had been there to work with me on these honors. While some of these areas may have been touched on before, the format and explanation of their importance in an accurate chronological timeline summary is important.

I had an appreciation of awards very young in my life as I had gone through Cub Scouts and attained the rank of webelos, the highest rank at that time before becoming a Boy Scout. My parents and Cub Scout leaders made it possible for me to have the appropriate experiences for this award. The religious award in Boy Scouts was the Ad Altare Dei Award, and I was fortunate enough to have the support of my minister and parents to receiving this award.

I had worked for years to become an Eagle Scout. If there had not been scoutmasters and assistant scoutmasters, I would not have attained this honor. I heard a saying when I was young, "You will forget the names of a lot of people in your life, but you will never forget the name of our scout leaders." The names Don Albright, Bill Schlotterer, Len Playko, Lance Young, John Leitz, and Walter Frederick were the names of those leaders. If there had not been merit badge counselors, I likewise would have never attained this goal. My father was always there, making sure that if the chance to pass a milestone toward the Eagle Scout wasn't present, he would find a way. Two of the hardest merit badges at the time were swimming and lifesaving. My medical doctor's daughter, Roberta Kaufman, was encouraging and supportive in passing me on these two merit badges. Herb Hart, the basketball coach and physical development teacher, worked with me on the merit badges related to sports and physical fitness. It had been fifteen years since a new Eagle Scout badge had been awarded in Willard. I can still see the packed room of people at Xavier Hall from my family, my neighborhood, and the community who were in attendance and took part in this impressive Court of Awards.

At John Carroll University, there were many organizations I had the opportunity to join. One of those organizations I did not have control over joining but was given the opportunity to be a member was the National Honorary Society in Psychology called PSI CHI. Fr. G. F. Williams S. J. was the head of the psychology department and the organizer and moderator of this new society on John Carroll's campus. Father Williams was always available and would meet with students on our turf, even the local pub, to discuss our concerns and our lives.

From 1971 to 1973, I and many other coworkers were extremely active on a statewide basis in an organization called the Ohio Athletic Association for the Mentally Retarded and Developmentally Disabled. I had the opportunity to work with many committed professionals such as Doug McVey and Barb Smola from the Northwestern Ohio area. Because of all our achievements, I was a member of the state board and was named the outstanding male member of the association in 1972. The Ohio Athletic Association was to become the Ohio Special Olympics. My roots thus go back to the beginning of the Ohio Special Olympics, and I have been fortunate to be able to be the co-meals coordinator. I was singled out to receive five awards from the Ohio Special Olympics and Wood County Special Olympics. One was in 1988; I was named the honorary coach of the Summer Ohio Special Olympics game because of the work of all the people on the meals committee. The summer games is a combination of five thousand participants, coaches, and volunteers and holds its summer games at Ohio State University each year.

It would not be fitting to discuss this section without giving credit to the person responsible for the Ohio Athletic Association and the beginning of the Ohio Special Olympics, Mr. Dick Ruff. Dick was missing from birth sections of his arms and one foot. Dick was the placekicker for the Ohio State Buckeyes in his college days. His physical limitations were not noticeable as he golfed, swam, and functioned as you or I do. Dick was a truly remarkable person and gave guidance to many young aspiring physical development specialists. Many of these young men became leading managers in the field.

While employed in the Toledo area, several talented people worked with the city of Toledo to start a recreation program for people with handicaps. The organization was one of the first of its kind in the nation and was called Toledo's Organized Recreation Program for the Community's Handicapped. Champion Spark Plugs sponsored a summer day camp through TORCH and recognized the founding board members for their contributions. Since I had no children around 1971, I was active with another Toledo-based organization, Big Brothers of Northwest Ohio.

I had many good experiences with Herbie and Kurt and was delighted to receive my five years of service pin.

While an employee of the state of Ohio at NODC in 1981, I worked with the staff to produce a program that broke down the various jobs within NODC. I documented responsibilities for the major jobs at the center and produced a grid that compared and contrasted the various positions chart. The system was judged as a top idea in the state of Ohio, and I was awarded a plaque for Meritorious Service for Heroic and Extraordinary Contributions to the state of Ohio. The award was worth several thousand dollars, but as an employee of the state, I was ineligible for the compensation.

Jim Moore was the mayor of New Rochester for as long as I can remember. There was never an election; it was just the fact that Jim was mayor. When Jim passed away in the late 1980s, people began to call me the mayor of New Rochester. Whenever any type of business came up associated with the unincorporated village, I would attend the meetings and make sure that citizens were informed on the progress of any projects. The last project was the inability of the village to drain water from its various properties. It is an interesting job that at times is very busy but other times is slow. I don't know that I will have to worry about my successor as I will not be in a position to push anyone for appointment.

In 1982 and 1985, Eastwood School awarded a VIP award from Pemberville Elementary School, and a scholarship was established in my name and the name of a local pastor, Larry Nelson. Since I was on the local parent-teacher board serving as a member and president, these facts must have contributed to my VIP award.

In 1990 I had the honor of being president of the Special Education Advisory Board at BGSU. Dr. Ed Fiscus, department chair, surprised me with a Special President's award. Although I received the award, the board was successful because of the efforts of the entire board.

Another surprise award was presented by four Eagle Scouts I counseled for their Eagle Scout Award. The scouts were Ed Hammett, son of Ed and Pat; Brian Hampshire, son of Jim and Nelore; Wes Sweeney, son of Bruce and Karen; and Mark Frederick, our son. The four boys worked hard for their award, and I was happy to see them achieve the honor. Their Eagle project was to establish the Block Watch program under the guidance of the Wood County Sheriff Department. This program registered Freedom Township residents in a program in which citizens watched their neighbors' homes for any possible wrongdoing. I appreciated the gift of an engraved plaque.

The next surprise award was from an organization that yearly honors individuals who do good things for others. The committee functions as a fine oiled machine. The awarding from the Black Swamp Humanitarian Awards Committee for Volunteer Leadership as their chairperson held a special place in my heart. The presence of both my sons, Joe II and Mark, at the awards ceremony made the event a bit more special.

It is evident that each of these awards involved the efforts of many other people. I hope all of them shared in the awards they have bestowed on me.

PART IV

Grandchildren

CHAPTER 13

Grandchildren

Everyone who has been a grandmother or grandfather knows that one of the greatest joys in one's life is being close to the grandchildren to whom they have been blessed. As the saying goes, we can spend time with our grandchildren, spoil them, and send them home. We have been blessed with two grandchildren, Zachary and Joshua. We will share some of the most delightful experiences we have thus far had with our grandchildren.

First Comes Zachary

Birth of Zachary

I was at work on the morning of December 4, 2003, and I received a call at work from Kathy informing me that Tara and Joe were at the St. Anne Hospital in Westerville, and Tara would be delivering our first grandchild within the next few hours. Kathy called me, and I finished a meeting and picked up the final accreditation report from Kaye, my staff member responsible for accreditation, which was due in Columbus at the state office within the next few days. I would then be on my way to New

Rochester to pick up Kathy and then to Columbus. I figured my part would be to put in time at the waiting room. Kathy and I picked up a quick lunch as Joe had called us again and said the labor had slowed down.

We entered the hospital, found the waiting room for the delivery rooms, and saw Peggy and Ed Mobley, Tara's parents, and her brothers Jeff and Ryan. Everyone was there but our son Mark, who was deer hunting in Southern Ohio. Within a few minutes, Mark appeared in full hunting gear before the birth had taken place. I was reassured by Joe that the baby wouldn't be delivered for the next two hours, so I had time to deliver the compliance document to the Department of Mental Retardation in Downtown Columbus. Kathy reminded me that the baby could come early so I shouldn't be spending much time talking to the people in central office. I took off for downtown, made the delivery, and returned in time for the birth. The birth was to take place a few minutes after I returned to the hospital. Joe came out of the delivery room all smiles and not saying anything. Everyone had looks of joy as Joe walked in, but no one except Joe knew what had transpired in the delivery room. Within a few seconds, Joe informed everyone that we had a new baby, Zachary Joseph Frederick. This was the first child on both the Frederick and Mobley family. Everyone was laughing, smiling, and just plain relieved and jovial that the birth was complete, and we did, in fact, have a new baby.

Unlike the birthing process that Kathy and I had gone through, where visiting was very restrictive, Tara and Joe had a birthing room, and everything was homey, and everyone was able to be in the room with Tara, Joe, and now Zachary. The baby was passed around. Joe was happy. Tara looked like a million bucks after just delivering the baby. The nurse and doctor were doing all the things they are supposed to do with a new baby. I noticed that Zach had my blond hair. This was to be one of the happiest minutes of all our lives.

The Racing Heart

A few months later, Kathy and I happened to be in Columbus for a work-related activity when we received a call from Joe that Zachary had a racing heart, and they were taking him to children's hospital. We found Tara, Joe, and Zachary in one of the small private waiting rooms. It seemed that Zachary would become very active as if his heart was beating really fast. An X-ray had been completed, and he was to go to one of the treatment areas. By this time, Peggy, Ed, Ryan, and Jeff, Tara's family, was there, and Mark, our son had made it to the hospital. It seemed like forever before we went to the treatment area that resembled an operating room. The treatment room was very scary. Within a few minutes, the room was filled with doctors, nurses, and people taking notes on the treatment process. Shortly after everyone entered the treatment area, Zachary had a spell, and his body began to shake. The doctors and nurses began to wrap his little body in ice so that his heartbeat would stabilize. Medications were given, and blood was drawn so that it could be sent to the laboratory at Ohio State to confirm the diagnosis. That diagnosis was that a virus had gotten into the bloodstream and caused the irregular heartbeat on Zachary.

We left the hospital, except for Tara and Zach, and the medication seemed to be working. The next day, we received a call in the early afternoon that Zachary was doing much better, and the blood tests confirmed the diagnosis that the irregular heartbeat was caused by a virus of unknown cause. That was the first and hopefully last time we are exposed to this medical complication.

First Fish

When Zachary was three years old, Joe and I decided that he was old enough to go fishing. We had some worms and an easy-to-use fishing pole, so we took off for Alexander's pond. The pond was a favorite for young children as one was almost sure that they would catch a fish. Many times, I had taken my wife's class fishing there, and everyone always caught a fish, usually a blue gill. On this particular occasion, we had baited up three fishing poles, each having a bobber, a hook, and a worm. We figured this would improve Zach's chances of pulling in a fish. Shortly after we had thrown in the line, there was a bite on one of the lines on the south side of the pond. Zachary took the pole and began to reel it in like a champ. It became apparent that this was not a small fish. I thought it must be a bass by the way it was fighting. Zachary reeled the fish in until it was next to the shore. Joe pulled up the line and the fish to find out that it was a two-pound catfish. Zach took one look at the fish and decided he didn't want any part of this ugly-looking fish!

A Phone Call from Zachary

When Zachary began to talk, he would like to call Grandpa and Grandma Frederick. On this particular call, Zachary was around three years old, and we were not home when Zachary called. Zach had had Mom or Dad dial the number, and a click came on the phone like someone was answering, but it was really the answering machine. Zach was very busy talking, and he said "Grandpa, Grandma, I love you." At this point, he heard the recording, and Zachary said, "Grandpa and Grandma, where are you?" I guess we should have stayed home.

On another occasion, Grandma was home to receive a phone call from Zachary. Zach said to Grandma, "When are you coming down to see me?" Grandma said, "We will be there after you sleep for two nights." Zachary asked, "Do you have any cookies?" Grandma responded, "Zachary, I always have cookies." Zachary then responded, "Grandma, can we stop talking now?"

In another phone call with Grandpa Frederick after Zachary had talked for a period, Zachary said, "Grandpa, my long talk is done."

In early 2008, I was talking to Zachary, and he said, "That's all I can say. Talk to my mom."

A Ride in the Cemetery

On February 24, 2007, Zachary, Joe, and Grandpa and Grandma Frederick were taking a ride around the country block. In the process of taking that ride, it was decided that a quick trip around Fish Cemetery was in order. Fish Cemetery is located behind and can be seen from Grandma and Grandpa's house. As we began to go around the cemetery, the adults began to reminisce about a fox's den that was located to the south of the cemetery. Since the fox had not been seen much in the cemetery area in recent years, the point was mentioned that the coyotes were replacing the fox in the area. Zachary saw a squirrel that was running through the snow and asked what had happened to the squirrel's tail as the squirrel had no tail. Nobody came up with an explanation as to why the squirrel had no tail, so Zachary said, "The coyote or fox got it (the tail) and buried it in the snow." That explanation was better than any explanation given by the adults.

Florida

On May 3, 2007, Tara, Joe, Zachary, Joshua, Grandpa, and Grandma Frederick took off for Pensacola, Florida, for a week's vacation. I was beginning to occupy my place in the van when Zachary saw some red licorice. He asked me for a piece, but Tara had told me that she did not want the kids to eat licorice in the car at this time. I told Zach he could have the licorice later. Zach said, "I can hold the red licorice and not eat it." I did not give Zach the licorice at that time.

The weather was beautiful, and we spent much of the day on the beach or in the swimming pool. At night, we would sometimes eat out and at times eat in. Tara had a friend, Amy, who lived in the area who was also in her wedding. Amy had a friend named Bill, so they both came over to swim and eat. On one afternoon, Joe, Bill, and I went to a large fish market and bought shrimp and fish for an evening meal. Some people liked salmon, others mahi-mahi, and others trout. Joe and Bill barbecued the seafood, and a delicious meal was had by all. On the next day, Amy and Bill came over to the resort to go swimming in the pool. Amy was swimming with Zachary and asked him if he was going to be a doctor when he grew up. Zach didn't give a response. Amy then asked if he was going to be a fireman. This question was right up Zachary's alley because not only did he have several fire trucks, but he also had a full-fledged fireman's outfit consisting of hat, coat, and boots. Zachary looked at Amy and said, "I already am a fireman!"

Later that day, I was assigned the task of watching Josh, our second grandchild. I was well aware of the proverb "Anything that can go bad will go bad." I was on my best guard with Josh because the cute little toddler was also the one who could produce actions that made me look like I wasn't doing my supervisory duties. Josh had been under my supervision for at least five minutes playing on the pool deck. Joe walked by, supervising Zach, when he asked me how Josh had received the skinned chin. Sure enough, Josh had a skinned chin. I did not answer the question but resolved myself to do a better job of watching Josh. Unbeknownst to me, Zach had found a stone on the bottom of the pool and placed it on the pool deck. I took Josh over by Zach to watch him swim. I couldn't see Josh's mouth, but Joe could and said, "Dad, Josh has a stone in his mouth." I don't know how it happened, but Josh found a stone and put it in his mouth. I had flunked child supervision twice in less than fifteen minutes.

About the same time of year, Kathy was babysitting with Zach and Joshua. Zachary looked over at Grandma and said, "Grandma, you are a good babysitter because you watch baby (meaning Joshua) and the trucks."

The Parade

Zachary and Joshua both love to play with their fire truck, police cars, ambulances, and other small cars and trucks. Earlier that day, Zachary had gone to New Albany grade school to help Tara set up her classroom. On this particular evening, Joe was watching his sons. Joe had convinced Josh to go to bed, but he was having a tougher time with Zach. Zach had his cars and trucks in a line on the kitchen table. Joe reminded Zach that he had promised him to go to bed. Zach said, "I can't." Joe asked, "Why not?" Zach said, "I'm organizing this parade."

"Speak, Monkey, Speak"

Zachary enjoyed talking. One day Joe was watching Zach. Joe then started to play a game that he learned with his brother, Mark, and father to quiet things down. It is called "Speak, Monkey, Speak." The game goes like this. The leader will say the following words:

"Order in the court,
The monkey wants to speak,
Speak, monkey, speak."

At this point, everyone is quiet, and the first person to speak is the monkey, and the first speaker also loses the game. Zach is learning not to be the monkey.

Playing with Legos

Zachary has a passion to play with Legos. He probably inherited this trait from his father and is good at pulling others into paying with Legos. On one day in October, Zach was playing in the living room of Grandpa and Grandma's house. Zach had just directed Grandpa by saying,

"Grandpa, you sit here and help." Then he said to Grandma, "Grandma, you are not helping."

Birthday

Zachary's fourth birthday was December 4, 2007. On that day, Grandma Frederick had taken him to the Dairy Delight for an ice cream cone. After coming out of the Dairy Delight, Zach said, "I need to go to the Hallmark Store." Grandma Frederick said, "Why?" Zachary said, "It is my birthday, and I think I need a card."

Later that day, Grandma and Grandpa called Zach to wish him a happy birthday. The phone rang, and Joe gave him the phone as Zach was in the bathtub. Zach took the phone and said, "The birthday boy is taking a bath."

Great Wall of China

One day Tara was taking the boys, Zach and Josh, with her to do an errand. As Tara came around a curve on I-280, she noticed a big wall that had been constructed. Tara said to Zach, "Look at this tall wall." Zach responded, "It looks like the Great Wall of China."

Crescent Moon

Kathy reminded Tara of how Zach had been eating his round waffle and had eaten all but one section that looked like a moon. As Kathy noticed that the waffle had now been reduced to a small moon, Zach confirmed her belief by saying, "Grandma, this waffle now looks like a crescent moon." At this point, Kathy is wondering where he got the word "crescent moon." Kathy decided that some things are meant to be a mystery, and crescent moon was one of these times.

One evening Kathy was putting Zach to bed. She took him to the window to look at the moon. She said, "Look at the beautiful moon, Zachary!" Zachary said, "Grandma, that is a crescent moon." Out of the mouths of babes!

Guided Tour in the Basement

Zachary and Joshua both love to go into the old basement of Grandma and Grandpa's home. Our house is over one hundred years old, and the basement is old and dark. One half is a wine cellar, and the other half is the furnace, fruit cellar, and storage. On this particular day in 2007, Zach had the idea that all children and adults needed to go on a tour of the basement. The first need for each participant was a flashlight. The next need was to have a name tag for each of the participants. After turning off the basement lights, we went down the steps. Everyone was very quiet. Zach led the pack, Josh was second, and everyone else kind of fell into the line of Joe, Tara, Grandma, Grandpa, and Mark. After passing through the wine cellar, the highlight of the trip was upon us. In the second room was stored Uncle Mark's deer decoy. As we passed the deer, Zach would touch the deer, and Josh would pet the deer, usually three times. The next part of the tour was to kick the big exercise ball. Josh, being a toddler, needed to be very careful because the connection of the two rooms had a raised bump that was tall enough for Josh to trip and fall on. After the tour was over, it was time to immediately start a new tour through the entire basement and observe each of the favorite points of interest again. This tour could be repeated many, many, many times.

Christmas Presents

Christmas for 2007 was to happen shortly after Zachary's fourth birthday. One evening in the middle of December, Zachary was listening to a nighttime story from his mother about the *Berenstain Bears*. In the book, it talked about the little bears going out and buying gifts for their mother and father. After the book was over, Zachary began to cry. His mother asked him, "Zachary, what is wrong?" Zachary answered, "I do not have any presents for Mommy and Daddy for Christmas."

Tara said that she would ask her mother, Peggy, to take him Christmas shopping. So four-year-old Zachary and his grandmother, Peggy, as well as his grandfather, Ed Mobley, went shopping. All did not start out on the right foot for the shopping outing, for as the three of them were leaving the car to go out to supper, the smell of dog-doo was very strong in the back seat of the car where Zachary was sitting. A further investigation showed that Zachary had somehow stepped in dog-doo, and it was all over the bottom of his shoes. The Mobley grandparents cleaned up the mess, and they were off to supper and shopping. As they began to walk through the various departments in the store, Zachary saw some bras and announced that he wanted to buy his mother a bra. Peggy said, "Zachary, Why do you want to buy your mother a bra?" Zachary answered calmly, "Because she only has two of them." Peggy moved on to the jewelry department and convinced Zachary to buy Mommy a pair of earrings. Daddy was to receive an ice scraper, and little brother Joshua was to open a play truck. The truck I assume was one that Zachary could also enjoy.

Shoveling Snow

In January 2008, Joe and Tara had put their house up for sale on Woodstream Boulevard. On this particular afternoon, Tara had allowed the boys to play in the snow. The boys had been out for their allotted time, and Tara wished them to come in the house before they could test their ability to stay out in the cold. Joshua was about ready to come in, so he was very compliant about entering the house. Zachary, on the other hand, never wants to leave the white stuff and continued to shovel snow long after his mother had asked him, "Please stop playing in the snow, and please come into the house." After two or three unanswered requests by Tara, she was forced to personally confront Zachary to come in the house to get warm. Zachary became somewhat emotional with Tara's request of leaving the snow in favor of the house and said as he also began to cry, "Mom, all I want to do is shovel the snow." Tara responded, "You can shovel snow another time, but you are cold and need to come in the house." This experience just goes to show us that working is no substitute for obeying mother's request, especially when the request is coupled with trying to keep us healthy.

The Fireman

Zachary loved playing a fireman. It so happens that in July 2008, Zach was playing with the hose. He could play with the hose with his parents' permission but not otherwise. On this day, Zach was playing fireman with the hose without his parents' permission. His father asked him what the deal was in playing with the hose. Zach said, "It was like this when I got here" (meaning the hose had water coming out the nozzle). It was pretty hard to take away the hose. Zach later told us he was kidding about the hose being out and on.

The Pemberville Fair

The Little House in the Cemetery

My wife, Kathy, was bringing the boys back to our house from Columbus to stay with us a few days and to go to the 2011 Pemberville Fair with us. The boys were excited about the fair for several reasons, one being that they each had a collection to enter in the fair. Zach had his pencil collection and Josh his jumping beans collection.

As the three of them were traveling through Findlay, Zach noticed something in the cemetery. He asked Kathy, "What is that little house in the cemetery?" Kathy said, "The little house is called a mausoleum, and people who die are buried there." Without missing a beat, Zach said, "I want that little house."

By the way, the boys also entered vegetables and several flowers in the fair. Each of them did well as they each earned ten ribbons.

Zach and the Fair—Again

It is August 2012, and the boys are here for the Pemberville Free Fair. Once again, the boys entered their collection. Zach had the shells he had collected from Pensacola, and Josh entered marbles. As usual, flowers and vegetables were entered.

Zach had shown an interest in the games on the midway the first night of the fair. The interest was more like a driving force that he needed to play toss games, or he didn't know what he would do. Kathy told Zach she was not going to give him money for the games as she felt it was a waste. Zach had his mind set on popping a few balloons with darts for a pillow with money printed on it. Kathy said she had a lot of jobs that needed to be done, and she would pay Zach for his time and energy. Zach agreed. Kathy offered the some proposal to Josh. Josh informed Kathy that he was not interested as he was planning on borrowing money from his elder brother when he was paid for his jobs.

Zach worked very hard on several jobs the next morning. When afternoon came and Zach had been paid, he was ready to go to the fair. Zach had been notified that he had won first place and best in class for his shells and was to have his picture taken for the local paper. I told Zach that I would take him to Pemberville for his picture, and we would see what he could do with his $15 in the midway.

We reached the fair, had Zach's picture taken, and then headed for the midway. Zach walked up to the balloon tent and told the proprietor that he wanted to play. He gave the man $5 and popped enough balloons to win a prize. Another $5 and he had a small pillow with a dollar bill printed on it. He won his prize. His prize was a very small pillow. However, Zach wanted the very large money pillow. Zach went through his money and the same amount of Grandpa's money, but he was beaming from ear to ear. He had won his big pillow! He looked at Grandpa and said, "I have to win something for Grandma." Another $15 and enough broken balloons put Zach in a happy mood with two prizes. It was a good day for Zach and a draining day on Zach's and Grandpa's wallet.

Now We Have Joshua

Birth of Joshua

The date is April 26, 2006. Once again, we received a call from Joe, our son, that Tara is about to have their second child at St. Anne's Hospital. Joe is back with Tara as everyone else had just said good luck to Tara before they went back to the waiting room. The cafeteria is nearby, so a few of us went down to have some pastry and a drink as we waited for the arrival of the baby. The wait was short again, and out came Joe with a big smile on his face. For a few minutes, he just looked around at everyone as they waited to hear the news about the new baby. Joe proudly announced that it was a boy, and his name was to be Joshua Ryan Frederick. Within a few minutes, the family filed into the birthing room to get their first view of this new baby, Joshua. Unlike Zach, Josh has dark hair like the Mobleys instead of the blond hair of the Fredericks. Unlike Zach, Joshua was going to redo the charts when it came to a challenging little boy.

Joshua's Independence

From the very beginning, Josh always knew what he wanted and, like his elder brother, went after it. From the beginning, Joshua was a very good baby. Shortly after Joshua was walking, he was into every room and every corner he wished to explore. He was an inquisitive little boy. It was on such a day that Kathy and Tara were child sitting with Zack and Joshua. Zach had been taken to preschool, and Josh was busy running around the house. Kathy and Tara were sitting in the front room when Josh came running in with a hot spoon that he gave to Kathy. Kathy felt the heat on the spoon and asked Tara where he could have gotten a hot spoon. Both Tara and Kathy went into the kitchen, only to find that Josh had somehow opened the running dishwater to extract the spoon. Later that day, Josh was found in the oven, only the oven was cold instead of hot.

Joshua's Ears

It was Christmastime 2007, and the Frederick family from Columbus was visiting Grandpa, Grandma, and Uncle Mark in New Rochester. The first night, Zachary came up with a bad ear infection and went to the emergency room for treatment. The second night, Joshua had an ear infection, and it was off to urgent care. Tara and Joe were in the urgent care waiting room when Josh decided to put on an act. He would go to Tara and whisper in her ear and then laugh. Joe received the same treatment. Finally, the nurse said, "You may come into the examination room." As Joe and Tara walked into the room, they were getting themselves prepared for the worst because Josh despised anyone looking into his ears. As the wise doctor came in, he told Josh that he needed to look into his ears. He went a step further by telling Josh that he was going to look into his mother's ears first. The doctor looked into Tara's ears and told Joshua he needed to look into his ears. Josh lay on his back and allowed the doctor to look into one ear and then the other. Joe and Tara couldn't believe their eyes as nobody had an easy time looking into Joshua's ears. The doctor then gave a shot to Joshua, and this procedure was not as easily accomplished. The doctor said that the shot would start working immediately, and it did.

No Horses in Our House

Grandma Frederick was in Columbus watching the boys. There had been much activity this morning. Grandma thought that she could calm things down. As Josh was beginning an activity in fast mode, Grandma asked Josh, "Hold your horses." This phrase means to slow down. Josh looked at Grandma and said, "We don't have any horses, Grandma."

Not Kathy

My brother Mike and his wife, Marge, happened to stop by our house near the end of July 2009. My son Joe was home with Tara and Zach and Josh. Our two families had always been together as the other brothers live out of state. Mike was talking to Kathy, and he addressed her as Kathy. Josh was playing near Mike, and he stood up and put his hands on his hips. Three-year-old Josh said to Mike, "She's not Kathy. She is Grandma."

High Five

One afternoon Kathy and I were watching the boys in Columbus. Josh and I were playing with his train set. Josh had completed the assembly of his train track and had done an excellent job. I told Josh that he had done a great job. I then told him to give me a high five. As I looked at Josh, I noticed that he had his right thumb in his mouth. His right hand was the hand that he usually gave me a high five. I had already started to give him a high five, so I continued my follow-through. Josh finished his high five by hitting my right hand with his right hand. His thumb was still in his mouth when he completed the high five.

The Stairs

One afternoon in the summer, Josh and Zach were busy in the house playing. Zach went to Tara in the kitchen and said, "Josh is doing something wrong." This was exactly what Tara wanted to hear! Tara immediately walked into the great room to see what Josh was doing. Josh was nowhere to be seen in the great room. Tara looked up and saw Josh almost at the top of the stairs on the outside ledge of the stairs holding onto the stair rails. Yes, Josh was doing something wrong!

The Barn

We had a big barn that I had built for Joe so he could store their tractors and equipment. Mark was on the porch with Josh. Mark heard a bloodcurdling yell from Josh and saw he had lower the roof on the barn and caught his finger in the crack. All the men child sitting were trying to find out how serious the finger was hurt so proper medical help could be attained. Josh was having no part of any investigation or any part of any treatment. He figured he did it, and it was nobody else's concern. We put ice on the finger, only to find out we were not going to inspect this finger. The finger did move, so we thought it must not be too badly hurt. Josh held his hand high for three days, telling everyone his finger was hurt but allowing no one to see it. The finger healed, but the basic principle of the curse of man had prevailed. If anything is going to happen, it will be when the men are on duty.

Playing in the Basement

Josh is to wear his helmet when he is riding his bicycle in the basement. One day in February 2010, Josh was riding his bicycle without his helmet, and he fell off the bike and hit his head hard on the concrete floor. After he had recuperated from his fall, he put on his helmet and proceeded to reenact the original fall. As he got up from his second fall in which he hit his head and helmet on the floor, he said, "That wasn't too bad."

God

Josh wasn't feeling well on Sunday morning, but it was thought he felt good enough to attend church. When we arrived at church, Josh was not doing well. Tara stayed with Josh in the vestibule. At the end of Mass, the priest is one of the first people out of Mass. Seeing the priest with all his vestments on, Josh said, "There is God." He did say it not only once but also many more times.

Easter Bunny

A week and a half before Easter when Joshua was four years old, he called Grandma Frederick on Daddy's cell phone. Joe did the dialing. Grandma answered the phone and was delighted to talk to Josh. Grandma asked Josh if he was on his way to school. He assured Grandma that he was. Grandma asked if Josh had seen the Easter Bunny. Josh replied, "Yes, Grandma." Josh went on to tell Grandma that he saw the Easter Bunny, and the Easter Bunny winked at him out of the corner of his eye. After the wink, Josh relayed that he and the Easter Bunny had a snowball fight. After the snowball fight, they had an egg fight. Josh's imagination continues to grow.

Santa Claus

Like all children Josh's age, he was very excited about Christmas. He had his Christmas list and was counting the days. Joshua had a difficult time sleeping the night before Christmas. Santa did come and brought Joshua many lovely gifts. When Josh was asked about Christmas, he shared with us that in the wee hours of Christmas Eve, he actually saw Santa Claus in his sleigh pulled by his reindeers and waved to him outside his bedroom window. What a night!

Sue's Cat

In October 2009, Sue, our neighbor, had a beautiful white-and-black pet cat. One day the cat had ventured into our yard. Josh saw the cat and asked the cat to come to see him. Beau, the cat, would not come to Josh. Josh asked, "Why didn't the cat come to me?" He then said, "He probably didn't come because he didn't know my name." Josh then proceeded to say "Well, I am Josh Frederick." The cat still didn't come to Josh on its own.

Great-Grandma Long

Joshua's imagination can be beyond creative. For example, one day he was with Kathy, and he began to tell her about his recent sleepover with Kathy's mother. The occasion was very special. Joshua told the story very sincerely by saying, "No one else was there but Great-Grandma and me at the sleepover." It seems they had a very good sleepover except for one small detail. Josh was never at Great-Grandma's for any type of sleepover. It didn't matter to Joshua though; he had a great time.

John Deere Tractors

Over the years, we have acquired a sizable collection of toys, especially John Deere tractors and implements. In the summer of 2010, Josh was playing with the barn I had made for his father over thirty-five years ago and the John Deere play things when he said to Kathy very convincingly, "You have so many John Deere tractors at your house that we should take some of those to my house so I could play with them. You have lots more John Deere tractors than we do, and if we took them to our house to play, we could bring them back to your house when we come to visit you." It was a good argument, but in the end, the John Deere equipment stayed at our house so that there would be something special for our grandchildren to play with when they visit.

The Mouse and the Sandbox

I had built a large sandbox at the boys' house that was over six feet by six feet. At night, a huge tarp was put on the sandbox so that leaves and other critters would not get in. The tarp had been successful in keeping out cats and dogs and usually was successful keeping out mice except for July 2010. On this particular day, the tarp was removed from the sandbox, and it was easy to see the tarp had not done its job. A family of mice had moved in. Josh was not a happy camper when he saw his father dispose of the mice. In fact, his words were very descriptive about how the situation should have been handled. Josh's words to Kathy were "My dad killed those mouses. They are so cute. We could use them for pets in the house." Josh obviously did not have his way on the mice.

The Snake

This is another sandbox story. Living in the country, the boys' sandbox was occasionally visited by a snake. Kathy and I were watching the boys that day. As we helped take off the tarp, we discovered a tiny black snake sleeping in the sandbox. We decided to relocate the snake. We caught it in a bucket and took it for a ride down the road. After we had gone a few miles, we decided to turn it loose in a field. As the snake hurried away, Josh said, "I'll bet that poor snake will really miss its mommy." We told Josh that the snake would be OK. That was really sweet that a little boy would be that concerned about a little snake.

Surprises

Josh and Zach were visiting our house before the Christmas season in 2010. I was in the basement working on my wine, and Josh came down the steps with a flashlight, searching the basement. I asked him what he was doing, and he told me, "Looking for the deer." My son Mark has a life-size deer decoy that he used for hunting, and the boys in the past had come to the basement to go on a hunt to find the deer. Josh also relayed to me that he was afraid.

I watched him go to the second room of the basement where the deer was stored. As Josh went into the room, he was looking to the left where the deer was not stored. I told him to look around real good as the deer was in that room. Josh had been looking for some time in all the wrong spots. Just as he was about to give up, he saw the deer. As he saw the deer, he jumped into the air and almost dropped the flashlight. He informed me that he was afraid of the deer as he went upstairs.

Later in the day, it was decided that Zach, Josh, Grandma Kathy, and I would go to the variety store in Bowling Green called Ben Franklin. Zach had a little money, and Josh was good at spending Grandpa and

Grandma Frederick's money. Ben Franklin has many kinds of toys that can be purchased. Zach was occupied with a stuffed animal toy, while Josh was looking at anything that had a price tag.

At one point, Josh picked up a wooden box and tried to slide the top open. After some effort, Josh opened the box, and a small plastic mouse jumped out at him and scared him out of his pants. After his first experience, Josh decided that he liked to be scared. Josh then began to open the box, and each time he did, he would jump and shout out words of surprise as the mouse came out of the box. It was my turn to open the box and be afraid as Josh laughed at me for being afraid. What a great day!

A May Visit in 2011

It was time to visit our grandsons as they were both on baseball teams, and this was the only time we could see them play this summer. Our son Joe was coaching both Zach's and Joshua's teams, so we were interested in seeing how Joe could be coaching two teams at the same time.

We went to Zach's first-grade class when we arrived in New Albany at a little before noon. We had stopped at Wendy's for his lunch and were with him at the New Albany Kindergarten First Grade School, where he was to eat lunch with us. Zach was also allowed to bring with him a guest, and he brought with him a very pleasant young lady classmate. Zach ate, as did his friend. It was time to go as Zach needed to get back to class.

Our next stop was at Joshua's school, the Jewish Preschool. As we were waiting for Josh to get out of class, we noticed Tara's niece walking down the hall to her nursery school class. I was standing by the door waiting for Josh to come out the door. It was not quite time for him to be leaving. As I peeked around the corner, I saw a young boy dart by the door. I looked again as did this student, and it was Josh. He smiled and said hi and was gone until he was dismissed. We left school with Josh and pulled up to Wendy's just as three New Albany police officers were leaving.

Policemen and firemen are favorites of both Josh and Zach. We watched the policemen leave.

The meals were ordered, and we began to eat after a brief prayer. Josh is a talker and began to amuse Kathy and I as soon as we began to eat. Josh could not wait to tell us about his Grandpa Mobley. It seems that Grandpa Mobley is a great juggler. In fact, he was recently at Josh's house, and he was juggling balls. Josh then said, "Grandpa Mobley is a great juggler, but he drops the balls." The story was so hilarious that eating stopped, and laughing began. We were all three laughing so hard about the dropped balls that people around were beginning to give us the "What is so funny?" look. Kathy and I had never heard about the juggler story and were wondering if Grandpa Mobley really did juggle and if he really dropped the balls.

No sooner had we calmed ourselves down from the juggling act than Josh began to tell us a story about his father. Josh said, "I had a question for my dad." Kathy and I both bit, "What did you ask your father?" Josh said, "I asked him how many chucks could a woodchuck chuck." This set all three of us into another laughing spree as that is a line that I always used, and it is always good for a laugh because nobody really knows how many chucks or bites can a woodchuck take. You really had to be there to appreciate the humor. It was time to leave before we got kicked out of Wendy's for making too much noise.

Now it was off to Josh's house. Josh decided to go outside and ride his two-wheeled bike. Kathy was with him. A few minutes later, in comes Kathy with a big smile on her face. I asked, "What happened now?" She proceeded to tell me that "Josh was riding his two-wheeler when he came by me and told me to look. I looked, and he was riding with only one hand on the handlebars, and he told me he was going to ride his bike in the circus using one hand." It wasn't a minute later that he fell off the bike, got up, and announced, "I wasn't going to be able to ride my bike in the circus."

The laughing jag started again for Kathy and me. Josh has a true gift of being funny!

Around that time, we stayed over with Joe and Tara and went to church with them on Sunday morning. It is customary for children to go up at Communion time and receive a blessing from the priest. On this particular morning, I asked Josh to go up to the altar with me. "No, I do not want to go up at Communion time." I offered him a quarter to go up with me. He said, "No." I offered him two quarters to go up with me. He said, "OK."

The Picture

One of the Christmas presents from Zach and Josh was a picture of the two boys in a wooded area near their home. Josh had his arm around Zach, and they were both laughing and seemed very happy to be together.

Kathy thought the picture should be in the living room displayed with other family pictures. Josh expressed his desire to have the picture displayed in the kitchen. Kathy assured Josh that the picture looked good in the living room. As Josh was leaving to go home to Columbus, he told Grandma, "I will check next time I come to see that the picture of Zach and me is in the kitchen."

New Albany Elementary School

Kathy and I had gone to visit Josh and have lunch with him as it was Grandparents Day. We sat down with Josh and a couple of his friends. Josh introduced his friends, and then he introduced Kathy and me. After he had introduced us, he followed up with "You know my grandpa is mayor of New Rochester?" His friend didn't miss a beat and said convincingly, "I know where New Rochester is." I just said, "Really?"

Zach and Josh

Emergency Vehicle

Tara had taken Zach and Josh to Tim Hortons in New Albany. It was a great treat for the boys to have a few donut holes and something to drink. On this particular visit, Josh was about twenty months old and appreciating more and more these trips to Tim Hortons. Tara had asked the boys if they wished to go inside the restaurant or just eat and drink their treat inside the car. The first decision by the boys was to have their treat inside the car. Well, this decision changed as soon as they had gone through the drive-through as going inside now sounded much more like fun than eating in the car. Tara picked up the food and drinks along with the two boys and their needed toys and entered the front door of Tim Hortons.

As they sat down at a table, both the boys noted that an ambulance had just parked outside the restaurant, and the whole crew of the emergency medical technicians (EMTs) was about to walk into the restaurant. This sight was heaven to both the boys, fireman and EM personnel and all their vehicles. Well, it just doesn't get any better than this. As the EMTs began to eat their food, Josh's and Zach's eyes were glued to their every move. Josh decided, without telling his mother, that he really wanted to get a little closer to the emergency people, and he jumped down from his chair, ran over to one of the EMT people, and used his famous communication tool, his hand applied to the EMT person's finger. His next step was to pull the person to the desired location, in this case, the big window. As Josh and the emergency person stood in front of the window, Josh used his other communication tool, his finger, to point to the emergency vehicle. The EMT person was very astute and asked Josh if he wanted to see the emergency vehicle. Josh has many words, but the one he was most adept at using was "Yeah." Within a few minutes, Josh and Zach and their mother were on their way to a private showing of the ambulance. Zach was a little shy on viewing the vehicle, but Josh must have figured that this was a once-in-a-lifetime chance, and he wasn't going to miss the chance to see every corner of this big vehicle. The boys and Mom thanked the emergency personnel for the tour, and the boys gave Daddy a blow-by-blow description of the emergency vehicle when he came home that evening.

Pemberville Fair

The Pemberville Fair has been a yearly event for the Frederick family since 1973, the year we moved close to the Pemberville community. Now that our grandchildren are old enough to appreciate the fair, we try to take them each year. One of the big events of the fair is the parade held on the Saturday afternoon of the fair. There are bands, baton twirlers, and the Shriners on small motorbikes, floats, and vehicles such as cars, fire engines, trucks, and emergency vehicles. One of the most popular personalities in town is the UPS man Pete. The parade lasts around two hours, and most of the vehicle entries have one common practice. Most of the people in the parade throw candy to the crowds lining both sides of the street. In 2008, Joshua was at the age where he could skillfully pick up the thrown candy in the street. Zach was very intent on picking up the candy. In fact, he had one and a half bags of candy at the end of the parade. Josh, on the other hand, had his unique approach of eating the candy as fast as was humanly possible. He would eat each piece of candy as he picked it up. Needless to say, Josh had only fifteen pieces of candy at the end of the parade because he was eating candy rather than picking it up and saving it.

Injuries Are OK

At the age of two and a half, Joshua had the ability to instigate an incident and then run. For example, it was not below Josh to hit his brother and take off before the scream of his brother had the chance to develop.

Therefore, it appeared to an unsuspecting person that Josh was an innocent bystander when, in fact, he was the main instigator. His parents were smart enough to thoroughly investigate incidents before laying blame. It also was not uncommon for Josh to be confronted with the evidence of his wrongdoing, and in this case, Josh would look at the accuser, open his large dark eyes, and say, "Sorry." The positive effect on Josh of not doing the act again after his "Sorry" was not so likely.

Josh did, however, come up with the short end of the stick on one occasion. Josh had mysteriously developed a very sore nose. No one seemed to know how the nose was injured, but it was. On the way to the doctor's office, Tara stopped to pick up Zachary at preschool. As Zachary got into the car, he was so glad to see Josh that he shut the door. Joshua screamed bloody murder because Zach had unintentionally slammed the door on his finger. Now Tara had two injuries to report to the doctor. One would have been understood, but two began to look a little suspicious, a fact Tara the teacher was well aware of. In the parking lot, Tara left her seat and went to the back seat to unbuckle the boys. As Tara approached Zach, she told him how sorry she was that he had hurt both his nose and finger. Josh looked up to Tara and said, "Be OK, Mommy." Upon entering the doctor's office, Tara began to explain the background on the nose, which wasn't very detailed. After the doctor had looked at the nose, he gave a prescription and was ready to leave. Then Tara casually mentioned the finger. If needed, Zach was able to collaborate Tara's story on the injury of the finger. The doctor understood the circumstances, looked at the finger, and ordered an X-ray. For your information, the finger was not broken.

Staying in Bed

Until after his second birthday, Josh had not once climbed out of his crib. As his age increased, so did Josh's attempts at risking his life and limb. Without trying hard, Josh could now leave his bed without any help from

Mommy or Daddy. One afternoon about one thirty, Josh had been put to bed at his Grandmother Mobley's house for a nap. There was a garage sale happening, so Tara was at her mother's doing a combined garage sale. Zachary looked at this practice with a great deal of pleasure as he was beyond such a mundane practice of taking naps. About fifteen minutes later, Josh could be heard on the monitor upstairs, saying, "No nap, going down stairs to play." Tara being the ever-present and all-knowing mother quickly slipped out of the kitchen and placed herself just around the corner on the stairs that Josh would be coming down. As Josh came around the corner on the stairway, Tara scooped him up by surprise and carried him up to his waiting bed for his nap. Josh did not come downstairs that day until Tara allowed him to do so AFTER his nap. Josh would have had a better chance of at least making it down the steps if he had not made his intentions known on the monitor or loudspeaker. Behind every young active boy is a waiting mother!

Wheels on the Car

Another incident happened around this time, and it had to do with the boys' Hot Wheels. Zach and Josh both have cars with rubber wheels. Somehow they learned that the wheels come off the cars. Once the wheels come off the cars, they frequently are hard to put back in place as the wheels stretch out. It was for these reasons that both the boys had been instructed not to take the wheels off their cars.

On this particular afternoon, Tara had given Josh a nap, and later he was playing with his cars. Josh was very quiet. Josh was sitting next to his toys. Tara walked in the room and asked Josh what he was doing. Josh replied, "Stay away, Mom. I don't want you to see me." Tara looked anyway and saw that there were three cars in which all the wheels had been removed.

Amish Country

In June 2009, it was decided that Joe, Tara, Josh, and Zach would meet their Great-Grandma Long, Kathy, and me in Amish Country located in Holmes County. We met them at Guggisberg Cheese store. Guggisberg is known for its baby swiss cheese. As we pulled up, we could see that Zach was real busy doing something around the gazebo located near the parking lot. As we walked closer, we could see two kittens under the floor of the gazebo. As Zach would get close to the kittens, they would go back under the gazebo so that we could see them but couldn't catch them. With the cats secured under the gazebo, we proceeded into the cheese factory. Cheese at Guggisberg is made in large stainless steel vats over thirty feet long. Once the milky solution is poured into the vats, there are large paddles driven by overhead chain drives stirring the solution so it eventually solidifies into cheese. It is a process that should be seen in person to be fully appreciated.

After lunch, more like a supper, at the Der Dutchman Restaurant in Walnut Creek, we proceeded to see a friend of my mother-in-law, Reuben. Reuben is an Amish carpenter and has been long-time friends with my mother-in-law and father-in-law. As we opened the door to Joe's SUV, Josh and Zach went straight for the playground area, where they found a sandbox. A sandbox is the ultimate toy to the two boys. Reuben has a shop where he sells a number of items, in addition to woodworking. A few of the items he sells are knives, lamps, and toys. As Zach and Josh came in the door to the shop, they spotted the toys section before the door had closed.

Zach walked over and immediately picked up a pack of plastic animals, marched over to the counter, and placed the bag on the counter, saying, "I want to buy this." Kathy asked him if he had money, and he said, "No, but I want them." Josh found a several piece John Deere tractor set, which was $29. Kathy said, "Josh, this is going to cost a lot of money. Do you have money?" Josh looked at Kathy and seriously said, "I need to take this to my mother's house." Each of the boys was bought a moderately priced toy.

As the day rolled down, we stopped by a bakery called Hershberger's on State Route 577. The pastries were heavenly, and just to the left of the bakery is an animal farm where anyone can for free see and touch the different animals. There are several goats, a draft horse, sheep, chickens, and ponies that could be ridden for a nominal fee. You guessed it; Josh and Zach were on those ponies in a second. It was an eventful day in which Josh was not able to take the expensive set of John Deere tractors to his mother's house.

Forget the Kiss, Mom

Zachary was enrolled in Safety Town in the summer of 2009. Tara and Josh had taken him to Safety Town and waited for the instructor to begin the program. Zach was sitting by some girls his own age. As the program was starting, Mom went up to Zach to say goodbye. Tara could see from Zach's body language this was not a good time for a kiss. Tara went up to Zach and gave him a small hug. Little brother followed Mom and gave Zach a big kiss on his lips. There was nothing Zach could do but take the kiss.

Wendy's

In the late summer of 2009, Kathy and I were watching Zach and Josh. We were taking them to Wendy's for lunch. As we walked in the door, their attention was immediately drawn to the donuts at the adjoining Tim Hortons. We convinced them that we eat first at Wendy's and then come back for a donut. Zach and I went up to order at Wendy's what I had been told to order for Josh and Zach. Somehow the order changed as I was doing the ordering. It would have been much easier for me to allow Zach to order for everyone.

Back at the table, I had gone to get something, and when I returned, there was ranch dressing on the floor, the chair, and the table. Evidently Josh had felt he was to open the ranch dressing when Kathy had already started to open it. The old adage that there can't be two bosses had proven to be true. Despite the loss of ranch dressing, there was still plenty of dip for the chicken nuggets. It was at this time that Zach noted that he had received a prize that was not to his liking. Zach and I went to the counter to exchange it when I discovered there were six people ahead of us. I got in line and then decided that I had already gone through the line. Zach and I went around the six people and exchanged the toy for one of his liking. Josh began to wiggle in his chair when all of a sudden, he fell off his chair.

At this time, Zachary decided to make a spitball and shot me using his straw. As the spitball hit me, the manager happened to be walking by. He looked at Zach and said, "You are having too much fun." A short time later, the manager came over to our table and looked at Zach with a slight smile. Everyone at the table had a laugh with the manager. Josh, not to be outdone by his brother, stood up on his chair. You guessed it; he slid on the chair and almost fell to the floor. Each of the boys was able to have a donut. This was accomplished after the right one was picked after much deliberation.

Glitter Glue

Predicting what is to be said or done by children is not an easy matter. On New Year's Eve 2009, Kathy and I were watching the boys so Mom and Dad could go out for the evening with Mark, Jill, and Bryan. Our evening was to consist of dinner with the boys at Bob Evans and then a few stories and then bed. After we had eaten at Bob Evans, we were to make a quick trip to Kroger's to buy some glitter glue. Glitter glue is pieces of glitter that come in a packet of liquid glue. On our way to Bob Evans, we were all discussing this glitter glue when I said that we would need to buy two glitter glues, one for Josh and one for Zach. Zach said that his dad said that "glitter glue is for older children or adults." Zach said, "Josh cannot play with glitter glue as he will make a mess." I braced myself for some type of disagreement between the boys when Josh calmly admitted, "I will make a mess with glitter glue." That was the end of that discussion; Josh knew his limits with glitter glue and was not afraid to admit it.

Names

One afternoon Zach and Josh were playing indoors. Zach was into full names that day, and he told Josh that his name was Zachary Joseph Frederick. Josh replied that his name was Joshua. Wishing to make the names full, Zach said, "Your name is Joshua Ryan Frederick." Something about this exercise was not to Josh's liking, and he rather loudly announced, "My name is Joshua." Zach didn't wish to miss a chance to instruct his brother and announced to Josh, "You are Joshua Ryan Frederick." At this point, Josh had had enough of this exercise and very loudly announced, "My name is not Ryan! My name is Joshua!" Joshua did not want to hear any more about his name, and the parents made sure he didn't.

Christmas List

It was October 2010, and Zach and Josh were talking about what they wanted for Christmas. Their mother gave them a few of the magazines she had received in the mail that had among other potential Christmas items, toys. Each of the boys was asked to circle those items that they would like for Christmas.

Tara brought the magazines with her the next time she came to our house in New Rochester. She gave the magazines to the boys and suggested they give Uncle Mark a chance to see what they wanted for Christmas. Uncle Mark opened the magazines and let out a big laugh. Kathy walked into the front room and asked Mark why he was laughing. Mark said that every toy in the magazines was circled except for baby toys and toys for girls.

The next suggestion was that each of the boys make out a list of toys they most would like to receive for Christmas. The lists were developed, and Christmas shopping for Zach and Josh was made much easier for all.

Cold Water

In 2011, Zach and Joshua were visiting our house. They were both very thirsty that day. They knew we had cold water in our refrigerator in a plastic container with a spigot on it. The narrow container had cost us less than $10. Josh had taken his drink from the container, and Zach was in the process of filling his cup when he told us how much he liked to drink from our plastic container. He also said that he would like to have one of these water containers at his house. Zach and Joshua had a very expensive refrigerator/freezer that had an ice maker and a water dispenser.

Kathy looked over to the boys and told them that someday their mom and dad would have enough money to be able to buy a water container like ours. They both looked at Kathy, agreeing that someday their mom and dad would have enough money to buy one of our water containers.

A Few Visits

Our grandsons remain a blessing for us. Zachary had just turned eight, and Joshua was five in 2011. We had "just the boys" a couple of times this year, and what fun we had. Zachary helped me weed the garden, and he did a terrific job. Joshua asked Grandma if he could have our house when he grows up and proceeded to tell us all the things he liked about our house, barn, and garden shed. He looked at Grandma and said after some thought, "I guess I will have children of my own." Grandma agreed. When they are with us, their favorite things to do include having a guided tour of the barn, looking for some secret places in this old farmhouse, and going to Bass Pro, Ben Franklin, and Beeker's store. They love playing hide-and-seek. That game is just as much fun and still as scary as it was when we were kids! We are usually pretty tired when they go home, but it is a good kind of tired.

The Lights in the Basement

Kathy, Zach, and Josh decided to go down to the basement in the kids' home in the early part of 2012. As they were about to go down the steps, someone turned on the lights. When they reached the bottom of the steps, they slowly proceeded toward the toys. The fluorescent lights in the basement came on very slow. Someone said that the lights were cheap and came on slow. Josh looked up at Grandma and said, "Don't worry, Grandma, the lights will get lighter."

An Unannounced Visit

In April 2013, I had the pleasure of attending a state of Ohio Special Olympics Committee meeting in Columbus. It had now been forty-two years that I had helped coordinate the meals for the Special Olympics participants and volunteers. I had never seen the Special Olympics offices in Columbus that were purchased in the mid-1980s. On the two-and-a-half-hour trip down, I came into some severe rain and winds. At one point after the Northwestern Ohio city of Carey, the winds were so severe that they had rocked my van back and forth to the point that I put my brakes on to try to minimize the effect of the strong winds. I was concerned that my van would tip over.

I went to the meeting, and when leaving, I decided to make a stop at Joe's house in Galena. As I began to come into New Albany, I saw a sign for Joe's road. My GPS said to go another direction, but the sign said differently. I disregarded my GPS. I looked at a road sign a few blocks away, and I was not on their road. I looked at the GPS, and it said Joe's road was to the right. I called them and reached Tara. I told her I was in the area and would be there in a few minutes. I said goodbye, proceeded down their road, and reached a dead end. I knew the road dead-ended at the other end, so I called again. Joe answered, and I told him my dilemma. He said go north, turn left, and then turn right. I was then on the right section of their road.

I arrived at their house a few minutes later. They had not told Zach and Josh I was coming. I walked up to their bedroom on the second floor and saw Zach's mouth drop and then say, "Grandpa!" I looked at Josh, and he was just staring at me in disbelief. Zach then said, "I suppose Grandma is going to walk in next." I assured him that Grandma was not with me. Josh, without losing a beat, said, "Have you got my birthday present yet?" I assured him it was in the process. With the inclement weather, I decided to start my two-hour trip home. Yes, I did experience several thunderstorms on the way home, but I safely arrived. I went to work on that birthday gift for Josh.

Conclusion

At the time of writing this section, both the boys are in high school. I am happy to say that they have grown to be good students and good boys. They enjoy golf and tennis and being with their friends. We have enjoyed watching them grow, and they are such a blessing in our lives. In addition, we also enjoy going fishing, playing euchre, and eating good food, including Grandma's special cookies!

PART V

Retirement Experience

CHAPTER 14

Retirement Years (2006–2011)

Retirement proved to have many activities not originally planned by Kathy or me. I had had some plans to write this book, and we had planned to do some remodeling of the house. The time required for the book, and for sure the time required to remodel the house was many times the planned time. In addition, there was time for our newly formed church, time for my various extracurricular activities, and time for my family. Each day of the week had its own challenges similar to those I experienced when I was working. This chapter will cover my immediate family, New Rochester neighbors, and our organizations that are so important to our lives, relatives, and friends and other interesting happenings.

Adjusting to Retirement

Some Days One Cannot Make a Nickel

Every once in a while, I have a day when many things seem to go wrong. I would bet that you have had similar days, hopefully not too many of them. On those days, I try very hard to turn around my experiences as I feel that when something goes wrong, I may have some responsibility for the negative happenings. December 27, 2007, was a day when I had a hard time finding positive happenings in my life. I hurriedly began the process and removed the cap on the first bottle of champagne and cleaned out the top of neck of the bottle with my small finger. I looked at my small finger and noticed that it was discolored because I had placed some salve on it the night before. Although I had cleaned my finger earlier, it didn't look good. I threw out the bottle of champagne because I didn't wish to serve possibly contaminated wine. In a short period, I had completed the whole case of champagne.

I was putting away the wine equipment when I noticed that there was an additive called acid that was not added to my last batch of white zinfandel that I had just bottled. I looked at my checklist to see if I had added it and noticed that I had not filled out my checklist and was not sure if I had even stabilized the zinfandel. Stabilizing the wine neutralizes the yeast in the wine and prevents the cork from becoming dislodged. Well, what else can go wrong?

My neighbor Sue Welty had gone to Pennsylvania to visit her daughter Carol and her family. As a result of this trip, I had been asked to house sit, and this included Sue's new cat. When leaving the basement, I lowered my head to miss the low beam and, having thought I had cleared the beam, raised my head. I heard a clink and immediately felt the beam come into solid contact with my head. My second headache of the day was on its way to a rapid fruition.

My second or third bad day, however you wish to view it, started with the occurrence of just one item that went sour. On February 21, 2008, Kathy and I were beginning to clean up two rooms downstairs in our house. We had given our dining room and our living room a facelift by putting coving around the ceiling; painting the walls, ceiling, and windows; and installing hardwood floors in both the rooms. There were five doors to be installed to cover storage areas in the two rooms. I had purchased some new hinges to install the doors on the frames, and the new hinges were exactly the same size as the old. This was a very positive discovery since this would mean that the old holes used by the old hinges could now be used to install the new hinges. Wrong, four out of five of the hinges would not line up with the holes on the new hinges. A twenty-minute job turned into a three-hour job.

That evening, I was invited to the New Rochester Men's Club Card Game. The cards were to be played at Tim Hoepf's house, a member of the club who lives in a nearby town of Bowling Green. Nine people showed up for the festivities. Tim's father, Ray, and brother, Terry, were also present as well as Lonnie and Neil Karns, Ed Hammett, Dave Kimmet, Scot Danielson, all neighbors from the New Rochester area, and me.

We had snacks, sandwiches, and everyone brought their favorite beverage. Well, what does all this have to do with something going wrong? Very easily, I did not have but one or two good card hands all evening. Let's go to the final game. My partner was Scot, and we had come from behind and were now tied at nine to nine with Ed and Dave in our quest to win the ten-point game, my first of the evening. Our partners had made spades trump. This means when spades are trump, if a spade is played, it will beat any other suite such as hearts, clubs, or diamonds except for a higher spade. I had what was called a good euchre hand, meaning I had a good chance of taking three of the five tricks. Any team that takes three tricks gets points regardless who has made trump. Well, the first trick was played on by the other three players, and my partner, Scot, had the trick with a high ace of hearts. All I needed to do was make an elementary play by allowing Scot to take the trick and saving my two good aces and my spade called a left bower, second highest card, and another smaller trump. I reached to play a king of clubs, which meant that Scot would get the trick, and I had a good chance of getting two more tricks. I reached for the king of clubs and played my nine of spades, which is trump. I played the wrong card, took the trick away from Scot, and wasted a trump. I led an ace, and the other team trumped it. Scot and I did not get three tricks because of my foolish playing. We lost the game because I just wasn't able to make a nickel that day.

Retirement Is Not to Be Easy

I am searching for the time in my life when things will be easier. That time would be labeled as time when I do not have to put out an inordinate amount of energy to have successes with my actions. As I was talking to my chiropractor, Dr. Jon, the other day, this very issue of an easier life was center stage. Neither of us was seeing an easier life anywhere in the near future.

It seems there are all these everyday little happenings that do not add credence to a more mature easier life. For example, I walked in the house one evening around Easter 2009 and heard someone leaving a message on our phone recorder. I increased my forward motion but didn't get to the phone in time to talk to the caller. I thought about the voice on the phone and decided that it was my cousin George Schlotterer. I would recognize his voice anywhere. Later that evening, I called George, and both of us were contributing small talk to the phone conversation until George asked, "Why are you calling me?" I kind of laughed and said I was returning his call from a message he had left earlier that day. Instead of George acknowledging the call, he didn't seem to remember calling me, and he certainly didn't remember why he had called me.

My wife, Kathy, was reviewing phone messages later that evening. She asked me if I had received the message from Butch Rothschild, asking me to return his call. I informed her that the only message I had received was from George. After a short discussion and review of the phone recordings, I admitted that George's voice was very similar to Butch's voice. Now I had two phone calls to make, one to Butch and one to set the record straight with George that he had not, in fact, called me and left a message.

The next morning, I unplugged my cell phone from charging and began to make a call to Butch. The phone went dead, and I discovered that the battery hadn't charged last night, nor was it charging now. We were off to the cell phone shop. At the store, I explained that my phone was dead. After explaining the phone workings, the associate told us that it was better if I obtained a new phone as my service contract was up, and I was eligible for a new phone. A little caveat was added that they could not find a battery like the one in my phone as my phone was obsolete, and so was its battery. The company had thrown out all the extra batteries. Things were going fine on the negotiations for a new phone until I was informed that unless my phone would charge, they could not transfer the contact numbers to my new cell phone. Silently, I was boiling inside because the last time I wanted my contacts transferred to my new phone, there was a compatibility problem between the old and new phone, and the contacts could not be transferred. I had to copy by hand all the contacts I had in my phone. Now I cannot even get to my two hundred or so contacts to either copy or have the contacts transferred. Kathy and I had spent around two hours, and we had nothing but bad news to share with each other. We did share this bad news with each other in great detail. These conversations did not solve our cell phone challenge.

One fact surfaced between Kathy and me; that was if we were able to find another battery, it might jump-start the cell phone so it could be charged, and then contacts could be transferred. We found another cell phone shop and asked if they had old batteries that would fit in our cell phone. Much to our amazement, he found an old compatible battery and plugged it in the cell phone. I thought I would faint as the new old battery did jump-start the cell phone. We traveled home and proceeded to charge the cell phone. As it charged, I thought I was seeing a miracle in progress.

My Family

Garage Sales

Every year or two, Kathy would ask everyone in the family to see what we owned but were not using as she was having a garage sale. Actually, we (the family) were having the garage sale.

When the boys were young, they would always have toys and usually some sports equipment for the sale. I would have tools and collectibles. Kathy would have clothes, glassware, and anything else she could receive from her mother and sister for the sale. The garage sales were always successful in terms of making money and getting rid of scarce resources we no longer needed. We usually found out that we did not miss the items that we had sold. The proceeds of the sale usually went to some family outing or purchase.

I remember one of the garage sales like it happened yesterday. Actually, it did happen very recently. There were so many varied items for sale. For example, Tara and Joe II sent us a high chair, a toy car, and a backpack. They were all in good shape, and they were to bring a good price. I had two winepresses and several winemaking accessories and other items I found in the garage attic. I wasn't sure if they would sell. Kathy's mom sent a twenty- to twenty-five-year-old space heater, a ceiling fan, some jewelry, and some rolled floor tile. Kathy had a very nice covered chair, extra material from covering the chair, several pieces of glassware, lots of jewelry, a dresser, and other household goodies. Mark had some used small radios, some toys, and an alarm clock. There were several other items, but my story centers around these items.

Before the signs were out on the five roads and highways near our house, buyers were ready to purchase goods at least an hour and a half before the published time in the local paper, the *Sentinel-Tribune*. As I returned to the house after I put out the signs, I saw that the driveway was packed with vehicles. I also discovered that both my winepresses were gone, several pieces of jewelry, glassware, and other odds and ends. After a successful first day, there still remained all of Tara and Joe's items, the space heater, the ceiling fan, the rolled floor tile, the covered chair, and Mark had not yet brought out his items.

The afternoon of the second day, all the items not sold on day 1 remained, and Mark did bring out his items. We had just told Tara and Joe that none of their items had sold at that time. A few hours into the supper hour, the high chair sold as did some of Mark's items.

The last day was Saturday, and all the items except the high chair and some of Mark's items had sold on day 2.

On day 3, Kathy had to take her mother home, so I manned the door. I sold several collectibles and the covered chair. When Kathy came home, we were getting close to closing the sale when a man looked at the heater and wanted to know how old it was. We said twenty to twenty-five years old. He said, "Sold. I wanted an older heater." He also bought the backpack of Tara and Joe. Another customer bought the expensive covering like that on the chair. The last customer bought the ceiling fan and took the rolled floor tile. To make a long story short, the garage was bare, and every major item, except for Joe and Tara's toy car, was sold, many at the eleventh hour. The total take was $575.25. And the items were scarce resources that we did not need. Isn't it great to be part of successful venture?

The Eagles

In February 2008, there were several storms that came through our area for the greater part of the first two weeks. One of those days I had retired for the day, and I noticed the wind howling outside my window. I have a hard time sleeping on those particular evenings, and this evening and all night was no exception. The next morning, I left the bed. I can't actually say I got up after a good night's sleep because I had not slept more than a couple of hours. Just about anyone I talked to that day starting with my wife and proceeding with people I saw downtown to my neighbors and other friends relayed my experience of the lack of sleep. I talked to my wine supplier at Home Winery Supplies in Dundee, Michigan, concerning the best time to bottle and cap my champagne. I explained to him that the wind we had in Ohio as well as the wind they had in Columbus according to my son Joe had been terrible the evening before, and he said, "I hear you."

Shortly after that, I talked to my next door neighbor, Terry, about the wind from the previous evening, and he gave me some disturbing news. Terry told me, "The bald eagle nest that was in a large tree about two miles from our house had been blown down and that all was left was the limbs and mud from the nest smashed on the frozen river." I asked if there were any eggs that had broken, and he said he wasn't sure. This is the time of year that eagles hatch their young. Later that day, I went for a ride with my wife and saw the mess on the ice of limbs and dirt that had been the eagles' nest. The eagles represent to me a symbol of our country and of beauty and hope for the future, and they are trying to regain and keep their status of not being an endangered species. This is a real downer to this area and one that brings to mind the possibility that the eagles may leave this area because of their misfortune.

My wife and I then talked about the catastrophe that the eagles had experienced a few years earlier. At that time, there had been another lightning storm a little later in the year than the present date, and the lightning had actually struck the nest, the mother and the two eaglets. Much of the nest had caught fire; the two eaglets and the female bald eagle had all been destroyed. For months, the male eagle would fly around, making a screeching-type noise, probably trying to find his family after this latest act of nature. We hoped that the male and female eagles were OK, and the eggs had not yet been laid. My neighbor John volunteers to help the eagle procreation, so he should know if the eagles will stay or leave.

While I didn't run into John, around the last of April 2008, I was returning home from Pemberville, and I noticed a spotter, someone with a large lens, viewing the nest. I stopped, and to my surprise, it was Sue and Chuck Frizzell. Chuck had recently retired from the Wood County Sheriff's Department after a stellar career as a detective. Sue had worked with me at Wood Lane as the computer consultant. Sue taught me most everything I knew about computers, including how to call her when the computer or I were not working properly. Sue recognized me and came over to talk. I asked her if there were any eaglets. She shared the good news that there were two in the nest. I, of course, shared this information with my family and friends. This was indeed good news.

Unemployment

With the recession in the middle of 2008, I was amazed at how much money my friends and I had lost in their investments. People had worked so hard to build up monies for their retirement, and within a few months, large percentages of their funds were gone. Who was to blame for this recession? The news continually reported that people were being given loans that their income would not be able to support unless the rise in housing prices was to continue and the potential income from the increase in their house value would give them equity. Buying homes that could not be supported by their present incomes was very common in the housing lending industry. At the time of purchase, this practice was not seen as a great gamble by either the buyer or the lender. Lenders were being encouraged, as the story goes, by the federal government to give loans so that every American would be able to own their own home. Unemployment was rising as products were not being bought since people didn't have or didn't wish to spend their money.

One of the very noticeable industries that were to meet up with the inability of selling their product was the big three auto makers. Because of the lack of consumer buying of Ford, Chrysler, and General Motors cars and trucks, huge losses were incurred by these auto makers. The price of gas rose to around $4 a gallon in early 2008 and had resulted in consumer cutbacks on buying certain cars and trucks. The American vehicle drivers were cutting back on all transportation. While the gas prices were high at the end of 2008, cars were not selling, and two of the big three, Chrysler and GM, were asking for and received bailout funds from the federal government so that restructuring and other adjustments could be made to the floundering automobile industry. Ford had already restructured and didn't need the bailout funds. Another one of the reasons commonly given that the big three were in trouble was that unions had been able to obtain high wages and benefits for the present and retired workers. Expenses by the CEOs of private jets and multimillion-dollar wages was not a positive factor for legislatures or the American people in granting bailouts.

Since Kathy and I were both retired, we had earned retirement, and employment was not a big concern. Other events in my life began to give attention to unemployment. The Modine plant in Pemberville, which employed over 250 people, was forecasted to close, and there would be no radiators made at this plant. It seemed every day when I watched the morning news, another major plant was closing. As I drove down the streets of Bowling Green or other cities, it seemed company names were changing, or there were more stores that had closed.

I was reading my e-mail when I noticed that one of my friends was sending me an e-mail, thanking me for putting him on my prayer list as a result of surgery he had on his hand. I had also mentioned to him that there had been many other positive successes from God and possibly for other people I had put on my prayer list. My friend finished his e-mail by telling me that my prayers must be working as his hand was doing well. He then asked me to keep praying for him as he was looking for a job. Since this man had been a successful attorney, I couldn't help but think that the employment situation was much worse than I originally had thought. It was back to the prayer list and asking God's help for him and others in need.

Farewell, Oh Great Tree

It was December 2008, just a few days before Christmas. Big trees had been a landmark of our property; some were there when we arrived, and others had been planted by us over thirty years prior. Slowly, the trees had begun to either be injured or destroyed by unusual natural disasters. The background on tree removal is as follows: thirty-five years ago, when we moved into our new residence, a tree at least three feet in diameter was dead in our backyard. It was close enough to our house and our garage that a good wind could push it in either direction.

I asked a number of neighbors to come over on a Saturday morning to help falling a tree. To the east of me, Sonny Castillo and Richard Lopez were in attendance, and from the west of my home came Jim Moore and Bruce Danielson helping me cut up the tree. Anyone who wanted wood could have it. Gene Walston and Jim Meyers were also present with many possessing their chain saws. Everyone arrived on time, and it was now time to cut down the tree. I decided the best way to fall the tree was away from the house and the garage into an empty field.

This was not to be as the tree was leaning very heavily toward the house and the garage. I had closely worked out my cut on the tree so it would fall in a forty-foot open space between the two buildings. I had just enough room to fall it between the buildings and not injure either of them. I needed a little help from God, and I got it. The cut was perfect, and the tree fell perfectly between the two buildings. That was a good show of skills to all my new neighbors. I was astounded, and I think my neighbors were impressed.

The Ice Storm

Several years ago, a huge ice storm had come into the area. The ice storm destroyed a number of our giant white pine trees. The loss of these pines was in a sense self-destructive. One of the top branches would break off because of the weight of the ice, and it would fall onto the branch below it and break off the next lower branch. This process would repeat itself until all the branches below the original branch that had broken were stripped from the tree. The result was the trunk of the tree with a few branches was all that remained. My father-in-law, Albert Long, was shortly on the scene with his chain saw, and he made short work of all the damaged trees. Gene Walston was here with his Oliver tractor to tie a long rope from the tree to his tractor so there was guidance to where the tree fell.

Another Ice Storm

A few years later, I was in Columbus on business, and I returned in time to give a lecture to Dr. Sharon Clifford's class at BGSU on mental retardation and developmental disabilities. When I arrived home after dark, I saw many branches from the trees down. My wife told me that our trees' branches were covered with ice and were burdened down by the storm. In many cases, the top branches broke off with many of these branches landing on the roof of our house, yet many were hanging on to the tree by a sliver. It would not have taken much for one of the branches to break loose and cause a chain reaction of falling ice-covered branches that could have possibly injured the roof, the eaves troughs, or the side of the house such as our windows. While we heard the branches shift in the middle of the night, we did not experience any roof or structural damage to the house.

The Old Trees

Within the past few years, two trees, the front maple and the English walnut, were succumbing to the years of aging and were rotting outward from the core. These trees were so large that I could not possibly take them down. I hired the local tree trimmer, Rick Beeker, to do the heavy work. Watching Rick and his crew remove the tree was like watching a fine-tuned symphony playing. They knew how to do their business, were proud of that fact, and never touched any of the other trees in proximity. As they took one limb out, there was another there so that they almost continuously and rhythmically eliminated the trees.

We are now at the point of dealing with the present injured tree that was by far the largest tree we had ever had on the property. On the night of the big ice storm in December 2008, Kathy told me as she came to bed that the swing on our giant hackberry tree was lying on the ground. I asked if any limbs were down, and she said there weren't any down in the afternoon. The next morning, I looked out the window toward our hackberry tree, and the sight almost made me physically sick. I saw several large limbs close to two feet in diameter on the ground. I dressed and looked closer at the tree to find that about half of the tree had lost its limbs. It looked as if one of the limbs higher up had buckled under the weight of the ice, and as it came down, the upper limb caused the lower limb to also crack and fall to the ground, similar to the method that destroyed our white pines. I took a closer look at the tree and discovered that the two limbs that had come down had pulled about twenty feet of the bark of the side of the tree down to the middle of the trunk. The survival of the tree did not look good.

I called Rick Beeker to assess the seriousness of the damage. A large branch was sitting on the roof of our garden shed, and I could not tell if the shed had been seriously damaged. Kathy and I had a number of errands to accomplish, and we didn't return home until about four o'clock in the afternoon. Terry Hoepf, my next-door neighbor, called me and asked if I wanted to go on a walk as we frequently took his dog, Jack, on this type of outing. I explained that the tree between our properties had been badly injured by the ice storm, and I needed to take off the large branch that was lying on the shed. I relayed to Terry that if the tree were to shift, it could destroy the shed. Terry said he would be over immediately so we could remove the large branch. As it turned out, there were other branches higher than the roof that also needed to be removed.

We were able to cut loose most of the branches from the roof of the shed that evening, and darkness prevented us from finishing the job. We decided that we would finish the job the next morning after the winter solstice observance at Denny Walston's. The winter solstice is the time in the northern hemisphere when the sun is farthest south of the equator, and Denny has erected what he called the bridge hedge at the proper positioning of the pieces of what was once a bridge had been established. The ceremony of the solstice was cut short this year as the sun was not out, and the temperatures were well below freezing. Denny wore his traditional monk's robe. Terry Hoepf and another friend, Allan Vaughn, and I all toasted this great day at about seven forty-seven in the morning. After pancakes by Denny, it was time to get back to the tree.

Terry and I began taking down the limbs over the shed piece by piece. After the limbs were cleared from the shed, Denny came over to help saw up the tree. I was scheduled to go to a soup and pie luncheon at Ellen and Dave Stoots, friends of ours, so I quickly tried to cut the last piece of wood. This was a huge mistake; I tried to quickly put a cut on the underside of the branch so that a clean cut could be made. As luck would have it, I cut too far, and the branch started to break loose, but it stopped and bound my chain saw in the limb. I tried several ways to get out the saw, but it did not move. I left the saw in the limb and found a wedge and a hammer. If I could wedge the branch so that the limb fell to the ground, my chain saw would be free. That plan did not work, so I used Denny's saw to cut off the limb that was almost cut off. The limb went down, and with the limb cut off, so was the pressure on the chain saw so I could pull it out.

Rick and I hadn't connected on cutting down or not cutting down the tree. I decided that I would try to cut down the rest of the two branches that were down but not separated from the trunk of the tree. I had one last limb that was sticking out about forty feet from the point I was going to cut it. I probably should have made two cuts at twenty feet instead of one at forty. I didn't opt for the twenty feet cut because it looked like an easy cut at forty feet. I began to cut the branch down from my aluminum ladder and didn't notice that I wasn't holding onto the branch as I had done for the previous cuts I had made. As the limb fell, it hit the ground, and I noticed it sprang back toward me and my ladder. As I watched the limb come toward me, I immediately felt the cut end of the branch hit my ladder, and I felt the ladder and myself sliding down the limb. A quick thought in my mind was I am going to be hurt very bad. Luckily, about ten feet back from the cut, my ladder took an abrupt stop; I had hit another limb growing of the branch I was on. That was the last time I was on a ladder in that tree.

A few days later, Rick Beeker did come to give his opinion on saving or cutting down the tree. The damage was extensive, so we opted to cut down the tree. Terry Hoepf said he would help pay for the removal of the tree since it was located on his side of the property as well. One of the remaining challenges was to find another tree from which we could hang the swing and tire swing. The maple tree in the back of the property was selected, and Rick was to come back closer to the summer to attach the ropes with his cherry picker. We made at least five cords of wood from the tree.

Losing Good Friends

Little did I know that I was going to lose two friends of mine in a few weeks. Dr. Dave Gedeon had served with me for years on the St. Thomas More University Parish maintenance committee. We had attempted many different jobs as a committee, and Dave's expertise in planning projects as well as carrying them out was invaluable. Dave's accident occurred a summer day when he was cutting down a large tree in the front of his house. As I understand the story, Dave was in the tree, had cut a branch with his saw, and was hit by a branch after sawing it off. Dave landed on his head and died shortly thereafter. Dave was such a safe person using his skills. I can only imagine what went wrong.

A few days later, another fall happened to my high school friend, John Wiles. John was in his shop repairing something from a ladder when he reached for a tool, lost his balance, and fell to his death by hitting his head. We will miss John at the next reunion because he was a swell person, and we'll miss seeing him at his beautiful farm and recreational areas. John provided the setting for the Friday night 1962 class reunion.

Tires on the Road

I was working on this chapter and writing about how there are happenings every day of our lives that could be used as material in a book. Our lives are so rich with interesting experiences. I had also just written the section on positive people and experiences and negative people experiences when it was time to go to my chiropractor, Dr. Wolph, for an appointment. As I was driving west down Route 6, I saw something in the road. As I looked closer, it was a large piece of tire that had come off a truck. I immediately pulled my car over, for the piece of tire was completely on the road, and anyone who hit it could be thrown into a wreck, or at least their car would be badly damaged. As I put on my hazard lights and began to cautiously get out of the car, I wondered how a piece of truck tire that long could have been on the road. I knew it could not be very long. I knew that Route 6 was a very dangerous road because of the high volume of traffic and especially because of the high truck traffic.

I looked to the west, and I saw heavy truck and car traffic. I looked behind me knowing that traffic was coming and fearing that if the east and west traffic passed, they would be passing each other where the tire was lying on the road, and I was standing nearby. I knew for sure that I had put myself in a potentially dangerous situation with the possibility of traffic coming from both directions and the westbound traffic being in the situation where it could hit the rubber on the highway. As I looked to the east, I saw that that there was a high truck carrying a liquid coming toward me. I looked at the rubber tire about ten feet from me and knew I couldn't pull it from the road to make the vehicle pass by safely. I took a few steps back, knowing that it was possible for the east and west traffic to meet at the rubber tire, and there would be no room to avoid hitting the tire and causing some type of accident with me close to the center of the action.

Again, I looked at the truck on my side of the road to see how fast and close he was. To my amazement and joy, the truck was slowing down and, in the process, stopping all the traffic from the east. I ran out on the road and pulled a very long piece of truck tire off to the side of the road. As I began to pull the tire, I noticed that it weighed about three times as much as I thought it should. I could not tell you if any traffic was coming from the west because I was focused on the tire and the east traffic. After pulling the huge truck tire off the road, I saw smaller yet potentially dangerous pieces of tire rubber. I looked to the trucker, and I could see that he was stopping for me to pull off the remaining two pieces. As I finished my task, I stood off the road and waved to the truck driver as he blew his horn to me.

I didn't want to think what would have happened to me if the trucker hadn't stopped the traffic from the east. I did not know this trucker, but he is my friend for life. Around three that afternoon, someone had sent an angel to me and assured me that I was not to be hurt while I tried to protect the other drivers on the road. I had already hit much smaller objects and had damaged my vehicle. I had to pull off the rubber tire; I didn't think it would be this dangerously exciting. I got in my SUV and saw the truck enter Interstate 75 toward Toledo. I will probably never meet this driver, but I would love to thank him for being my partner in removing the tire pieces and keeping me and others safe.

A Reality Check, Hospitals

Over the years, I have been in several hospitals both for myself and for other people. The emergency room is usually the point of entry for quick service or admission into the hospital. One can develop a reality check on one's self instantaneously in the hospital. The usual conclusion for me is that other people coming in are many times in greater need than me. Also, I was not always sure of who or why someone was in the emergency room, but my assessment was that something was of a much more serious nature than why I am there. In the fall of 2008, I was in the emergency room at six fifty in the morning to have tests done on my abdominal area. I had checked in and was waiting my turn. An Amish family of four came into the emergency room. The mother and father and young girl all had what I would consider normal smiles and body movement. The young boy of five was walking with his head down and kind of scuffling his feet, giving me the impression that all was not well. It became apparent to me that the cute little Amish boy had something wrong with him. I was concerned that it might be serious. In any case, seeing a young boy in the emergency room so early in the morning assured me that something was going to happen to the boy. I instantly felt sorry for the family and thought I must be in better shape than the boy.

Let's face it, anyone in an emergency room doesn't need to strain their ears or eyes much to hear enough from somebody else about what is wrong with another person. Seeing a bloody towel on the arm or leg or other part of the body indicates that someone else is probably worse off than me. Watching someone vomit or holding their head as if they have a headache or seeing people come in by ambulance or, worse yet, helicopter can usually mean that something is very seriously wrong. In any of these cases, I always think that there is someone else that is in worse shape than me, and I had better appreciate where I am and not complain because things appear to be pretty good for me. So if I want a true check on how well am doing, the emergency room is a good place to go.

Lady the Cat

On November 26, 2008, Kathy came to me as I was waking up in the morning and told me that Lady, our calico cat, was in the garage, and she could hardly walk. She informed me that we needed to change our plans of going shopping in the morning and go instead this evening because we needed to take the cat to Dr. Jones, our veterinarian. Lady had been gone for a few days, and when she returned, she was very sick. Lady is the type of cat that doesn't like to be touched by just anyone. My wife, Kathy, and son Mark are two of her favorite attention givers.

I had borrowed a trap from my friend Keith Madaras on Monday. Keith was not home when I called, but his wife, Janice, told me that she knew I really needed the trap, so I should come over to the house, and she would find one. It was important I had the trap Monday because the vet's office had told me they could work the cat in on Tuesday all day, but Wednesday was very busy, and Thursday was Thanksgiving. I had set the trap Tuesday morning and opened the garage door so Lady could come in the garage, and in the process of taking the tuna bait, she would be trapped in the live trap, and we could transport her to the vet. There was no Lady in the trap most of the morning. Just before lunch, I checked the trap, and it had worked; it had caught a cat. The problem was that it was the wrong cat. I had caught a white cat, not a calico cat. So here we are on Wednesday morning, and Lady had come in the garage, and Kathy put down the garage door so we could catch her.

I called Dr. Jones's office, and it had a 9:30 a.m. appointment open. It was now 8:00 a.m., and we had about a half hour to figure a way of confining kitty. Kathy told me that she thought Lady was so weak, and she wanted to pick her up and hold her while I drove to Dr. Jones. We walked into the garage, and Kathy went over to Lady, talking to her the whole time and was able to pick her up. In the car went Kathy very slowly and very carefully. By this time, Lady was meowing strangely, and Kathy and

I agreed that it was a cry of pain. I started driving to the vet. As I drove, my mind began to wander. It wandered to Lady, and it wandered back to the time that Lady first came to our house. I noticed Lady and told Kathy that I wanted to see if Ed and Pat Hammett had wanted to adopt more cats. I located the cat transporter and picked up Lady and began to put her in the carrier. As I put Lady over the carrier, I noticed she was struggling and uncooperative. As quick as lightning, Lady decided to bite my hand between the thumb and pointer finger. I dropped Lady and called the on-call doctor to see what I needed to do. I was told to quarantine the cat if it was needed to aid in treating me. I told the doctor I couldn't pick the cat up, let alone quarantine the cat. We kept the cat, and now we were taking this once young beautiful cat to the vet for assessment and treatment.

I pulled in Dr. Jones's driveway with Lady continually meowing as if to say "I am very sick." I told Kathy I would go in, and when Dr. Jones was ready, I would come to the car and tell her the doctor was ready. I walked into the vet's office and immediately picked up the smell of Dr. Jones's waiting room. There was another Cocker Spaniel being treated, and during the treatment time, two more cats and their owners came in. One gentleman was from Portage, Ohio, and he had a striped cat. In talking with him, I found the cat was his wife's, and there were two cats in his house. The other gentleman had a white cat. The owner thought the cat was experiencing a shutdown of its kidneys, and he had been in a week to see Dr. Jones for a month. Dr. Jones came out about 9:50 a.m. My appointment was for 9:30 a.m. Dr. Jones called out a name like Bunker as the next gentleman to have his cat seen. Mr. Bunker said this gentleman was before me, meaning that I should go in first. I had talked to both the gentlemen in the waiting room, and they knew my cat was very sick. I thanked the man for allowing me to go first and went to the car to ask Kathy to come into the office. Because of the fact that there might have been a dog or another animal that might have spooked Lady and caused her to run, Kathy was staying in the car to avoid this scenario.

We went into the examination room, and Dr. Jones almost immediately determined that Lady was very sick. We could have some or many tests done, have expensive or not-so-expensive treatment depending on her condition, or have her put to sleep. I told Kathy and the vet that I thought we should have her tested for feline leukemia, and then we would make a decision. Dr. Jones told us that he would have the test results when we returned in an hour. Kathy and I left the office and talked about the options. We decided that a definite decision would be made after Dr. Jones gave us the test result, and we knew more about the options. We traveled to Dr. Jones's office again, and as we walked into the office, we braced ourselves for the worst. Dr. Jones told us that Lady did not have the untreatable feline leukemia, but he had examined Lady in more detail. Lady is a very sick cat and is suffering trauma, possibly neurological damage or possibly a brain tumor. The unsteadiness that Lady was observing when she was walking and his examination pointed to these variables. Kathy and I talked through the options with the vet and decided that we would have Lady put down as the prognosis was not good. Dr. Jones agreed and began to prepare the injection for Lady. It was very emotional in the treatment room for Kathy and me. Dr. Jones injected the fluid, and Lady quietly went to sleep.

We chose to take Lady home for burial. We left with Lady's body, and I immediately went back in time. I directly went to the time when I had taken our miniature French poodle to Dr. Jones Senior and had to have her put down. We had Missy for twelve years, which was shortly after we were married. That was a sad occasion, and this was a sad occasion. When we reached home, Mark was not available, so I waited until later in the day. I told Mark about the cat, and at the same time, Kathy came into the dining room. Mark and Kathy started the grieving process up for the second time that day. I buried Lady and hoped to myself that I did not have to deal with a pet or human death for some time.

A Memorable Christmas

Kathy and I were attending a discussion group sponsored by our new parish, Blessed John XXIII, in November 2008. Some of our friends of thirty years plus were there—Don and Gerry Sternitzke, Meg and Roman Carek, Fred and Dorothy Sneider, and some new friends. We were sitting around the Sternitzke dining room table enjoying dessert and drinks when Meg Carek, a member of St. Vincent de Paul Society, relayed to us that the needy families being canvassed for our Christmas Giving Tree all had the same need this year. St. Vincent de Paul is an organization at Blessed John that does wonderful acts of help for people whose need is to pay for utility bills, car repairs, clothing, or food. They are not in the position to help themselves. Meg's point was that she felt because of the economy this year, the families were asking for one item from the church's Giving Tree, and that was food gift certificates.

I looked at Kathy and could see by her smile that she was thinking of the same idea I was, and that was the original year of the Giving Tree at St. Thomas More in 1981. As the story went, the boys, Kathy, and I had gone to Mass the morning of Christmas Day. Marla Overholt asked us if we could deliver three Christmas packages to families around the Fostoria area. Marla is the type of person who brings sunshine to every room she enters and is always talking with a smile. This sounded like an appropriate act to perform on Christmas Day. We were on the way to my mother's house, and this would give our two sons, Joey and Mark, a new experience in how some of the less fortunate families lived at Christmas. We loaded up the presents and food and shortly pulled up to one of the homes where we were to deliver the Christmas goods. We knocked on the door and were invited into the home. As I looked around, I could see that the front living area had been turned into a bedroom so the two young girls could have a place to sleep. There were a few other rooms I could see; all of them seemed very cramped. As I put down the groceries and my sons laid down the bag of presents, one of the three children, a young boy of eight, began looking in the grocery bags. As he looked into the bag with groceries, he said, "Wow, there is bread in the bag!" My family was surprised that bread would be such a surprise to anyone because there was always bread, unless we had run out, in our house.

We entered another home in the country, on a road I had never traveled. The day was very cold, windy, snowy, and icy, and this house was sitting in the middle of a plot of land with no protection from the elements. As we knocked on the door and began to enter the house, we immediately noticed that the home we were entering was very warm. As we told the family we were from St. Thomas More and we had presents and food, our eyes began to roam around the room. We noticed that the home was almost dark from lack of lighting, and in the middle of the room was this large coal heater. The temperature was really hot close to the heater, and I felt uncomfortable with the young children walking close to it. I was also somewhat uncomfortable with the heavy coats we were wearing. There were three children, two girls and one boy, none of them over the age of eight or nine in the home. One of the young girls was smiling, and it was easy to see that she was in need of extensive professional dental attention.

As I began to talk to the mother, she informed me that their water was obtained by going outside the house to the barn, which was around one hundred feet from the home, and after filling the buckets, they were carried by a family member back to the home. The freezing of the water source was a concern in the cold weather we were experiencing. The last point and the most disturbing one made by the mother was that this family was being evicted in a few days from this home, with no other place to live.

The last house in Fostoria was not as uncomfortable to see as the first two. A very important lesson learned by our boys that day and reinforcing a belief that Kathy and I already knew was that we are fortunate, and we need to help those less fortunate. I will never forget the smile on the young girl's face.

The Landfill, Recycling, and Scrap Metal

There is a saying "Habits die slowly." That must be true in this case because when Kathy and I lived in Mansfield, Saturday morning was the day we went to the landfill. It was enjoyable, and we parted with our food and drink containers, boxes, and just plain old junk.

Now that we live near Bowling Green in Wood County, we have three stops instead of one to take care of our different types of waste or junk. Each place we go to depart with our waste is another story. The first stop we usually take is to go to the scrap metal yard or to the E & M Recycling. This yard is located near Portage. When one walks into the yard, he is so overtaken with all the different metals in the yards. There are old cars, tons of scrap metal, aluminum siding, batteries, and about any metal you think could be worth money. When I sell metal there, it is a routine to recycle the scrap metal and the aluminum pop and beer cans. The first step is to find a parking spot along Route 25 south. Next, I try to take all the pop cans and scrap metal in at one time so I don't have to make two trips, and so I can sell everything I brought.

As I walk into the building that I am going to sell metal, I have to walk slowly and carefully as both inside and outside, there is debris everywhere, and there are few places to walk. When I have my metal weighed, there are three or four different people I have talked to who work in the yards. They are the workers who weigh you in and make out a slip and those who pay you. While the person is weighing me in, I always stop talking because I want to obtain credit for all my metal.

The person who does the paying is the most interesting person in the yards. I have talked with him for some extended periods, and I always find him most interesting. The man with the money seems to be the boss, and he is also the one who runs all the big equipment such as the crane. When I am paid for my metal, the man with the money pays me with cash from a wad of bills that would choke a horse. I wouldn't have any idea how much money he has in that wad, but it is around three inches thick in diameter. The last visit I had at the scrap metal shop, I had an extended conversation with the boss. He was explaining to me that he liked to camp. I asked where he camped, and he pointed to a good-sized camper sitting in the middle of the scrapyard. He said he enjoys camping in the scrapyard. He then told me they had a large fire in the not-so-distance past in the yard. I asked him what happened. He said he was in the trailer early in the morning, and he heard some noises, and the trailer caught fire. It burned in a matter of minutes. He thought that some raccoon had made its way into the fuse box and shorted out the wiring in the trailer, and that was the end of the trailer.

The second stop we make is the county landfill. I sometimes take brush, trash, and junk to the landfill. The process of unloading the trailer is to back up the trailer to one of the six unloading sites that are located in front of the dumpsters that hold the junk. Once the trailer is close to the dumpsters located below ground level, and then the gate is put down next to the dumpsters, and then I would unload my junk into the dumpster. The last time I was at the landfill, I saw a Toyota 4Runner with a trailer similar to mine. So the cars were almost identical as were the trailers. As I began to talk to the person unloading the Toyota 4Runner, he also noticed that the handcarts we both had were identical. The minimum charge is $15.60 for what is termed solid waste. When I leave, I must pass over the scales the same manner when I came into the landfill. If all I have is brush, I can unload the brush with the other natural vegetation. If I have both junk and brush, it goes to the dumpsters.

The last stop is recycling glass, papers, and steel cans. The last time I went to the Bowling Green Recycling Center, it was so busy that I had to wait for someone to leave. There are around five spots that recyclers can park outside the center. Unloading the various recycling materials is done by simply carrying in the materials and placing them into the right containers. I have gone to the center all hours of the day and night, so it must be open twenty-four hours a day. One time years ago, I was at the recycling center and was going to put something into the container for scrap metal. Another person was next to me, and I saw an antique chair on the back of his pickup. I offered the metal I had for the antique chair, and we were both happy. One never knows the deals one can develop at the landfill, metal recycling yard, or the recycling center.

The Tooth

It was July 2009 in the evening when I was performing my "get-ready-for-bed activities." One of those activities was flossing my teeth. Flossing had not been a problem with me as long as I was to maintain this practice. As I was flossing, I noticed that after I had flossed the second tooth from the back, I felt something in my mouth. I fished out the piece of hard substance and realized that I had pulled out about twenty-five percent of my tooth by flossing it. I felt around with my tongue to see where the tooth had come from, and I discovered that the last tooth I had flossed was the culprit. The hole felt like the Grand Canyon, but I knew from past experience that space in a tooth tends to magnify itself. I called the next morning, and the receptionist very kindly made an appointment with the dentist. As I walked into the dentist's office, I could not help but think of the former dentists in this building, and those were Drs. Cheryl and Gary DeWood. For years, they had taken excellent care of my teeth compared with a previous childhood dentist who had practiced very crude methods, by today's standards, on my teeth. Luckily, when I lived in Willard, Dr. Piller provided me great care. In Mansfield, Dr. Marshall and Dr. Picard were accomplished dentists. So now I was walking to a patient station to ask Dr. Shawn Thompson to fix this tooth that had lost a large part of its existence.

Dr. Thompson came into the room and examined my tooth. He immediately conferred with me on how to fix it, and we opted to use a computer machine that takes dimensions off the existing tooth and actually comes up with the new dimensions to repair it. I asked how a tooth could split like this one had, and he assured me that since I had a small silver filling, it was possible for the silver to expand over years and fracture a tooth. This was very possibly the cause. It all sounded so easy and so exact that we made an appointment for the next opening he had available. I was extremely relived that Dr. Shawn was able to repair rather than replace the tooth.

As I came into the room, I tried to think only of the very competent dentists I had experienced instead of a dentist who was probably doing the best he could at the time. He did cause lots of pain and lots of apprehension about drilling and treating teeth with no novocaine. The assistant came in and placed a piece of cotton with a numbing solution on my gums. A short while later, Dr. Shawn came into the room. I had my eyes closed. As the dentist began to work, it seemed he was outlining something on my tooth. As he left my mouth, I opened my mouth and saw something silvery vanish. I asked what had just happened and was informed that I had been given an injection to numb my tooth. I couldn't believe that the dentist had given me shots into my gums, and I felt and knew nothing about what was happening, even though I was present.

The drilling of the tooth to make sure that the tooth was ready to receive the crown proceeded for a short while. The drilling began again, and I was informed that another section of the tooth had fractured. With the computer having taken all the dimensions needed to make the new tooth, I was invited to observe the machine make my new cap.

The machine consisted of two sets of drills with water shooting onto the tooth to cool it as my new crown was being made. When the crown was nearly complete, the machine shut down. A drill was replaced, and we were on our way. The machine stopped again, and a filter was blamed for the stoppage. After replacing the filter, the machine went forward for a few minutes. The independent machine was now asking for a new block so my tooth could be made again. Luckily, the tooth crown was complete, and it could be finished by the dentist. The crown fit like a glove, and I was done just in time to make it to my next appointment with my chiropractor, Dr. Jon Truman. As I left the dentist's office, I reflected on the professionalism of Dr. Shawn, his assistants, and his office staff. The tooth fit perfectly, and I had not a pain in the process of placing a new crown in my molar located in the top right side of my mouth.

My Sixty-Fifth Birthday

It was October 2, 2009, when Kathy and I had come into the back door of our house. I thought I heard two people talking, and that was strange because Mark was home by himself when we had left for our ministry helping with Mass at the Otterbein Portage Valley homes. I walked into the kitchen as my younger brother Mike from Cleveland came walking into the room. I asked him why he was in this neck of the woods. Mike does many handyman-type jobs since he retired from his teaching profession, so I figured he must have a job in the area. No sooner had I gotten the words out of my mouth than my other younger brother from Connecticut, Bob, walked into the room. I did not comprehend immediately why they were in my house and asked Bob why he was here. They both just looked at me, and a light came on in my head; they were here to help me celebrate my birthday. I didn't remember seeing any vehicles other than our vehicles. It came out real soon that Mike had picked up Bob at the Cleveland Airport, and he had parked his truck behind my old garage. It also came out very clearly that Kathy had sent letters and talked with each of my brothers, my sister, and my brother-in-law about a weekend celebrating Joe's birthday. I later found out that there were instructions in the letter about what phone number to call so I was not tipped off about the surprise.

This gesture of kindness hit me like a ton of bricks square in my heart. I was awestruck that Mike and Bob would come to my dwelling to help me celebrate my birthday. I knew that this was Kathy's doing, and I was more than delighted to be able to have this time with my two brothers.

I was to find out that there were to be many more surprises before the weekend was out. Later that afternoon, I saw a vehicle come into the driveway. A few minutes later, in walks my elder brother Walt. Walt is from the Raleigh, North Carolina, area. I couldn't believe he had also come that distance to help me celebrate my birthday. As the talk began, Mike shared with us how he had bought an industrial-type mixer for his wife, Marge, at a flea market. I asked him if it looked like the KitchenAid blender I had in the cupboard next to me. I opened the door, and Mike said it was like that, only it was an Osterizer mixer. We enjoyed eating that evening a nice supper. Deviled eggs were one of the first items served. I remembered seeing Kathy make deviled eggs that morning and asked her why she was making deviled eggs. She said something like she had eggs and felt like it. She usually made deviled eggs for a special affair, and I knew of no special event going on that Friday. I missed that clue. She also served chicken sandwiches bought from the Dairy Queen. A few weeks earlier, we had bought the chicken for the sandwiches, and she told me that we really needed to have them on hand for company. That statement made sense to me, and I missed that clue about by party. The last clue I missed was that we were cleaning the house with nobody coming. This party was in the planning for over six months, and I had no clue that anything was happening.

A few games of cornhole completed the outside evening activities. Cornhole is a game in which beanbags are thrown at a hole in a board, and the person who either gets it in the hole or keeps it on the board closest to the hole is able to score points. Mike is usually the champ, but he was not quite as good as Bob and Mark as they were victorious over Mike and Walt. As the game progressed, Bob had fun showing his Harry Potter insignia on his wrist. The insignia is a scar that looks just like Harry Potter's scar that looks like a Z. Bob shared that when he wants to get the attention of his children, he grabs his wrist and yells out that something bad is about to happen. This action is usually used when Bob wants to sidetrack some potential misbehavior by his children.

The rest of the evening consisted of drinks, cards, and a whole lot of talk about a whole lot of memories. Walt was unbeatable in cards, and luckily, he was my partner. Walt had several go-alone hands and seemed to be able to make trump successfully on about every hand. Mike and Bob were not happy cardplayers. Losing was not Mark's game, and for sure, it was not Bob's. Many of the memories shared turned into kidding one another about their various actions from the past. Filling the evening hours into the early morning hours was not a problem. After sleeping quarters were found for everyone, we settled down for a short night's nap. We needed to be up early in the morning because we had a full array of activities starting with eggs, bacon, fried potatoes, and drinks. We were up early, and we were all taking up on the kidding where we had left off the night before.

After the breakfast, Mark informed me that we were going to load up our guns and ammunition as we were scheduled to do some serious shooting at our friends, Pat and Cliff Martin's, shooting gallery. We left a little after nine thirty and traveled to a rural area near Willard. On the way, we stopped to pick up my brother-in-law, Fred Eldred. Fred loaded up his pistol, shotguns, and a rifle that was the Hungarian version of AK-47. The AK-47 is an assault rifle, and it is very powerful.

A trip back a farm lane at Pat and Cliff's led us to a stream. On one side of the stream were a number of targets, and on the other side was a very nice six-man shooting table. Before long, the rifles were ringing out their message. The pistols followed suit, and in addition to a .22 pistol, a magnum .38-caliber pistol came out of the case. I knew the .38 magnum pistol was different from the .22 pistol as it nearly broke my eardrum as the first shot was taken. We shot several rounds of .22 cartridges, and then we got serious about the .38 magnum. The .38 magnum had a lot of kick, and when it hit a plastic bottle, the bottle would fly several feet in the air. We then got out the AK-47 rifle and began to pulverize every target available. A hedge apple was shot, and the apple almost disappeared. Another plastic bottle was hit by the .38 pistol, and it flew ten feet into the air. A cookout was next, and my favorite picnic sandwich, the hotdog, was grilled over the open fire. It certainly was my day. Drinks, dips, snacks, and beef jerky rounded out a perfect meal.

We completed shooting pistols and rifles and moved on to shotgun shells. Cliff had a portable clay pigeon thrower on two wheels. We shot at the pigeons, having one person as the first shooter and the second as the backup, who shot only at clay pigeon not hit by the first shooter. While we were not pros, we had a good time trying to be pros. The early afternoon ended, and so did the shooting of over 1,000 bullets and over 150 shotgun shells.

It was off to the Havana Tavern. The Havana Tavern was the hangout that my family used for a few drinks and a good evening's entertainment. As we walked in the side main door, we observed that there was still a pool table. The shuffleboard and pin ball machines were gone, but the place had the same mystique of many past years. After a drink of beer, a quick trip to St. Joseph's Cemetery in Willard and a few prayers for my mom and dad followed. A visit to the site of my twin's final burial site and a prayer completed our Willard area excursion.

We had an hour ride to New Rochester, and we were to eat supper around six thirty. When we arrived home, there was time for another game of cornhole. Mike was able to get back his magic touch and began winning in his usual style. In the middle of the game, another car came into the driveway, and there was my baby sister Ann. It was good to see Ann as she and I were about the same age, and we were very close in our years at home. Supper was served with beef tenderloin as the main course. Ann brought, now get this, a lemon pie, a butterscotch pie, a strawberry pie, and a lemon birthday cake. Walt brought three boxes of sixteen-millimeter movies my father had made. Many memories were rekindled as the movies were shown. Walt had to leave for home after the movies. Another evening of euchre took place, and six-handed euchre was played, but the game was not as competitive as Friday night's games. Another late night of one thirty ended the Saturday evening events.

Sunday was a light breakfast, and Mass at Blessed John followed. A trip to Grand Rapids provided one more surprise, a breakfast/brunch at La Rose Restaurant. A beautiful deck overlooking the Maumee River could not be enjoyed because of the adverse weather. The food and ambiance inside was a good backup environment at La Rose. After returning to our home, Ann took off in the early afternoon, and Bob and Mike left around three thirty. They did not leave until 140 stalks of cornstalks were cut and loaded into the bed of Mike's truck. Mike is big on Halloween decorations. Faye Sherman gave us the OK to pick the cornstalks as her sons Dean and John were unavailable. It is such a great feeling to live among people who are so generous and kind with their time and energy. What a wonderful birthday!

Why Am I Tired?

While I was fortunate enough to have an abundance of energy, it was not uncommon for me to be tired in the middle of the day. I had always thought that it was common to be tired if one worked very hard. I found this fact not to always be true. The first of October in 2009, Kathy and I were returning home from a trip to her mother's in our new minivan, a 2008 Honda Odyssey. There were only thirteen thousand miles on the speedometer a month previous when we had bought the car. The car was in great shape, and the price was right. Within a few miles of our house, I became very tired and began to fall asleep. Kathy saw the car beginning to go over the center line and shouted, "Joe!" I immediately woke up and pulled the car under control.

This incident brought to mind another incident that had happened with my son Mark in June 2008. We were returning from the Ohio Special Olympics Summer Games in Columbus where my family and others were responsible to provide meals to the participating athletes and their chaperones. The largest number of meals served was at lunch on Saturday in which five thousand people were offered lunch. My day on Saturday started at around six o'clock for breakfast and ended after six o'clock supper with meals provided by Ohio State Food Services. Since our group usually enjoyed some evening activities, the weekend was not a time to catch up on one's sleep, so I was usually dragging after three days and three nights.

As Mark and I were traveling home on Route 23, I suddenly became very tired and began to doze off. I didn't doze off for long because my car drifted into median, and the terrain was anything but smooth. I worked my way back to the road, giving Mark a pretty bumpy road. This was the first time in recent years that I had dozed off, so I decided that with two occasions of drifting off, I needed to find out the cause of this dangerous dozing. I was lucky on two occasions, but I was concerned about the possibility of number 3. The possibility of an accident while dozing was not an option.

I met with my family doctor, Dr. Jon. He thought my first course of action was to have a sleep test. This possibility did not excite me greatly as sleeping away from home was not my most favorite activity, especially when I knew that someone was watching my every move through the monitoring system.

I was to meet with Dr. Louis after I had completed my life history on medical issues as well as a special section answering questions on sleep patterns. I wasn't aware of many issues such as movements in my legs in the middle of the night. For Pete's sake, I was asleep, not observing what my body was doing. After many sessions, I did complete the many pages of questionnaires. It was then time to meet with the good doctor. In the meeting between Dr. Louis and Kathy and I, it became very evident that the doctor was not entirely satisfied with the answers I had given on the questionnaire. Several of the questions were asked verbally, and I felt that I was not the first patient who had not sufficiently answered the questions on the initial survey. The good doctor was most patient with my responses. At the conclusion of the interview, the die was cast; I needed to be evaluated by the Toledo Sleep Disorder Center. I felt things were getting kind of serious because the doctor was now throwing out a label for my condition, sleep apnea.

After this meeting with the doctor on October 29, 2009, arrangements were made for my sleep test on November 12. This testing was moving along very quickly, and I began to wonder about the seriousness of this sleep apnea. The date for my sleep test arrived very fast. Before I knew it, I was driving down Holland Road, looking for the sleep center at about seven in the evening. Since it was dark, I was paying particular attention to the street numbers, which were almost entirely nonexistent. I did find a number close to the one I was looking to find, and since I was running a little behind schedule, I turned into the parking lot thinking I could find the office more safely out of traffic. I pulled around the building and in the back expected to locate my office. It turned out that the parking lot was designed like a maze. I tried going around the building, only to find that there was no way to go to the right. Instead, there were solid brick walls and fences that blocked my way. I was now a great distance from the main road I used to enter these parking lots, and I was not going to admit defeat in finding my office complex. I was pushed into going to an opposite direction I wished to go, and you guessed it, I had no idea which direction to go so that I could go back to the entrance.

I was in the middle of a mess as it approached the time I was to be at the sleep clinic. I traveled through a number of parking lots; none of which led me to a main road. I traveled from one parking lot to another, always meeting the wrong parking lot. By the grace of God, I entered a parking lot that looked like the one next to the Toledo Sleep Disorder Center. I looked at my clock, and it was time for my appointment. I looked closely at the building next to me, and the sign said Toledo Sleep Disorder Center. I parked, gathered my clothes for the evening, and approached the door.

A thought hit me. *What do I do if the door is locked?* Well, the door opened, and I was in the building. I saw no one in the halls, nor did I hear anyone. I stood in the middle of the building and wondered what I should do next. After a few minutes, I started to walk down the corridors. After several investigations, I had no office to enter. I walked down the last corridor, and I saw a sign that said Toledo Sleep Disorder Center. I walked into the office and saw a sign that said, "Please be seated. Someone will be with you." After a short wait, I was admitted. A few minutes later, I was in this room with all these long covered wires. The nurses scooped a solution out of a jar on the end of a wire and attached it to my head. Other wires were attached with tape on my legs and my chest. One electrode was attached to my chin with a piece of tape. I looked like something from outer space.

The other three people in the evaluation with me went to bed shortly after 10:30 p.m. I couldn't believe that they expected me to sleep with all those electrodes stuck to my body. Also included in the study was having someone observe us sleep all night. The night passes quickly, and before I knew it, it was morning. All the electrodes were removed. Along with the tape came the first few layers of skin from my chin.

I called the clinic in the afternoon to obtain the results. Sure enough, I was spending more time going to sleep than I should and less time waking up. I was to be tested in early December for a CPAP or a continuous positive airway pressure machine that monitors and helps the flow of air into my body. I returned a short time later to have my all night test with the breathing mechanism that would help me breathe better and thus not be tired during the day. The test with the breathing machine meant I would have a hose and connecting nosepiece with openings for my nostrils so that it could be decided if the machine was needed. I also had the electrodes applied to my body for a second time. I mentioned to the nurse that the last time, the tape had removed skin from my chin. The test was given, and in the morning, I was again awoke at six o'clock. All the electrodes were removed, and a smaller patch of skin was removed when the tape was removed from the chin area. I was told I would be called by the O. E. Meyer Company to fit me for a sleep machine.

The company called, and I was fitted with the nose mask for the machine. A few days later, I noticed after my shower that my chin was bleeding where the tape had been taken off earlier in the week. I put a Band-Aid on the small sore and proceeded to bed. The next morning, Saturday, I awoke and was going to shave. I tried to pull off the Band-Aid, but it wouldn't leave my skin. I finally loosened a corner on the and pulled it off. As I pulled the Band-Aid off, I felt a sharp pain on my chin. I was faced with a bleeding chin several times the size of the first sore.

The following Saturday was the day that a feature article on my homemade wine was published in the *Sentinel-Tribune* by reporter Bill Ryan and photographer J. D. Pooley. Kathy. Mark and I attended Mass at Blessed John XXIII. Many parishioners complimented me on my newspaper article. The article quickly took second stage as they asked, "What happened to your chin?" I wish I had not used that Band-Aid. Sometimes one thinks they have made a good decision when it turns out that they couldn't have made a much worse decision.

A Slight Inconvenience

Every now and then, there is an experience that happens, and it makes one think about those things we take for granted. This experience was one such curve in the road I experienced one Sunday evening while returning from my son's. I should include my grandsons Zach and Josh because they were part of the visit to Columbus over the weekend in October.

On the way home from my son's, I usually need to use the men's facilities around Delaware. There is a McDonald's located on the north end of Delaware, and it had a restroom to which I had made many previous visits. We pulled in the parking lot, and I told Kathy that I would return shortly. As I walked into the restaurant, one of the employees was leaving, and he held the door open for me and wished me a good day. I walked to the restroom, and as I opened the door, I noticed the lights were either very dim or not on. I removed my sunglasses, thinking this was the problem, but it wasn't. I went into the dark men's restroom and discovered more darkness.

I looked around for the light switch but found none. I had never noticed before that there were no switches in many of the public restrooms, so I couldn't turn on the lights. By now, my fluid elimination system had gone over the acceptable time limit that I could control my bladder. I opened the door as wide as possible to allow light in the restroom. I focused my eyes on the urinal and jetted toward my goal. I was very lucky. I found the urinal in the pitch-dark and was able to utilize it in a safe manner. I tried to flush it to see if there was water, but I could not activate the urinal. I noticed that no other male was coming into the restroom. This was a double-edged sword since I really didn't want anyone else in the dark with me, but on the other hand, another person would have confirmed that I wasn't the only person foolish enough to be in a McDonald's with no power.

Light or no light, my mother had taught me that I was to wash my hands after using the restroom. I made my way to the door and opened it wide. I focused my attention on the sink and the hand dryer. I left the door open and rushed to the sink, found the soap dispenser, activated the soap machine, and activated the water. After washing my hands in total darkness, I tried to find and did find the hand blower. For probably a good reason, McDonald's does not have paper hand towels in bathrooms, or I would have been out of the restroom in a flash. As I walked into the serving area, there was a lady sitting in one of the booths. She told me that the lights were out, and I could not order any food. We left a parking lot empty of cars and a McDonald's employee telling people that we could not order any food as the electricity was out.

Christmas 2009

Christmas for the past several years has followed the pattern presented in the next few paragraphs. Christmas each year starts with the opening of presents before the big day. Two weekends before Christmas is usually a party with the Long family at one of the relatives' houses. This year it was at Agnes's, Kathy's sister, in Norwalk. Tons of food, drinks, and presents are a requirement for this early Christmas celebration. Kathy had bought both of our grandchildren, Zach and Josh, a remote control racing car for this occasion. Not only did the two owners of the cars have a good time seeing the race cars spin on their rear wheels, but also people of all ages enjoyed the experience.

My son and his family had our Christmas exchange the weekend before Christmas at our house. It is amazing how fast those presents are opened. Joe, Kathy, Mark, Joe II, Tara, Zach, and Josh all received more than their share of presents. Watching children open gifts and play with their toys is for me the highlight of the present-opening experience.

The next big event was helping to put out the luminaries on Christmas Eve. This year was the twenty-ninth year that we had the pathway for our Lord with candles placed in gallon milk jugs. It is a most beautiful sight seeing the attention being given to baby Jesus through the cooperation of the New Rochester Community. Most of the residents in and around New Rochester donate $10 so that six hundred candles can be placed along the roads of our little settlement. The process starts at one o'clock in the afternoon of December 24 with the lighting and placement of the candles. The entire evening into the wee hours of the morning allows any person who wishes to drive through our candle display the opportunity to view this magnificent sight. The year 2010 is our thirtieth year of placing out the luminaries, and talk is already being heard about increasing the candle display.

Church on Christmas Eve was at eleven o'clock. Kathy, Mark, and I attended Blessed John XXIII to celebrate the birth of the Christ Child. The belief in God and His many powers is very well felt at Christmas. The Christmas celebration in which baby Jesus is God made man is more than an awesome belief and experience. The other great event is the resurrection of Jesus after His death on Calvary. God died for all our sins. At Easter, He then went to be with His Father in heaven so we can enjoy eternal salvation.

Christmas Day for several years has been the day that my brother Mike; his wife, Marge; and daughters Mandy and Melissa get together for steaks and crab legs. Kathy, Mark, and I are participants as is my brother-in-law Fred Eldred. This year Mandy brought her new husband, Mike Pritts, and next year we hope to see Missy's new husband, John Porvaznik, in attendance. Everyone present at Mike and Marge's feel very lucky to be able to share food, drink, and cards. The cards played are none other than euchre. The stakes of winning touch the pride of every player as winning becomes all important. I had the chances of winning two games of euchre, but brother Mike invoked his house rules and took away my sure bid on both these occasions. Next year is another chance to be part of the winning team.

The following Sunday, we celebrated Christmas with my brothers and sisters. We have been enjoying a meal and a gift exchange for over ten years in the Sandusky area. My two brothers, Walt and Bob, have the farthest to travel from Raleigh, North Carolina, and Danbury, Connecticut, respectively. In past years, there had been many homemade Christmas gifts, but this year purchased gifts were the norm. I took the prize for the person who brought the most homemade gifts. I brought a bottle of the aperitif, cherry bounce, smoked homemade fish, homemade horseradish, and homemade wine.

The party went well until everyone was getting ready to leave. The four boys were standing around doing small talk. My brother Bob and Mike got on the kick of celebrating either Walt's or my seventy-second birthday. My father died when he was seventy-two, and each of the boys was in hopes that Walt and, if not Walt, I would meet and surpass their seventy-second birthday, thereby giving hope that all the boys would live longer than our father. It was decided that all the brothers would meet in Raleigh, if Walt were to attain the age of seventy-two. If Walt didn't reach the age of seventy-two, when and if I did, all the remaining brothers would come to New Rochester. I was hoping both my brother Walt and me would win the contest, and we did.

Help with My Writings

There had been several facts for the book concerning my JCU college years that I wanted to confirm with one of my former classmates. I had been gathering questions for several months and was thinking I should make the phone call to my former college friend, but I didn't.

One day I had this unusual feeling that was pushing me to call my former college classmate, Don. My wife had been on a mission trip to Guatemala, and I had several irons in the fire I wanted to complete in her absence. The urge to call my friend became so great that I felt I had to make the call now. I made the call, and no one answered. I thought I guess this phone call is not to be made today. I rechecked the number and found I was calling the wrong number. I called the right number, and Don's wife, Peggy answered my call.

She immediately told me that Don had been very sick for several months. I knew immediately why I had this unusual urge to call my friend; he is very ill. His wife asked if I wanted to talk to my friend. I said, "I sure would," before she had the question out of her mouth. As she handed the telephone to Don, I could hear her say in a very upbeat manner that one of his college roommates was on the phone, and it would be good for him to talk with me.

My conversation started with needing help on my book. As I said the words, I immediately shifted gears and started to ask about my friend's health. There was not even a question in my mind my friend's health was much more important than my book. I wasn't sure where to go because I wanted to be supportive of my friend and not in any way to make him feel worse than he was already feeling.

We had a good conversation, but the subject matter was difficult as a definite prognosis had not yet been reached. I hoped the lengthy conversation and supportive information I had was helpful. I briefly went over the information I needed for the book. He said he would think about the answers. I told him I would pray for him, and I would be in regular contact.

It had been three and a half years since our last conversation. I felt like I had been part of a small miracle because the conversation seemed to be helpful for my friend. I believe without a doubt that the urging to make and the content of my conversation I was giving was influenced by a force much higher than me. It also reminded me that I needed to call one of my high school friends who had lost his wife in the not-so-distant past.

The Sequel to Help with My Writing

In this section, we will see how one project leads to many while the most important concern does not always get the attention it needs, something we all see in our lives.

It had been around ten days since I had called my college roommate Don for information needed in my book, and I had been plenty worried about his health. The urge to call him was once again very strong. I had to call, and I had to call now. It was February 23, 2010. The phone rang, and no one answered. I thought in my mind, they must be out, and the doctor was the most likely place to be as Don did not sound like he was up to joyriding. I didn't leave a message. I thought that I wasn't sure when they would get back, and if they had news on Don's health, they would be tired. and I didn't want to bother them with a call back. I would call back tomorrow.

When tomorrow came, I was very busy with a project for the Knights of Columbus called the Eggstravaganza or egg hunting event with many other added events. Talking with Don took second place as the Eggstravaganza was proving to be more than I had anticipated. That is what happens when everyone wishes to make a project better.

Also, the previous night was the Knights meeting, and there were several items that I as one of the quad chairpersons and the rest of the committee presented to the council. All the items we presented were approved as was the new budget. Joel, a quad chairperson, had investigated candy prices in about every store in the area; Brad, another quad chairperson, was investigating the bunny costume; Mike, also a quad chairperson, was organizing the various age groups; John, the other quad-chairperson and master of ceremonies, was organizing the entertainment and working with me to plan the Easter egg hunt. Another committee member, Terry, was making sure that all facility issues were addressed.

With a team such as this and several issues to be addressed in one month, there was much to be done. At the initial meeting, several other issues had come up that needed attention. I had just finished a lengthy memo to the committee and the Grand Knight, Wayne, explaining in detail all the decisions we needed to make. Having set up a tentative meeting in two weeks, the next step was to call Blessed John and reserve the meeting room with the secretary.

In addition to the egg hunt, I needed to find out information about the family voted by the Blessed John XXIII Knights of Columbus as the Family of the Month for February 2010, Brad and Mary. The Brad and Mary family had just returned from Guatemala with a delegation of

Blessed John church members who spent a week working with a project to help the coffee bean business better function. The project was a new road for transporting the coffee beans.

Not only had Brad and Mary adopted a child from Guatemala, but also their other daughter was adopted from China. They are involved in the Guatemala project and other church and community projects, so I needed some demographic data to complete the application process for them to receive the Family of the Month Award. I called the secretary at Blessed John and told her the information I needed. She asked if she could call me back. I said, "Sure."

It had not been more than a few minutes, and my phone rang. I figured it was the parish secretary; I was dead wrong. The person at the other end said she was Peggy. The Peggy who came to mind was my daughter-in-law, Tara's, mother. As the person talked, it did not sound like Peggy Mobley, my daughter-in-law's mother. It turned out to be Peggy, my college roommate's wife. I was about to receive much information in a short time. I was more than interested in what Peggy had to say as ten days ago when I talked to Don, he was a very sick man. Shortly after I talked to Don in February, he had gone to Columbus on the encouragement of both their daughters in Columbus to see what was wrong. This was the first information I heard about Don's stay in Columbus. I found that Don was operated on shortly after arriving in Columbus, and the future was uncertain.

A week later, I visited Don in Columbus shortly after his surgery. At the hospital, Peggy described to me some of the difficulties Don had gone through with his heart. Two of the valves in his heart were infected, and they had a vegetation-like substance growing on them. Some of the growth had flaked off and could be causing negative results as they migrated through the body in the blood. Don was a very sick man who was under very competent care. If Don was to have a new lease on life, Ross Heart Hospital would be the place for this to happen. His family had worked hard to get him appropriate medical treatment. As I saw Don barely conscious, my heart went out to the family.

Don's major difficulties had become manageable two months after the surgery, and he was to be transferring to therapy to St. Rita Hospital in Youngstown. Two months away from home is a long period for Don and Peggy. Don sounded good the last time we talked, and Peggy was very encouraged with Don's progress. Discussions on the book were not possible. I see a trip to Youngstown in the near future.

Good Works

Good works and examples of good works seem to jump into my eyes as I walk by printed matter. I was walking by the dining room table while composing this section. On the table was the February 2010 issue of the *Catholic Digest*. I saw a picture of a nice-looking couple who turned out to be Jamie and Karen Moyer. I could not pass up looking at the article. I found that Jamie is a pitcher for the Philadelphia Phillies. They have eight children and are active in establishing a bereavement camp to help kids through the period after the death of a loved one. They hope to have sixty camps by 2012.

Both are active Catholics. When they see people being overwhelmed by the world, they think, *I'll bet a trip to the children's hospital would change that.* With their many active personal and charitable projects, Karen explained her life like this: "It's truly how I live life. I get the most out of it. I think it's such a gift. My days are always full. I'm always one to tell my kids to make it a good day instead of have a good day." The article was inspiring, and my hope is that the inspiration will be an actualization of spinning many of us into action. Please read the article. By the way, Karen has been around sports her entire life. Her father was former Fighting Irish basketball coach Digger Phelps.

Tucked away in my files was another example of "good works" in the June 21, 2008, edition of the local newspaper the *Sentinel-Tribune*, as reported by staff writer Jordan Cravens. The article was titled "Tontogany group gives family $14,555." The money was raised at an auction by the Ohio-based Tontogany Sons of the American Legion and was presented to Sandy Woodbury, whose husband, Billy, is a member of the American Legion.

The funds were for nursing home care needed after complications from diabetes caused Billy to lose a foot, and an infection spread to his spine, paralyzing him. Ultimately, Billy was forced to live in a nursing home for his needs to be met. The monies came largely from a spaghetti supper and an auction. Steve Powell, also a member of the local American Legion, presided as auctioneer at the event in which people were said to be pretty generous. "Such generous behavior was shown by a man who bid $210 for a homemade pie, later giving it to the second highest bidder." Incidentally, Billy was at the auction with roughly five hundred other people. This was Billy's first outing in over a year. It is easy to see that examples of "good works" are present in newspapers and magazines in more than one year's time.

Helpful Hints

From time to time, I run across various sayings in e-mails and other written material. One of the sayings that caught my eye came from an unknown author. It said, "Judge your success by what you had to give up in order to get it." There is a lot of truth in this statement as I have yet to see many times in my life that success was easy. Do you agree?

Another saying was "Maybe . . . you should try to live your life to the fullest because when you were born, you were crying and everybody around you was smiling but when you die, you can be the one who is smiling and everyone around you is crying." This is certainly a different twist to birth and dying.

The Garage

From Fast to Slower and Longer

I had always been a very fast talker, worker, and anything else that could be done fast. I would multitask and thus be able to get twice as much accomplished. May 8, 2010, proved to be a day of awareness for me regarding my fast actions. I awoke at seven thirty-two to a windy, dismal morning. I would have preferred that the day was sunny as I was painting our entire garage. By entire I mean ceiling, side walls, and floor. As I reached the bottom of the stairs, Kathy informed me that the robin's nest outside the back room window had been blown off the lattice and was lying on the ground. She was concerned about the eggs. I put on my coat and went outside to survey the damage. I located the nest on the ground, and behind the lattice, I saw three robin eggs. I had put on rubber gloves so as not to give any human scent to the nest or the eggs. I had been told when I was young that if you touch baby eggs or any other type of baby, the mother will not raise them. The chances of the mother coming back and sitting on the eggs was near zero. The possibility of the eggs being good since the mother had not sat on them for at least an hour was near zero. The eggs would certainly be cold by now.

I decided to pick up the eggs gently and place them in the nest. I took the eggs in the house where it was warm and asked Kathy for some of her thin wire used for plant arrangements. I began to take the eggs out of the nest and got into too big a hurry. As I was taking out one, I also had picked up a lose piece of twine attached to the nest. I picked up the egg, and in the transfer, the twine pulled my hand and caused my finger and thumb to crack the egg. The egg went on my hands and on the side of the window. I quickly proceeded outside to wire the nest on the top cross section of the lattice. The faster I had the nest up, the quicker the robin could get on her eggs. As I was putting on the last wire, Kathy informed me that the nest was originally down two cross sections. I had a few uncomplimentary statements on doing all this work for nothing and losing valuable time I should be using painting the garage. I moved the nest down two sections, finished the wiring, and walked into the house to get the eggs. I placed the eggs in the nest, and already two tasks had not gone right. My fast action of putting up the nest wrong before checking with Kathy on its previous location and breaking the eggs was not the outcome I had desired.

It was on to the garage and painting the trim. As I was working on painting around the supports holding up the rails to the overhead door without taping the metal on the ceiling, I noticed I was painting on the metal supports. This was exactly what I did not want to do. I then took the time to tape all the metal, so I didn't paint it. As I was painting the ceiling and wall corners, I was again in a hurry, and I began slopping paint on the floor.

I wasn't aware until later that my fast actions caused the closet to collect some droppings from my earlier paint job. I had painted the closet several months before and didn't need to paint. The paint droppings had dried, and I tried to chip it off. I noticed that the paint drops I had slopped on the closet had come off, but so had the original paint. The color of the closet was different from the paint I had dripped on the closet. I knew I didn't have any paint to paint my sloppy fast painting earlier in the day.

It was now time to paint the cover for the steps in the ceiling of the garage. I pulled the door down, only to find that the trim needed to be caulked. There goes another fifteen minutes. I found that the file cabinet was covered below the door, so I pulled down the cover so I could caulk the trim. I wasn't about to waste time moving the cabinet, so I stepped on it and began to caulk and then paint. As I was getting down from the file cabinet to get on the ladder, I grabbed the ladder for support. That was a very poor move because the steps flew out of their resting place and hit me in the head.

It was now time to paint the wall that was located next to the top of the garage door. I had to open the door to be able to paint the boards. As I raised the door, the wind was blowing very hard. The wind was swirling in the garage, and all my plastic drop cloths were blowing out of place. I reset the drop clothes and began painting. I was behind schedule, so I painted faster. As I painted faster, I began to paint places I was not to be painting such as the springs to open the garage door. I loaded up my paintbrush and again began to paint fast. As I painted faster, I lost control of the brush, and it flew to the ground full of paint. Luckily, the brush fell on a drop cloth. As I tried to gain some ground I began tripping over items on the floor. I was in such a hurry I wasn't even looking where I was going.

I was now painting behind the refrigerator and the freezer. I unplugged both and painted behind them. I intended to plug in the two cords as soon as I was done in that area. About four hours later, my son Mark opened the refrigerator and asked me if it was working since the light was off. Instantly, I remembered I was rushing to get the painting done and must have forgot to plug in the cords.

We went to church that afternoon to five o'clock Mass. As I sat down in church and reviewed my day, it became very apparent to me that I was trying to go too fast and was not gaining anything from this type of fast action. There was more than the wasted time at trying to wire the bird's nest and breaking the robin's egg, both attributed to fast actions on my part. I had always had great luck with working fast, but for some reason, it was not working. I was getting a message that I needed to slow down and work a little longer. I credited God with the awareness that at sixty-five years old, I needed to slow down a little. If I didn't, I was sure that other tasks would not go the way I wished.

The Memorial

For years, my sons and I had a chance to attend the Memorial Tournament in Columbus. The golf tournament was held at Muirfield, a golf designed by Jack Nicklaus, also known as the Golden Bear. The first year we attended the tournament, we had won tickets donated by a classmate by the name of John Morris. John had after that first winning experience always invited me to bring my two sons as guests of his at the tournament. John was a retired FBI agent and also coordinated the security for tournament. At the 2010 tournament in June, rain was a force to be addressed.

There were days that the play was delayed and some that ran smoothly. The last day is always the big day for me because someone is going to be the undisputed winner. We were watching the teams come in at the eighteenth hole. We always had stood in front of the clubhouse. There was a pathway between the fence and the clubhouse where the players could walk behind the spectators undisturbed. This was one of the easiest spots to get players' autographs. While we stood facing the eighteenth green leaning against the fence, there were other, mostly older people, who sat in their seats to our left. Sitting allowed the people in that position to relax a bit, but people walking by would on occasion stand in front of the people sitting in their chairs and block their view of the golfers. On this particular day, a few younger adults stopped in front of the people in chairs. I looked to see if they were blocking their view. Sure enough, the young adults were blocking the view of those elderly people sitting behind them. Even when the police came to ask the view blockers to move a bit to the side, the two spectators complained that next to them, people were not getting out of the way of other spectators behind them. The police walking patrol explained to the blockers that they were blocking the view of people in chairs behind them while the other spectators were not. After a few words, one person moved over to barely allow the people in the chairs to see, and the other young man knelt down to open up the view.

This went on for about fifteen minutes until several friends of the original two young men joined them. The new friends were now standing in the same spot that the first two spectators had been asked to vacate. I waited to see if the police would intervene or if the two men who had been asked to move would tell their friends of the standing rules or if the elderly people would say something. Over the years, I had learned that one of the consequences of taking actions meant one was placing one's self in an uncomfortable situation. If I were to say nothing, I would live with guilt for having not used my communication skills. If I approached the young men and asked them to be considerate of the elderly people behind them, I would experience anxiety in approaching the situation. I was really boiling inside at this point because of the inconsideration of the gentlemen. I decided to approach the four to six much taller than me young men and ask them to please open up the view for the older people behind them.

I tried to be as nice as I could when I approached the young men. I reminded the two who had talked to the police about keeping the view open and asked everyone to please move over a few steps. As I walked away, the young man doing most of the blocking called me a four-letter expletive. I continued my walk past my standing spot and found two uniformed security personnel. I explained my concerns, and they immediately talked to the offenders. As I listened to the security officer, I was struck by the apparent lack of respect for authority of the young men. Finally, the young men were told to open the viewing, and the next time, the police would be taking more serious measures. A few minutes later, more young men were beginning to stop in front of the elderly people. They were being asked to move on by the elderly viewers. As one of the young men came by me, he began to badmouth the elderly viewers. I politely asked him, "Please watch your words." Immediately, the young man said to me, "What did you mean watch my mouth?" I ignored the comment and tried to enjoy the rest of the tournament.

The confusing factor to me was that in both cases, the young men were violating, in my judgment, other people's rights. I was not asking for their firstborn, just a little respect and compliance. I felt I had the choice of doing nothing or doing something. For me, doing nothing was contributing and allowing an injustice to take place, so I had to do something.

The Cats

Kathy and I are both of the Roman Catholic faith. One of the privileges we are able to enjoy is being Eucharistic ministers. This means we can give the Body and Blood of Christ to other Catholics. We believe that Jesus Christ died for all of us on Good Friday on the cross in Calvary. This death was necessary because we were marked by original sin when we were born. Original sin was first earned by Adam and Eve when they ate the forbidden fruit that God had told them not to eat. This original sin was passed on to all descendants of Adam and Eve. For all humanity to be able to enjoy eternal salvation or heaven, God made man as Jesus Christ to give of His life so that He and all of us could live again. All of us must be baptized to rid us of original sin. We all must die, and when we die, we have the opportunity to spend eternity with God.

On the third Friday of each month, Kathy and I, along with Jerry and Gerry, Sue and another Kathy, conduct a Communion service at Otterbein Portage Valley Homes. We have between fifteen and twenty people attend the service. To have the service, I usually go to our church, Blessed John the XXIII, to pick up the hosts or the Body of Christ. The route that I usually take is Route 582 through a little town called Dunbridge, Ohio. Dunbridge is basically at the crossroad of two roads with another street or so being lined with twenty to thirty homes. As I came into town, I slowed down as the speed limit decreases. On this particular day, I sensed that I really needed to slow down. As I slowed down, I looked out of the corner of my eye to make sure nothing was going to run in front of my car.

On the left side of the road is a ditch that is probably fifteen to twenty feet deep. There is a guardrail except for when a driveway goes into a residence. Sure enough, I saw a blur running beside the right side of my car in the same direction as I was traveling. As soon as I saw the dark object, my vision was cut off because the object disappeared behind a huge bush. Thinking that the object might turn to the left and come onto the road, I put my foot on the brake to gradually slow down.

Just as I put my foot on the brake, I saw a brown cat come onto the road and run in front of my car headed to a driveway on my left. I placed more pressure on the brake to make sure I wouldn't hit the cat. As the cat was passing to the left side of my car and going into the driveway, I immediately saw a white cat with dark spots on the side of its body. I placed more pressure on the brake as the cat began to run in front of and very close to the car. I watched the cat to see if I was going to hit it. As the car came closer to hitting the cat, it swerved to its right, missing my car, and went into the driveway to my left. I had barely missed the second cat, which I was not aware was chasing the first cat until I saw it in front of my car.

This was a particularly strange incident because before the cats suddenly came in front of my car, I was expecting something to happen. When it did happen, it was as if somebody took over my body to have me miss the cats. I have heard that some people become so close to God that God in essence takes over their lives. The whole experience from anticipating that something would happen until it was over was a rather calm incident for me as it happened. If God took over this incident for me, I would be happy to have Him take over more of my life because it was a very pleasant experience.

The Beauty We Create

Dan Gibson published a story on the Wonderful Cracked Pot. My friend Cliff sent me the story, and after reading it, I knew that it fit well into this publication. The story is centered in India and is built around the water carrier called a *bishti*. As the name suggests, every day the *bishti* carried water in either two pots located at each end of a bamboo pole or leather pouches carrying up to thirty to forty gallons of water.

The Wonderful Cracked Pot

Once there was a man who carried water every day from a stream to his house. He carried it in two large pots hung on each end of a pole slung across his neck. He called them his "wonderful pots."

One pot was perfect. It was always full of water at the end of the long walk from the stream.

The other pot was cracked. It leaked and always arrived at the house only half full.

One day by the stream it spoke to the man.

"I am ashamed of myself," it said.

"Why?" the man asked.

"Water leaks out the crack in my side all the way back to your house," the pot said.

"Because I'm not perfect, you can't bring home two full pots of water. I'm a failure, just a cracked pot."

"You should not feel that way." the man said. "You are not a failure. You are a wonderful pot. And, you can prove it to yourself."

"As we return to the house today, look carefully alongside the path. When we get home, tell me what you saw."

All the way home, the cracked pot paid attention to everything he saw. At home the man asked, "What did you see?"

445

"Flowers," said the cracked pot. "I saw lots of flowers."

"Yes you did. Aren't they beautiful?"

"Yes" said the pot. "But once again, half the water I was carrying leaked out. I'm sorry."

"There is no need to be sorry," said the man. "Tell me. did you notice where the flowers were growing?"

"Well yes," he said, a little puzzled. "They were only on my side of the path, but none on the other side. Why is that?"

"For all these years," the man said, "I have planted flower seeds on your side of the path. Every day as we walked back from the stream."

"Ohhhhhhhh!" the pot interrupted, shaking with excitement. "I watered the seeds through the crack in my side, and the seeds sprouted and the flowers bloomed, and..."

"Yesssss," said the man, who was as excited as the pot. "Because you are the way you are, everyone in the village can decorate their homes with beautiful flowers.

"Each of us is a cracked pot in one way or another." he said. "But there is still no limit to the beauty we can create."

I have always been astonished at the implications from this type of story. At times, I have had people come back to me and say, "I was really down the other day, and the time I spent with you helped me get through the day." While I have heard of a few times I was fortunate enough to spread beauty in the world, I can only try and hope there were other times that all of us have spread beauty for others' benefits.

Holiness

When it comes to spreading beauty in the world, there are several people who come to mind. On a very pleasant summer day in late June 2010, I was reading a magazine that is published by the Knights of Columbus called the *Columbia*, and as I leafed through the magazine, my eye caught an article on Blessed Teresa of Calcutta. Blessed Teresa is known for giving beauty or services to the very poor. She has always been an inspiration to me of love, commitment, and holiness. In the article, Mother Teresa "recognized that a key to holiness is to do small things with great love." Later in the article, Mother Teresa "expressed her appreciation for the work of the Order, (Knights of Columbus)." She said, "Holiness is not the luxury of the few. It is a simple duty for you and for me."

These two statements helped me put in perspective what holiness can be in today's world. The first statement is indeed easy to identify with, doing small everyday things that we all do, with love. Holiness in the second quote is seen as a duty for all and is not a luxury. These were two simple approaches in understandable language for a word not always easily understood or known to be practiced.

Fishing

Fishing has always been a favorite sport in my family and in my life. While I enjoy fishing on Lake Erie, the waves and intense sun have made it less enjoyable. The lake is the place that I am able to catch and eat the fish as opposed to river fish, which are not as plentiful, and their nutritional value and taste is questionable.

On this particular evening, Mark and I were going to fish in our favorite spot in the Portage River. There are three branches to the Portage River, and since I don't care to tell the exact location, I will just say that it was one of the branches. The location of the spot is about thirty minutes from the house. This distance allows a quick decision to fish and the access at the same time. The river is located close to a major highway, and therefore, noise is a bit more than desired. The breathtaking beauty of the environment, rock formations, wildlife, and good fishing outweighs any negatives.

As we drove down the lane leading to the fishing spot a few days before July 4, 2010, we noticed that there were no other cars parked along the river. That was a good sign. We passed the area, which was a drain for the surrounding area, and noticed that a spot had been cleared out in the woods next to the drain area and next to the river. We also observed that the large water pump was sitting in the cleared area, and six- to nine-inch hoses were hooked up to the in and out sections of the pump. Mark pulled the car into the clearing and parked beside the pump.

We went to the rear of Mark's Toyota 4Runner and began to put our waist waders onto our legs and then our feet. We now had our fishing poles and tackle in our small plastic tackle boxes filled with lures that fit neatly into the pouch inside the front of our waders.

On one of my first casts, I was snagged on the bottom. I was using a spinner and a grub-type lure. I worked my way through the water to the lure. As I worked my way through the water, I began to feel and stumble over large rocks beside and beneath my feet. I finally reached the lure after several near misses of falling over rocks and concrete and was able to retrieve it unharmed. The next time I got caught on the bottom, I was not as lucky. Actually, the next six times I was caught on the bottom of the river I lost my spinner and my grub lure.

I looked up at the sky and saw a large black bird flying the route of the river. It looked like an eagle but had no white head. Its tail was tipped in white markings. I asked Mark what it was, and he said it looked like an immature eagle. Later research with my wife and my bird book confirmed that Mark was correct; it was, in fact, an immature bald eagle.

Meanwhile, Mark had caught a large and smallmouth bass, a large rock bass, and a couple other smaller fish. I had taught Mark and Joe II everything I knew about fishing, and now Mark was catching fish while I was not. Mark must have learned his lessons well from my instruction. I felt good that Mark was having good luck fishing.

As I was busy tying new lures on my line, Mark made a signal to me and pointed up stream. There was a beautiful doe and a very small fawn crossing the river. The doe looked at us a few times as she crossed the river. She took one final look at us, took a drink as did the fawn, and were in the woods disappearing as fast as they had appeared. A few years earlier, we had seen a doe and a fawn at the same spot, so we wondered if this was the same doe and a different fawn.

As we were fishing, I looked downstream and saw the back side of a baby raccoon and two other baby raccoons disappearing from the river into the woods. Mark told me he saw a mother, a father, and three small raccoons. About a half hour later, I noticed a single raccoon come down to the river, swim to the other side, and vanish into the woods.

A root beer float provided us both with a refreshing treat on the way home. When we reached home, we put away our tackle and rinsed off the waders. I went to the basement and felt a pain in my left foot at exactly the spot I had felt uncomfortable in the river with my waders. I began to think more seriously about getting new waders as hurting my foot is not a pleasant thought and a less pleasant experience.

I took a shower, and as I was drying myself off with the towel, I realized that I had been near much poison ivy. I didn't think I had been exposed to the poison ivy, but I couldn't afford to take a chance. I dried myself and went to the basement and found my Fels-Naphtha soap. Something in this soap kills poison ivy if you wash within a few hours of exposure. I took my second shower feeling a little negative about taking two showers but feeling better that I might have avoided the dreadful poison ivy itch. It was a pleasant evening even if I did not catch any fish. Being close to nature at such a short distance from my house was as positive an experience as I could have hoped for. Spending quality time with my son was even more important and enjoyable.

CHAPTER 15

Retirement, Vacations, and Other Events

Vacation in 2010

While the Joe and Kathy Fredrick family spend time together throughout the year, the amount of time is limited and does not always allow for extended growth for the family. In August 2010, a cottage was rented at a not-for-profit community on Lake Erie called Lakeside, Ohio. The cottage was owned by one of our relatives, Ron and Amy and their five boys and a girl. The cottage could sleep ten people, and it is so located that a view of Lake Erie is present. The vacation lasted from August 3 until August 7 for Joe; Tara; their two boys, Zach and Josh; and our other son, Mark. Kathy and I stayed for another day, August 8, and needed to be home on August 9 for another vacation with my brother Walt and his wife, Judy, into Canada in their motor home.

August 1, Sunday

Kathy and I arrived a day early at the Methodist-based Chautauqua community on the shores of Lake Erie. The community is based on religion, education, culture, art, and recreation. The gated community offers programs based on the entry fees for vehicles and adults and children. Our first task on Sunday was to register the children for activities available to their age group. Since we were to leave Lakeside for many of our activities, the participation in community activities for our grandsons was somewhat limited. After settling in, we decided to take a trip downtown. One of the enjoyable means of travel is the golf carts that come in many sizes. We found a store that offered a weekly rate for a six-passenger cart, and we snatched it.

Later that evening, we walked on a path that is close to the lake and offered us a view of the lake and the sun. Since it was the appropriate time, Kathy and I found a comfortable bench, and along with many of the Lakeside residents, we enjoyed one of God's beautiful creations, the sunset. Water has the ability to make a sunset more than it is away from the lake or ocean.

August 2, Monday

Kathy and I had Monday morning to ourselves, so we traveled downtown to see what was happening. The shops were open, and the pier drew everyone to its presence by the lake. Soon, it was time for Kathy's mother, sister Agnes, and Agnes's granddaughter, and daughters Amy and Laurie to arrive for a visit. We picked everyone up at the main gate in our six-passenger golf cart. Everyone seemed to enjoyed the open view, protective roof, and wind in our faces. A quick tour of the houses and downtown area prepared everyone for some cheese and drinks on the front porch of our rented cottage.

In the early afternoon, a restaurant was successfully sought, and everyone chose their favorite meal from the menu. A wonderful afternoon with our relatives ended in the early evening. The relationships renewed through conversations and laughter helped prove that people, not material goods, is the true basis of happiness. There was also meaning in this revelation event. You might say, "What is a revelation event, and how do people become an expression of it? A revelation event is any happening by which God becomes a tangible reality in the lives of ordinary people. God was everywhere during this and other visits that week, and so was His beautiful world and our loved ones.

Taking in the sunset was a planned event for Monday evening. As we walked down the wide dock, there were people enjoying the sun, talking, fishing, and all seemed to be anticipating the setting of the sun. The fishing on the pier was producing a few rock bass, some sunfish or blue gills, and mostly the inedible fish. Gobies are a small fish possessing little beauty in appearance but occupying fisherman's time and possibly providing bait for larger fish.

As sunset approached, we decided to find a bench where we observe the magnificence of God and nature. I spotted a bench partially occupied by two women. As I approached the two women to see if we might share their bench, one said that "Anyone who was familiar with Sloppy Joe's was welcome to sit with them." I looked down at my T-shirt and saw that I was wearing my Sloppy Joe's T-shirt from Key West, and I understood her comment.

The four of us immediately launched into a discussion of diving and Key West. Both our new acquaintances were more than nice. The lady who did most of the talking said she was from Pittsburgh and was a medical employee. I did not find out the occupation of the other lady, but she was a scuba diver like me and had dived at Key Largo, Florida.

In the middle of the discussion of Key West, one of the ladies asked me if I was familiar with the graveyard that had housed a young lady loved by a scientist. I said I was faintly familiar with the story. As she explained the story to refresh my memory, I found my memory was refreshed. As the story goes, a young lady in her early 20's was sick and enlisted the help of a doctor. An epidemic of tuberculosis was taking place at that time in Key

West. The lady contracted the disease and died from it. The doctor who treated her fell in love with her, and he took the body from the building in the cemetery which he had erected for the young lady's body to his home. The scientist/doctor reconstructed the body and covered it with wax. Several years later, the doctor was exposed. The body was secretly buried, and the doctor was not prosecuted. Many more details are available in a video. It was time for our newfound guests to leave as they were leaving for Pittsburgh early in the morning. We had enjoyed our new friends, and we never did obtain their names. It was for us an experience we would not easily forget.

August 3, Tuesday

Tuesday was me and Kathy's day to have fun. Since no one else was present, we had nothing planned until later in the afternoon. Originally, Joe and Tara were to come late in the morning this day, and a day on Kelly's Island with the circus would have been lots of fun for the boys. Since Joe, Tara, and the boys were coming later in the afternoon, it would have been hard to make it on time to the circus. Besides, the boys had just been to the Ringling Brothers Circus in Columbus.

Kathy and I wanted to explore the downtown shops we had missed on Sunday. Kathy had her eye on a small shelf for the kitchen but wasn't sure that she wanted it enough to purchase it. A bicycle ride and golf cart ride are always lots of fun and relaxing activities.

We were very excited about seeing the grandchildren, Tara, Joe, and Mark. The call finally came in the late afternoon; Joe, Tara, and the boys were at the entrance gate. I made my way to the entrance and found everybody from Columbus in good shape. As I directed them to our cottage, I could see the boys looking at the large golf cart. I imagined that they were waiting for the first chance to get a ride. I was correct. When we arrived at the cottage, the first thing the boys wanted to do was ride the cart.

We ate supper and made our way around Lakeside with the golf cart. Kathy and Tara wanted to visit some shops, and the men wanted to ride around. Taking in a shuffle board game preceded the sunset on the lake. I had been a fair shuffleboard player in my younger days, but Joe showed me that I needed some practice. The boys went to bed, and Tara and Joe took on Kathy and me in a game of euchre. Let's put it this way, Kathy and I did not have the best cards in playing euchre that evening.

August 4, Wednesday

The day started with a bright and hot sun. The boys were up early, and so was everyone else. After breakfast, we made plans for a visit to Marblehead and Johnson's Island. We stopped at the Marblehead lighthouse. The lighthouse is a majestic site located on several large rock formations next to Lake Erie. There we ran into Kathy's sister, Agnes; her late husband, Lloyd's, daughter, Candy; and her daughter, Breanne. Next, we were off to Johnson's Island, formerly a prison for Confederate soldiers in the Civil War and now a vacation resort. Several prisoners lived on the island, and many were buried on the island. We looked at the many beautiful homes built around an abandoned stone quarry.

It was now time to go back to Lakeside and go swimming. The boys did more playing in the sand than swimming in the lake. Each of the boys was so busy when they played. They were in constant motion, a trait that I acquired from my mother, and you can obviously see how the boys obtained this trait. That evening, Kathy and I again took on Joe and Tara. The cards were in our favor, and we showed Joe and Tara who the real all-time champs at euchre were, at least that night.

August 5, Thursday

The big day of fishing and swimming at the place of Kathy's Uncle Bo at the lake had finally come to pass. We arrived around noon; Mark also arrived at the same time. The fishing lines were baited and thrown into the lake, so we hopefully could catch some big fish. The swimming started from the beach, which is situated to the right of the fishing pier. As Joe and Uncle Mark took the boys into deeper water, it became clear that the boys' attention was focused on a large rock located in the neighbor's swim area. Within a few minutes, everyone in the water was slowly finding their way to the big rock. Unfortunately, many sharp rocks impeded our ability to rapidly approach the big rock. We went slow and tried to minimize injuries to our feet caused by the sharp rocks. Everyone finally made it to the rock and conquered it by sitting on the rock.

Ron and Claudia, Kathy's cousins, came down for part of the afternoon and enjoyed time with Kathy. Ron's brother, Jim, also stopped by, so Kathy had some time with many of her cousins. We left before suppertime and picked up a Subway sandwich for Zach and Josh. Steaks were awaiting us back at the cottage, and I displayed my culinary skills. The steaks were from Frobose Meat Market in Pemberville, and they grilled up beautifully. Everyone agreed that the steaks were some of the best they had ever tasted. Since I grilled the steaks, I would not call any of the others a liar on this subject.

August 6, Friday

I couldn't wait to see Zach and Josh taking the ferry ride from Catawba Point to Put-in-Bay. Put-in-Bay is located on South Bass Island, and like many other islands, it is very intriguing, interesting, and relaxing. The boys thoroughly enjoyed the ferry ride over. When we arrived, we found that we could not rent a golf cart by the dock. Joe II took a ride to town, and within twenty minutes, he had a large golf cart ready to pick us up. Since Mark had worked on Put-in-Bay when he was in college, he knew the island like the back of his hand. One of the first stops we made was at the Department of Natural Resources fish exhibits. As we pulled into the parking area, a friend of Joe, Landry Sheets, pulled in with his daughter on a golf cart. Everyone enjoyed seeing the fish native to Lake Erie.

The trip downtown included a stop at Heineman Winery. Mark's friend and our friend, Kevin, works at the winery and enjoyed serving up some of the vino to us. Kevin is very busy these days as he will be getting married in October to Leslie. Funny thing about this marriage is that Kevin was working at Heineman when Leslie was taking a tour of the winery by Kevin. The rest will be history. Later that evening, we ate at the Boardwalk. I love lobster bisque, and the Boardwalk makes the best bisque. Zach and Josh enjoyed feeding the ducks off the deck with oyster crackers. It was a great day for everyone, and I think everyone would love to go back.

August 7, Saturday

Everyone was planning to leave Lakeside as the end of our rental was fast approaching. Joe, Tara, and the boys and Mark traveled with us to the Mon Ami Restaurant and Winery on Catawba Point early Saturday afternoon. We had a luscious supper, and then it was time to say our goodbyes. I believe the entire family will be talking about our summer experience at Lakeside and the surrounding area for years to come. Kathy and I are grateful we have the resources to help provide this type of vacation for our family. Kathy and I had to pack and get things together at the cottage before we left on Sunday. It was a great vacation, and it will be tough to beat this year's vacation on the shores of Lake Erie.

Vacation to Quebec in 2010

A week before we were to depart for Lakeside, my brother Walt called me and asked Kathy and I to go with him and Judy to visit the shrines around Quebec, Canada, the same week we were to be in Lakeside. We, of course, couldn't go that week but made plans to leave with them on August 10, two days after we came back from Lakeside. Walt and Judy had asked us to go on other trips with them in their motor home, but we couldn't break away. While these two vacations were very close to each other, it made sense for us to enjoy the trip. My parents had taken us to the shrines in Canada when we were very young, but this was the first chance I had to see the shrines as an adult.

August 8, Sunday

Kathy and I left Lakeside about noon and drove home. We received a call from Walt saying that they would be in Sunday night instead of Monday. I told Kathy they would be in Sunday. Kathy said we would leave with Walt and Judy on August 9, Monday, instead of Tuesday, the August 10. Walt and Judy arrived in the afternoon at our house, and we made plans to leave the next morning. Kathy and I had never traveled in a motor home, so we talked with Judy and Walt in the evening about what we needed to know.

August 9, Monday

As we pulled out of our driveway, we estimated that we would be traveling around 1,800 miles on this trip. We traveled through Ohio, Pennsylvania, and into New York. In the late evening, we found a campground near Niagara Falls called Niagara Campground and Lodging.

We unlocked Walt's pull car and took it into the Niagara Falls area. We found an Italian Restaurant, and Kathy and I had spaghetti, and Walt and Judy had fettuccine alfredo. Since we wanted to see the falls from the Canadian side, we crossed over into Canada. The border patrol or customs looked over our passport. While they could look into our car for possessions we should not possess, they didn't. It is pretty hard to get a smile from these officials. I made the mistake of offering some M&M's to the ladies in the back seat during the interview, and I was told in no positive terms to give my attention to the guard.

There had been a shower earlier in the evening, and still, people were walking everywhere at Niagara Falls. Parking is very expensive, and I am not sure if the mist present was from the falls or the remnants of the early shower. We stopped and quickly went over to the wall to see the falls. Because of the mist, it was hard to see the falls, so we were on our way back to the motor home.

August 10, Tuesday

The next morning, we were up and out of the campground very early. We usually ate breakfast in the motor home, which saved time and money. We traveled through New York into Canada. In the late afternoon, we began to look into our camping directory for campgrounds around Montreal. We found a St. Charles Sur Richelieu in the book, called them, and after losing the call, called again and reserved a site. A Mimi was an owner who spoke much French and enough English for us to understand her. When we arrived at the place the campground was to be, we saw a campground with another name. We went to the end of the road, only to find out that we had missed the right campground. We later found out that the campground had changed its name, and the book had the old name.

That evening, we traveled into town to eat as we were extremely hungry. The first restaurant we found was about two times more expensive than we wished to pay. We traveled down the St. Lawrence River and enjoyed all the beautiful homes on the river. Even in the darkness, we could see a great deal of each home.

We decided to go back to the motor home and have some wine, cheese, and sandwiches. I had brought a few cooked hot dogs, so that combination was fine with me. A little euchre topped off the day's activities with Judy and Walt eventually winning.

August 11, Wednesday

Another early start placed us north of Quebec City at Sainte-Anne-de-Beaupré. Before going into the main church, we visited the kneeling steps. The kneeling steps are around forty steps, most having relics in the facing of the stairs. One starts at the bottom on their knees and says a prayer on each step before going up another step. We walked into the basement of the Basilica and visited the various stations. The places to light candles were many. One spot was like a cave, and it was very hot in that area.

We proceeded to the main part of the church where a service, I assume Mass, was taking place in some foreign language. As one walked into the main church, there were several crutches hanging that had been given to the church when these people were cured of their illness or disability. The main altar was very large, and to the left was a special round kneeling station with a golden saint at the top of the kneelers. Around the statue and the kneelers encircling the statue were several crutches. I was reminded that over fifty years ago I had prayed to St. Anne because I had a very bad case of poison ivy. I was cured in a short period after a prayer to St. Anne, the mother of Mary. We visited the gift shop and bought a few mementos.

We traveled off the main road close to the St. Lawrence River. On the back road, we saw a French restaurant that we used for our lunch meal. The food was fantastic, and the service was great. We had a soup and a salmon sandwich.

It was time to find a campground, and we found one near Quebec City. It was named the Do Maine Au Grande. They had a large swim area and three hundred campsites. We found a nice restaurant for supper and once again played cards after dinner. Kathy and I must have won that evening.

August 12, Thursday

We were up early and ready to go to St. Mary du Cape. I had not remembered fifty years ago that the Basilica was so large. The original church was on the grounds, and a magnificent Basilica was present. I had remembered two stories about the Trois Rivieres, and the first was about how the people attending the church had not been very faithful to their religion. One day the pastor was praying before the altar when he looked up and saw a pig walk in front of the altar with a rosary in its mouth. A rosary is a method of Catholic prayer. The pastor interpreted this crossing to mean that the congregation needed to be better Christians. The praying of the rosary was emphasized, and a beautiful bridge with eight giant rosaries on it was erected on the grounds of the church over a large gully.

The next story is that two priests and a deacon were praying in front of a plaster statue of St. Anne. As the three men prayed, they noticed that the eyes on the statue that had always been shut were opening. The interpretation followed that a new larger church was needed. Plans were made to construct the church, but the blocks needed to build the church were on the other side of the river, and they had no boat large enough to bring over the blocks over the river.

The congregation began to pray for the St. Lawrence River to freeze over so the blocks could be transported. The cold months were coming and going. January came and went with no ice. February came and went with no ice. In March, a great winter storm came, and a large ice bridge formed on the river. The blocks were transported to the St. Mary side of the river, and the new church was built.

We found a second French restaurant after leaving St. Mary and had another enjoyable meal. That evening, we got lost going to the Rue eau Acres campground, which had about three hundred campsites. Once again, I had hot dogs, and the others had wine, cheese, and peanut butter sandwiches.

Negotiating off-road directions was a difficult task, and buying gasoline for the motor home was especially not an easy task. I can remember one gas station in Woodstock, Ontario, we pulled into. The gas pumps were facing a vertical instead of horizontal position to the road. Trying to pull in and out a motor home towing a car was almost impossible. We almost took the station with us as it blocked our exit. We also would not be popular trying to get gas and blocking other gas pumps.

August 13, Friday

Friday was to turn out to be our last day on the road. We stopped at a McDonald's for Judy and Walt's coffee and a drink for me. Kathy always drinks Tab soda after breakfast. While the waitress didn't speak English, the person standing behind us did, so he ordered our drinks. Interestingly enough, I could order the smallest or largest drink, and it all cost the same.

We proceeded toward Detroit and decided to stop for supper. We found a quaint place in the country for lunch. There were bicyclers eating there. It was easy to see that they all had their fancy racing bikes, their hats, their gloves, their spandex clothes, and their backpacks. I was navigating with the map and noticed a spot where the road went close to the water. When we reached the spot called Picton, Canada, the road dead ended into the lake, and there was a ferry transporting vehicles to a dock. We could see that it would cost us twenty miles to go back and circle around the area. We really didn't want to wait for the ferry and pay the crossover fee. We went around the detour. That was not the end of our traffic problems. We began having trouble with traffic as we approached Montreal. At times, traffic stood still as we lost time and fuel on both sides of Montreal.

The trip through customs at Detroit wasn't any better than on the trip over. They actually came on the motor home to see what we had stored. They found nothing, but we discovered we had a great trip. It is always good to come home.

Other Happenings

Little Happenings May Be Frustrating

It was the end of August in 2010. Kathy and I were returning from Upper Sandusky, Ohio. We had met my son from Columbus and dropped off our two grandchildren, Zach and Josh. This stay was the first overnight one for our grandchildren without either of their parents. We had a wonderful time fishing in the neighbor's pond with the boys and Mark. Each of the boys had caught several good-sized bass and bluegills. A visit to the Toledo Zoo provided some educational and fun activities. We took a mini safari and saw kudu, zebra, giraffes, gazelle, and wildebeest while riding close to the animals on a small railroad. Snakes and many tropical as well as freshwater fish were able to be seen at proximity. The day was capped off with an ice cream cone.

Joe arrived at the restaurant at about the same time we did. We had supper together at Wendy's. Tara is a teacher, so Mom could not join us as she was busy organizing her classroom for a new school year. After leaving the boys and Joe, Kathy decided to make a trip to the grocery store on the way home. I dropped off Kathy at the Meijer store, and since I needed gas, I went to the Meijer gas store. As I pulled up to a pump, I noticed that gas was priced at a reasonable rate.

After filling up, I went into the gas station to check a Powerball ticket I had purchased a few weeks ago. I saw a machine that I had never used to check the ticket. It said to put the ticket into the machine. Since I had already put the ticket into the machine to see if I had won, I did it again. One of the clerks must have been watching me, and they said to put the bottom section of the ticket in the machine. The ticket looked like it had two bar codes, and guess who put in the wrong part as I only play the lottery about two times a year.

I then went into the grocery section of Meijer to find Kathy. I found her and helped her finish up shopping. At least I thought I helped her finish shopping. We began to leave the grocery section and go into the pharmacy area located across one of the main aisles. As Kathy crossed the aisle into pharmacy, I told her I would be right back as I forgot to get some M&M's for a sick friend. My friend dearly loves peanut M&M's, so I thought that was the least I could do for someone who had just had their second brain surgery. I found the candy and fast footed it back to where I left Kathy. I crossed the main aisle going into pharmacy and began looking for Kathy. I went through the entire pharmacy and no Kathy. I turned my attention to the rest of the store that we had not yet shopped. I went through the entire store and no Kathy. I waited near the cash registers because I knew she eventually would need to pay for her groceries.

After a few minutes, I saw Kathy coming down the main aisle in groceries. She asked me what I was doing up front because she was waiting for me in the main aisle between the groceries and pharmacy. I had looked everywhere but that aisle because I thought she had left groceries and was in the pharmacy last time I looked.

We began to check out, and I was looking for a place to dispose of a sweet cherry pit and the stem I had sampled when I came in the front door. I saw a wastebasket under the open register to our right and thought I would put the pit and stem from the cherry into the wastebasket. It sounded like a good plan to me. I quickly pulled out the wastebasket as I didn't want the cashier seeing me at the next cash register. I began to throw away the cherry stem and spit out the cherry pit as I pulled out the wastebasket. As I pulled out the wastebasket, I received a big surprise; the wastebasket was full of hangers. It was not a wastebasket for trash but a basket for hangers. I had already thrown the stem into the container and had pushed it back under the register. I had tried to stop my spitting of the cherry pit into the wastebasket when I noticed that the basket was back under the register, and I was more than halfway through the spit as the cherry spit dropped to the floor. At this point, I knew not where either the stem or the pit had landed.

I began to load the groceries into the shopping cart and wondered where the pit and stem had gone. After loading a few bags of groceries, I turned to the next register and pulled out the wastebasket to see if the stem was in the basket. I couldn't see it. I pulled it out again a few seconds later. The stem was in it, so I pulled out the stem and went to the restroom where I knew a bona fide trash can was available. I threw away the stem and washed my hands. It was back to loading groceries. I loaded a few more groceries, but my mind was occupied with the missing cherry pit. I went over by the vacant cash register, looked around, and saw the pit. I didn't want anyone to turn their ankle by stepping on the pit, so I picked it up. It was back to the restroom for a throwaway and handwash. I ventured back to the groceries and quickly loaded up the rest of the groceries. The top of the cart was full, so I put a gallon of bottled water on the rack below with the potatoes.

I took out the groceries, being very careful not to hit any bumps and lose the gallon of water. I am a professional at hitting bumps and losing gallon jugs. I made it to within five feet of the van when I hit a bump. As I looked down, I saw the gallon of water leaving the rack. I picked it up and put it back on the lower rack until I had opened the van. I had everything loaded but the bag of potatoes. I tried to pick up the potatoes, but they would not move off the lower rack. I got down on my knees and looked to see what the problem was. It seemed three of the potatoes had fallen between the crack in the lower-carrying rack, and then they must have rotated so they were sideways and thus caught in the rack. I carefully rotated each of the potatoes until I had freed the potatoes from the rack. I then lifted the potatoes and loaded them into the van. I hoped I was ready to arrive home, unload the groceries without incident, and complete another task I had started earlier in the day. I knew that it was not an unusual occurrence for me to have challenging situations arise when I go grocery shopping. I just hoped I was home safe.

Bad Things Happen, but They Could Have Been Worse

Once a year in the late summer or early spring, I powerwash our home. The house is covered with vinyl siding, and it attracts dirt. It wouldn't be so bad that it attracts dirt, but the color of the siding is a bright yellow. I found a cleaner that works on the house but have been told to keep the solution off windows, or it will stain the windows if not properly washed off.

It was a bright late summer day in 2010, and I had been working on the house for the second day. I have three high peaks that must be washed, and I am careful to take no risks while I am on the ladder. I had climbed the extension ladder to within four feet of the top of the peak and began to spray the covered section of the roof. To spray this section, it was necessary for me to reach out with my sprayer and cover the section that was parallel to me only out a few feet. As I sprayed over my head, I felt some of the spray penetrate the top of my glasses, and as it touched my eyes, it stung. I didn't think much of the stinging, but as my sight slowly began to become cloudy, I knew I needed to do something. I quickly went to the other side of the house and began to wash out my eyes.

Kathy came in the kitchen and wanted to know why I was washing out my eyes. I explained, and she said she wanted to check the precautionary on the bottle of the cleaner. After the precautions were read, I found I had another fourteen minutes of eye washing. I washed out my eyes and began to see a little better. I went back to my house cleaning, but this time I had airtight goggles, not my eye glasses, as protection. The more I washed, the better my eyes became.

Just as my luck with the eyes got better, I tried moving the extension ladder, only to find out my careful moving patterns with the ladder were beginning to not be so safe. As I was sliding the top of the ladder around the corner of the house, the ladder was located in thin air. Since I was holding the ladder up, that meant that the full weight of the ladder transferred directly to my body. Since I was not expecting the weight of the ladder, the ladder came down on me and rested on my head. I regained my composure and managed to push the ladder off my head and to a safe position on the ground. I decided very quickly that the next time I was to move a ladder around the corner, I was to take the ladder down, carry it around the corner, and then reset the ladder.

That evening, my eyes were both very sore. I went to bed with much better eyesight and awoke with my sight completely restored. While temporarily having my vision cloudy and hard to see, it could have been permanent, and it could have been worse to permanently lose my sight. Also, the scratch on my head from the ladder could have been worse by causing a broken bone. I had a pretty lucky day with someone watching over my good health.

The 2010 New Albany 10K Walk

For several years, Tara, my daughter-in-law, and I had competed in this 10K walk. The previous year was a pleasant day, and we enjoyed the walk. The total mileage in a 10K is 6.2 miles. Being in condition through ongoing practice is important. I tried to walk whenever I had a chance, but I am sure I could have put more effort into preparing for this race.

Tara and I were up early the day of the race. Zachary was also up early as he was to walk in the one-mile run for very young walkers in connection with the New Albany Walk. We arrived at our usual time and waited for the race to begin. It was rumored that around three thousand walkers were to participate, making this the largest walking event in the United States.

As usual, people were packed like sardines in the starting area. Tara and I kept close to each other to have enough room in front of us so that we could clearly see the people to the side and front of us. From previous years, we knew that if you didn't watch others' feet, you were likely to end up on the pavement due to tripping over other people. As the race started, Tara and I were very successful in staying away from other walkers' feet. We carefully approached the start line and worked our way into a start that wasn't dictated by other walkers. The situation we avoided was getting boxed in by walkers ahead of us and not being able to set a good pace.

I took the lead and worked us into positions that gave us the freedom to make good time. For the first one-half mile, we were cruising along and holding a position that was advantageous to our plan of walking. As soon as I began to get comfortable with our position, I began to feel something tugging at my right foot. The further I went, the more my hip and leg hurt. I went for a mile bearing the pain and hoping my pain would lessen. I offered a prayer up to my God, asking Him for the strength to finish the race. A little over two miles and my leg began to feel better. I continued to see more people pass us as my leg was causing me to work doubly hard to stay in the race.

I prayed harder and relayed to Tara that I was feeling better. Another mile and we were approaching the three-mile mark. My leg received a new jolt of pain, and we were only about half done with the race. The next three miles caused me to be very tired, injured, and in great pain. I never gave serious thought to giving up the race. Tara asked me on the second half of the race if I wanted to stop. I briefly explained to Tara that quitting was not in my vocabulary. The overcast weather in the early portion of the race was now becoming sunny and much hotter. I pushed on knowing that my leg was out of place, and therefore, one leg would be shorter than the other. Since I was not going up or down many hills, the leg pain was somewhat tolerable. As the sixth-mile marker came up, I automatically did what I always do in a race, put on the speed for a good finish.

As Tara and I began to weave in and out of the walkers ahead of us, we began to pass several groups of walkers. We had easily passed five groups of walkers as we both hit the finish as close as possible together. Our time was one of the best we had produced in all the years of walking the race.

We found Joe II, Zachary, Kathy, and Josh at the finish line. We were curious how Zachary's walk had gone. It was good news in that Zach had a great walk, run, stop, and go. I downed three containers of water and juice as I literally had nothing to drink that morning, and I had gone light on my breakfast. Food and water are avoided before the race as stopping to use the restroom rapidly takes time off one's ending race time.

We arrived at Joe and Tara's house, and it was decided that we would begin to take down one of the dead trees in the front of their house. I was not in any position to walk around, but I took it easy and was able to pick up the branches that came flying off the dead tree. As we cleaned up the yard and hauled away the brush, it was a good feeling to know that despite the pain, I was able to pull my end of the work.

After a great supper, we had a six-person wiffleball game. Tara, Josh, and I played Joe II, Kathy, and Zach. It was a great game, everyone hit and fielded well, and we were then on our way to New Rochester.

On Monday, I had several appointments from St. Marys, Ohio, to Findlay and then Bowling Green. I had a few minutes to visit my chiropractor in Bowling Green and make it to my five o'clock meeting with the Black Swamp Humanitarian Committee. I walked slowly into the meeting, but after my appointment with my chiropractor, I was at least walking.

Garage Sale on September 16–18, 2010

Each year, Kathy usually executes a garage sale. Kathy's garage sale becomes everyone in the family's sale as we are asked to contribute items. While we will harvest the sales, we are also asked to spend time selling the items. Kathy is very organized, and the sale runs smoothly.

Kathy has control over most items connected with the sale such as what to sell, how much, store hours, and who works at what times. Although Kathy works most of the time, she needs backups if customers are very numerous or someone other than Kathy knows the item to be sold. This particular year, the weather had been beautiful until the afternoon of the first day of sales. The rain came, and the customers didn't.

My responsibility is to place and maintain the signs. The weather had a big effect on signs this year. There had not been rain for weeks. The ground was like solid rock. Pounding in the stakes to hold the signs was a near-impossible task. After the signs were placed, the rain and an accompanying windstorm blew away several signs, and many of the poles were knocked down or loose. On one occasion, I was replacing two poles and stapling a sign about a mile from my house at Chad's house. I used a pipe with one closed end to pound the wooden stakes to the ground. The hard ground forced me to pound the stakes very hard.

On this particular day, I had just finished securing the second stake. I was making a considerable amount of noise pounding the stakes. As I laid down the pipe hammer, I had this funny feeling that I was being watched. I looked around and immediately saw why I had this feeling. Chad's two large draft horses had journeyed from the top of the hill, probably being attracted by my stake pounding, and were both standing next to the gate a few yards from me, staring at me working. I couldn't help but laugh, and eventually I thanked God for the unusual sight of two horses spending part of their day, giving me their undivided attention.

On Friday afternoon, we had asked our son Mark to watch the garage sale while we went to Otterbein Portage Valley to conduct a Catholic Communion service. Several of the residents were not able to come to the service, so we took Communion to them. One of the most unusual experiences of my life was to take place that afternoon. One of the residents had fallen and hurt his ribs. I took Communion over to his room, and we talked about his recent rib injury. Before we give Communion, we say a prayer with the resident. This particular resident had a beautiful Labrador dog. The dog was very active until the resident and I joined hands to say the prayer. As we started the prayer, the dog came over to us, lifted both front paws in the air, and rested them on the resident and my hand. The dog did not move until we had completed the prayer. It was like a small miracle to me inspired by a force higher than myself.

Going back to the garage sale, twice a day, I checked the signs to see if they needed attention. This year turned out to be the year of the signs because I spent a considerable amount of time fixing signs. On Saturday morning, I was taking in the garage sales when one of the neighbors informed me that one of the big signs had the wrong date on it. There were two signs that the neighbor had taped over last year's dates with this year's dates. One of the new date signs had become wet with the rain, and the sign peeled down, exposing last year's incorrect date. I had already fixed one of the signs three times, so I was looking for number 4. I checked the sign I had been repairing and found it had the correct date listed. A look at the second large sign showed that the dates for this year had been completely removed, and the wrong dates from last year were exposed. This time I stapled the correct sign containing this year's dates.

Overall, our garage sale was very good. We had more customers than ever except for the Thursday afternoon rain time.

A Small Miracle

I spend a considerable amount of time on my hobby of making wine. While making wine can be fun, it can also be challenging and frustrating if the process does not go as planned. The first process was making champagne. I had been making four cases of champagne, two for about nine months and two for about six months away. The challenging part of making champagne with these four cases was that the champagne was not clearing. Champagne is cloudy because there is sediment in the bottle. To clear the bottles, I must turn the bottles upside down in the case so that I could work the sediment to the neck of the bottle on the cap. Champagne is different from other wines because the yeast is kept alive so that there will be bubbles in the wine. After fermenting the champagne, I placed it into a bottle and placed a cap on the bottle to keep in the pressure. In this case, the four bottles did not have champagne that was settling in the cap of the bottle.

I had promised earlier that I would provide champagne for all the guests at the wedding on Put-in-Bay for the toast. Well, the time was rolling around, and it was about a month before the wedding. Since the champagne was starting to settle, I told the groom, Kevin, that I would be able to provide the champagne as promised. I couldn't wait any longer to tell Leslie and Kevin; it was either yes or no. I took a risk and said, "Yes, the champagne would be ready for the wedding." I continued to work the sediment into the cap. It was now two weeks before the wedding, and I did not have the champagne ready. I went to a two-times-a-day clearing process. At one week before the wedding, mysteriously, the champagne did clear. I was degourging or removing the champagne on the Wednesday before the Saturday wedding day. I thought a small miracle happened because the champagne was ready a few days before the wedding.

The second small miracle happened in connection with fermenting pink Catawba wine. On a Tuesday morning, I traveled to Sandusky to

Firelands Winery to pick up five gallons of pink Catawba juice to make wine known by the same name. I brought home the juice and put in the sugar, the yeast nutrient, and the yeast. The next day, it should be bubbling. The juice was not working. I let it go another day and called my wine experts in Dundee, Michigan. He told me to put in a certain chemical. I did just that, and nothing happened. Two days later, I called Dundee again, and I was told to put in more sugar. That did not help. I called two days later, and we decided to put in some yeast booster. Still, no help. Two days later and I called, and we decided that more yeast might start the fermentation. It did not. Two days later, I then decided that a second dose of yeast booster would be good after going to the wine store in Bowling Green. I also left a sample of the juice for analysis. I went with a third dose of yeast booster. I am now at day 10, and I saw a few bubbles. The wine store proprietor in Bowling Green called me and said his analysis showed I needed to add a certain chemical. The fermentation took off, and much to my surprise, I didn't have to throw out the juice. Yes, this was to me a small miracle.

The Wedding at Put-in-Bay

The champagne for Kevin and Leslie's wedding had been sent over on the ferry on Friday, October 1. Kevin is employed at Heineman Winery, and Leslie is a nurse in a hospital. We met the 11:30 a.m. Miller's Ferry at Catawba Point. Luckily, we didn't have to wait long to board. As we were boarding, our son Mark was walking down the path beside the cars being loaded on the ferry. He saw us, and since we were in the line next to the walkway, he transferred his luggage over the fence to Kathy. It was beginning to drizzle, so he was off to the boat.

The trip over was a pleasant ride, and when we reached the other side, we drove up the hill from the ferry, and I felt very relaxed being on the island. We arrived at our lodging, the Bay Shore Resort. After checking in early, we began to dress for the two o'clock wedding at Our Lady of Sorrows Catholic Church. We opened the curtain and discovered a beautiful balcony and an even more beautiful view of Lake Erie. The view was breathtaking as we watched the waves hit the shore below our third-story room.

Mark had the room next to us, and he experienced the same beautiful view. It was now time to go to the reception room and cool the champagne before going to the church. We arrived with many other people we knew and would get to know at our destination the wedding. As I looked around the church, my eyes fell upon an acquaintance I had not seen in years, Joyce and Hub Reed, who now lived in Apple Valley, Ohio. They really enjoyed their home close to a good-sized lake. As I looked toward the back of the church, I noticed Denny and Barb Layman. They were parents of Mark's very good friend, Brent. We lost Brent a few years ago because of a heart disorder. It was a big loss to so many. As I looked back further, I saw Louie, owner of Heineman Winery. While Louie was a successful businessman, he was also an interesting person who could keep my interest for hours.

The service began with two singers, Kevin's brother Jody and Jody's fiancée, Natalie. Both Jody and Natalie are actors on Broadway, and both sang with such great talent and volume that I thought the roof of the church was in danger of being raised off its rafters. The wedding proceeded, and at the appointed time, Kevin was escorted down the aisle by his parents. A memory was brought back to me as I had wanted to have Kathy and I escort our son Joe down the aisle at his wedding. We must have been ahead of our time. Leslie was escorted down the aisle by her parents, and the service proceeded as it should with not a negative sight or sound in the church.

After the service, it was off to the Heineman Winery, and everyone had a coupon for a drink. I was happy that I was able to find more than one drink before traveling to the yacht club. Barb and Denny were traveling with us to the winery and the yacht club for the reception. A drizzle had found its way to Put-in-Bay as we left the winery. The toast was given by Kevin's other brother, Keith. The sparkling wine was provided by the Frederick Wine Cellar. I have never received so many compliments at one time for my champagne. With the rain and my vehicle, I was to provide rides to the Jet Express boat many times that evening.

The next morning, it was to Frosty Bar for breakfast. The breakfast was fantastic as was the conversation with Kathy, Mark, and two of Mark's set of friends, Josh, Joey, Matt, and Christina. I also saw the wine master for Heineman, Ed, and had a few words with him. He had a few words for me, and the most significant was his unsolicited compliment on the champagne at the wedding I had made. That was truly a compliment; it does not get any better than this.

It was time to catch a ferry, and we pulled our car into line. We didn't get on the Miller's Ferry on the first boat. Since Mark's car was on the mainland, he did make the first boat. In fact, we missed the second boat by three vehicles, but we did get on the third boat. I was a little concerned because there were gale winds and waves of ten feet crashing over the ferries. We loaded on the ferry, and I was immediately greeted by that old acquaintance of mine, seasickness. I was extremely fortunate that my old acquaintance did not pay me much of a visit that day. It was on the mainland and home after another successful outing.

Retreat

In the Catholic faith, there is a practice called a retreat. The purpose of the retreat is to get away from the busy everyday world and to spend time with God and the guidance of a spiritual counselor to renew one's relationship with God. Retreats can be as short as a day or for several weeks. My friend Mel Wicks asked me to attend a retreat with him in Bloomfield Hills, Michigan, at the Manresa Jesuit Retreat House.

I had not been to a Jesuit retreat since 1966 at John Carroll University, so this was like a coming home experience for me. I was looking forward to pulling together some lost experiences in my relationship with God. The retreat lasted parts of three days, starting on Friday evening and finishing on Sunday at noon. The organization of the retreat centers around spiritual talks, and then there is time for meditation on the topic just covered or topics of importance to the participant.

I was particularly interested in deepening my relationship with God, which to me meant having a more fulfilling ongoing prayer life, a goal I had strived for in the past but never felt as comfortable with as I wished. It turned out that this particular retreat was custom made for me. The central theme was prayer and several approaches to prayer. My counseling with the spiritual directors helped me immensely to see how I could better approach prayer.

I learned very quickly to recall ideas that I had known as a child but had let go by the wayside. The first idea is that God made me, and since He made me, He had a responsibility to me, He loved me, and He is always with me. He is on twenty-four-hour call, and He will be there for me. I have trust in God, and He is there to help me. A very important virtue that I constantly need to develop is the ability to listen to God so I know what He is saying to me. The second part of listening is accepting and being thankful for God's gifts to me. These gifts include anything beneficial I have in life. Many of these gifts I didn't ask God for, but God took care of me. Listening is a form of love and one I needed to work on each day.

Among the helpful ideas I received that weekend was the idea that since God made me, He also made all the people in the world. Some of the people who had gone before me, I felt reasonably sure they were in heaven with God. Since I felt comfortable with talking with some of these people while they were on Earth, why not talk with them as they are now probably in heaven with God? It is a form of prayer with and through these people to God. This type of prayer may allow me to have a better image to pray with than the abstract image of God. In prayer, I need to allow time for

God or other saints to speak back to me. I have the ability to talk so much that I may not be giving a chance to receive feedback.

One of the most powerful exercises I went through in this retreat was a healing service. This healing service gives one the chance to tell God what they desire to have healed in their or another person's body. One of the priests relayed how he was halfway around the world and went through this healing exercise for a relative of his with cancer of the mouth. Shortly after the healing exercise, he received word that the young man was cured. My son's headaches as well as three other friends' physical disorders were foremost in my mind. As I approached the priest to have his hands laid on me and the oils of healing the sick placed on my two hands and my head, I felt an exhilaration of unexplainable proportions. This exercise opened up to me many new possibilities in the art of healing, one that I plan to study and pursue.

Lost Ring Found

In the early 1980s, a friend of mine, Diane Myers, had lost her wedding ring while she was working in the garden. Nothing happened until a new neighbor, Les Litton, moved into the house. Then on September 23, 2010, he found the wedding ring while gardening and called us to see if we knew to whom the ring might belong. We did and notified Diane of the find. Everyone was happy as the ring found its original owner.

Our Relatives

Schlotterer Reunion

Going to the family reunion is a fun activity. There were originally sixteen children in the Karl and Lucille Schlotterer family in Willard. My mother was the eldest. As of August 2008, there were five of the six living brothers and sisters present at the reunion. Families have traveled from Pennsylvania, Illinois, Iowa, North Carolina, Arizona, and Ohio. Kathy and I try to attend the reunions and were glad to attend this one held in Ashland, Ohio. Karl Schlotterer, who is Uncle Joe's son, is the one who runs the show. He does a very good job and keeps the meeting on task. Incidentally, Uncle Joe is my godfather and namesake. At the family meeting, there was a motion to celebrate the fiftieth year of the reunions next year, 2009. Although there have been more than fifty reunions, they went back to a date marking one of Grandma and Grandpa Schlotterer's anniversaries as the starting date for the fiftieth celebration. The motion passed to have the fiftieth reunion celebrated next year, 2009.

It was good to see everyone even though the day went fast. Almost every family had a representative there. I didn't see anyone from Bill's family and Rose's family, and to the best of my knowledge, these might be the only families not to have a representative. There were lots of games for the kids. The kids were able to find candy and money on various hunts. I believe they had an auction for the adults, but we needed to leave early. Adults also had a guessing game involving guessing the number of people present. I guessed 98, and I think the number was 107 or 108. Aunt Nancy's husband, Henry, won the big prize. A good time was had by all. Unfortunately, seeing the relatives more than at the reunion usually is at a funeral.

Engagements

My younger brother Mike and his wife, Marge, had two girls who had as of November 2008 both been out of college and working for a few years. The elder daughter, Missy, lives in Washington, D.C., and is employed as a writer. The other daughter, Mandy, is a mechanical engineer and lives in Pittsburgh. In 2008, Mandy's boyfriend called up Mike and asked him if he would like to play a game of golf. Mike said that would be fine, and a date was set. Come to find out that during the golf game, Mike asked if he had any objections to Mandy becoming his bride. Mike gave his blessing to them, and a wedding date was set for the year 2009.

Mike told me the following story. Missy also had a boyfriend, and in the same year, John asked Mike if he wanted to go golfing with him. Mike was a little suspicious, but he said sure, he would go. Mike chose to go to a golf range that Mike has a two-year-old pass to play two nine-hole rounds of golf. Mike called the golf course and asked if the pass was still good. The person who answered the phone said he would honor the pass, but he was leaving in an hour, and he wasn't sure if the next worker would honor it. Mike is known to be extremely thrifty, so he was very concerned that he and John get on the move. In fact, Mike always has concerns about money and will do about anything to get a bargain on a purchase. Mike told John they needed to go leave for golf—now. Mike was wondering as they got in the car why John wanted to go golfing in the first place. They went to the first tee, and Mike pulled out his driver, placed a tee in the ground with a ball on the tee, and approached the ball. As he approached the ball, he felt a flutter of wings on his shoulder and looked on his right shoulder to see what was there. Mike looked and found a small yellow bird. The small bird opened its mouth and said, "Cheap. Cheap," and flew away. Mike got the message, and I got the joke. Yes, John did ask for Missy's hand in marriage, and Mike was two for two in accepting new sons-in-law.

Weddings

Weddings have always been a big part of our family. They have been a social event, a religious event, and a very happy event. Within a year of August 2009, we were to attend four wedding of our relatives. Each wedding was unique and had its own story.

The First Wedding and Reception

Pittsburgh was the site for the wedding of my godchild, Mandy Frederick, and Mike Pitts on August 15, 2009. In fact, all my living brothers and sisters and spouses were present for the wedding of Marge and Mike Frederick's youngest daughter. The wedding was held in a woods located adjacent to the Bella Sierra Banquet Room. The ceremony went well, and the dinner was about to begin. I had been asked to make the champagne for the toast and had transported around fifty bottles of my best champagne. I wanted the champagne to be a success for Mandy and Mike. I also had some interest in the success of the champagne. I had asked three people to open the champagne—Bob, Mark, and Mike Frederick. Seven people were recruited to serve. Since people have different tastes for wine, I was concerned that the dry and sweeter champagne might not be to people's liking. I decided to serve mostly medium and sweet champagne. That was my decision, and I stuck to it.

To add a little class to the event, I had asked my two sons and my nephew Matt Frederick to serve the parents' tables and the head tables. I had three choices of wine for them—dry, medium and sweeter. The remaining 140 guests were served medium and sweet champagne, but there would be no choice as time was limited. I think that it is common for anyone who has made something to be eaten or drank to have doubts if people will like their product. To me, the champagne had the best color, fizz, and, I thought, taste.

I was very surprised with the results of the champagne as everyone couldn't say enough good about the champagne. In fact, I was a celebrity of sorts throughout the evening as people made it a point to meet me and compliment me on the wine. It was truly a memorable evening.

However, all good things must come to an end. I needed to get the champagne bottles together, and I wanted to keep the corks as I could reuse them. The corks fit the bottles so well that pliers could be used to open the bottles. Mark and I had taken all the ice chests and accessories out to the car so that we didn't need to do so later. One of the servers came up to me and said that I had left my corks in the kitchen where we had opened the champagne. I put them on our table so as not to forget them. This was a very bad move.

The next morning, we left the motel for home. Upon arriving home, I noticed that my champagne corks were not in the ice chest, and I must have for the second time forgot them. I also noticed that my camera was gone. My luck had taken a turn for the worst. I thought I had last had my camera in the hotel, so I called the hotel and was forwarded to the housekeeping department. I left a message and called the banquet hall. I also left a message at the banquet hall as it was Sunday. I called my brother Mike to inform him of the lost camera in case he was to get a call about the camera. Somehow I knew that my camera would be found. My bad luck changed on the Monday following the Saturday of the wedding when I received a call from the hotel telling me they had found the camera. I concluded that there are still honest people in the world.

The Second Wedding, Reception, and Travels

In the spring of 2010, my niece Becky and fiancé, Kenny Munday, were to be married near Middlesex, North Carolina. Kathy, my son Mark, my brother Mike, my brother-in-law Fred Eldred, and I were to journey to North Carolina for the festive event. The ten-hour trip was routine except for a wreck that had just happened on the Virginia Turnpike and a steaming truck a few miles later. The wreck involved two vehicles, a banged-up car that was facing a guard rail on the right side entrance to the interstate, and an SUV that looked like it had hit the car in the rear. The lady driving the car was walking on the road and looked like she was not feeling well at all. The cause of the wreck to us was undetermined. We looked on and felt lucky as we began to see the northbound traffic behind the wreck stopping. It had always been my observation that seeing a stopped line of traffic in the opposite lane made one feel much better about life than being in the line of vehicles with no motion.

A short time later, a conversation came up about coincidental happenings in life. Mike relayed to the captive audience that he and his wife, Marge, were vacationing in New Orleans. They had decided to take a guided tour of the city. The first stop was a bar, where they received a two-for-the-price-of-one drink called the Hurricane. As they proceeded through New Orleans, they visited a parade in progress. As they were watching the parade, Mike heard a girl's voice shout, "Mr. Frederick!" Mike looked toward the sound and discovered one of his daughter's friends, Racheal, from Cleveland.

Another coincidence shared on the trip down was from Mark, and it involved him and his brother Joe. Our cousin Cassandra Barrett lived with us for a short period when she was attending BGSU. The following summer, her family invited Joe and Mark to visit them in sunny California. The plane ride out revealed much nature to the young men. They shared their time with two young ladies also traveling to California. Their vacation proved to be much fun as they were exposed to the California way of life. One particular day, a trip to MGM studio was planned. The boys thought the tour was interesting and were even speechless when they encountered the very same two young ladies they had sat with on the plane while traveling to California.

Another unique happening occurred as a result of an incident both to and from North Carolina. We had stopped in West Virginia for lunch when three Harley-Davidson motorcycles with four riders pulled into the Submarine Restaurant where we were having lunch. The jackets had Hells Angels on the back. We watched with interest as the group interacted with each other. We began to talk to them about their place of origin and their destination. They were from Cleveland and were going down South. They left, and we left.

The wedding was simple but meaningful. Good foods and drink as well as music are always a hit. I had the privilege of bringing some of my homemade wine and serving it. My brother Mike, brother-in-law Fred, and son Mark rounded out the foursome of bartenders. We enjoyed an extremely busy evening and compliments on the wine and our service. Once again, the importance of family emerged as most meaningful.

On the way back to Ohio, we were traveling along on the interstate in Virginia when we saw three motorcycles driving in the rain. We questioned whether these motorcycles could be the same ones we saw on the way down. We caught up with the cycles and found that the three motorcycles and the four riders were the ones we had met on the way down South. Unbelievable!

The Wedding Shower

Wedding showers are big, and weddings are even bigger. On February 20, 2010, I traveled to Cleveland with Kathy. The occasion was that my niece Missy was to marry John Provaznick on May 29, and today was the wedding shower. I was traveling with Kathy so she didn't have to travel alone, and it also gave me the opportunity to take 165 of seven ounce champagne bottles filled with cabernet sauvignon to Missy so she could label the bottles for the wedding reception. Also included in the trade was a case of regular bottles filled with cabernet sauvignon to be labeled and used as gifts to the wedding party. Kathy and I arrived at the restaurant, Mallorca, and parked across the street in a vacant parking lot that we were told to park in the invitation. We sat about five minutes, and in pulls Mike, my brother, and his wife, Marge. They unpacked the pickup truck in record time. Mike parked his truck on the street. I left my van and shouted to Mike that he was to park in the parking lot where we were parked. He said that he trusted the street more than the parking lot in terms of being charged for the park.

Kathy and I moved our van to the street to comply with Mike's thinking. I stood with Mike outside the restaurant parking cars and opening the entrance door. Standing out in the street and motioning people to pull in front of the door was somewhat of a power trip. The control over the street diminished with not knowing all the people coming to the party. We had cars parked in what seemed about half the city of Downtown Cleveland. Luckily, we did not run into any tickets by parking in areas that we didn't feed the meter. My son Joe and Tara came from Columbus for the party. We found parking places on the street and checked to see all the cars were parked where needed to be parked.

The party began, and Mike, Joe, and I began our own party by eating in the restaurant. It is important to remember that Mallorca is one of my very favorite restaurants. The service is beyond reproach, and the food and drinks are unmatched in their good taste. The waiter took our order, and there was not one order the same. My Joe had shrimp, Mike had frog legs, and I had mahi-mahi fish. It is one of my favorite fish dishes, and Mallorca's seafood is among the best entrées available anywhere. We had our salad after ordering our meal when I was beginning to run out of beer. The waitress asked if I wanted another beer. I said I was not quite ready. A few minutes later, another waitress asked if I wanted another beer. I still was not ready. The first waiter came back and asked if I was ready for another beer. I figured I better order it now. I ordered the beer, and as the waiter left to get the beer, another waiter walked by and asked if I would like another beer. I told him I had just ordered the beer. That is the type of service we had that day. The waiters constantly wanted to see that you were happy.

John, Missy's future husband, came out of the party room to have a quick break from the festivities. While I had been part of a husband-wife wedding shower, I had never been in the room very long with an all-female, except for the groom, wedding shower. John seemed to be weathering it all very well.

The three of us left for a few minutes to find a particular liquor. Joe was interested in buying a bottle that was served in Mallorca called Ferreira Duque Doirinha, an almond liqueur. We searched for the liquor in a large wine shop but found nothing. In the second shop, we entered and found the liquor and purchased it. We went back to the restaurant and decided to take a ride around Downtown Cleveland since we could see it would be a while before the shower was over. We knew perfectly well that we would be called back to the restaurant to take care of the cars and other heavy stuff as soon as we reached another destination. Just as we had planned it, no sooner had we reached Downtown Cleveland than we received a call that the shower was over, and we needed to get back to the restaurant. All the cars were located and brought back to their rightful owners. The presents and other decorations were taken to Mike's truck.

One of Mike's fellow teachers came with and went home with Mike and Marge. I had had a truly enjoyable experience visiting the house of Mike's fellow teacher on a previous Christmas. She decorated her entire house with mostly antique winter-related items such as snowmen, angels, and animals. You name it, she has them. Back to the shower, we found that the winners for the closest guess of the number of olives in a jar was won by Allysia, a student at Baldwin Wallace, daughter of Al and Karen. Barb Frederick from Danbury, New Hampshire, guessed the most spices by smell and won that prize.

Barb followed me to Mike's house, and Mike's daughters, Missy and Mandy, and the future groom, John, all came at the same time for a party at Mike and Marge's. Chris, Marge's sister; Chris's husband, Jake; and their daughter, Jackie, also stopped by for the party. I learned all I wanted to know about the car business from Jackie and was impressed with her knowledge of the car business. A conversation on snorkeling and scuba diving with Mandy and Jake was very informative and enjoyable for me.

The issue of the upcoming wedding of Missy and John was discussed. Jake was talking about getting his room reservations for the wedding near Washington, D.C. When he found out that the reduced rate for the rooms reserved by Missy and John were reduced from $299 per night, he committed to calling for reservations at the new rate of $99 as soon as possible. Everyone was looking forward to a good time at the wedding. It is amazing to me how weddings bring out the best in all of us.

The Third Wedding

There is nothing like a wedding, especially when the wedding is near Washington, D.C., and a few days of sightseeing preceded the wedding.

Pre-Wedding Experiences in Washington, D.C.

Missy's wedding was scheduled for May 29, and we scheduled our trip to D.C. on May 26. At 8:00 a.m., Kathy, Mark, and I pulled into Fred Eldred's driveway near Willard. For several months, we had been planning this trip, and now it was happening. The trip was beautiful with mountains, red bud, and dogwood trees in blossom forming an almost continuous chain. In Washington, D.C., traffic was congested, and we moved at a snail's pace for some time. We finally arrived at the Hilton Garden Inn in Arlington, Virginia, checked in, and decided to go to Central Station, the place that all the trains converge. As we pulled into the hotel, we noticed several motorcycles parked out front of the hotel. We found out later that that was a motorcycle parade scheduled for that Sunday called Roaring Thunder. It would have been nice to see the several hundred thousand bikes in the parade.

We left the hotel and caught the subway two blocks from the hotel. Trying to figure out how to get a pass at one of the machines to board the train was a story all its own. As we entered Central Station, we approached confusingly the many vendors. After a few wrong turns, we found that the night tour we were interested in taking was not in the location the brochure showed it. When we found the twilight tour, we were surprised to find that we had time enough to eat a quick supper and then board the bus for the tour of Washington, D.C. We found a pizza shop and quickly ate.

We boarded the bus and picked what we thought were good seats. The tour was beginning. The Washington Monument was outstanding in terms of beauty and history. We also saw several of the other major landmarks in D.C. We were a bit disappointed that we could not cross the Washington Bridge to see Arlington Cemetery at night. A traffic accident prevented us from crossing the bridge that evening.

On Thursday morning, we decided to take in the visitor center at the Capitol Center. Since our tour of the Capitol was in the afternoon, we decided to eat in the dining center. Since the weather was so hot outside, we called Rep. Bob Latta's office and asked if we could meet Rob, our tour guide, in the visitor center instead of his office complex.

Rob gave us a tour of the Capitol Building, and we watched a committee hearing in the House of Representatives chambers. Several conversations were going on as the official business was being conducted. Dinner that evening was in a pub located near our hotel, and the food was excellent.

On Friday morning, we visited the Museum of Natural History. It was our intention to be at the Hope Diamond display as early as possible. We were at the display shortly after the museum opened, and we were not the least bit disappointed. The Hope Diamond was larger than I had thought it would be, and it was beyond description. Other displays were magnificent such as an emerald as large as a football, but the Hope Diamond took the cake. We visited other displays in the insect area, the dinosaur age, and many other informative and well-done displays. We could have spent days in this one museum of the Smithsonian, but we had other fish to catch.

Our tour of the White House was in the early afternoon, so we caught a quick lunch and were in line for the White House tour. Caitlin from Representative Latta's office, had done a marvelous job of coordinating our various tours to the government buildings. The wait to visit the White

House Visitor Center was much shorter than we anticipated. Security was tight as we were checked when we entered the center, and we were checked again by name as we went into the White House. Every person who entered the White House needed to have their name in the book that security checked at the entrance.

We had heard that the tour of the White House was not that big of a deal from some of the other people we talked to in D.C. From the moment we entered the White House until the moment we left, we were totally enthralled at what we heard, what we saw, and what we experienced. The Blue Room, the Red Room, and the State Room all had their own stories as did the other rooms we visited. In one of the rooms, there were some gold furniture. The story was that President Buchannan had sold ninety-six pieces of the gold furniture when he was in office. When an attempt to find the furniture was made years later, only thirteen pieces of the furniture were able to be obtained. On our way out, we were walking through the White House back lawn, and there was nobody else walking in that area. It was a unique feeling to be at such a famous place and have it to ourselves.

After the White House tour, we grabbed a cab to Arlington Cemetery. We found a place on the bus and saw the Eternal Flame at Pres. John F. Kennedy's grave. We also saw Bobby and Ed Kennedy's graves. The Tomb of the Unknown Soldier was probably the most solemn place at Arlington. The precision of each movement that the guards took was impeccably accomplished. The changing of the guard every thirty minutes in the summer was a sight that I will never forget. It is truly an honor for each of the soldiers to guard the tomb.

Since Memorial Day was Monday, there were a couple of battalions of army soldiers placing flags on every grave in the cemetery. Once again, I will never forget seeing that sight. Friday evening was a time to party as my brother Bob; his wife, Barb; and their offspring—Megan, Mike, and Matt—had come in from Connecticut. The conversations were pretty loud as old stories were told, and corrections to the stories were constant.

It seems no one can get the story right the first time or according to everyone's memory.

Someone brought up the time that I got stuck in a bean field at two o'clock in the morning. The issue came down to which girl I was dating at the time. No stone is left unturned in the Frederick family.

The big day of the wedding came, Saturday. Kathy and I decided to take a walk on Saturday morning and came upon a farmers market in the parking lot across from the hotel. There were vegetables of all kinds as well as antiques, fruit, and plants. I was taken by a plant called cat whiskers. The whiskers on the plant looked just like cat whiskers, so I had to have it. The next day, I made it a present to our neighbor lady, Sue, for having watched our house in our absence. Another unusual article for sale was sponge mushrooms. That was the first time I had seen sponge mushrooms for sale. It was time to get ready for the wedding, so we went back to the hotel to get ready for the big event.

The Wedding

Since there are not many places to park vehicles in D.C., we took one of the shuttle buses to the wedding. As we arrived, we could see that the building had been around for a few years and had an attractiveness that only age and good care could make shine. The wedding was on the main floor and was set up in one section of the very large room. All the young ladies had a glow to them as they took their parts as maid of honor and bridesmaids. The smile, the dress, and the beauty of the bride was a sight to behold. I must mention that John was as handsome as anyone present, including me. The ceremony was largely written by Missy and John. The message to each other was sincere and to the heart. The vows were public and private.

After the wedding, a bit of an unusual reception was held on the roof of the building. There was a large bar overflowing with cocktails and enough hors d'oeuvres to have been a substitute for the sit-down dinner. It was sunny yet not too hot. Everyone was smiling and having a good time. John and Missy had the opportunity to work the crowd with interruptions from the music. I would have planned something like this at my wedding if it had been available. There is always our fiftieth anniversary.

After the hors d'oeuvres and drinks, we were invited to the main floor, where the workers had converted the wedding area and the rest of the hall into this beautiful banquet area. There must have been around five different stem glasses for champagne, water, white wine, red wine, and of course, a spare for after-dinner drinks. The silverware was the same order as the glasses—forks for salad, main meal, dessert, and one to grow on. It was truly elegant and the food delicious. Did I mention that the bride is a food editor for one of the D.C. papers? The service was outstanding. One needed to not think of what they might have wanted to eat or drink because if they thought about something to eat or drink, the waitress or waiters would have it served.

Dancing was wild and crazy. You name it, it was on the radar scope of the DJ. It was fast, it was faster, it was slow, and it was rock and roll. Once again, my niece Megan and I enjoyed some fast dancing. Our various moves seem to coordinate despite the forty-plus years age variance. There was no cake for this reception. Dessert was gelato and was it good. Patches to cover one eye appeared out of nowhere. Was this for the Pittsburgh Pirates? At the exit were the small bottles of cabernet sauvignon from Frederick's Wine Cellar. Yes, bottles of wine were a gift of love from my family.

After the reception, we adjourned to Mike and Marge's room for an after-reception party, similar to the one the night before.

Fishing with the Waves

Since my brother Bob, his son Matt, Mike, and my son Mark were interested in going fishing, I contacted my good friends Butch Rothschild and Ed Hammett. Butch is my best childhood friend, and Ed is my neighbor. Ed is also known as the shepherd as he raises sheep. The other fisherman on board was Butch's son-in-law, Paul Brunner. Paul is one of the best fishermen I have known as he can catch fish when no one else can. We were to go fishing the Tuesday after Mandy and Mike's wedding out of Catawba Island. Butch and Ed both have boats over twenty-five feet, so they are good-sized boats and can withstand the waves of the shallowest lake in the Great Lakes, Lake Erie. Both are experienced boatmen, and I certainly trusted their abilities to manage a boat safely. Spirits were high as we boarded the boats and headed toward the Canadian border north of Kelleys Island to fish. The word was that they were catching eleven- and twelve-inch perch, which is a huge perch. As we hit the lake, we couldn't help but notice that the lake was very choppy with at least two to four feet waves.

As we approached the proper coordinates on the GPS, we dropped anchor off the back of the boat. The lake seemed to be getting choppier the longer we tried to fish. Actually, the fishing was becoming more of a hold on to the siderail of the boat so you will remain in the boat. Fishing for perch is usually done by having two hooks with minnows about eight inches apart on an apparatus called a spreader. The spreader keeps the baited hooks apart.

As I began to fish, I noticed several variables had come to the forefront. The first variable was the fish were taking my bait because I could not tell with the movement of the boat if I had a bite. The second was the boat would go up and down, and as it came down, it would hit the water, creating this fountain of water. This fountain of water was then depositing itself in the boat. I was sitting where the water was deposited in the boat and was very wet after the third onslaught of the splashing water into my lap. The third variable was that the boat's anchor could not dig into the bottom of the lake as it was continually being jerked by the waves. We had reset the anchor once, and now we noticed that the anchor had once again pulled loose, and we were drifting toward the Canadian line. Fishing in the Canadian waters required that we have a Canadian fishing license, and we had not one license on either boat. The fine for fishing without a license I am told can be the loss of the boat and all fishing equipment. As we were approaching the Canadian line, we noticed that the Homeland Security boat was speeding directly toward our boat. Seeing this action, Butch said, "Pull in your lines." Butch at the same time was pulling in the anchor. When Butch had half the anchor rope in, the Homeland Security boat took a look at us not fishing and pulling up the anchor. We must have met the letter of the law because they left us in a burst of waves. We didn't catch many perch, so Butch said, "We are getting out of this place for a calmer fishing area." By this time, I was very dizzy and probably green, but I was holding my own and didn't look much worse than the rest of the fishermen.

We arrived at the next spot, which was on the west side of Kelleys Island, and began to fish. The water wasn't near as choppy as the first fishing spot, but the waves were still very active. After about fifteen minutes, my mouth began to salivate, and I knew what was going to happen. After a few sessions of losing my breakfast, I quit the vomiting. I didn't miss a beat, from vomiting to fishing. As soon as I was done losing my cookies, I picked up my rod and reel and caught three fish in about two minutes. We caught 110 perch, and everyone thought Bob and Mike should take the fish back to Connecticut. We traveled to Port Clinton and had the fish cleaned. The fish were cleaned before we had finished our beer in the local tavern. Amazingly enough, nobody gave me a hard time about vomiting. I think they didn't bring it up because everyone else was on the brink of getting sick. Nonetheless, a good time was had by all.

Dave's Retirement Party

Forty-six years is a long time to spend in one job. This was how long my brother-in-law, Dave Long, had worked for Modern Tool and Dye (MTD), also known as Midwest. The company is known for the manufacture of several different outdoor machines. Some of the machines manufactured by MTD were lawn mowers, riding mowers, snowblowers, and lawn edgers. As near as I could figure out Dave's job, he worked in the timekeeping department and was also responsible for company parties and fundraisers. At least this is what I had heard, and the slideshow at his retirement party verified these facts.

As Kathy and I pulled into the parking lot at the varsity club in Willard to attend Dave's retirement party, we discovered that we could not find a parking spot. If all or most of the cars present represented people who were attending the retirement party, Dave must have been a popular person. After several trips through the lot, we finally decided to look in the back of the building. There was a spot that looked like the last parking spot available next to the dumpster.

The inside of the restaurant was as crowded as the outside, and yes, most of the people were there to honor Dave. As Kathy and I walked into the party room, most of the people were unknown to us. We saw a few people we did know: Dave; his wife, Diane; and their mothers, Laetta Long and Jeanne Matteson. Later, we saw Dave's son Eric; his wife, Angel; Dave's daughter Hilary; and her husband, Jim Crawford, and their family. My sister-in-law Ag Balduff and her three daughters—Amy (Dave Weisenberger), Beth (Rick Fritz), and Laurie (Kim Haughawout)—and their families were also present. I had prepared a roast speech for Dave because the invitation said roasts and toasts would be given. My words were to be kind as I was going to emphasize Dave's management skills. The first skill Dave possesses is to ask others for input into decisions. The second skill was to take actions once the direction is set. The third skill is seeing things through to completion.

I also wanted to share with the group how on one of our first double movie dates with Dave and Diane, he had asked me at the intermission what I thought of his sister Kathy. He was obviously following his three management skills by obtaining input from me, thanking me for my input, and seeing that he was following through as a good brother. Another memory of Dave I had was one morning around three o'clock, I was dropping off Kathy after a late party at my brother's in Mansfield. As Kathy was going in the front door, Dave was leaving for work out of the back door.

At the party, there were many stories being told about Dave and others. I heard not one negative comment on Dave. A few other interesting actions at my table were one of the attendees at my table told another to clean up. I asked what that meant, and they said to be quiet. Another mother was telling of a rather challenging situation she had encountered when their son was first going out for sports. A note came home from the coach asking the parents to be sure that their son had the right size cup or jock strap. Since the father was out of town on business, the mother took the son to the sports store. She asked the clerk for an athletic cup. The clerk asked what size. Without skipping a beat, the son yelled out large. The son's perception and the reality of the size were two different measurements. Reality was much smaller than his perception.

The party would have been the type of party anyone would have wanted for their retirement. The food and drinks were excellent, and the man of the hour was most deserving of all the positive actions and comments given that evening.

The Retirement Party at Work

The second retirement party for my brother-in-law Dave was held at his place of work MTD at noon on January 15, 2010. This retirement party was a little different from the first party held at the varsity club. From the time Kathy and I walked into MTD at eleven o'clock until the time we left around two thirty, we have never seen a workplace so happy to see Dave able to retire yet sad that they were going to lose him after forty-six years of employment. When Kathy and I arrived, we were escorted by the front guard to Dave's office. Within seconds, all these people were coming to his office to see Dave. Most of them, both men and women, were congratulating Dave and giving him a hug and some a kiss. A few would shake his hand instead of giving the hug, but that was the minority. As I watched, people from Dave's department, human resources, approached Dave and gave him congrats, hugs, long hugs, and a few kisses.

On the way to the party room, Dave was pulled aside by many people for a few words, more handshakes, and hugs and for those who could not get to Dave because of the machinery, or there were waves. These waves were not just ordinary waves; they were friendly waves with big smiles that said "We wish you well, and we are going to miss you more than you or we can imagine." Literally everyone was trying to get a piece of Dave. We are talking about a plant that employs nine hundred people.

The conference room was reached after all these goodbyes were said. Kathy, her mother, Diane's mother, Dave's wife, Diane, and I all left his office together. We were in the conference room ready to eat when Dave finally came in several minutes after the set time. The potluck was made by all the employees. There was seating for over 120, and most of the chairs were full. Several workers were not able to attend the party because of the assembly lines that were still running.

After eating the delicious meal, one of the managers asked for everyone's attention, which he obtained in a matter of seconds. The ever-smiling Dave was given a special service plaque, a picture of Diane and him, and two metal sculptures. It seems a welder at the plant can do smaller sculptures. In Dave's case, they were both related to his OSU football team. The first was a football with OSU and Dave's name, while the second was a person climbing a ladder and the words OSU. Dave was also handed a leaf with his name and number of years he worked before retirement.

After the luncheon, we went to go back to Dave's office and waited for him to put his leaf on this large wall tree and join hundreds of other retired employees. Dave was to put up his leaf at 1:30 p.m. Dave was nowhere near his office at a few minutes before 1:30 p.m. His coworker, Sarleen Slone, called the cafeteria to tell him he was going to be late. Well, Dave did make it to his leaf ceremony and did successfully attach his leaf to the wall tree. Kathy, her mom, Diane, Dave, and I were to then take a tour of the company on a golf cart with Dave driving.

The tour was to be brief according to Dave. Remember all those employees who couldn't come to the party? Well, those employees lined the route of the golf cart. When those employees saw Dave coming on the golf cart, you guessed it; they waved, hugged, kissed, or shook his hand. It was an extremely positive experience seeing one man so beloved by his fellow employees. I was very happy for Dave. As I thought about my very nice retirement party, people were cordial and wished me well. But there was not the ever-present display of public affection. It was an afternoon to remember. By the way, we did finally make it through the plant on our tour. The tour had to be one of the longest in the company's history.

As I reflected on Dave's retirement party, I felt very comfortable with the manner in which the employees and Dave had this true experience of being very nice to one another. It seemed that there was trust and faith in this work atmosphere of one another, and that translated into helping others with their habits of giving positive interactions. As I walked in the factory to the men's restroom, every person looked me in the eye and said or gestured hello. The experience was very positive and reinforced the idea that I personally believe that people can give and receive and feel comfortable with an outward expression of positive interactions to others routed in inward positive feelings. I dare say that I saw many actions related to a giving love, and these examples were so moving that thoughts of working in this environment were present.

The Neighborhood

Abandoned Cars

In a period of twenty years, we had brushes with three vehicles that had been in our neighborhood. The last one was in November 10, 2007. I was going to my neighbors Heidi and Rick to pick up some eggs, and I saw the sheriff's car pulling into Lonnie's area by the river. As I passed the sheriff car, I looked into the river, and there was a van sitting in the river. I went to Heidi and Rick's house and picked up my eggs. I told them about the car, and they seemed to think that the emergency vehicle they heard early that morning was going to the van. I went back to my house and ran into another set of neighbors, Mary and Jim. They told me that the van did not have a key in it, might have been stolen, and was running. I went back to my house and got my camera and took a picture of the van on my way to the store in Pemberville.

On the way back from town, I saw a wrecker trying to figure how they were going to get a van out of the middle of the river.

The second abandoned car was found by my son Mark in Hammett's woods, one of our neighbors who lives about two miles from us. This happened about 1998. Mark was going to town, and there was a fresh snow accumulation of four inches on the ground. As Mark went by the woods, he noticed a vague set of tracks going into the thick of the woods. Mark parked his car and followed the tracks into the woods. After going one hundred feet, he thought he saw something. As he approached a group of trees, he saw a car in the middle of them. As he looked around, he tried to figure how the car had been able to pass all the trees and still keep its movement into the woods. Mark came back to the house and told us about the car, so we called the sheriff, and they had the car towed. It seems this car was stolen.

In 1987, Kathy and I were taking a walk on our old double bridge when Kathy said to me that she saw something in the river. I looked over the side of the bridge and could make out a door and a hood of a vehicle. We called the sheriff and explained what we had seen in the river. A few days later, a wrecker came out and pulled the pieces of the vehicle out of the river. I think this car was stolen and cut up by the thief. I never did find out why they had dumped the parts in the river.

Familiar Faces from the Past

It has always been a positive and uplifting experience for me to unexpectedly see people I knew from the past. I have few people whom I have negative relationships with, so it is a treat for me, and I believe them to renew old acquaintances. Talking to persons I had once known in the past is a gift of giving and receiving. When I visit my hometown, Willard, which is rare since Kathy's brother Dave and his wife and her mother are about the only relatives we visit, we do go to St. Francis Xavier Church. There, we occasionally see a few people I knew when I lived in Willard such as Butch Bogner, who worked for my father; Mrs. Don Albright, wife of my former scoutmaster; and a few of the families I remember such as Don Perry and Mr. Schloemer. A few words at church make for a nice visit.

Other people share my feelings on seeing people from the past. For example, I was having my haircut, and I relayed my thoughts on this topic to Faye Coe, my hairdresser, about the positiveness of seeing people who were in our lives but reappear. She told me that during a recent Christmastime, she and her husband, Dan, were in the new Tim Hortons restaurant in Bowling Green when in walked a girl, not living in this area, with her family who was in her confirmation class at St. Paul's Church in New Rochester several years earlier. One never knows when one is going to see a person from the past.

Another example of by chance meetings was when the boys were younger, we were in Orlando with my mother, Kathy, Joe, and Mark. As I walked up to the concession stand, there was Jim Moore, mayor of New Rochester, and his wife, Jackie. On another trip returning from the South, we were flying home and waiting for our plane in the Raleigh terminal. We had been visiting my brother Walt; his wife, Judy; and their children in Middlesex, North Carolina. We were approaching the waiting area when Kathy noticed a familiar face, Dr. David Jump, a classmate of hers at Willard High School in Willard. After catching up on family news with Dave, we were on our separate flights to Ohio. It was a positive experience talking to Dave.

Seeing people from the past is similar to seeing old landmarks and buildings except the landmarks and buildings don't talk. I recently visited my hometown while attending the funeral of my elder sister, Mary Lu. I had the occasion to visit the downtown area and noticed that there was not too much familiar. In the first block on the northwest side, the pool building owned by Mr. Jim Joyce was not open. The bakery, jewelry shop, and Capozzies shoe store, with the X-ray machine for feet, is gone. In the next block on the west side of the street, Hermie Ott's Sporting Goods was not there. The antique store and paint shop were gone. The theater was closed. On the other side of the street, the bar next to the city hall was closed. The clothing store was gone. The drive through bank was closed, and the main bank is no longer the Willard United Bank. The Hallmark Store and Jackson's Drug Store is closed. Many of the stores have changed ownership such as the Grill is now a Mexican restaurant. Uncle Dudley's Restaurant is located on a side street and is still in business. When I go in Uncle Dudley's, I am lucky to know one person. My former neighbor

Madeline Kostoff or Chuck and Brenda Ryman are about the only people I usually know there. Change is a matter of the present.

Fourth of July 2007

On the Fourth of July, watching the fireworks at BGSU was always a special treat. Beating the traffic after the fireworks was not a treat. On this particular year, we were invited down the road from our house to Ed and Pat Hammett's for a barbecue in the early evening. Our other good friends, Terry and Lori Hoepf, Tim Hoepf, Ellen Walston, and our son Mark, were in attendance. The evening was topped off with Ed's homemade chocolate ice cream and my ice-cold Rebel Yell whiskey.

Kathy, Mark, and I decided that we would go to the church parking lot in New Rochester because we could avoid the crowd and see the pyrotechnic display that was about seven miles away. The terrain in Wood County is extremely flat because of the fact that the area was at one time the Great Black Swamp.

As Kathy and I pulled into the parking lot, we noticed Mark's car and another car. As we approached the people in the dark, we noticed that it was Shelly and Denny Walston. Denny is a sheriff deputy. They are both fun people, especially Denny.

It was, of course, dark, and we noticed that a person had walked onto the far end of the parking lot. I told Denny that I was going down to see who it was, and I wanted him to cover me in case there was trouble. He said no problem. As I approached the person, I noticed it was John, another neighbor. John is among other trades a plumber. John still retains his long hair, which had been popular for many years gone by. I asked John to join us at the other end of the parking lot for the fireworks. By this time, not only were the Bowling Green fireworks on display, but also two private fireworks to the north and one to the south were going full blast.

As we began small talk, John relayed two stories to us about how he was picked up for nothing and almost arrested twice. The first was with the Wood County Sheriff's Department and the second with the Pemberville police. The Wood County Sheriff noticed that John had a right turn signal burned out. John went to the rear of his truck to see if it was out, and the sheriff told him to lean up against the hood of the car. The sheriff deputy cuffed John and eventually gave him a breathalyzer test. He had not been drinking and was let go after much questioning.

A short time after that, John was stopped because he was going too slow according to the Pemberville Police. A police officer from Lake off duty came upon the scene and said John was drinking. Once again, he was handcuffed and taken to Bowling Green for a breathalyzer test. Once again, the alcohol level was insignificant. While the Bowling Green Police tried to find a reason why John was drinking, John was eventually released. I felt rather uncomfortable that someone who had done nothing wrong was being treated like a criminal.

The Shoot

Once a year in the summer, usually the middle of June, Terry Hoepf would have a party at his establishment. Terry lives in an old renovated school house, and it is beautiful. The party would usually begin at one o'clock, but guests didn't arrive until one thirty or two in the afternoon. Terry would also have a fire because people like fires as do supervised children. The day was going well, and bratwurst and other side dishes were also served. After the meal, the shoot began. The shoot consisted of clay pigeons being thrown out over the back field, and the guests would try to hit the birds, as they were called, with shotguns. If one were able to hit the clay pigeon, it would usually break into my pieces.

The afternoon continued to be sunny and fun. At about four fifteen, our luck ran out, and the rain picked up. There was a dash for the large garage. Kathy, Mark, and I left the party to attend church, and then we returned for supper. As we began to eat, Terry's mother and father, Mick and Ray, arrived. They were visiting each of the guests when they came to the lady next to me. The lady walked up to Mick and said, "You probably don't remember me, but I bet you remember my father." The lady went on to tell Mick that she was the home nurse for her father when he died. Mick remembered her father, and the lady immediately said that Mick had sat her down about a day and a half before her father died and told her what to expect. The lady said that she wanted to thank Mick again for helping her deal with her father's death. The lady reminded Mick that she had sent a letter to the editor thanking all the people for helping her father, and she had a special thanks for Mick.

The conversation then switched to the manner in which nursing was done for the terminally ill. Mick made the point that she was very restricted twenty years ago in giving help to the terminally ill or what is today called hospice. Mick was asked the question about the freedoms nurses had twenty years ago. She told us that doctors twenty years ago would not allow nurses to do much. When a patient died, the doctor, not the nurse, pronounced them dead. Mick relayed how she asked a doctor if she could pronounce the person she was giving services to dead when the proper time came. The doctor said no, and within a few days, the doctor was called in the middle of the night to pronounce one of his patients dead. The administration of medication today allows nurses much more responsibility than they had years ago. I was amazed at the small amount of power given to nurses twenty years ago. Times have changed for the betterment of the patient, family, doctors, and nurses by giving more freedom to the nurses. I was also amazed how Mick was given so many positives. I can see now even more than ever how Mick was and is a very accomplished nurse who had helped many people over her career.

The Book

One summer evening in 2008, Kathy had gone to visit our neighbor Ellen Walston. I received a phone call shortly after she had left, and it was Kathy. She said that they needed me at Ellen's house. I immediately went to Ellen's house as something sounded suspicious. When I walked into the house, they said they wanted me to look down the hole where the old cooking range had been removed in preparation for the new range. I stepped into the wall and, with a flashlight, looked down into the open hole. At the bottom of the bricked-in structure, there was what looked like a book. I could not get to the book and decided to go home and find a fishing pole, a lure with a treble hook (a hook with three barbs), and a weight to snag the book and bring it out of the hole.

Upon returning to Ellen's house, I tried to snag the book with my hook. Kathy and Ellen were talking about the possibility that Gene might have placed the book there when the house was remodeled, and the book could function as a time capsule. Gene was Ellen's husband and had died about seven years earlier. Gene was also a trickster and would have delighted in such a task as placing a book in a hole, to be discovered several years after he had planted the book. I hooked the book on my third try and pulled it to the top of the hole, only to have it come loose from my hook and fall back to the bottom of the hole. I hooked the book two other times, but each time it pulled loose from the hook. The fourth time I hooked the book, and it came to the top of the hole. I grabbed the book carefully and released it from the hold of the hook. We all three looked at the book that now appeared to be a small book while in the hole, it looked like a large book.

The title of the book was *The Truth That Leads to Eternal Life*. There was no message written in the book, and we still had our belief about Gene placing the book in the hole and not identifying himself. In fact, it would have been more enjoyable for Gene to leave us guessing rather than for us to have a concrete solution to the origination of the book.

One More Hard Luck Story with a Good Ending

To have daily activities become success stories, I have found that I must keep on trying to solve the problem, and that means don't give up and try new options or solutions when the obvious does not work. One evening I was hooking up a new inside antenna for my neighbor and friend Sue Welty. The new wire hooked through the VHS player into the TV. I had just taken off the old wire and hooked up the new wire to the VHS. It should work right; wrong. The picture was worse than when I started. After several checks of the system, I noticed that the VHS machine was turned on. I thought that if I turned it off, that would help. I turned it off, and my neighbor has never had a better TV picture. I didn't give up, I didn't become frustrated, and I tried other solutions until I found one that worked. This is a simple procedure with mighty results.

A Walk with Jack

Over the years, the idea of exercise has been a more than important practice. In high school, I was a distance runner. My first several jobs involved physical development. I then began to run until I realized while teaching in the early 1990s at BGSU that swimming would be a better exercise than running for my knees. After I decided to leave college teaching, I began to power walk. Walking has been my exercise for several years.

While at times I walk by myself, I tend to walk faster than when I am with others. My neighbor Terry took up walking because his large dog, Jack, needed the exercise. Jack is mostly black, white with some white, and is larger than but not a German shepherd. When we walk, we do so in about any type of weather, and we usually go around two miles each day. Sometimes my wife, Kathy, or son Mark walk with us.

Walking with a dog along a road requires safety for us and for Jack. When a car passes us, we usually stop, and Terry gives Jack a command to sit. Most cars slow down when they see us and Jack, but there is always the exception. Some cars continue their fast regular speed, and others, it seem, according to my judgment, think it is wise to go a bit faster. I guess they think that if they go by faster, there is less time for anyone to go in front of the car.

We try to walk every day between four thirty and six thirty in the evening. The wind usually slows down in the evening, and in the summer, it is a bit cooler. Our walk goes through Fish Cemetery located behind our house. If we don't walk to the cemetery, we walk down North River Road toward Pemberville. We usually turn around at Linda and Paul Rolf's, but at times, we walk further to the Pat and Ed Hammett farm. At times, the Hammett home turns into a neighborhood bar, where the price for a drink is nonexistent. While walking near the road and woods, at times, we have seen squirrel, fox, deer and an eagle.

Another less traveled route is to walk along the Portage River located on the property of Sonny and Gloria Castillo and Richard Lopez and Jane in front of our house. Another river route is to the left of our property on Laura and Bruce King's land. Various waterfowl such as wood ducks and Canada geese can be observed. Regular birds such as cranes, crows, and hawks can be seen. Raccoons and squirrels are also seen on these properties.

These walks are very important to us because of the wellness activities, and I need the walks to keep up my stamina for the yearly 10K walk that Tara and I participate in each year at New Albany.

Our Friends

Friends are people who offer support and kindness to others. In other words, they give love and are in line to receive love. Many of the stories in this section are of examples of kindness and support.

George and Betty Weekends

Part II

George Schlotterer is my first cousin. I have known him and kept in contact to date. George attended the same college I did, John Carroll University, and we were in each other's weddings. Periodically I had visited George and Betty when I was on business in Columbus, and Kathy and I had visited George and Betty wherever they lived. This is the story of our yearly outings together. I have chosen to put this section under friends since Betty and George are relatives, but they are also close friends.

2007, Avila, Indiana

Upon arriving in the Fort Wayne area, we traveled with George and Betty to meet Amy, Ron, and their four boys and one girl to attend one of their son's basketball games. George and Betty's daughter, Amy Sarrazine, is a registered nurse, and Ron, a medical doctor, so a medically oriented family would be a safe assumption. In a short time, their family would be adding its sixth child. The games went fast and were enjoyable as the boys played, and Ron coached.

It was off to Auburn to the Auburn Cord Duesenberg Museum. It was a tempting stop, but we didn't have the time. We would have loved to see "It's a Duesy" car, but that was not to happen. Around the corner was a Sandra D's restaurant, and this fit our era of dining before hitting

Avila. We made a quick stop at a local antique shop to feed our particular shopping passion.

My grandfather Karl and great-grandfather Charles Schlotterer were from Avila. In fact, my mother was born in Avila and spent many years of her youth in that area. We met George's brother, Leo, and his wife, Deb, in Avila, and we traveled the area looking for our ancestors' footsteps and found a few.

My great-grandpa Charles Schlotterer owned a bar that we thought we had discovered until we looked closer at the original picture we possessed and found the columns in the front of the present bar did not match up to the original picture of the tavern. Since we had already had a few brews in memory of our great-grandfather and grandfather and told the patrons in the bar that it was our great-grandfather's bar, we did not feel like admitting our error and arousing some embarrassment on our premature statements. We did look and did find another building close by that seemed to better fit the picture, but it was not presently a bar. We decided to let sleeping dogs lie and turned our attention to a nice restaurant that our great-grandfather also owned at one time. After finding the restaurant, we knew a sure thing, so we made reservations for supper.

A quick trip to the American Legion where Leo, George's brother, was a member brought us to time for Mass. We attended Mass and, after church, made a beeline to the altar area. George had wanted to show Kathy and me some of the memorabilia in the back of the church in the sacristy where the priest dressed. Old plaques and documents helped fill in time before we ate supper. A conversation with the priest continued in the sacristy. Most people have interesting stories to share about their life; the priest was no exception. He told us of his chaplain years in the service and how he met and dealt with his many challenges.

By now it was turning dusk, and we had not toured the cemetery next to the church where relatives were buried. As we pulled in the cemetery, we noticed a large structure. We went directly to the building and were greeted by large locked iron gates. We could see in the gates but not well. It made sense to me that there was another entrance. I found another door and opened it, and we explored the inside. It was getting darker, so I tried to close the door I had opened to enter the structure. The door wouldn't close, and I was in a pickle. I immediately wondered if this was a trap, and I was going to get caught. I saw no other car coming, and I continued to rapidly work on closing the door. Finally, the door was secured, and we were out of there.

I was named after my uncle Dr. Joe Schlotterer, and I had never seen his grave. Bingo, just as the lights were coming on around the cemetery and the darkness was beginning to set in, George found my uncle Joe's gravestone. There was a baby's gravestone of the same last name, so that must be why Uncle Joe is buried in Avila. Our dinner reservations were ready, so we hurried to the restaurant. The meals were everything we expected.

A visit to George's brother, Leo, and his wife, Deb, in Fort Wayne was next. We had an evening of conversation, eats and drinks, and more conversation. Our childhood football and baseball games of the "Frederick vs. Schlotterer" were topics of conversation. We stayed in a motel that evening and watched George cash in his points for a free stay. Early the next morning, we were to visit Amy and Ron's house.

As I walked into Amy and Ron's home, I easily noticed another very positive happening. Ron and Amy took time with each of their children, even as they were showing us through the house. The message I discovered was that family was a very important variable in this house. The effort that was taken interacting and respecting each child was planned and deliberate. It was good to see that a solid foundation for their children was being built by these parents. This family unit was alive and well. It brought back memories of my parents who made sure that their children would have a strong family foundation for a good life.

I enjoy unique antique collections. Ron's large collection of antique rubber vehicles was right up my alley. Many of the vehicles he pulled out of his collection were made at the nearby Auburn Rubber Company. Since Ron grew up near Auburn, his collection held special significance to him. We then bid farewell.

On the way home the next day, we stopped for lunch in McClure, Ohio. Todd, brother to our neighbor Terry, owns the restaurant. The food and drink were both enjoyable, and this concluded our weekend together.

2008, Traders World

Our surprise destination this year was Southern Dayton. We did not know where we were going until George said to look at all those animals on top of those tents. We looked and saw giraffes, monkeys, and other animals. We asked what that was. George said, "Traders World." We were to find out that it was like a big antique store where many of the people specialize in certain projects. There were rows and rows of displays. When one thought we were getting to the end, there was still more for sale.

We had a good time and bought a few items, but we were more interested in the home-cooked meal and company. We left the next morning for home.

2009, Michigan

It was our turn to plan the weekend for George and Betty. George and I were both raised at least part of our lives in Willard, a railroad town originally for the Baltimore and Ohio Railroad. We knew that there were trains, and we knew that there were many other attractions they would be interested in seeing. We started out early on a Saturday morning, and we headed for Greenfield Village in Michigan.

When we arrived, we decided to go to the village first. In the village are many house-like dwellings in which displays are housed. I spent some time in the Thomas Edison display as I have always had an interest in Edison's inventions. Thomas Edison was born in Milan, a town a little over thirty minutes from Willard.

We saw most of the exhibits in the village, and then we turned to the museum. Once in the museum, it is hard to leave since there are so many different and interesting attractions. We particularly enjoyed a remodeled diner. The Rosa Parks bus in which Rosa refused to go to the rear of the bus and sit only with people of her African American decent was on display. There was a house in a circular-type pattern that was extremely efficient. There were farm machinery, trains, cars, furniture, and much, much more. The ride home was filled with talk about the many objects we had seen. An enjoyable dinner at the world-famous Tony Packo's in Toledo was enjoyed. Tired legs helped us go to bed at a decent hour when we reached our house.

2010, Centerville

On Saturday morning, we left Betty and George's house, and we were off to a kitchen supplies shop. We spent some time there, and after a few other shops, we found a large bookshop. A few more shops and we were back to Betty and George's for a fine meal and drinks. The weekend turned out to be a relaxed time as we didn't take a trip to any noticeable destination.

2011, Fremont

On Friday evening, George and Betty arrived at our house at around seven o'clock. We had supper at our house in New Rochester. The main course was fish, Lake Erie perch that Mark and I had caught the previous summer while on a fishing trip with my friend Butch and his son-in-law,

Paul. We have a method to bread fish that is dynamite. It goes like this: We thaw the fish, and then we recheck the cleaning of the fish to extract any bones or scales. The fish are then double washed in water and placed in a bowl of flower. After the fish are covered with flour, they are placed into a bowl of raw eggs and milk mixed. The final phase is placing the fish into ground cracker crumbs. Oil is heated to five hundred degrees, and two or three fish fillets are placed flat into the oil for a minute on each side. The fish are now golden fried and ready for consumption with homemade french fries, coleslaw, and usually a Jell-O salad or fruit salad.

The next morning, as I was starting breakfast, I received a survey call from the phone company on the recent delivery process of the new phone book. It was like a message from an angel as my experience with the delivery of the phone book had left much to be desired. The phone books were delivered on the same day as a large snowfall and had been placed on the ground. As I cleaned the approach to the mailbox, I noticed something was caught up in the snowblower's blades. I pulled out the item and immediately noticed I had just shredded the phone book. This was the first of two such books to meet their fate in the snowblower. I was a bit upset that the phone books were placed on the ground in the path of my snowblower. I dictated my story, and the phone company representative wrote down the information. It was a most fulfilling time for me as I never thought I would have the opportunity to tell my story to the proper person.

It is back to the breakfast of fried bread dough, a specialty of mine. Fried bread dough is frozen bread dough placed in a bread baking tin and set into a warm spot to rise overnight. In the morning, hot oil in a frying pan is used to place a piece of the bread dough stretched out to as thin as possible and then placed into the pan. When served, it is browned and then butter and syrup or honey is placed on the fried dough for flavor. It is better than good.

Now we are off to Fremont to see the museum and home of Rutherford B. Hayes, the former president of the United States. The home was in the process of restoration and had many very interesting spots. Everyone who lived at or visited the home had a job or work to do. Mrs. Hayes was a seamstress, cook, and gardener according to our guide. She had a special room upstairs that she could view her flower gardens; unfortunately, she didn't have much of a chance to use the room. The president spent several hours a day reading and walking according to the guide. The museum contained many thousand books as well as a collection of cannons, swords, guns, and ammunition. A display told how President Hayes became president by one electoral vote over his opponent.

After Mass, we visited one of our favorite downtown restaurants, Trotters. The food and drinks were great as was the company and the weekend.

Jerry Trabbic

Jerry Trabbic was our friend. He may also have been a relative or neighbor who attended our church, but we were friends. Some of us were old friends; some of us were new friends. With Jerry, he knew us all as a friend. Old friends had little preference over new friends. Jerry had a gift; he would walk into a room and start shaking hands with new friends and old friends. He would talk with you whether he knew you for one minute or years. Jerry could, as the saying goes, work a room as good as any politicians. I have watched Jerry's brothers and his father, Cliff, walk into a room and either renew friendships or make new friends. Jerry had some excellent role models in this respect. Jerry would have given Will Rogers a run for his money because Jerry, like Will, could say, "I never met a man I didn't like."

Another point that needs to be made is Jerry cared deeply about people. He would listen to you, and he would respect your point of view. He was not a judge but a cooperator.

Jerry had enrolled in Wood Lane Industries and was working and making great progress. Jerry was off a short time from the workshop because of an illness. He wanted to go over to see all his fellow workers at the workshop, so Don took him over. After his visit, I asked Don how his visit went after being absent for a period. Don said Jerry walked into the shop and said something like I am coming back as he raised his hands in the air. I hear he received a very warm verbal reception from his fellow workers. One could see that Jerry loved his fellow workers. One could also see that Jerry had endeared his fellow workers to him, and they showed this support.

The middle of March, I first heard that Jerry's health was not so good. My first reaction was a selfish one: I will miss Jerry. My second thought was he was doing so well. That all changed, and we are here to give Jerry his celebration of life.

I am proud to say that I knew Jerry. I am even prouder to say that Jerry was my friend, and I really loved him, and I am going to miss him. I am sure that everyone who knew Jerry would say these words.

Buzzards

Over the years, we have had a combination of friends who have been work associated from either Kathy or my place of employment. In this case, we had known Greg and Angie Bair because of my place of employment at the Wood County Board of Mental Retardation and Developmental Disabilities. Allison was their daughter, who is now married. In fact, I had the honor of making and helping serve several cases of champagne for Allison's wedding reception. It was a large reception and took around a dozen friends of the Bair family to serve the champagne in the Columbus-based wedding. Angela is an occupational therapist and works at a neighboring county board to the south of us, Hancock County. Greg is the CEO of the Wood County Residential Homes, which served people with mental retardation and developmental disabilities in Wood County.

Periodically, the Bairs have invited a number of guests over to their home for informal dinner parties. While some of these parties have been in the winter to beat the winter blues, one time a year in the summer, they host a gala event called a buzzard party. What is a buzzard party other than drinks, food, and conversation? Well, everyone has the opportunity to watch the around one hundred buzzards who fly in to roost in the trees behind the Bairs' home in suburban Bowling Green. The interesting part of seeing the buzzards fly in is that they do not all come in at once, and this means that the fly in is spread over a long period in the evening. In fact, they also come in rather slowly as they circle the tree that they intend to stay in for the night. The second interesting factor is the number of buzzards. As the buzzards circle in and then land, the trees slowly become full of buzzards, and there is a feeling of awe as so many large birds become so closely visible in the trees close to their home. The third factor is that the buzzards are not bothered by all the people walking near the trees. As people talk, walk, and make noise, the buzzards seem to be saying, "You don't bother me." It is a great feeling and sight to behold all evening the landing and continued presence of around one hundred buzzards. This is another unique experience that we would not have known, if it were not for the Bairs.

Larry and Carol

2007, the Spitzer Ghost

Every year Kathy and I go on a road trip with our friends Carol and Larry Moore. In 2007, this was our twelfth trip. The bed-and-breakfast we stayed in was located near Downtown Medina, Ohio. There were four rooms available upstairs to rent. On Friday night, we were the only couples in the home, but on Saturday night, there was an additional couple.

During the day on Saturday, we planned to visit the Cuyahoga National Park. Our sister-in-law Marge had told us that her sister, Chris, was a guide at the park, and the word was it was a worthwhile venture. We arrived early for the train, not wanting to miss it. We boarded the train and enjoyed a beautiful ride enhanced by the wonderful sunny weather and warm air. As we passed numerous nature preserves, it was pointed out to us that beaver were part of the habitat. While we did not see the beaver, we did see their dens. There was a house we left the train to visit, and I believe they called it a canal house. There was also a lock for boats in that area. Lunch was experienced at a small rural-type restaurant off the train route.

On Saturday evening, my brother Mike and his wife, Marge, came over from Parma, Ohio, to the bed-and-breakfast for a wine and cheese party, and then we went out to supper. Since Mike and Marge were in costume and had a costume party to attend, they left early in the evening to attend their event.

Larry, Carol, Kathy, and I went to bed somewhere around 10:30 p.m. Larry and Carol heard creaky noises outside their door before midnight in the hallway and thought it was the third couple. In the middle of the night, I heard the creaky floors in the hallway for several hours and left the bed on more than one occasion to make sure the door was locked; it seemed something wasn't right. My wife heard someone in our room, and for much of the night, she heard creaks made by someone in the hallway.

We contacted Rob, one member of the other couple, and he informed us they didn't come in until after midnight, and they were in bed at two o'clock. Rob also mentioned that when he was up between four o'clock and five o'clock, he heard creaking in the halls. I checked, and no one in our party was in the halls all night after they had retired.

This was a very interesting experience and one that I would like to go back to the bed-and-breakfast and see if I cannot only hear the ghost again but also see the ghost.

Larry talked to the innkeeper about the noises. The innkeeper reluctantly said, "Yes, we have ghosts!" The place has been covered in the national news, national TV, and numerous "haunted" books.

On the way home, we found a restaurant in the middle of nowhere that served good food and drink. The building was interesting in that it was very old and resembled a school or a former government building.

In the afternoon, we happened upon a back road. The road became narrower and more primitive the further we traveled. We walked into the woods at one point and were able to see hills and water in the distance. Thankfully, the road came to an end at about the same time our patience on riding the road was coming to an end. A few turns and there was a cemetery at the intersection of the roads. We explored the cemetery to find a different but not significantly different cemetery. That evening, we were back to the game of finding an available place to eat. That game didn't last too long, so supper was eaten at a reasonable time.

2008, Shaker Village and the Kentucky Horse Park

Our trip into Shaker Village in Kentucky was a long and in the end dark trip. As we were approaching the area where the bed-and-breakfast was located, the night continued to darken as the curves and other back roads began to increase. When we arrived at the bed-and-breakfast, we were greeted by the owners and decided we were all too tired to do much else than sleep.

The next morning, we were off to the Shaker Village of Pleasant Hill, Harrodsburg, Kentucky. The Shaker Religion had one belief that ultimately led to its demise. That was that they did not believe in men and women having sexual relations. This ultimately led to no offspring except for outsiders who became shakers.

The makeup of the buildings ran true to form as the men and women slept in separate areas. There were a number of remarkable practices in this community. They had running water and agitators in their mechanical wash machines. In 1820, they had musical concerts. Their historical animal breeds and heirloom vegetables were noteworthy. Their broom making, spinning, weaving, and woodworking were important parts of their life.

One Early Sunday morning, we were on our way to a horse farm in Kentucky. There were several horses boarded at this farm and several that had won many prestigious horse races. The surrounding physical structure was of hills and green grass. The majestic image of Man of War and Secretariat are just two of the greatest race horses on display. Also on display are the trophies and memorabilia from many of the great jockeys of all times.

2009, Traverse City

The leaves in the fall are very pretty in the Traverse City area in Michigan. Kathy arranged for us to stay in a log cabin–type home near Traverse City. As we began to look for a place to eat downtown, it was apparent that there were several restaurants in the area. The restaurants were very busy. We finally got lucky and were able to find an available booth. We had found that finding a place with an available opening is the way dining is in Traverse City. We also found that we were called leaf peepers.

The next morning, it was time to leave Traverse City. We did have one sight to see, the mother and two babies at the Sleeping Bear Dunes National Lakeshore. The story goes something like this: There was a large fire in the area. The mother was with her two cubs who suddenly took off into the water as the fire was approaching them. The mother found two piles of sand close to each other that were the babies, and the mother became the third large mound of sand.

On the way home, we stopped at the Pine State Park, where there were trails to be hiked. We hiked the trails and at the end entered the gift shop. I found a Petoskey rock while not having to go to Petoskey, Michigan, to find one.

We chose a route that we thought looked good for leaf peeping. The leaves were at their best. We had chosen and guessed the best route we could. Along the way, we discovered a winery, and we found a few bottles that looked inviting. We then went home.

2010, Cincinnati

We left New Rochester at three thirty on October 8 for a destination unknown to Kathy and me. In the early evening, we arrived in Cincinnati. The bed-and-breakfast we were to stay in was located in the gaslight district north of Cincinnati. The couple who owned the establishment had taken a rare night off, and the female proprietor's mother opened up and showed us the inside of the structure. As we walked up the two outside flights and three inside flights of stairs, my leg and hip injured from the Albany Walking Race a few weeks earlier began to cause me pain. As I thought of two more days of up and down these steps, I thought of even more pain.

We immediately noticed many unique remodeled areas in the building. A table and chair set located outside the first floor was one. Many art pieces on the floor and on the walls, small and large pieces of furniture from interesting points of origin, were also observed. Kathy and I took the third-floor apartment and Larry and Carol took the second floor. As Kathy and I looked closer at our rooms, we noticed that the bed was elevated considerably from the floor. Upon closer inspection, we saw a small step stool on Kathy's side of the bed to aid us into the bed. The only other concern was we might roll over in the bed and fall onto the floor. Kathy chose to use the step stool into bed, and I choose to lay on my back and scoot into bed. Neither of us fell out of the bed.

We went out that evening to a restaurant recommended by the owner's mother and watched the Major League Baseball playoffs while we ate. We were in Cincinnati, and the Reds did not play well that evening. While the Red fans were somewhat critical of their teams playing ability that evening, the four of us decided to watch our words as we were not natives to the area, and the natives might take offense to outsiders' views on their Reds. On the walk back to the bed-and-breakfast, we stopped at a jewelry/clothing store. I walked in the door and turned to the right, only to find out too late that the next room was about three inches down from the floor of entrance. As I stumbled down to the next level, a sharp pain shot up from my calf muscle to my injured hip. I absorbed the pain for about a minute and tried to move through the store. I made it to the door and back to the bed-and-breakfast, up the five sets of steps, and kept hoping that the pain would subside. The pain was not reduced, but I found out that there are several hospitals in the neighborhood where I could be treated. I could be sure of the many hospitals in the area when I heard the sirens at night.

We rode around Downtown Cincinnati seeing many young children in Halloween costumes. We assumed there was a large Halloween party taking place. We then traveled back to our bed-and-breakfast just in time to see the beautiful gas lights illuminate.

We walked up the sets of stairs and decided a game of euchre would be good. My leg and hip were bothering me, so I thought food would take my mind off the pain. I asked the other boarders present if I could eat anything I wanted in the refrigerator and was assured that anything in the refrigerator was fair game. I fixed Larry a few strawberries and had a few myself. As I was finishing my bowl of strawberries, in walks the owner. She had this funny look on her face, and I asked if it was okay if I had eaten the strawberries. She said something to the effect that if there are enough for breakfast, it would be OK. There were more strawberries in the refrigerator, but I thought I would only drink the liquids in the refrigerator and leave the other food alone.

The next morning, we were on our way to the Cincinnati Museum Center. The center houses several different museums. The first area we walked into was the giant entrance to all the centers. It was here we learned of the large transportation system of railroads that came though this terminal. Later in the day, we were to travel to the top of the structure and see the railroad system that presently operates this large transportation center. At one time, 462 trains came through this center. Questions were answered by volunteers who were familiar with the center. I was wondering who would take these volunteers' places in thirty or forty years. We also toured the upper level of the entrance area.

Another museum we saw was the Natural History Museum. There were animals, natural items such as stone-type structures, and mineral displays. Within this center was a display involving bats. We saw a demonstration of bats flying in a netted area, and there was a bat cave around eight feet tall. We found bats can eat between three thousand and five thousand mosquitoes a day.

It was off to the Ohio River to see if we could find a spot to eat close to the water. We wanted to eat and watch the barges, speedboats, and other recreational boats pass by our spot. We found an excellent place to eat and were able to see the river and boats go by. After dinner, we discovered that there was a beautiful paved walking path.

On Sunday morning, we were off to see the National Underground Railroad Freedom Center near downtown. We were excited about seeing this display, especially seeing how they would portray the underground tunnel. It was not to be; the center is closed on Sunday. We started our trip back.

2011, Akron and Dover

On Friday, September 9, 2011, at 3:30 p.m., Carol, Larry, Kathy, and I left for Akron, Ohio. Kathy and I knew where we were going, but Carol and Larry had not a clue. We traveled for two hours and pulled into the driveway of a beautiful Tudor mansion in Akron. At one time, Akron was known as the rubber capital of the world, and my father had worked at Goodyear Tire and Rubber Company for a short while in his early years of employment. The lady who owned the bed-and-breakfast was an exceptionally cordial and helpful person. She guided us to a very nice restaurant in Akron called Papa Joe's, and the restaurant proved to be everything that we had been promised, including a very popular and desirable name, Joe's.

That evening, we snooped around the beautiful accommodations and ended up in our suite. Larry seems to be the most accomplished snooper, and you never know where he will turn up next. We had an attached sitting room to our bedroom and decided to play a game. We had brought a fun game called right, left, and center. The game goes like this. Each player starts with three coins, and when the dice are thrown, a combination of pass to the right (R), center (C), left (L), or a dot comes up. A coin is passed to the left, right, or center pot. One more possible and desirable space on the die is a dot meaning one keeps the coin. The game is played until only one person has a coin(s). We played several games, and most everyone won a game.

The next morning, we visited the Stan Hywet Home. The home was built by the president of Goodyear Tire and Rubber Company in Akron, F. A. Seiberling. The mansion has over forty rooms and is situated in the middle of many acres of lands and gardens. The flowers were beautiful, and the grounds were used for many public gatherings as well as people interested in flowers. We saw the makings of at least two weddings that day. The greenhouse had many unique flowers and rubber plants from throughout the world. I was especially interested in the rubber plants as my father worked most of his professional career at a manufacturing plant that made rubber gloves, balloons, and other rubber products.

Late in the afternoon, we toured Downtown Akron. One of the more impressive sights was the silos from Quaker Cereals, which formerly stored its grain that was to be turned into merchandise. These towers are now being used as apartments. Someone was very creative in this conversion. It was then off to supper at Rock's Restaurant, kind of a sports bar that offered a wide variety of food at a reasonable price. Gyros are my weakness, and I had to have the scrumptious gyro salad.

As we entered our bed-and-breakfast, we saw the large party that was in full swing. Everyone was dressed for the occasion. The men were in their coats and ties and the women in their "Sunday best." I had talked to one of the men organizing the event earlier that evening on my way to dinner and found that the party was being sponsored by the Knights of Columbus and was titled "the Ladies' Night Out." Since I was invited to observe the party as a fellow Knight, I immediately began to walk around and observe what was "happening."

Everyone was more than cordial in explaining the organization of and the events taking place. The events consisted of an informal dinner, raffles, and a race in which six dice where thrown, and when their number on the dice came up, each of the lucky six people playing the game would inch forward on the track. One person would complete the game first. Each of the winners was then pitted in the final rounds so that the winner won a handsome gift card.

I was talking with one of the Knights, his wife, and another wife about the party. They expressed their interest in what the rest of the mansion looked like. I offered them a tour of the upstairs and introduced them to the people I was traveling. The conversations were so cordial that I thought I had known these people forever. It was with a fun evening and one I set my mind on taking back to my Knights of Columbus Council. My last-minute invitation to the party offered me a chance to an event that I will long remember.

Sunday was the day to say goodbye to the owner. As we were getting ready to leave, the owner told us a few stories about the mansion. One was about a wedding that took place. The bride had planned to have all the people in attendance be ushered to the living room. The room was capable of holding the crowd, and that is what happened. The preacher, the groom, and the best man were waiting at the other end of the property. The bride came down the beautiful stairway located in the middle of the mansion. She kissed her mother, and as she began walking toward the end of the house where the groom and preacher were, she had the ushers follow her and her father to the wedding. It must have been a sight to see as all the people walked in procession behind the bride and her father.

The second story was about a professor who lived in another town and once a month would come to Akron to teach. Each time he came, he would stay at the mansion where we were staying. In the afternoon, he would at an appointed time leave for the university, and after the class, he would return to his hometown miles away. The professor had missed a couple of months teaching because he had a severe heart attack and needed to recuperate. His health had improved, and he had come back to teach in Akron. On this particular class day, it was getting around the time for the professor to leave for his class. The professor was nowhere to be found. The owner knocked on the door, and no one answered. She was concerned and tried to open the door with her key. The key worked, but the hand lock prevented her from entering the room.

The time was coming closer to the start of the class, and still no professor. At this point, the owner called the police. The police came and informed the owner that the fire department, not the police department, was needed. The fire department came and decided to use its ladder to access the windows outside the second-story sitting room. The fire department opened one of the windows, and when they entered the living room, they saw the professor sitting in a chair. The professor explained that he went into the living room and shut the door to read. When he went over to leave the room, the doorknob came apart, and the part of the doorknob with the metal opener fell on the other side of the door, essentially locking the professor in the living room.

We were now on our way to Dover, Ohio, to see a collection of carvings done by Ernest "Mooney" Warther. This gentleman was an amazing person. He would carve to scale railroad engines and some cars out of ebony wood and ivory from elephant tusks. They were remarkably well done and with precision that seemed impossible. One of the ways that Mr. Warther earned his living was to sell kitchen knives. His family has carried on the museum and the kitchen knives to this date, and both of these are part of the museum open to the public. To my knowledge, not one of the train carvings has been sold. His wife had a large collection of buttons, which were mounted on large boards for display in a separate small building.

We began our couple hours' trip back to Pemberville. We noticed a large lawn sale about halfway home. We did stop, but we did not buy many articles. We stopped at a country diner on Route 224 near Bloomdale. The food was great, the service excellent, and our hunger was satisfied until our next meal.

2012, Indianapolis Museum

Kathy and I had no idea where we were going for the weekend. As we headed west toward Indiana, we were completely at the mercy of our tour planners. We came close to Indianapolis, and I thought, *What is in Indianapolis besides a football team?* I found that we were to be visiting the Indianapolis Speedway. That sounded different. We went to our bed-and-breakfast and unloaded our belongings before going out to supper. We played cards that evening and got to bed for our always busy Saturday.

Next morning, we were off to the speedway. We wanted to take a guided tour, but the track was scheduled for time trials. The weather was not warm enough, so the track was not used. We toured the museum, which was loaded with the Indy racers memorabilia. Winners were pictured from the beginning to the present. There was even a race car to hop into and have our picture taken. We went out for a late lunch at a deli that had more food and people eating than I would have guessed. We looked around the city and enjoyed the variety shops and other spots of interest.

After breakfast on Sunday, we went back to the speedway as there was a bus tour that went on the track. After a lap around the track, we stopped and looked around. I had heard the term "the Brickyard," but I didn't know it originated at the Indianapolis 500 Speedway. It seemed the entire track was made of bricks originally, and when the track was redone, a three-foot strip of bricks was left at the finish line. It was a great feeling to be on the bus as it circled the empty bleachers that held approximately four hundred thousand spectators. It is said that this speedway is the highest-capacity, stadium-type facility in the world.

The ride and tour was great, but we had war memorials to see. One was downtown and was called the Soldiers and Sailors Monument located on Monument Circle. It was open to the elements and offered a step or elevator access to the top. It paid tribute to American Revolutionary soldiers from the Hoosier State as well as the War of 1812, the Civil War and the Spanish American War. It is near three hundred feet high and offers at the top a great view of Downtown Indianapolis.

Thinking we had seen the most elaborate war museum in town, we journeyed to the Indianapolis World War Memorial and Museum. This overpowering building occupies five city blocks and has three floors of displays on wars from the Revolutionary to the War on Terror in Afghanistan and Iraq and pays tribute to Hoosier soldiers and the influence of Indiana on these conflicts.

Of all the impressive displays and structures, the third floor blew me away. At least sixteen marble columns somewhere around forty feet high and three to four feet wide dwarfed me as I gazed at them. I tried to think how they were put on the third floor and could only speculate that they were hoisted in place before the roof was closed. It was a good day and good weekend. It was time to go home.

2013, the Ohio State Reformatory

I had had the privilege of going through the Ohio State Reformatory when I was teaching at the Richland Newhope Center in December 1968. There were two very memorable events at the time. One was not being able to go through the hospital as an inmate had been stabbed by another inmate. The other was viewing the world's largest freestanding steel cell block in the world. It housed around 1,200 prisoners.

Kathy and I planned the trip to the reformatory in Mansfield as it was closed, and we thought it would be a unique and interesting event. We stayed in a bed-and-breakfast in Ashland, a neighboring city. As we drove up to the Jenny Wade Bed and Breakfast shortly before dark on Friday evening, the owners came out to meet us. That had never happened before. As we began to talk to the proprietors, Ken and Dianne Hammontree, we found we were in for another surprise, the lives of Dianne and Ken. Dianne had lived in Ashland for many years. She was a dog trainer and had written a book on dog training. Ken had been a minister, a draftsman, a guard at one of the newer prisons located behind the old reformatory, and was a provider of services to developmentally disabled people. In addition, he would dress like about thirty famous people and would impersonate them. On Sunday, we had breakfast with General Patton.

On Saturday, we were at the reformatory at 10:00 a.m. The gate opened about 10:30 a.m., and we wanted to be as near as possible to be first in line as the guided tours had a limit to the number of participants. We learned quickly that the old prison was owned by a nonprofit group, and there were only a few employees. The guides were all volunteers.

We began our tour of the buildings that centered around the movies of *Shawshank Redemption* and *Air Force One*, neither of which had any of us seen. Shawshank used, among other settings, the warden's office, the parole board room, the escape tunnel, the 1886 west cell, the grounds, and the "hole." The 1886 west cell, which held around seven hundred prisoners, was used as a Russian prison in *Air force One*. Also used was the front lawn in *Air Force One* as a landing site. The stairs were beginning to get to us.

Another tour and my favorite was the west cellblock, the world's largest freestanding steel cell block. Around 1,200 inmates were in this cellblock. Two men, two cots, one toilet, and one washbasin in a room barely big enough for the contents was each cell. There was also a small desk. When leaving the cell, the prisoners needed to push the cot away from the bars, or an inmate might reach through from outside and pull the desk over with a coat hanger and empty the personal contents of the desk. The Catholic chapel was located high in the structure, and all inmates went to church on Sunday.

The last tour was exposure to the west attic, the overflow room for prisoners who had not yet been assigned their cell. In the large and long structure, the inmates were detained with no bars between the prisoners and the guard. A ratio of 1 guard to 150 prisoners was not inviting to me as a job. At the far end of the long attic, it was hard for the guards to know what was happening. Several writings on the wall were available for interesting readings produced by the inmates. The stairs had pretty well done us in as we proceeded to a restaurant around Malabar Farms, home of Louis Bromfield, author, conservationist, Pulitzer Prize winner, and innovative scientific farming pioneer. The dinner was outstanding, and the rural ride to the bed-and-breakfast was most interesting for people who were used to the Black Swamp flatlands of Northwest Ohio.

The last day we went to Mansfield and the Richland Carrousel Park. There were thirty horses and twenty-two other figures that included four rabbits, cats, ostriches, and bears and one each of a goat, giraffe, lion, zebra, tiger, and hippopotamus of mythical origin. As I sat on a horse for my first ride, I felt like a kid. The music was right, the horses were beautiful, and the entire carrousel could not have been more perfect.

A tour of an antique shop in Downtown Mansfield helped end our exciting and tiring weekend.

Other Happenings

Class Reunion

The class reunion of 2007 was our forty-fifth at Holiday Lakes near Willard. The big problem with going to a reunion is that it is so hard to talk to all the former students of the class of 1962 and then to try to see the teachers who are being swarmed by your fellow students. I did briefly see my former gym teacher and his wife as well as my junior high science teacher. Maybe the next reunion in 2012, there would be more time to have discussions with this teacher. We sat close to my junior high science teacher and had a chance to talk to him about his farm of very black soil and his brother. His brother, a friend of mine, had passed on earlier in 2007, and I missed seeing him at the reunion. Reunions give one a chance to catch up; unfortunately, part of the information is about those classmates who have died.

While I have attended most of the class reunions, I have not maintained as close a relationship with my classmates as would have been desired. There was a problem with distance, and we have been very busy with our family, professional, and community activities. With all our different experiences, the class has moved in different directions. As I reflect on my classmates, I must say that I truly enjoyed them and felt we treated one another fairly.

Willard Dairy

A little over a year after my retirement, I had traveled with my wife to visit her mother near Willard. Kathy had developed the habit of spending a day with her mother about once a week. During that visit with her mother, it was decided to visit her neighbors Shorty and Justine Knoll. Shorty had lived across the road from my wife and her family for all the years she could remember. Kathy had babysat their four children and had continued her relationship with Shorty since childhood. Shorty's first wife, Annie, had died of cancer several years previous, and Shorty then married Justine.

I was having a conversation with Shorty in his garage about some of his milk bottles. He had collected them for years, and last summer, I had bought a Schodorf mini bottle for my cousin George Schlotterer. George is a history buff in many areas, one being Willard-related memorabilia. As I was talking to Shorty, I realized that there were two dairies previous to Schodorf and the Willard dairies. I had heard of neither the Clark nor the Blinzleys Dairy. Shorty had a milk bottle from all but the Clark Dairy. Shorty shared with me that after Clark and Blinzleys left town, both Schodorf and the Willard dairies were located in Downtown Willard. Schodorf was on the main street, Myrtle Avenue, south of the Pool Hall, and the Willard Dairy was originally down the alley where the Brunswick Grill was to be located. All this was very interesting to me since Bob Schodorf was a friend of mine throughout high school and college, and his father was employed at one time with the Schodorf and Willard dairies.

The Circus on an Island

Any trip to Lake Erie is an event to remember. Kathy and I had been close to the lake as we both were raised about thirty miles from the Lake Erie shores. While the mainland has become very commercialized around the lakeshore, the islands have a little more room to spare. When we have a chance to go to the lake, we try to take advantage of the opportunity and enjoy the day fully, knowing that we would be very tired that evening. On Monday morning, the first week of August, we were invited by a lifelong friend of mine, Butch Rothschild, and his wife, Phyllis, to go to Kelleys Island to see a circus. Yes, a circus on an island in Lake Erie. Monday morning was a pleasant cloudy day. It was to have been sunny and ninety-three degrees. Before the projection of ninety-three degree weather, it also was to be a day that my son Joe II and Tara as well as their two sons, Zachary and Joshua, were to travel with us to the island. Since the weather was not projected to be conducive to two children ages four and two being in the sun and the closed-in big top, they did not attend.

Kathy, our son Mark, and I boarded the ferry at Marblehead at 11:30 a.m. and made the twenty-minute boat ride to Kelleys Island. We toured the island with Butch after a picnic with him and his family. Butch and Phyllis's daughter, Christie, husband Paul, and daughter, Chris and Chris's friend made up the rest of the group. Butch and his family came over from the mainland to Kelleys on his twenty-seven-foot boat.

After lunch, the tour included riding on a golf cart around the island and seeing the glacier grooves carved into the rock. There were also a number of interesting homes and cottages to view.

The circus started at 4:00 p.m., and we enjoyed the Bengal tigers, elephants, many jugglers, acrobats, and other talented performers. All the concessions such as popcorn, snow cones, drinks, cotton candy, and glowing light toys were present in great numbers.

We boarded the ferry at around 6:30 p.m. and were back to the mainland at 7:00 p.m. After a delicious meal at the Whippy Dip in Woodville, we were ready to go home tired and full. This was a day of friendship, adventure, and appreciation of what God has given us in our natural surroundings.

Panera Bread

I do not often have the opportunity to see and speak with employees whom I have known over the years. Even rarer is it for me to have a chance to have a more than passing opportunity for a meaningful discussion. On October 14, 2008, I did have the opportunity to talk to two former employees from the Wood County Board of Mental Retardation and Developmental Disabilities. This rare opportunity came about because of the following happenings. I had a number of errands to run, errands such as returning the scuba diving tanks to Toledo, purchasing some needed items from Home Depot, picking up my belts from my leather specialist Glen Haught, and washing the car. When I was in Toledo at the dive shop, Kathy called me and asked if I wanted to go to lunch with her and her mother, who was in town visiting. I said thanks, but no thanks because I was afraid I had so many tasks to do I wouldn't be able to complete them if I went to lunch.

I was feeling a little bad about not going to lunch with my wife and mother-in-law, so I stopped by the restaurant where they were to have lunch, Panera Bread, in Bowling Green to see if they were there. I didn't see their car in the parking lot, so I walked into the restaurant to see if they were there. I walked through and didn't see either of them, so I decided to leave. As I was leaving and walking in front of the restaurant, I heard someone tapping on the window. I looked up, and there were Linda Smead and Rodna Metz. I was really elated to see them as it had been over ten years since I had seen either of them. I walked back in and asked them what they were up to these days. We had a nice conversation talking about retired life, and we began to talk about remembering the good times and people and remembering things that were not so good. The essence of the conversation is we all missed the many good people in our lives, but we didn't miss and needed to forget the things in our lives that are negative.

As we talked further, one of the two women made a statement that was so truthful and accurate that it stopped me in my tracks. They said that not remembering the bad things in life is so hard but so important for happiness. As we talked, I felt that the three of us had had very negative happenings in our lives and were striving to not remember these happenings as they were doing no good to any of us in dealing with life. As I thought later, it is good to forget negatives after one has worked through them. As I thought about the world in general, there must be several or even most people who would have a better existence if they did not remember the negativism in their life. Deal with them we must do, but to let them destroy us when there is little we can do about them needs to be rectified and not remembered.

A Fish Story

In the summer of 2009, my friend Butch Rothschild invited me and my son Mark to go fishing with him and his son-in-law, Paul. We had an early start and were fishing on Lake Erie by 10:00 a.m. The perch were biting slowly, but they were biting, and we were close to catching our limit of thirty perch per person. As I was baiting the hook with a minnow, I placed my fishing pole on one of the pole holders. I reached down for something, and as I did so, I touched my pole. Within a fraction of a second, I saw my pole going over the side of the boat. I grabbed for the pole but missed it. Yes, I had lost my new fishing pole in thirty feet of Lake Erie water.

I borrowed a fishing pole, and we continued to fish, and shortly before we were to leave, Paul said, "Look what I have." I looked and saw my fishing pole hanging on Paul's fishing line. We pulled in the fishing pole. When we looked at my pole and saw something we did not expect to see, a live fish was caught on one of my fishing hooks. Had I not been there, I would have doubted the truth of this story. Without Paul, this story would not have occurred.

Although our fishing was good in 2009, in the fall of 2010, the same four people were out fishing, and we all caught our limit of 30 fish or 120 total perch. The size of the fish was the most amazing part of this story because over half of the perch were jumbo fish, the largest group of big perch that I could ever remember catching.

Baby Fox

A few years ago, a couple named Andrew and Kelly and their two children had moved into the Oliver and Grace Walston house, which is located just north of Fish Cemetery. Kelly had remarked on occasion how people who lived to the south of them were good neighbors. One evening we met Kelly while on a walk.

The couple has two children, a boy and a girl. In addition, they had two dogs that had previously been seeing eye dogs for people in need of this service. One dog was blond and the other a shaded black. The dogs are exceptionally well mannered and often take walks with Kelly during the evening.

Another evening earlier in the summer of 2009, Kelly shared with Terry and me a story about a baby fox. Kelly was walking near the woods when she heard something screaming. She walked to the source of the problem, and there was a baby fox with its foot caught in some tree roots, and as a result, he had fallen into a hole. Kelly found a stick and managed to free the fox. Since that time when Kelly is on a walk and the rescued fox hears her voice, it will come out of hiding and stare at Kelly. Kelly did some research on foxes because different neighbors were hearing strange animal sounds in the middle of the night and other times. Kelly was able to match the sounds made by the animal to the sounds on the Internet of fox noises. The sounds matched a fox establishing its territory. Kelly then began to experiment with different fox calls and has had some response to her calls.

How Do We Influence People?

Cliff and Pat Martin are some of our friends from back home in Willard.. A few times a year, we go out for dinner with them. One sure event is their wedding anniversary. The first part of 2010 we had made arrangement for them to travel to New Rochester to go out for supper. The restaurant is up to us to choose, and choosing has become harder over the years as we have eaten at many of the restaurants that we both like in our area.

Kathy and I talked about the possibilities and looked hard at the steak or beef type of restaurant as that is usually Cliff's favorite. Several years ago, we had taken Pat and Cliff to Whitehouse, Ohio, to a restaurant that is called the White House Inn. One of its specialties is prime rib. We called and made reservations.

We did not tell Pat and Cliff where we were going as that is one of the little games we play. It was obvious that as we pulled up to the restaurant, this is where we were going to eat this evening. As we walked in, the political signs and decorations we had seen before came back to our memories. Cliff was pleased with the restaurant as it had many beef entrées to offer. One of the prime beef orders is so large, like a whole roast beef, that if you order this entrée and eat everything with the dinner, you don't have to pay your bill. I am not sure if anyone had earned a free dinner, but I knew I couldn't even begin to eat half of the serving.

The interesting part of the evening came as we talked about our various abilities as parents. Our conversation centered on Cliff's ability to make about anything. Cliff was in the process of completely tearing down a tractor and reassembling it. I had a power washer, and it had stopped working. I couldn't fix it, but Cliff did. Cliff had started from scratch and built toy farm machinery such as discs and watering devices.

The conversation turned to my ability to fix most items that are broken except gas engines that drive machines such as a power washer. I am also known as the stain master as I can get about any type of stain out of clothing.

As we talked about our children and how they had learned from us, it was pretty well agreed that we don't always know how we influence our children when they were young as we don't always know how our parents influenced us.

As parents, we can only hope and pray that our children learn the good things from us instead of the more negative.

Audrey Hepburn

Bill Williams, a financial consultant, a member of my church, and a friend, daily sends e-mails of interest to many people in the Bowling Green and Perrysburg. This is a list Audrey Hepburn wrote when asked to share her "beauty tips." It was read at her funeral years later.

For attractive lips, speak words of kindness.
For lovely eyes, seek out the good in people.
For a slim figure, share your food with the hungry.
For beautiful hair, let a child run his/her fingers through it once a day.
For poise, walk with the knowledge that you never walk alone.

People, even more than things, have to be restored, renewed, revived, reclaimed; never throw out anyone.

Remember, if you ever need a helping hand, you will find one…at the end of each of your arms.

As you grow older, you will discover that you have two hands, one for helping yourself and the other for helping others.

Audrey said it well, and her words help support the ideas of this book.

A Fishing Miracle

Life and the person I feel responsible for giving me life, God, give all of us surprises. Sometimes the surprises are expected and other times there was no clue at all that the surprise would happen. The date was November 15, 2010, and the place was Lake Erie between Perry's Monument on the west side of Put-in Bay, Ohio, and east of Kelleys Island. I was at this site because my good friend, Butch Rothschild, had called me on the phone earlier this week and wanted to know if I wanted to go walleye fishing on the boat named Erie Drifter.

I had been out fishing with another friend the previous week, Bruce, and we had covered most of Lake Erie, searching for perch. We caught five perch the entire day. As Butch was asking me to go, I thought it was the middle of November, and it was getting cold, and I recently didn't have much luck fishing on Lake Erie. Why freeze on the lake and not catch any fish?

Butch relayed to me what a great captain the boat had at its helm. He also told me that the captain is serious about getting fish. I looked at the website ErieDrifter.com and was pretty impressed with the boat, the captain, and the fish caught from the Erie Drifter. I checked with my son Mark to see if he wanted to go, and he had to work. Butch had asked me to go several times earlier in the year, and sometimes I went, and sometimes I was not able to go. Butch already had Paul, his son-in-law, going and another friend by the name of Steve Burkhalter. I knew Paul was fun to fish with and is an excellent fisherman and is always there to help others out in the fishing process. Butch is my longtime friend and fun to be with on the same boat.

At this point, I had two questions: where was the wind going to be coming from that day, and what was the projected temperature? The temperature was to be close to sixty, and the wind was to be out of the south. While the temperature was a bit cold, the wind was to be out of the warm south. I said I would go.

I hate to get up early in the morning. On this particular day, I had to get up at five thirty to be at Catawba Island by seven o'clock or seven fifteen. I was up, dressed, packed my clothes and drinks, and was off for Catawba Island. My temperature indicator in the car said thirty degrees. I reached the bait store where I was to hook up with the others at a few minutes before seven o'clock, and it was dark.

I reached down for a pen in the tray beside my seat and felt something bulky that was usually not in my tray. I turned on the inside light, and there was the cell phone that I shared with my wife. Kathy was to have the phone that day when she visited her mother an hour from home, and tomorrow she was going to be in Columbus. She needed the cell phone both today and tomorrow. I called Kathy and told her about the cell phone. Since I had the phone, I thought why not use it?

It was now a few minutes after 7:00 a.m., so I thought I would tease Butch a bit. I called Butch and asked him his location and why he wasn't at the bait shop as it was 7:00 a.m. Butch was uncharacteristically silent about why he was late. I gave him a bit of a rough time about being late and said goodbye. The funny part of this conversation was Butch wasn't to be at the bait shop until 7:15 to 7:30 a.m. Butch must have forgot the time he was to be at the bait shop. I figured I had pulled one over on him.

Within a few minutes, Butch, Paul, and Steve were at the bait shop, and we took off for the dock. The captain was waiting for us and telling us how great a day we were going to have. The boat was a 2007 Sport Craft 302. The ride out to the fishing grounds was to be the smoothest boat ride I could remember on any fishing expedition. The captain was an easygoing, fun-loving person named Tom Straus. We loaded up and went out about eight miles from shore.

The boat had special planers for troll fishing. Planers are floating devices positioned on both sides of the boat with a line connected to the boat and the other end to the planer. On this line was to be attached clips, and the clips have snaps that hold the line from the fishing pool until a fish strikes. When a fish strikes the lure, the fish and the lure take off, and the fisherman reels in the fish. We had four fishing lines on each side of the boat or a total of eight lines in the water.

As we reached our first and what was to be our only fishing area, it was only about ten minutes before we had our first hog or lunker fish, an eight-pound walleye. A hog or lunker fish is an extremely large fish. I looked at the size of this walleye and remembered when I got a second place award for a six-pound walleye that my son Joe netted for me off Uncle Bo's beach in Vermilion. I had never been in a boat that a fish this large was caught. I began to wonder where this all was headed with a start this positive. Within a few minutes, another hog walleye was caught. This pattern repeated itself until we had twenty fish in. One was twelve pounds, five were ten, and all but four were over three pounds.

Everyone, including the captain, was just looking at one another and not believing what they were seeing. We quit fishing about three o'clock; our boat fish box was full. The twenty fish had filled the fish box. The captain was saying that this was the largest catch of big fish for this season. That put all of us on the top of the hill.

We lined up the fish on a metal pole, and they were so heavy they broke the pole. We then had anyone with a free hand hold up the fish that didn't fit on the pole, and the picture was taken. This was one happy group. We loaded up the fish and were on our way to Butch's house in Plymouth, Ohio, to clean the fish. As we were setting up the tables to clean the fish, we decided to lay out all the fish on the tables for one last picture. The pictures were awesome. As we looked at the display of fish, all we could do was pinch ourselves and convince ourselves that this whole experience was real.

We cleaned the fish in about an hour. Cleaning fish this size is not easy because they are slippery, they are big, and their bones are big and strong. It was the most work I ever put into cleaning fish. When the fish meat was gathered and weighed, there was an unbelievable forty pounds. Forty pounds of fish meat meant there was at the minimum eighty pounds and probably over one hundred pounds of live fish. If converted to market value, we would have had enough money to pay for the charter. The fish were divided up by Paul, and everyone was more than happy with their two full bags of fish fillets.

I thanked God for allowing us to have such a successful day with the fishing but, more importantly, the good time we had with one another in a most positive expression of brotherhood. After a delicious supper made by Phyl, Butch's wife, it was time to call it a day. The sad part of this outing is that it will be pretty impossible for any one of us to have a repeat performance with this degree of success. We may fish again with success, and we may have good luck, but a successful fishing day such as this is probably a once-in-a-lifetime occurrence. Yes, we have the memories, and we will smile when they come into our minds.

In fact, our adventure coming to our minds would be very soon after the fishing expedition as captain Tom produced his brochure for the 2011 year. Guess who was on the front page of the new advertisement. It was the four walleye fishermen and our twenty more than large fish. As I listened to people describe the picture, one comment I heard was about me and my clothing. At work, I always dressed up in my Sunday best. When I was relaxing, I did as was shown in the fishing picture, I dressed in the oldest clothes I had. I enjoyed being comfortable, even though I may not have looked the best.

The Trip Down South

We have relatives and friends in North Carolina. Our first stop will be my elder brother Walt and his wife, Judy, who live near Raleigh, and five of their six children also lived in that area. Our second stop was to be at a friend and former coworker, Jerry and Linda Johnson. They live in a golfing community near Wallace, North Carolina. The third stop was to meet up with Bonnie and Jim in Fayetteville. From their house, we would travel to Asheville to tour the Biltmore Estates, home of the Vanderbilts.

Walt and Judy

As we reviewed our itinerary, our trip into the South was filled with many anticipations with our relatives and friends. The flowering crab trees, dogwoods, and red bud trees were in full and majestic bloom as we made our way South. Here and there, we would see a few azaleas beginning their appealing show of colors. The mountains were large and attractive as we traveled through West Virginia. The trip lasts eleven and a half hours without breaks. Road construction was minimal until we reached Winston Salem, where traffic slowed to a single lane.

The first evening at Walt and Judy's is usually a quick trip around the Frederick compound to visit as many of Walt and Judy's children as possible. Trace (Walter III), Denise, Angie, and Becky all live on the family compound near Middlesex. Peter lives in a nearby town, and Jackie lives in Idaho. The first home to be visited was Trace (Walter III) and Rene's house. One of their daughters, Krystal, was a few weeks over due with the first grandchild and great-grandchild. She was to be induced the next Sunday if she had not delivered the baby by then. Her husband, Chris, was on leave for a few days from the army, so the pressure was on to have that baby.

I had recently bought a new smoker for meat and fish. I passed around samples I had made of fish, deer, and beef jerky to see how everyone liked the taste; they did. I made a note that smoked beef would be a good present to my brothers and sister for next Christmas. Trace and Renee's other children—Dutch (Walter IV), Stephanie, and Caitlin—were also at home for our visit.

The next visit was to Denise's house. Tommy (T/J) and Nicholas (Nick) were both in the house with Denise, while Heather was outside with a friend, learning how to change the oil in her vehicle. It was late, so the visit to Becky and Kenny's house would have to wait for another day.

On Wednesday morning, an in-service was being presented by Renee to the Shutterworks staff on marketing the various types of shutters. This included not only the shutters made by Shutterworks but also those that could be purchased and installed by Shutterworks. I had the distinction of introducing Renee. My comments were brief, somewhat comical, and yet of a serious nature. Since Walt and I were to meet the ladies for breakfast, we opted out of the meeting a bit early.

Breakfast is a big event after most of the ladies have just completed a session at Curves. Some of the men enjoy time conversing with one another. I was involved with an interesting conversation over my breakfast with a friend of Walt's, Gary. Gary was filling me in on how he could control his sump pump, the temperature of his home, and his home security from any location. It was time for the women to visit a large outlet mall, where the women took the opportunity to make purchases of their liking. Walt and I went to a few antique stores and ended up buying nothing. All the women—Kathy, Judy, and Angie—beat us at the game of making the most purchases.

It was now Wednesday evening, and we were to attend a soup supper and the Stations of the Cross at the local Catholic Church. There were three choices of soup: bean, chicken, and taco. I had the first two, and they were excellent. The Stations of the Cross is a solemn ceremony commemorating the crucifixion. Since I had attended the service when I was young, it was interesting to see that the words and songs have remained the same. Memories of days gone by crept into my head as I looked around and saw many members of my family. The ceremony was memorable.

The next day was Thursday, and Walt, Denise, Renee, Becky, and I were on our way to the fairgrounds in Raleigh to set up for the home show.

Everything was ready to go for the display of their plantation shutters, so we loaded up the truck in the rain. Our luck with weather was cut short with cold and wet weather most of our stay in North Carolina. After a quick breakfast, Walt's treat, we arrived at the Raleigh Fairgrounds amid a continuous downpour of rain. We were in hopes that we could unload the display inside the exhibit hall. Trucks were going in and leaving the building. Lady luck was on our side as we were able to take the truck into the building and park near our display site. Unloading was as smooth as loading. The Shutterworks display looked inviting and attractive. I had done many displays for organizations I had worked or volunteered for in the past, but this was a new twist, the commercial display.

Thursday evening was eating out at a restaurant pub where my nephew Peter was playing a gig. This meant that he was playing the guitar, harmonica, and any other instrument while singing for a private party, in this case, a birthday party. Walt, Judy, Angie, Kathy, and I met Pete's wife, Julie, and their two children, Hannah and Peter, at five at the restaurant. We had a delightful meal and enjoyable conversation. After the meal, we were invited to attend the gig and the birthday party. Pete's music was enjoyable, and he played some tunes familiar to me.

On Friday afternoon, we visited Becky and Kenny's house. Ryan and Ashley were also home, and we had a nice visit and played with their two new small dogs. It was time for us to leave for us to go to supper and the home and garden show and then get ready to leave the next day.

The home and garden show had something for everyone. There were two giant buildings, each filled with some type of commercial product. There were tiles, granite, bricks, HVAC systems, eaves troughs, vinyl siding, water softeners, wood products, bathtubs, water basins, paintings, shutters, and many more useful products. It was a great show, and hopefully all vendors developed many good leads from the visitors.

Linda and Jerry

We left Walt and Judy's house so that we could arrive in Wallace, North Carolina, at around 1:00 p.m. As we pulled up to the golf course community where Linda and Jerry lived, it was impossible to miss the beautiful shrubs and trees in the allotment. The gated community meant that we didn't get in the grounds unless our names had been given to the front desk by Linda and Jerry. We began to go into the inner sanctum when we decided to review Jerry's directions to the house with one from the gatekeeper just to be sure.

It was good seeing Linda and Jerry. Since it had been over ten years since I had worked with Jerry, we had a lot of catching up to do. We sat for hours, finding out where our lives had gone. There are few events in life as enjoyable as talking with friends that one has not seen for years. Linda and Jerry's house was very inviting and contained many nice furnishings and many golf-related decorations, all carefully chosen. As we were talking, something began hitting one of the windows in the room. As we all looked at the window, we saw a bluebird perched on a feeder after hitting the window. Jerry explained that the bird had for years came to the window and had probably seen its reflection in the window, causing it to fly into its image. As I looked out into the lawn, I saw a black squirrel with a white nose and white tipped ears. Jerry explained that this was a monkey squirrel.

Jerry then took Kathy and I for a tour of the grounds. We were amazed to see the size and beauty of the many impressive acres of housing, golf grounds, streets, and woods. The various bridges and the large clubhouse added to the splendor of a setting called River Landing.

That evening, we had supper at the golf club. The choice of and taste of the food was superb. We took frequent trips to the bar to see how the NCAA Men's Basketball Tournament was proceeding. Butler won over Virginia, and UConn beat Kentucky in the semifinals.

The next morning was Sunday, and Kathy and I decided to take a stroll around a small portion of the golf course. There were a few groundkeepers working on the greens, but the golfers had not yet reached our hole. The fairway and green looked picture perfect to us. If we were golfers, this course looked like as challenging and well-kept as any we had seen.

Later in the day, it was to Wrightsville Beach. An auto tour of the city surprised us with many older well-kept homes. There were many interesting shops and a big surprise for us as we came near the water with a look at the USS *North Carolina*. This had to be the largest military ship I had ever seen. The last stop was a restaurant on the beach where we had drinks and supper. Back at their house, we watched more NCAA Women's Tournament action with Notre Dame beating UConn and Texas A&M winning over Stanford.

Bonnie and Jim

It was early Monday morning when we left Linda and Jerry's to arrive at first Fayetteville and then Asheville. Fayetteville is the home of our friends Bonnie and Jim. Kathy and Bonnie had been friends since they met as contestants in the Miss Huron County Beauty Pageant in Norwalk. While Kathy had visited Bonnie a few years ago, I had not been to their home in Fayetteville, which is south of Raleigh.

Jim showed me around the house, and I observed many remodeling projects he had successfully undertaken. Since I had not worked on tile, I was particularly interested in those projects. We had at least a four-hour drive ahead of us to reach Asheville, so we started on our way. Jim rode with me, and Kathy rode with Bonnie.

We had gone the majority of the trip when I noticed that my car was losing power. I looked at my gas gauge, and I was out of gas. I had been talking with Jim and wasn't watching my fuel indicator. As the car continued to slow down, I saw that within a mile, there was an exit. I also noted a sign that indicated there was a gas station at the exit. I didn't touch the brake pedal and continued to look for the exit. At this point, I was hoping for a short road from the interstate downhill to the gas station.

We reached the exit and began to descend toward a filling station. There was only a stop signal between us and the gas station. As I reached the stoplight, it changed from green to red. I had to stop. I asked Jim if he would push me when the light changed across the road and into the filling station. He pushed me with the help of another passing motorist through the stoplight and partially up the hill where the car came to a dead stop. At that exact moment, a pickup truck stopped ahead of me and asked if he could help. Jim asked him if he had a belt to tow us. He did, and he pulled us up to the vacant gas pump. I gave the pickup driver a tip for his trouble, thanked him, filled up the car, and we were on our way.

Bonnie had arranged for us to stay at a bed-and-breakfast in Asheville. We found that we had a house for our stay. A wine party was held in the yard of the main bed-and-breakfast shortly after we arrived. While the wine and munchies were good, I had my eyes on one of the largest and most beautiful set of waterfalls I had ever seen in the side yard. I collected many pointers on the construction of the falls and pools, and it was time for supper.

The weather was threatening, so we took our umbrellas to the nearby downtown area. We found a pizza place with a large patio. As we were ordering, we noticed a few raindrops. Some of the tables had large umbrellas on them but ours did not. We asked for an umbrella, and we were happy we had because it began to drizzle a short time after we ordered. The meals were good, and we headed for home to watch the finals of the Men's NCAA Basketball Tournament between UConn and Butler. UConn was to be victorious.

Tuesday, April 5, 2011, was to be the day we toured the Biltmore Estates. The Biltmore Estate was built in 1895 by George Vanderbilt. The estate covers eight thousand acres of land. While there were many attractions in the estate, Kathy had for years wanted to see the house and the gardens. I was interested in seeing the winery. As we rode the bus from the parking lot, it was a breathtaking sight to see the home for the first time. From the time I entered until the tour was completed, I was fascinated with how anyone could spend the amount of money that had been spent in this home. The grounds offered many varieties of trees, bushes, and flowers. The upkeep on the buildings and grounds is massive.

The last part of our tour was the wine cellar and shop. The making of the champagne wine was particularly interesting to me, and I found a few helpful hints that I will use in making my champagne.

That evening, we happened upon an Italian restaurant. The food was very good, and the waiter turned the channel on the television so we could see the finals of the NCAA Women's Basketball Tournament. Until the final few minutes, it was an exciting game in which Texas A&M beat Notre Dame. We had our final conversations that evening as we would be going home the next day.

We said our goodbyes, and Kathy and I were on our way home. As we entered Kentucky, Kathy noted signs for bourbon distillery tours. We picked out the closest one, Wild Turkey, and before we knew it, we were standing in front of massive vats of primarily corn mash fermenting. Distilling was the next stage before bottling. We finished the tour in the tasting room and were surprised to see the assistant master distiller for the company, Eddie Russell. He was as nice a person as could be, and he even signed my bottle of bourbon. This was the only major stop on our trip home and one that we will not forget.

Organizations

Over the years, I had the pleasure of being a member of many community organizations. In this process of belonging, being an active and participating member was always important to me. One of my parents' favorite sayings was "If you are going to do it, do it the right way." As a result of following this saying, I had the pleasure of joining and being active in many service organizations, and in many cases, I was given the pleasure of holding an office. I have already talked about my experiences with the Special Olympics programs on a state level and the maintenance committee at St. Thomas More Parish. I now wish to share experiences with other organizations. My experiences with all these organizations had one factor in common; every time I gave to an organization, I would receive back more than I had given.

Black Swamp Humanitarian Awards Committee

Background

In 1987, I was invited to be a part of an organization that was in the formative stages in Wood County. Dave Miller, editor of Bowling Green's paper, the *Sentinel-Tribune*, and Betty Montgomery, Wood County prosecutor, were the two organizers. The first awards were held in 1989 to recognize people for having done good deeds for other human beings. Any person living in the county or if their action happened in Wood County was eligible to be considered for the awards. Today there are four awards—Good Samaritan, Service to Others, Beyond the Call of Duty, and Life Risk.

As of November 2008, there have been a total of 292 awards given by the committee. Of all the service areas that I had the good fortune of being involved, the Black Swamp Humanitarian Awards compared with any other organization as being representative of the two goals my parents had set up for me and my siblings. The first is to give to other people and expect nothing in return. The second is to enjoy life, use one's time wisely, and set a good example for others.

I always enjoyed the entire day anticipating the award to each recipient after their story of giving had been presented. I think that sometimes I don't appreciate the gift that God has given in making the awards possible. Nor do I appreciate the fact that God had given me the chance to be part of this movement of recognizing others for their giving to other human beings. The joy of seeing the awards and the possibility of the general community displaying positive actions by modeling the award participant's actions offered the hope of the duplication of the actions being rewarded. The possibility of other people reading or hearing about the actions of others and the good probability that other people would give of their talents to others as the award recipients had given made the possibility of many more positive actions to other people. These awards most readily pulled together the teachings of my parents. Reading a few of the examples of the awards should give you a much better understanding of the purpose of this organization.

The information contained in the Humanitarian Awards becomes public information. Since the potential award winner had the option of refusing the award, by accepting the award, they accept the recognition that goes with the award. The information on the awards is public at several phases of the ceremonies. At the ceremonies, the information handed out in the summaries of the awards and the information presented in the awards is public. The information is widely distributed in the *Sentinel-Tribune* and, at times, other public media. In many cases, the information on these events is public information contained in police, fire, and other public body reports. Therefore, entire names and circumstances are used in this section.

Awards

On the evening of October 23, 1988, Jamie Welty and two other teenagers were walking down Zepernick Road near New Rochester. Fog was coming in very heavy, and the evening was approaching darkness. A speeding car without its lights on was approaching the three walkers. Jamie became aware of the speeding vehicle as it was very near them and pushed the other walkers out of the path of the vehicle just before it whizzed by them. As the story was finished, quietness came over the room as people realized how serious this incident was. Jamie received the Life Risk award for his action. The parents of the two teenagers who were almost run over by the speeding car were very happy Jamie was there to save their sons' lives. Robby Ruck was one of the teenagers, and our son Mark was the other. This close call came and left as fast as it came. It was indeed a very good day when Jamie saved our sons.

On August 13, 1993, Julie Martini noticed a car on its side in flames in Perrysburg Township. Julie, a lady of small stature, somehow pushed up and opened the driver's door and assisted Crissa Abke and Kimberly A. Loutzenhiser escape the flaming car. Both occupants and Julie escaped with minor injuries. Julie received the Life Risk award. One does not want to imagine what would have happened to the two persons in the flaming vehicle if Julie would not have been present. Julie was not able to be present at the banquet, but her parents, Tina and Joe Martina, did attend. As this award was presented to her parents, I had a hard time understanding how Julie could have ever opened a heavy car door with the law of gravity pushing the door down. In fact, understanding how many of these award-related incidents happened is baffling.

On Tuesday, December 29, 1998, Coast Guard Petty Officer Eric Mueller, a Coast Guard rescue swimmer, was deployed to Lake St. Clair to help rescue eighteen fishermen stranded on a rapidly sinking ice floe. Eric was lowered into the icy waters of Lake St. Clair and swam to the floe and loaded the individuals one by one using the helicopter hoist. He accompanied each person on the hoist and rode with them into the helicopter again and again until they were all safe. With the wind chill of five below zero and the battling hypothermia as the floe continued to break up, they were not on the helicopter and off the ice any too soon. The four-hour operation took place at night. Eric received the Service to Others award. With the weather and ice conditions, one could only imagine how much longer the fisherman could have survived.

At the 2004 awards, it was reported that Eric and Becky Walls were traveling west on U.S. Route 6 one morning when they noticed a white van parked in the driveway of their neighbors Julie and Bob Heuerman. The vehicle fit the description of a vehicle used by burglars in recent robberies. The couple then called Julie Heuerman at work to tell her about the suspicious vehicle that looked like it was marked to look like a garage door installation van. Mrs. Heuerman told the couple they were not having work done on their garage door. The nominators then pulled into the neighbors' driveway in time to see the burglar run from the home, enter the van, and flee eastbound on U.S. 6. The nominees called the sheriff while following the van. The sheriff's deputies ultimately stopped the van and arrested its occupants, who were in possession of Julie and Bob's jewelry. The nominees were awarded the Good Samaritan Award. It is easy to see that if the two persons had not intervened, the question would be how much more of the Heuermans' possessions could have vanished.

At the November 12, 2010, awards at Nazareth Hall in Grand Rapids, one of the attendees remarked near the end of the program that she could see God's hand in all the twelve awards given that evening. I looked back over the awards and had to agree with her. For example, when Andrea Amonette, Katie O'Neil, and Teresa McCormick pulled Ayden Brogan's purple and unresponsive body from the bottom of the Perrysburg/YMCA Pool on July 8, 2010, and helped save his life, God was present. The same was true when Sara Lewis saved a mother and three children from a riptide in Daytona Beach, Florida. When Scott Miller and Joe Gonyer, employees of Cooper Tire in Findlay, freed pregnant Kristina Baumbarger from hanging upside down in her car after an accident by kicking out the windshield, cutting seat belts, and pulling her through the windshield to a safe haven until the ambulance arrived, one could see God's presence. By the way, this was the first time since the accident that Kristina had the opportunity to thank the men for helping her to safety.

It was easy to see God's presence as the story of Kelly Pickard, who has multiple sclerosis, was relayed. Tom Pendleton and Richard Marten received a Good Samaritan Award for pulling Kelly out of a deep ditch as the water began to fill her automobile. Mary Sue Miller, a scuba diver at White Star Quarry in Gibsonburg, Ohio, ran into trouble in forty-five feet of water. As she was being rescued, her diving buddy released his weights, and he went up, and Mary Sue went back to the bottom. It was ten minutes later before she was rescued and lived. Mary Sue felt she had a lot of people helping her, including Weston, Ohio, EMT Alan Oberhaus. As I talked to Mary Sue after the ceremony, it was easy to see the faith and belief she had in others. I also saw God's hand in this most unusual rescue.

Dr. Stacey Rychener received a Beyond the Call of Duty Award for being concerned about her coworker Kandy Current at home. Dr. Rychener went to Kandy's home to check on her and contacted 911 as Kandy didn't seem right. Kandy wasn't right; she had a major stroke, and Dr. Rychener's actions saved Kandy's life. I saw God's hand in this incident as well as the incident in which Michelle Gilford jumped in the cold Maumee River water on October 9, 2009, to save George Albert's life.

As the stories are told and the awards given at the banquet, I stand in awe of the goodness of other people, a goodness that I feel comes from God.

Observations

It is easy to see, feel, and know some of the results of these awards to the recipients. At the award ceremony, there are many emotions shared. A chill coming down one's spine is not unusual. In the end, it is very gratifying for the committee to be a part of making public the good that the award winners gave to the involved people being assisted. Likewise, the recipients have displayed the role model to the community. Being the chairperson of this committee allows me to see the many good results that come from other people's actions being identified, explained, and rewarded. It is truly an experience of receiving more than was given.

The other amazing part of this committee is that it is composed of a cross section of various professions who surround a central core of law enforcement officers, emergency personnel, and firefighters who periodically meet to identify worthy recipients for the awards, plan and carry out the banquet, and see that proper respect and recognition is given. The board members are very involved and very positive in dealing with the recipients, their families, the victims, and most notably their fellow board members, who totaled fifteen as the committee celebrated its twentieth anniversary in 2008.

As the years progressed, there were to be other recognitions that were received by the Wood County people. The Wood County Spirit Award was given to people for giving their time on a long-term basis. My friend Gene Walston was recognized with the Farming Award because of his many years of membership and leadership in this area.

In Bowling Green, there was an award for youth, the Positive Start Week awards. Many Bowling Green students, 102 in 2010, in the seventh and eighth grade, were honored for the good things they had accomplished in the local paper the *Sentinel-Tribune*. Many students are recognized for their grades, volunteer activities, skills, treatment to others, extracurricular events, skills, and positive attitude.

The city of Bowling Green presents two awards, the I Love BG Award, given to a citizen who has majorly given to BG, and the Athena Award, given to the person who has given in many ways to the community. A professional associate of mine, Melanie Stetchberry, received the female Athena Award. Several years ago, I had the honor of hiring Mel into the regional office of the Department of MRDD. There cannot be too many awards for exemplary service to other human beings.

Blessed John XXIII

Background

Blessed John XXIII is a new Catholic Church located south of Perrysburg, Ohio. Because of the fact that the area served by Blessed John had a large population of Catholics but did not have a church that could serve this population, Bishop Blair of the Toledo Diocese asked Fr. Herb Weber in 2006 to be the pastor of this church and build first a Family Life Center to be used for services and eventually build a church. Until the Family Life Center was built, Masses were said at Perrysburg High School, Christ Lutheran Church in Dowling, Ohio, and St. Paul's Lutheran in Haskins, Ohio.

Lecturing

On November 10, 2007, Kathy and I as well as our son Mark were going to church at Christ Lutheran Church. Since Blessed John XXIII did not have a church yet, they used other available churches in the area. On this particular day, I walked into the church and saw two babies in the second row. They were twins about nine days old. As I looked at the twins, a feeling of joy and a feeling of loss was present. Like so many times before, I thought of my lost twin and felt a presence of this twin that I had never seen.

We took our seats, and the service began. As the procession walked by us, we noted that there were no lectors present. Kathy actually brought this to my attention. Since our priest Father Weber was not able to be at church because of an operation, other persons would have to double up their shared responsibilities. I walked to the back of the church and went up the side aisle to the front and asked Marla, the coordinator of such activities, if the lectors were there. She and I checked the sign in sheet, and sure enough, no one had signed in, and in less than five minutes, someone needed to be giving the two readings to the many parishioners in church. I volunteered that Kathy and I would read as we are both lectures.

I walked back to my seat. Anyone who has been to church knows that one does not walk around church during the services unless one has a job to carry out. Well, I was getting a lot of eye contact from the parishioners, and I merely smiled back to say everything was okay. I informed Kathy that we were going to read, and she said that was fine except she had not practiced. Immediately, the thought passed through my head. *What if there are long, hard-to-pronounce words or short words that can be pronounced various ways? I need to get the right one.* Well, Kathy and I sat there uncomfortably about not having practiced the readings. The fortunate part of the readings was that they both came within a few minutes. Kathy had a rather long reading, but it went well. As I began to go up to read, I saw the two twins in the front row, and I asked my twin for some help. Well, I went up to the podium and got through announcing the "A reading from the second Letter of Saint Paul to the Thessalonians," but halfway through the reading, there was the word "perverse." I pronounced it okay, but I felt like a hypocrite talking about perverse from the pulpit in front of all those people. While it temporarily put my mind off track, I rebounded and finished with the best reading I think I had ever given. The strength and confidence I received from my twin was most appreciated. I was also to give the petitions reading after the sermon. I frantically looked on the pulpit for the list of petitions, but it was nowhere to be found. As I left the pulpit, I, by chance, looked on the altar, which was beside the pulpit, and there magically appeared the petitions sheet. After the petitions reading, I felt very good about having read so well, but as I left the pulpit the second time, I tripped on a cord and stumbled a little. That cord brought me back to reality and humility!

Commitment to My God

I was able to access an opportunity that I had not been able to do so a year previous. The opportunity was to attend a retreat in lower Michigan at St. Francis de Sales compound. The retreat was in November, and the skies were beginning to look like snow and cold weather. I arrived at the retreat house around 11:30 p.m. I was to have arrived at 7:00 p.m. but had the Black Swamp Humanitarian Awards Banquet at Nazareth Hall. Counting the 19 awards this year, there had been presented 279 awards in the last thirty years. Nazareth Hall was for years a Catholic military school and had closed its doors several years previous. Arriving at the camp in the middle of nowhere was not a big negative as Don Burkin Sr. was guiding me into the camp on his cell phone for about the last twenty miles. I would place no bets on my safe arrival had it not been for Don's intervention.

The fellowship began that evening at midnight when I arrived. Help to carry my belongings was abundant. I felt like some kind of person with special distinction as almost every participant was curious about my safe travel in the evening because of my banquet commitment. The next morning at breakfast, the feeling of brotherhood and friendship was present from not only the men I had previously known from Blessed John's but also from the people I had not had the pleasure of meeting. Several of the participants were also in the program. Each of them shared a different part of my Catholic faith and my relationship with God, Jesus, and the Holy Spirit. The Catholic teaching is that God the Father, God the Son, and God the Holy Spirit are all one and are called the Holy Trinity. A difficult concept to understand, but if one is praying or communicating to any of the three, they are speaking to God.

Significant discussion on the practice of daily prayer with God was an important and necessary concept so that the happenings of the day, challenges, and my needs could be shared with God. Something that I had never been good at was asking for God's intervention in the good and not-so-good happenings in my life. Asking for God's guidance was another of my needs, and I worked on and am still working on my relationship with God. The hardest part of prayer for me is listening to God. As the sessions moved on, the concept of God putting the right people in my life was intriguing. God being with me and for me is a powerful concept to believe in and to practice.

Christ living through me was a very humbling practice. The idea that God gives to me and I to Him brings down to earth the great love God has for me and I have for Him. Talking about these topics makes me a little uncomfortable because while I believe in a close relationship on one hand, on the other, I ask why God wishes to be so committed to me. I also look with pride that I have certain gifts and that God gives me these gifts and will help me use these gifts. Each of us must make our time and our conversations with our God daily to live a happy, fruitful, and accountable life.

During the retreat, in the evening, each participant was given around seven letters. These letters came from our family and other participants in the retreat. As I read my wife's letter, I was overtaken by the writings and the spirit of the writing supporting me in this venture with God. It is truly an adventure that I should take more often to sort out my life under the influence of my God. Other letters were also very supportive from the team providing the retreat. I felt renewed and ready to practice the leanings I had acquired as a result of the weekend. The men who were participants in the retreat had formed a bond of friendship and commitment to a wholesome Christian life. This friendship is sincerely expressed each time I see one of the participants from this weekend.

St. Louis Soup Kitchen

Kathy and I had the opportunity to work at St. Louis Kitchen in Toledo once a month with other people from the Blessed John. Most of the regular workers we had known for years. For example, Meg was a summer nurse at Wood Lane when I was employed there, and Meg's husband, Roman, was the head of the Counseling Center at BGSU and were members of our previous church. Mary and Bill Batechelor were the coordinators of the program. Don and Geri Sternitzke both worked in education and attended our previous church. Scott Regan was also a member of our previous church and is the life of the party, using his background in drama to keep the interest of the group at a high level. Other workers come on a less frequent schedule. Our job was to prepare a lunch for between 200 and 250 people, some children but mostly adults, many who were homeless. The pleasure of being there is because I enjoy the experience, and am beginning to make a few acquaintances with some of the patrons.

In February 2009, I was to have an experience that I cannot explain. Tuggie and Larry Ryan were new workers. I was explaining to Larry, standing next to his wife, Tuggie, on how to use the dishwasher. I had just told him that the only big problem he would experience was if there was soup, and the plastic soup bowls were used. Washing these light plastic bowls is a nightmare. They jump everywhere in the washer and many times don't dry well because they flip over and fill with water. They also fly out of the holding tray. I had just finished with my orientation with Larry when it was announced that the plastic bowls were going to be used for the soup. I made a big deal out of the negatives I had just explained to Larry when the boss of the center came walking through. My explanation of the perils of using plastic bowls must have caught her ear because she substituted other bowls for the plastic bowls.

I was still working next to Larry and Tuggie when a terrible noise came out of the garbage disposal. I had a disposal at home, so I knew to shut down the disposal, put on my gloves, and begin to feel around in the disposal for the problem. I did just that, and I found a few nuggets of something that were identified as small bones. We turned on the disposal, and the sound was better, but there were still bones or something in the disposal. The disposal was shut down a few more times, and each time I would wait before putting my hand into it to clear it. On one of these occasions, the disposal was shut off, but something told me it was still running. I checked the switch, and somehow the switch that was turned off was now on. I had a weird feeling in my body about what could have happened if I had not checked the disposal and shut it down. The thoughts I began to have about what my hand would have looked like if I had put it into the running disposal were horrifying. I certainly was glad that I had checked the disposal before I put my hand in. I, to this day, cannot explain how that switch went from off to on. I even saw the switch being turned off.

Small Miracles

I have relayed to you how many situations in my life were negative and not so easy to deal with. I would now like to look at the plus side of some recent happenings in my life. A few years into my retirement, I had been asked to serve Mass. While there had only been a few funerals at our church, I was asked to serve a few funeral Masses at Blessed John XXIII. I told Father Herb I hadn't served for years. He said that he would have a run-through with Roman, the other server, and me. The day of the funeral, Kathy and I were running a little late, and I missed the practice with Roman and father. Roman guided me through the service, and it went pretty well. A few months later, I received an e-mail from Marla Overholt asking me if I could serve for a funeral that Friday. I said yes, but I would like another server to be present as I hadn't served much lately.

I arrived at the church early and looked for Father Al, our substitute priest. Father Herb, our full-time priest, was not able to preside over the Mass as he had just had some surgery and was recovering. I found Father Al and told him that I was a server when I was younger, but I only recently served. Father Al is a very positive person to be around as he always tries to make you feel like a million dollars and is very successful at his attempts. Father Al has another admirable trait. When Father Al is around, everything is okay. If something goes wrong, you would never be able to tell it by Father Al's actions.

It was a few minutes before the funeral procession arrived, and there were no other servers to be seen, and Father Al asked me to light the candles. I began to ask him many questions about my job as server. He answered my questions and many times told me he would tell me when it was time to do a certain task. We discovered that the funeral party was at church, so I picked up my cross on a staff and led the procession, including the casket, and began the journey down the aisle. I was thinking ahead about what my next task was after I had placed the cross in the holding stand, and it was to find the holy water container and the sprinkler. The procession went well into the church. I walked slowly and ended the procession by the placing the cross in its holder.

Next, it was time for me to find the holy water. I did so and watched the people coming into the church. As I looked around, my heart sank. I had not lit the candles. Mass had started with all the people now in the church. I whispered to Father Al that the candles were not lit. He calmly asked me to light them. I gave him the holy water container and sprinkler to hold until they were needed. At that point, I needed a small miracle to light the candles. I don't think too many people noticed the unlit candles as the service was just beginning. There was another complication; I wasn't sure where the candlelighter or the matches might be stored. I immediately started the long trip to the sacristy, which is a good distance from the altar. I began what I hoped would be an easy task, finding the candlelighter and the matches. I looked far and wide for the candlelighter and found it; now where were the matches? They were nowhere to be found. I heard Father Al progressing through the opening prayers and kept thinking that I was going to miss my jobs because I was looking for matches. I also thought, the sooner I lit those candles, the less noticeable it would be.

I asked the secretary if she knew where the matches were, and she said she didn't. The thought hit me. What would I do if I couldn't light the candles? Panic was first and foremost in my mind. There were all those people in the congregation, several being Catholic, and many of them had to be wondering why there were no lighted candles. In a last attempt, I scanned the room that I had already thoroughly surveyed, and as I looked into a box, I saw that there it was. I found the butane lighter and tried to light it. The igniting mechanism involved pushing a sliding tab on top of the lighter and pulling a trigger at the same time. The sliding tab was not moving. I tried again, and it still wasn't working. The secretary was about to try the lighter when it started. With the candlelighter ready, I proceeded to the casket area and began to light the Easter candle. As I lit the candle, Father Al said the words "Now we light the Easter candle." I proceeded to light the other candles on the altar. I stored the candlelighter and made it back to the altar to hold up the book for Father Al to read.

The next significant task I was to perform was lighting the charcoal so that it could burn the incense. After the consecration or the part of the Mass that wine and bread are turned into the blood and body of Christ, I walked to the sacristy to start the charcoal. As I approached the charcoal, I couldn't help but think of the story that Father Al had told me before Mass about lighting the charcoal. It seems that at a church north of Perrysburg, the server had gone to light the charcoal in a room adjacent to the altar. As the boy ignited the charcoal, it started sparking, as it usually does. This time the sparks flew on some papers close to the charcoal and began to burn. Father Al continued the Mass as he noticed the flames. He quietly asked a person who was a firefighter to take care of the fire. Other people were enlisted by the firefighter to help with the fire. While the three extinguished the fire, the EMS and fire department also arrived on the scene. Father Al continued the Mass through all the excitement of the fire and at the end of Mass informed the parishioners of the fire.

The story about the fire faded as I took a few precautions in moving anything flammable away from the place where I was going to start the charcoal. I picked up the same lighter I had used before, pushed forward on the safety device on top, and clicked the trigger. The lighter did not start after several tries. I shook the lighter and found that it appeared to be empty. One more try with the lighter and the same result occurred, no flame. I was beginning to get a little concerned because the charcoal had to be lit soon so that it could produce smoke as the incense was placed on the hot charcoal. What a spot to face. As an outdoorsman and Eagle Scout to boot, I couldn't start a fire. I began to quickly and frantically go through all the drawers in the sacristy. As luck or a small miracle would have it, I found a whole box of blue tip matches. As I struck the matches, I would place them in a strategic position around the charcoal. Some of the matches broke off, but most of them did start. After I felt the charcoal was started, I took my place by the altar with the vessel that held the charcoal. When it came time to put the incense on the hopefully hot charcoal, I watched closely to see if the incense burned. The incense did burn, and I was a happy camper. I had a few small miracles that day and hoped that I didn't need any more help in a crisis.

Later, a friend of mine congratulated me on lighting the Easter candle at the same moment that the priest talked in his reading about the lighting of the Easter candle. I told him that I had not lit the candles as I was supposed to have done. He said that nobody in the congregation would have known that I was late lighting the candles as the timing of the lighting and the readings made it look like a job well done. After that conversation, I decided to tell very few people about what really happened. I knew God's role was responsible for the perception by many of a candle lighting that looked very appropriate and to me was a form of a miracle.

Yes, some of the examples of the most significant beliefs I have of God's influence in my life is buried in the last and next few paragraphs. It seems to me that as I grow older, God is kinder to me. He helps me out when I am in need of His help. These times I have called small miracles, and I have a few that I wish to share. There was a time many years ago that I was in graduate school and was scheduled for my internship in educational administration for my specialist degree. The location was the superintendent and assistant superintendent's offices in the Toledo Board of Education. As I checked on the fees for the course, I found we needed $550. We had maybe $100. Kathy and I had a rule on money. We only borrowed money for our house and our car. I had mentioned to my father that I would have to put off a semester doing my internship because of our monetary shortfall. At the time I was not asking nor was I thinking of asking for money, but we were just keeping my parents informed of my progress. We received an envelope a few days later with a check from my mother and father. It was for $550.

Do you remember the wedding at Put-in-Bay in the fall 2010? I had promised my friend Kevin and wife-to-be Leslie that I would provide the champagne for the wedding. The rest of the story is that champagne usually takes about four months or so to make. There is the making of the champagne and the degorging or the extracting of the sediment after it settles in the neck of the upside-down bottle. For some unknown reason, two of the cases of champagne were going on eleven months and the other two cases on six months of having settled the sediment and thus being able to complete the champagne making process. I had told Kevin and Leslie that I would try to have the champagne ready for the wedding. I knew I could be in trouble since the champagne had not settled as it should. When it got to one month and there was some clearing but not enough to degorge, I took the risk and said that I would have the champagne ready. Two days before the wedding, the last case of champagne was cleared, processed, and picked up the very same day to be transported to the island. God was the one who made that champagne clear, and He was doing it on His timeline, not mine. His timeline did get the job done; it was not as soon as my timeline.

Another example of a small miracle was a few days after the wedding at Put-in-Bay, I delivered the remarks to around two hundred people at the dedication of the Dr. Thomas Bowlus Life Enrichment Center near Luckey, at the Otterbein Portage Valley Homes. Dr. Tom was the founder of the entire complex. The new complex was a $475,000 complex that can be used by the residents for many social activities such as cards, relaxation, pool, and many others. I was the chairperson of the board, so that was why I gave remarks. Doing a good job was my goal as I always wish to use the skills God has given me in the best way possible. As I started my remarks, I noticed that I was looking more at the audience and less at my notes. As the remarks proceeded, I received energy and words from some place that I knew not where they came. After the remarks drew to a close, I began receiving many compliments from the audience on how well my short speech had been given. It did not take me too long to realize that in this case as in many examples in my life, God had decided He wanted to be more involved. It certainly wasn't a coincidence in any of these examples that God was taking a major part in my actions. A miracle, yes, I would call all these events and many more like them small miracles.

Baptism

Baptism at Blessed John is a very special event for the baby, parents, sponsors, congregation, and Father Herb. It all starts at the entrance of the church. Father Herb welcomes the baby, parents, and sponsors and introduces them to the parish and has a short ceremony. The baptism party then proceeds down the aisle with the servers, lectors, and Father Herb. Somewhere near the middle of Mass, the baptism party is called up to the altar for the baptism by water. In addition to the baptism by water, the holy oils are administered, and a candle is lit to be a guide for the parents to be good parents. After the baptism is complete, one of the most wonderful experiences of my life takes place. Father Herb is given the baby by the parents. All the baptism party but the baby and Father Herb then go to their pew.

Father then places the baby in his arms so that the baby can see around the church. As Father begins his formal presentation of the baby to the parishioners, he begins walking through the entire church, displaying the new baby to the entire assembly. On some aisles Father Herb must walk backwards so the baby and the parishioners can see each other. As the baby is presented, there is a smile on everyone's face and sometimes even on the baby's face. When father reaches the back of the church, there is a large window, and on the other side of the window are the children looking at Father Herb and the baby. The children coming from Sunday school also have smiles painted on their faces. It is such a beautiful event there are tears of joy exhibited by both male and female parishioners. During the presentation, I feel like time has stood still, and this is definitely one of the most beautiful experiences of my life. Father Herb then stops in front of the parents and gives the baby a kiss on the forehead. On one occasion after a baptism was held at Mass, Kathy and I were talking about the beautiful baptism ceremony and Father Herb's procession with the baby. Kathy remarked that all the babies seem very content with the presentation to the parishioners. In fact, she remarked that she has never seen a baby cry during father's presentation.

Evangelization

The Catholic Church has talked about evangelization but that it about as far as it has gone in this area until recently. Essentially evangelization is sowing the seeds of our religion and hoping for growth. Some programs are more involved with nurturing the seed than others. The essential elements of our religion is that God loved the world so much that He sent His Son, Jesus, to live, die, and be reborn in this world. Blessed John XXIII Parish was to become involved in a nineteen county evangelization movement under the direction of the Diocese of Toledo called Spirit of Jesus Alive Today. The overall coordinator of the program is Sr. Joyce Lehman, a friend of ours from the very distant past. I could not wait to see Sister Joyce as she is a lovable and positive person. As the program developed, we added more people to the core team of Fr. Herb Weber, Emilia de la Pena, and me. The names of four additional people were added, and the training proceeded for the core members.

I traveled to St. Paul's in Norwalk for the training. I liked to talk with people to see if anyone from Willard, my hometown, was present. As I began to ask around, I couldn't find anyone from Willard St. Francis Xavier Church. I found out later that Willard had canceled coming to this session. I was hoping to see someone I knew from Willard at the training.

As the training began, I wondered if I had locked my car door. The meeting was located near the downtown area, and there could be many people walking by my car. They would not have to look too closely to see that my car was open. I couldn't remember locking the door. A few minutes later, I began to think about my car again. I was more convinced than ever that I hadn't locked, and I knew my checkbook was inside the car. I hated to leave the training because I needed to know all the information being presented. I decided to try to forget the car until the first break and then check it. The first break was not until halfway through the program or an hour into it. A break was announced, and I jetted out the front door, ran to my car, and tried to open the door. It was locked, and nowhere did I see signs of anyone trying to enter the car. I ran back and finished the training. I resolved myself to the fact that I need to be more careful in locking the door. I was able to focus my attention better on the training in the second half or hour.

The Blessed John XXIII Evangelization Committee met a few weeks later. As usual, a conflict between my committee meeting and dinner commitments arose. Kathy and I had some friends from North Carolina, Bonnie and Jim Hicks, and we had promised them that we would take them out to dinner when they visited us. Kathy knew Bonnie because they were in the Miss Huron County Beauty Pageant together, and they had maintained their friendship over the years. I was concerned how I could leave the meeting when I had the information from the Norwalk meeting to report. I had to leave the meeting after an hour to get to the Biaggi's Restaurant, where we had reservations.

As the meeting started, I was a little uneasy about leaving the meeting early. So I informed the group that I had friends from out of town, and I had to leave in an hour. The conversation developed in such a way that I could make my report and still leave in an hour. I am amazed at times how a force can make things happen so that all the variables come together. For me, the force is my God.

The Good Samaritan

If there were Bible verses that I would say are very important in guiding my life, I would have to cite Luke 10:25–37 as being some that are near the top. On July 11, 2010, Father Herb read the passage on the Good Samaritan at Blessed John XXIII Parish. As the passage was read, I knew that what was being read was very important to my life. While I was not a Samaritan, a Jew who had married a Gentile, which would have made me a religious outcast in the eyes of other Jews, I am, however, a person who believes in helping others in need when the time arises. When the Samaritan found the Israelite mugged and half dead, unlike two travelers before him, he took care of the beaten man's wounds himself and cared for him.

The reverend Roger Karaban in his weekly column relayed that Jesus told His followers that responding to someone in need is more important than even religious rules and regulations. He did a survey of his freshman religious students to see what they would do if they came upon someone in need such as a person in an automobile accident on their way to the last

Sunday Eucharist. Stopping to help the person would mean they would miss Mass. The majority response was that they would say a silent prayer for the person in need as they passed the accident. A few said they would leave Mass at Communion and see if they could help at the accident. I nor the author thought that the class really understood the lesson from the Good Samaritan.

Guatemala

One of the mission projects through Blessed John was a trip to San Lucas, Guatemala, a trip Kathy decided to take in 2010. After hearing Kathy's stories, I can almost see the gleam in the eyes of the impoverished children and the beaming faces of the smiling adults in Guatemala.

I learned much from Kathy about a third-world country. What one eats and drinks was closely monitored. Kathy also talked about building roads as one of the main activities of the volunteers from Blessed John. Reminders of the civil war in Guatemala of a few years ago are in the parish church.

Any volunteers will never forget the hospitality, and faith of the present Mayan descendants can be seen through the blood of martyred priests who live in San Juan and are trying to build their community so they are able to live in an acceptable economic, social, and cultural setting.

Kathy's Trip

Kathy has told me many times about her love of the people, the environment, and the culture. An example of the remembrances that Kathy brought back to the United States are scarfs, table runners, and other tapestries she bought in Guatemala.

Kathy's reports on her trip were so moving that Mark, my son, and I signed up and were accepted to travel to Guatemala in 2011 to stay and work out of the San Lucas Mission under the leadership of Father Greg, pastor of San Lucas, Toliman. Father Herb and fourteen other parishioners also made this trip. This is that story, a story that would move anyone to examine their life as they experience firsthand what a few days in a third-world country is really like.

Joe and Mark's Trip

As part of a mission trip, I was pretty well convinced that I would gain more from the experience than I was giving. As the trip unfolded, I saw every day and probably every hour how God through the people of Guatemala was giving me many lessons on life, one being how much more I had in the material world than I needed and the other being how happy people can be when they have very little.

February 11

A total of fifteen people, including myself, from Blessed John XXIII left the Quinta Hotel for the Detroit airport at five thirty. We had arrived in Detroit around ten o'clock the previous evening after a Mass service and a van or Suburban ride from Perrysburg. I had roomed with Mark the previous evening as I would be doing for the entire trip. I was happy to see that Mark was moving around as he was getting over a flu bug he had contracted the day before we left. The previous night, I was not sure he would be able to make the trip.

All the airport security and ticket checks went well. The first flight was to Houston Bush International Airport with a flight time of just over two hours. A layover of one hour and twenty minutes would put us on a three-hour flight to Guatemala City. Our travel would become more exciting at this point as members of the mission would be at the airport to meet us and transport us and our luggage to our final destination. As we walked into the reception area, we were met by two men from San Lucas Mission. There was a pickup truck and a van. With all the luggage loaded and secured on the pickup, we boarded the van.

The ride through Guatemala City proved to be a stop-and-go experience peppered with dust from the unpaved roads. It would have been more dustless to close the windows, but the vehicles had no air-conditioning.

We ate supper after we arrived and found the food to be good. We had a meat soup as the main course. After supper, we had a discussion with Father Herb, our leader. We were informed that some of us were to work in the vegetable garden tomorrow morning, while others would be moving rocks to build a road. It was becoming more evident that the other participants from Blessed John were very special people who cared a great deal about the other people on the trip.

February 12

About four o'clock in the morning, there was a production of the "roosters." The rendition of cock-a-doodle-doo was loud, frequent, prolonged, and unmistakably familiar to those of us raised on a farm. The big difference was that on the farm, the roosters crowed at the break of dawn. The crowing was obviously much earlier here. We never did find the reason for the earlier crowing in Guatemala. We were to find that roosters are very common in this area. We were also to find out that the showers were very different at the hotel with a mixture of hot and cold water not necessarily under the control of the person taking the shower.

Working in the Vegetable Garden

Our first morning of work consisted of spending time in the vegetable garden. There was a large pile of small stones in the middle section of the garden that needed to be moved. This was accomplished by some workers shoveling and others holding the bag open until they were partially filled. The bag was then transported to a hole that needed to be filled. The hole was somewhat filled about the same time we ran out of stones. The work was accomplished in a fast manner.

After working in the vegetable garden, we had the opportunity to see the coffee bean project that was located on the hill above the garden. The coffee beans come in with a shell on them. The coffee is cleaned and the outer shell removed. The yellow bean is then dried on concrete slabs and then shelled. The gold or green bean is then roasted, and most of the beans are sold to large coffee companies. Some of the coffee is packaged in smaller bags and sold through parishes such as Blessed John XXIII, thus eliminating the middle man. The tour was helpful in that we now knew the major programs operated by the mission.

Getting to Know Our Surroundings

Today was also a day we were to become familiar with our surroundings. In the afternoon, the group took a leisure walk around Lake Atitlan located near San Lucas. One of the first sights we saw was a number of women from the village doing their laundry in the lake. There were large stone slabs located out a few feet from shore, and the women would scrub their clothes with soap on the large flat stones until they were clean. We also noted laundry basins of probably concrete on the shore.

As we walked around the lake, we observed some boys in canoes full of seaweed they had gathered and were taking to shore. We assumed for fertilizer. As we continued our walk around part of the lake, we could still hear roosters crowing. The other very familiar sight was dogs of all sizes wandering the streets and roads. There were many beautiful flowers that resembled some of the common varieties we have back in the States.

In our tour of the city, we discovered for sale cold bottled Coca-Cola. A Coca-Cola plant is located in the area, and Coke is easily available for consumption for the right price. Cold pop is available in the small shops in the downtown area. Our tour of the area also introduced us to very colorful vegetation, plants, and flowers. Coffee plants are very common. Mountains and inactive volcanoes were also present.

February 13

It was time for us to visit some of the surrounding villages. We boarded rather large boats and arrived at the first village, Panajachel. There were several shops, but we were more concerned in seeing the Church of St. Francis.

Finding St. Francis was an interesting venture. Since the river had overflown its bed during a recent storm, it had gotten completely out of control and wiped out the bridge. With no bridge, our options were few, one being to cross the remaining river barefoot. That was exactly what we did. We took off our shoes and socks and walked across a small running river. Everyone made it across with help from others. I made it with the help of a friend, Joe. Since we had a time finding St. Francis, we were lost. We took rides on the tut-tuts to the church. A tut-tut is like a golf cart only there is one driver with two or three passengers in the front, the vehicle is enclosed, and they have one speed, fast. The cost was about fifty cents for a one-way ride.

We arrived at St. Francis Church. As I walked down the aisle, I observed a large Soroptimist of Christ. This is Christ lying in a glass case like he is in the tomb. In the aisle, I observed a middle-aged lady on her knees praying and moving from the back of the church to the front of the church and then back again. She never left her knees during her prayers. My knees hurt, and I was not even kneeling. It was time to get back to the boat as we had two other stops on our agenda.

Our next stop was San Catarina. As we approached the village, we could see many houses in the side of the mountain, actually built into the mountains. We paid a brief visit to the Church of St. Catarina. Many statues of saints were located around the altar. It was then off to San Antonio.

San Antonio was the third stop. St. Anthony Church is located at the top of the mountainside overlooking the lake. There was an unknown ceremony taking place; it might have been First Communion. Whatever it was, the people were dressed up. As we watched the activities at St. Anthony's, Mark and I had our pictures taken with Lake Atitlan in the background.

It was back to San Lucas. Father Herb was going to go swimming in the lake, and I and another man were interested in going with him. As we approached the lake, we found a dock, and we were able to jump in. I was being very careful entering the water because the lake was very cold, deep, and polluted. I tried hard to keep my mouth shut as I swam. I did a few rest strokes to get accustomed to the water. I decided that I was going to do a regular or crawl stroke. As I began my forward motion and turned my head from side to side as I swam, I tried hard to keep my mouth shut and the water out. It didn't work. Somehow my mouth opened, and a large wave hit me. That was the end of keeping the polluted water out of my mouth and avoiding some type of infection. Leaving the water proved a challenge for me as there was no ladder to the floating dock. Thankfully, the other two swimmers helped me out of the water.

The group took a walk downtown, and we discovered an ice cream shop. The ice cream at the shop was a little like gelato and was very tasty. There was a computer shop where we could e-mail people in the States for a nominal fee.

Near dark before our group meeting, one of the other gentlemen brought to my attention that there were large bats flying in the sky. I watched for the bats, but they were hard to clearly see. I was happy to find a shop where I was able to buy a cold orange pop. It tasted really good.

February 14

In the morning, I could hear bells calling me to the church for Mass. As I walked into the San Lucas Catholic Church, I noticed that there were several near life-size statues on the side aisles. Behind the altar, I could see on the wall seven statues of saints. There was a large group of magicians who were to provide the music for the Mass. I counted ten members in the band. There were two priests, a seminarian, and seven servers to perform Mass proper. During the Mass, people were very attentive to the proceedings.

Father Herb was one of the priests co-celebrating the Mass, and I felt like an important person with him standing in front of all the Mayans speaking to them in Spanish. The different cultures present were very united in terms of worshipping as one. At the time in the Mass where everyone greets others by shaking hands, the instant unity of people from far different nationalities was very heartening and impressive. It had been a very moving Mass.

In the morning, we were to receive an orientation from one of the volunteers on staff. The presentation was very interesting, informative, and essential. The presentation was divided into three phases: why we were here, the ground rules, and the background tour.

Why we were here was pretty straightforward. We were in San Lucas Mission in solidarity. We were here on an equal relationship with others. We will walk with the people of San Lucas. They will tell us their needs. We will treat others with respect. We will learn to talk with them. We will develop relationships with them. We will largely work as laborers.

The ground rules are we do not want to be ones who give handouts to the Mayan Indians. Once they receive handouts, they will expect them. We are to be in by nine o'clock and not be by the lake at night. The ice cream shop is the farthest point we go at night.

The background on the area is as follows: The Mayan people are 90 percent of the area population. A goal is to provide dignified opportunities for the Mayan population. The Mayan people will tell us what to do. In the area, 5 percent of the population own 80 percent of the land. Workers are paid nominal fees by the landowners, which is not fair. A goal of the mission is every family will have three acres as their own. Tuition for the school is based on ability to pay. The programs at the mission are 99 percent funded by donations.

Next tours to the various facilities were given. The Women's Education Center was built so women could learn how to better cook, sew, keep house, learn other skills, and socialize with other women. The facility is well constructed and very pleasing to the eye.

The hospital is located at a different location. There is an operating room and other treatment facilities. There are a few full-time physicians and foreign doctors who come to perform various operations. As an example of the growth in treatment over the past few years, the number of surgeries last year was 60, and the most recent year was 105. Operations are commonly hernia, cyst, hysterectomy, and others.

The coffee operation had been explained earlier in the week and was also explained today. We saw the bags of coffee ready to be roasted as well as the roasting machine. We were off to lunch and then to work.

Hoeing

A few of us chose the hoeing detail. We were to hoe the vegetable garden with a hoe blade that was about three times the size of the American hoe blade. After the outside perimeter of the raised beds were hoed, the handwork of pulling the small weeds growing in the vegetables was to be accomplished.

Carrots, onions, and radishes were the major vegetables grown for the mission. The rest of the workers were busy transporting rocks to make a road or a side wall for the road so that the rain would not cause erosion of the road. It is important to remember that the region we were living in was close to the equator. This meant that the sun was more directly overhead and produced a more direct heat.

Debriefing and the Evening Walk

As usual, Father Herb had a debriefing at the end of the day where people had a chance to share their thoughts on the day. After the meeting, I told Mark I was still thirsty and wanted to find a soda and possibly something to eat. The street outside our hotel offered no open shops. As we began to travel over a few streets, we noticed that there were streetlights. We also noticed that more light would have offered us more safety. We began to find a few open shops but not the kind we were interested in. As we continued to walk, we were aware that we did not want to stray outside our boundaries, whatever they were. As we continued to walk, we noticed more people walking the streets. I began to feel a little uncomfortable in this strange surrounding as I had $75 in American money in my pocket.

I was closely scrutinizing every person I passed in the street. A few feet ahead, I heard two dogs growl at each other and begin fighting. Immediately, other dogs arrived on the spot to investigate. The dogs confined their fighting to themselves, and for that, I was grateful.

We then realized that we were approaching the town square, a bit farther from our hotel than I wished to travel. The thought of taking a tut-tut back to the hotel was becoming very attractive. I wasn't sure that I wanted to trust a tut-tut driver. My mind was brought back to the present as I saw many people walking in the town square. Mark found a taco stand and began using his Spanish to order himself some food and a soda for me.

The tut-tut alternative again came back to my mind. I then thought of how everyone was being friendly to us. Besides, I was taller than most of the Mayan people, and Mark was a real giant. We began to walk back to the hotel after we decided that walking was looking safer.

As we arrived at our street, a group of six young men stopped at the crossroad ahead of us. When we reached the crossroad, we walked beside the group and didn't even take a good look at them. We reached the hotel. It looked to us that there is little to worry about on the streets of San Lucas. The next day, we found that we had gone a bit far from our hotel. There was a reason for my uncomfortableness the night before.

February 15

The Market

At 7:00 a.m., I was ready to go to the market. I met Sue and Russ at the front of the hotel, and the three of us were off to the square. In a foreign land, I always feel more comfortable traveling with people I know. As we walked into the market area, some shops were set up, some were in the process, and others spots were vacant. We were to discover that there were at least two major parts or sections to the market. Some vendors brought boards to display their jewelry, while others used the bare ground.

There were various displays of produce such as pineapple, avocados, radishes, apples, onions, carrots, peppers, parsley, potatoes, lettuce, and watermelon. There were meats available, cooked and uncooked. Some of the largest displays were clothing and weaved materials made into scarves, table runners, blankets, and other assorted items. Commercial toys and trinkets were on display. It was interesting and fun watching the vendors unload, display, and sell their wares.

The vendors are always very friendly and use their smiles and their skills to make a sale. At one point, I was near leaving the displays, and since taking pictures is a touchy area, I had no good picture of the fruit. I noticed Father Herb nearby, and he arranged it with one of the vendors that I could take a picture of their fruit. I gave the lady five quetzales for her trouble. As I walked away, I thought, *I bet she would have posed for the five quetzales.* I missed that opportunity for a good photo shot.

As we made a turn in the market, we noticed a cemetery next to the market, and the four of us walked through an open door into the cemetery. The cemetery was unusual as many of the sites had mausoleums or burials above the ground. Some were single sites, and others were doubles or more. Several looked like they were family plots as many vaults were placed on top of each other. While some of the vaults were white, others were yellow, blue, or other colors. It was a magnificent display of colors, flowers, and other decorations. The site reminded me of burial grounds in North Carolina, but the colors there were usually white. It had been a great early morning seeing the market and the cemetery.

Working with the Rocks

As I left San Lucas Mission to go to the work site, I began to think of the stories I had heard about the most recent tropical storm, Agatha. Several days of rain had turned the area into a literal mudslide. Once the mud began to push down the mountainside, it would gather trees and homes with the mud. The most devastating happening was when the mud would gather or bury people. The aftermath of the loss of homes proved the need for temporary homes before permanent ones could be provided.

One of our assignments was to work at this temporary site so that some housing would be available. As I rode in the back of the pickup truck to the work site, I had a moving experience. It was a gratifying feeling to have the opportunity to help people so desperately in need. It wasn't money we were giving; it was our sweat and sore muscles. It was truly a Christian experience in which my whole body felt good. What an opportunity for our group to experience.

At the temporary work site the first day, our men worked by carrying broken rocks to a huge ravine made by the mud sliding to stop further erosion. The site for the temporary housing was originally covered with rocks several feet by several feet. The rocks were broken up by hand with chisels and hammers by the Mayan men. There are few machines as work is usually done by hand. Next to the ravine was the temporary housing site. The women were busy making the new women's center ready for the grand opening, which was just weeks away.

The Civil War

In the afternoon, one of the Mayan women who had been a victim in the civil war gave a firsthand account of her experiences. The military in the 1960s was very leery of the guerillas. The guerillas were people opposed to the military, and if you were a guerrilla or spoke about helping the poor, you were killed. The poor were also seen at times as opposed to the military. It was not uncommon for the military to come into a home and take usually the man who was suspected. The military would then beat and kill the man. The next day, the body of this person might be found along the side of the road. The Mayan lady presenting these stories relayed how her husband had been taken one night by the military and was never found.

Another story this woman told was about the time that there were eleven orphans who had seen their parents killed. A driver and this Mayan lady went a distance to bring back the children to the orphanage. After picking up the children, they all started back for the San Lucas Mission. There were checkpoints the military had set up. At the first checkpoint, the driver told the military the family was going home. They let them go through the checkpoint. At the second checkpoint, the military saw the children, and the driver told them that they could look in the car if they wished. The military let them go through. At the third checkpoint, the children and the Mayan lady were praying the rosary. They made it through the last checkpoint and home safe and sound.

February 16

Children's Mass

We started out our day by attending Mass at the San Lucas Church. As the music started, there was one distinguishing feature that I noted: the singing by the children was very beautiful. I had never heard any group of people sing so well from the heart. In addition, the boys and girls were attentive to the Mass. It was a pleasant and memorable experience.

Finishing the Rock Job by the Temporary Housing

After the children's Mass and breakfast, it was time for us to go back to the temporary housing site to complete our work with the rocks. Before we left, it was time to take a picture of the group. Today we needed to take rocks around some of the temporary housing to fill in the rest of the open ravine. We loaded the wheelbarrows and wheeled them to the site that needed the rock fill. Once again, some Mayan workers split the large rock of four feet by three feet with chisels and hammers while a few of our people tried to do the same with sledgehammers. The women continued their work of readying the new women's center.

Reforestation

Father Herb and Linda from our group knew the man who ran the reforestation project in San Lucas. In fact, I learned that the reforestation project had been renamed after Linda, from our group, sometime after Linda's visit to the project last year. Since we had the afternoon open, we decided to visit this project. As I understood, the project is to incubate many different types of plants and trees to be transplanted into other needed areas. The controlling of erosion is another big use of these plants.

We walked into the compound looking for the director. Unfortunately, he was away on business. We met one of the workers and saw many beautiful and varied plants and trees. Seeing this garden set in the middle of housing, which was a normal for San Lucas yet not affluent, was quite a dichotomy. It was a pleasant experience but did not trump the evening's activities in San Lucas.

An Evening in San Andres

The trip to San Andres was around twenty minutes long. It seemed like about forty-five minutes as the road was full of holes. As we traveled in our non-air-conditioned van in the late afternoon, I for one was wishing the ride was over as the driver skillfully tried to maneuver the van around the many potholes. Before we reached the village, I looked to the side and saw a huge ravine. I asked some questions and found that the ravine was made from a recent large storm that had wiped out the village of San Andres.

When we arrived in San Anders at the base of the hill where the church was located, a most moving experience took place. The bells of San Andres began ringing and continued to ring until our van was parked at the church. The only reason for the sound of the bells seemed to me was that Father Herb (Padre) was with us, and priests and Mass are not regularly scheduled events. Father Herb exited the van with his Mass in the bag, meaning he carried everything he needed for Mass in his bag. People greeted him with great reverence. All this attention spilled over to the other fourteen people from Blessed John XXIII Parish.

As Father Herb readied for the Mass, the wine needed for the Mass was not able to be found. The guitarist asked what was not right. Father Herb explained he could not find the wine, and it must be back at the mission. The guitarist told father not to worry as he had a motorcycle, and he could be back with the wine in a few minutes. He was correct, the Mass proceeded in a few minutes with a large portion of the church full.

I had not been able to find a restroom before Mass, so I, by necessity, left the service to find a men's facility. As I went out the front door and looked to the left of the church, like a miracle, there was a latrine on the hill. As I got about halfway up the hill, I heard and saw two large dogs barking and chasing me. I quickened my pace and made it to the restroom just ahead of the two dogs. As I was preparing to leave the latrine, I thought, *God, please take care of those big dogs.* I peeked around the corner of the door and saw nor heard the dogs. I walked out of the latrine and back to church. Thank God, the dogs never reappeared.

One of the unique parts of the Mass in this location is that incense is used several times. In fact, large amounts are used so that the church is filled with the fragrance of incense. Near the end of the Mass, Father was checking with a server to see that this was the last time incense would be used. The server responded, "Yes, Padre, this is the last time we use incense, so fill her up."

As we left the church, I looked up at the sky, and there was one of the most beautiful moons I had ever seen. I watched that moon as we traveled back to the mission and wondered about the being who had made this world.

When we reached the mission, there was a good meal and an excellent group discussion to complete a wonderful day. Evenings are such a peaceful part of the day. It is a time to reflect on the day and all that God has given to us.

February 17

The last formal day of work was Thursday morning. I was given a choice of jobs this day, and I took the one that seemed to me to be the easiest. The job was described as digging out a cistern. The cistern was now twenty-feet-plus wide and over fifteen feet deep. The final depth was to be twenty-seven feet, so we knew we were not going to complete the job. The granules of dirt seemed easier to handle than the large rocks of the past few days.

As Joe, Steve, Rusty, and I approached the hole, we saw that the bottom was near full of broken-up rocks that needed to be removed. It became apparent that we were not going to dig dirt as rocks, and not much dirt was in the hole. We organized ourself and decided that one person would be picking up the large rocks from the bottom of the hole, and the next would be on the ladder, handing them to the two persons at ground level. When we were transporting small rocks, the two workers in the hole would both be throwing the rocks to the two persons at ground level. Periodically, the jobs were switched so everyone had a chance to do all the jobs.

Also in the hole were two employees of the mission. Each of them was chiseling the large three-foot-by-five-foot boulders. The chiseling made it possible to have the rocks in a manageable size to be either thrown or handed out of the hole.

For two hours, the four of us passed, threw out of the hole, or piled the rocks. I had no doubt that the pile of rocks was going to have some useful future as everything is used and not wasted in this area of Guatemala. The work was at times partially shaded. The temperature was eighty to ninety degrees, and the workers were hot, sweaty, and becoming a bit tired. Around eleven o'clock, we finished the job of removing the rocks. Our ride back to the mission came at the same time.

When I reached my room at the hotel, I immediately prepared for a shower. I was very dirty, and the shower was the only thought in my mind. I turned on the shower and was about to walk in when I noticed there was no water. Since I was not properly dressed to leave the room, Mark found an employee of the hotel, and somehow hot and cold water appeared. I love to shower, and this shower felt great as it removed the dirt from my body.

After lunch, we were off to travel to a neighboring city to take in the sights. The city we were to visit was Santiago, known for its many shops, and this was our last chance to spend any Guatemala money on gifts for ourselves or others.

There was a priest in Santiago, Guatemala, near San Lucas named Fr. Stanley Rother. He was originally from the United States and decided to leave Guatemala when the civil war was active. When he went home, he decided that he needed to return to Guatemala. He reasoned that as a shepherd, he could not leave his flock. He came back, knowing he was on the military hit list, and stayed in the church proper. Each night he moved from one room to another to provide some protection to himself.

One evening the military came in to arrest him. Father Rother had vowed he wouldn't be taken alive as he did not wish to be tortured and be forced to give up the names of some of the people the military wished to take captive. One evening the military came to the church, found Father Rother, and killed him. Father Rother went with a struggle.

The presenter explained how she found Father Rother's body in a small room near the church. There was blood on the floor, which she swept up and put in a jar. This blood was still in a liquid state ten years later. She also found the bullet hole in the floor and blood on the wall. His body was buried in the United States, but his spirit remains in Guatemala and is buried with his blood.

As we left the church, we noted in the large courtyard where bands and chairs were being set up for a service. We found that it was a charismatic service in which hundreds of people were expected to participate. It was on to the shops. There were shops that sold clothing, arts, crafts, paintings, wood carvings, shawls, hats, toys, produce, and about anything else one could imagine. The merchants were very persistent in trying to sell you goods, and the negotiating system is the price setting standard. It was back to the mission and time for dinner.

Dinner was to be our last major meal together for the trip. Reservations had been made at the nicest restaurant in the city. The restaurant was located near the lake and was nicely landscaped and attractive inside as well. The conversation and food were appropriate for our last evening in Guatemala.

It was in my mind and I would assume others that the group and the setting in Guatemala was drawing to a fast close. While the friendships that had been formed would be rekindled from time to time, the setting would never be the same. I enjoyed the evening with one of the best fish entrées of my life and a group of parishioners I would never forget. From the time we had first met to organize the trip until this last meal together, God had provided for all of us relationships of a positive and supportive nature. I must admit that I felt a bit funny eating this excellent last meal while around this restaurant, there existed people who might not have had a good meal.

February 18 and 19

It was up and out of the mission by 6:30 a.m. A breakfast of rolls and jam were tasty and consumed rapidly. Traveling had its drawback for me as I was at the age where holding liquids in my bladder for any length of time is not going to happen. Limiting liquids was an event the night before traveling. The ride to the airport in Guatemala City was filled with beautiful countryside, mountains, and people. The two-hour ride seemed to go much better for me to the airport than from the airport. The restroom break about halfway to the airport was a welcome relief for me.

At the airport, we had several forms to fill out. Declaring what we had bought in the country and a security tax were two I remember. While waiting in the airport, I like to amuse myself by talking to people waiting for their flight. This day was no exception as I met a man and women from Texas who had a trucking business. They ran the business for thirty years. Their associated expenses had been $9,000 a year but had gone up to $20,000. Freight cost had become the biggest increase in his costs, and they had not been able to pass these fuel costs on to customers. He had to sell his equipment at a low price while the economy was also down.

Upon boarding the plane in Guatemala, my last name was called on the public address system. I knew that this was not good. As the security person came back to my seat, I thought, *What did I do now?* I asked the worker if he needed Joe or Mark Frederick. He said Mark. Mark went with the person. I had about a dozen plastic containers of honey I was bringing home, and I had carefully packed them, so I was happy it was not my baggage being checked. When Mark came back, I asked what it was about. He explained to me that it was my luggage, not his, that was being checked. I immediately asked about the honey. He told me that the honey was found, and the inspector went to his boss to see if it could be taken into the States. Mark worked for Homeland Security in the Columbus Airport, so he was familiar with what was and wasn't legal. Mark brought forth the fact that the honey was processed, so it was legal for it to go to the States. The head inspector agreed with Mark, so I could keep my honey.

Toward the end of the flight, I met a Fr. Carlo Alberto Titotto, who had worked with migrants for over twenty years. Father was from around Venice, Italy. We had a conversation about gypsies or tinkers as they are called in Ireland. His travels were around the world. I wished I had more time to talk to father, but we were in the Bush Airport in Texas.

I claimed my bag and checked to see that everything was OK. It wasn't. Somehow the upper section of my suitcase was wet. I could not tell what the liquid was that had saturated my suitcase, but it was only wet on the outside, not the inside. I rechecked my suitcase into the United States system where we were now headed for Detroit. Our flight was pleasant as

Mark and I sat next to a lady who worked as a human relations director with a company associated with auto parts.

We finished our flight and found it very cold as we boarded our van back to Perrysburg. It was the wee hours of the morning when we arrived home, but we made it safe and sound. I immediately had a cold glass of water and two glasses of cold milk.

CHAPTER 16

More of the 2006–2011 Era of Retirement

Knights of Columbus

In 2008, I joined the Knights of Columbus organization. This is an organization of Catholic men whose original purpose was to have insurance for widows and the surviving children. Today, in addition to the insurance program, there are many family- and service-related programs. The organization also gives aid to the needy and promotes social interaction with members and their families and educational, charitable, and other socially related projects. It was a no-brainer for me to feel and know that this organization represented by its members would easily coincide with my life goals of enjoying each day and giving to others.

My father and elder brother were Knights, and knowing my father and brother the way I did, this organization would also be for me. My father had been a Fourth Degree Knight, which is the highest degree. Membership in the Fourth Degree allows one to be a guard for various church-related events. The guard outfit is very colorful, even for a person who is color blind such as me. When I was in college, I had gone through the first three degrees but had never gotten further involved in the organization due initially to my educational commitments. One of my friends, Mark, was a state officer in the K of C, and for years, every time I would see him, he would ask me when I was going to get active. I worked with Mark's wife, Kelly. Mark was beaming the night that Blessed John the XXIII Council 14502 and Perrysburg Council held a joint ceremony, and I was involved. Perrysburg K of C had been very helpful to Blessed John Knights in helping us start. My son Mark also joined the council, and I was extremely proud as my father must have been forty-four years prior.

K of C Activities

The third Monday of the month was the date set for our monthly meetings. The Grand Knight, Wayne Vreeland, had worked like a trooper pulling together all the variables necessary to start a K of C Council. The election of officers was a loose and enjoyable process. If one was interested in an office, they would say so, and if there was no opposition, they were elected. I chose the advocate position. I also volunteered for the community activities director position as the activities were such that I thought my skills and gifts were most closely aligned to this position. One of the most notable factors present in the organization is the willingness of the members to remain committed to the cause of the organization and to positive relationships with one another. An atmosphere of charity is evident even when different viewpoints are present.

The cross section of members has not hindered the development of healthy relationships among the members while the organization was in its early development. A truly Christian atmosphere is readily observed as members interact during the meetings with one another as well as in the various projects in process or completed. An example of more friendship developing is evident as the members assemble after the meeting for refreshments and snacks at a local nightspot. I was a little behind the group in going to the pub. As I walked in and sat down, Mike, another officer, told me that the waitress was going to greet me from the bar, which was at the other side of the building. He said that the waitress was then going to ask "What does the new guy want?" I wasn't sure I believed him until the waitress greeted me and asked, "What does the new guy want?" Another interesting fact was that the beer was served in different sizes, but the largest was a fishbowl bigger than any that I have ever seen, and I had at one point in my life collected fishbowl beer mugs.

Interesting conversations have developed as members talk about their lives and world happenings. One interesting story related by my friend was about a patient suing two medical doctors because they had not given him all the medical treatment he felt he deserved. In the courtroom, the patient bringing suit had a heart attack as he was giving testimony. The two doctors being sued by the man in distress had the advantage of the two physicians jumping over the wall, separating the audience from the judicial section and then performing CPR on the person bringing suit against them, and they successfully saved his life. The judge dismissed the case.

A look at the diversity of the projects scheduled could be compared with the different personalities of its members. For example, early on, there was a fundraiser for Fanconi anemia, a genetic disorder that severely attacks a child's bone marrow. There is presently no cure. Approximately $2,400 was raised by this project. One of the members' daughter and another member's granddaughter had battled the disease since birth. Barbecuing for the annual church picnic of several hundred people was a lot of fun despite the hot sun. Participation in a soccer activity and a prayer for life assembly are the projects of this group and are all examples of activities happening in the first six months. The Grand Knight has the members in constant motion pursuing activities involving the family and the practice of the Christian faith. It is very easy for me to be committed to this group as they enjoy each day and are givers to others.

Otterbein Portage Valley

When my mother was in need of a structured living setting, we had visited many such facilities. One of the facilities was Otterbein Portage Valley or OPV. I had been a committee member on the board for a few years. Unfortunately, my mother did not meet certain criteria for admission. As a result, Kathy and I met with our good friends Jerry and Linda Johnson. They had experiences with a facility in Green Springs named Elmwood Homes. As a result of this meeting, our mother did go to live at Elmwood and did enjoy the facility and programs the rest of her life.

Meanwhile, I had been elected to the board of directors at Otterbein Portage Valley and in early 2000 was elected chairman of the board. After a break of a few years, I was asked to come back as the chairperson of the board. The following are some of the experiences at OPV.

The Life Enrichment Program

In the middle 2000s, the residents of OPV agreed that there was a need for a gathering room or a commons room that they could talk, play cards, play pool, or just drink a cup of coffee. At that time, there were a few patio villas or homes empty, and rather than build new, it was thought that we could use the existing structures. Larry Moore was the chairman of the board, and he began to pull together support for a new building. Vacant villas worked for a period, but they were not for the long term.

The resident council under the leadership of Dean Ruemelle was becoming increasingly more active in their pursuit of a new center. In March 2007, Ken Ault, the chairperson of the marketing and development committee of the OPV board, devoted his committee's time to the construction of a gathering center. Ken was to see through the entire project with his committee.

On July 31, another core committee became active, the fundraising committee. Joan Hankins, a resident; Pat Gory, OPV fundraiser; Tom Keith, director; Diane Ruder, corporate fundraiser; Ken Ault and Larry Moore, past chairpersons; Rev. Pete Johnson, some employees, and I began meeting to see where we needed to go with this project. We were not sure where to go at this time. We did know that something needed to be done. We pulled in Wilbur Hesselbart, a longtime board member and successful fundraiser for many organizations. Arlene Layman, who knows most people in Wood County and many in the surrounding areas, was enlisted to serve on this committee. Other OPV board members were Charlie Shanfelt and Bernie Shanchez. Denny Henline, a local businessman and son of Ken, an original board member, was recruited. All this expertise was essential to the project as it moved forward.

A resident's steering committee was also established to assure the residents knew and would inform other residents, their families, and other appropriate people where this project was headed. A resident, Joe Abel, agreed to be the chairperson of this committee.

With all these committees in place, a $475,000 goal was established for the center, and a project outline was finalized. A fifty-one-page presentation was developed, and pages and pages of founder and prospective donors were developed as we didn't want to miss anyone in the fund drive.

It was at this time in 2008 that we visited several Toledo area-based facilities that offered such a gathering room. On a hot summer afternoon, Otterbein Portage Valley through Pat Gory paid off the volunteers for their efforts in this project by buying everyone a super special ice cream cone. Pat was to leave us, and Barb came on board as fundraiser and said, "It is not if the project is going to go but when." The Ridgestone Builders were hired as the contractors and were to do a job so well that I marvel at the beauty of the room every time I see.

The groundbreaking ceremony was held on April 20, 2010, with a large crowd in attendance. The dedication was October 4, 2010, in a packed building. At the dedication, I had the opportunity to make some remarks. Since the building was named after Dr. Tom Bowlus, the founder of the Otterbein Portage Valley program, I couldn't help but pay tribute to all the original board members who had mortgaged their home so the money could be borrowed to enable the Portage Valley Homes to become a reality. Of all the commitments I have known in my professional and private life, this commitment of offering one's home as collateral for the start of a project ranks as the most unbelievable.

Dr. Tom has a dedicated wife, Maryilyn, who is always there to support him. Maryilyn used her skills to write a book on the origination of Portage Valley titled *The Building of a Dream*. The residents and their families, board, staff, and the community were proudly present in supporting everyone involved in the project. Seeing the support present that day, in my concluding remarks, I was honored to remind the crowd that "Anything that is worth doing is worth doing the right way," and I gave "A big thank-you to all who helped do it right."

Communion Service

Several years ago, Kathy and I had the good fortune to assist Father Herb and four other people on the first Friday of the month at two o'clock in the afternoon for Mass. Our jobs were to help the residents to the chapel and help with readings and offering help when needed to the residents. On the third Friday at two o'clock, the volunteers conducted a Communion service. Again, help was provided by volunteers for the twenty people who attended. As time went on, it became apparent that morning would be a better time for the services. In 2011, the times were changed for both services to ten o'clock in the morning. The arrangement worked out better for everyone involved.

It was also in 2011 in May that a state of the Otterbein Portage Valley Banquet was held. The purpose of the banquet was twofold. One was to update residents where the organization had been and where it was going. The second was to recognize staff and volunteers for their services. At this banquet, an award called the Second Mile Award was given to the church that has given the most to OPV in the past year. The church chosen was Blessed John XXIII. Not only did Blessed John XXIII provide church services at the Pemberville Otterbein Portage Valley Homes, but they also provided services at the Otterbein Avalon Homes in Monclova, Ohio, and the Otterbein Homes in Perrysburg.

The award was most humbling for Blessed John XXIII to receive. Six of the volunteers were present at the ceremony to receive the award on behalf of the parish. As I listened to the other volunteers, I was moved and agreed with their summation of the award. It was the feeling of the group that they received more from being involved with the services than it gave. The award was not really expected, but it was nice for the church.

God Spoke

The volunteer banquet was held on April 17 in the Life Enrichment Center. I knew that I would have a part in the presentation of awards as the chair of the board and found out that that part was to give a brief welcome to the one hundred honored guests. I had a few minutes to come up with my remarks. I have always been careful to have my remarks on paper, just in case my memory isn't as sharp as I would hope it to be. The administrators office was open, so I walked in to obtain some privacy and found the administrator, Tom Keith, had the same idea as me and was working on the opening prayer. I sat down and began to write.

As I began to write the central theme of my talk, I wrote that "At Otterbein Portage Valley, our guideline is giving to and for others." I looked at the first draft of my comments and immediately said to Tom, "God wrote these words I will be using this evening." I knew that God was with me and these words. The words came very easy, without effort, and were appropriate and accurate. It was a good feeling to have such a close encounter with God, and when I think of God, I often think of the presence of my lost twin. Thank you, God, the brief presentation went very well.

A Trip to Connecticut and the Big Apple

The end of October in 2010 was the date set to visit my brother Bob and his wife, Barb, in Brookfield, Connecticut, near the well-known city of Danbury, Connecticut. We left from Willard with my brother-in-law Fred around 8:00 a.m. on Thursday, October 28.

We rode in Fred's 2000 Cadillac. The car had plenty of room to put on miles since it had only around thirty-four thousand miles on its speedometer. The ride was extremely colorful with many remnants of the fallen leaves as well as the ones still on the trees. Pennsylvania is known for its many mountain ranges, and the Alleghenies and Appalachian provided us with great scenery. This scenery was familiar to me because as a kid traveling to Reading, Pennsylvania, my father's source of ancestry, the mountains were the status quo in terms of scenery.

We had not become lost or taken the wrong route that day until we were two miles from my brother's house. We missed the right street, and then that behavior became the norm of travel for us until we reached our destination. We arrived a few minutes later than scheduled to Barb and Bob's house but were in time for an excellent home-cooked meal.

Since Bob is a connoisseur of fine drinks, we were kept busy giving requests for drinks, and Bob was kept busy filling them.

The next morning was Friday, and Bob had taken off work to help us sightsee. Sightseeing is exactly what we did after a trip to Bob's local shooting range. While Bob had clearly been practicing with his pistol, Fred and I came in a close second. Franklin Delano Roosevelt had a home at Hyde Park, New York, on the Hudson River as did Cornelius Vanderbilt.

The Vanderbilt mansion was our destination that Friday morning. Cornelius made his fortune in transportation, probably best known for owning the New York Central line. Cornelius and his wife, Sophia, were said to entertain at their Hyde Park summer home. The grounds were peppered with beautiful flower gardens, and below the mansion on the Hudson was a railroad the Vanderbilts originally used to carry in supplies for the building of their summer home. On the second floor was a birthing bedroom room used by the family to display the birth of a newborn baby. This reminded Kathy and me of Versailles, where royalty shared the birth of their babies to many to make sure their birthright to the throne was properly documented.

Speaking of well-known, in the afternoon we visited Rhinebeck, New York, where a few weeks earlier, Chelsea Clinton was married to Marc Mezvinsky. Rhinebeck is also the home of the oldest inn and restaurant in the United States. Since we were there and since we were hungry, we did eat at the oldest inn and restaurant. After our lunch, we were off to the specialty shops in town.

A quick trip later in the afternoon to a local winery finished the afternoon sightseeing. The next day we left to visit some local sites, one of my favorites is Stew Leonard's grocery store. Stew has prided his store so customers expect the best in quality. The most in quantity is another happening as when there is one of an item, there is usually many. A trademark of Stew's is samples and relaxation. Most departments have eats for the customer to sample. The division of products was into separate rooms such as dairy, cheese, seafood, and meats, to name a few. This helped one to concentrate on the product at hand. I loved the atmosphere of the store as well as the products. The kiddies enjoyed pressing the button to see large stuffed caricatures talk, sing, and amuse, especially the younger patrons. After Stew's store comes his Stew Leonard's Wine Store. Once again, quality and quantity prevail.

Sunday was the day we were to go to New York City or the Big Apple. After a look at Rockefeller Center and the skaters, we did a quick tour of the Lego Center. It was time to eat, so we headed for a well-known restaurant called Becco. I have noted that restaurants in New York are of a modest size or at least the ones that I have been fortunate enough to partake in their cuisine. Becco was true to form. I noted on the menu that they served an entrée called Osso Buco alla Becco. This was veal to me, and that was what I ordered. I was in for a bigger treat than I could have imagined because the serving was very adequate, and the veal was the best I could remember ever eating. In fact, everything, including the service, was first class. This food experience put us in excellent shape for our next venture, *Jersey Boys*.

Walking into the theater helped us realize that we were on Broadway, and we were at one of the top-rated musical plays in the world. As the first act unfolded, I was sure that the talent I expected in this play was present without a doubt. The singers were more than talented, and as I listened to the songs I had known in the sixties, it was clear that I was completely infatuated with a performance that I could not have hoped to be any better. For a time, I felt like I was in the sixties. The beautiful presentation of the music had me hoping that the show would never end. The show did end, and at that point, I could see that others had enjoyed the performance as much, if not more, than I had.

It was hard to do anything else that day that would measure up to the previous events of the day. Bob did try to make our late supper as special as possible, and our trip to a local pizza shop was certainly enjoyable. Once I adjusted to the largest piece of pizza I had ever eaten, I knew the day was full. The trip home the next day was filed with more beautiful leaves, mountains, bright scenery, and an adequate supply of Halloween candy from Barb's stash. After leaving Fred at home in rural Willard, we paid a quick visit to Kathy's mom. We knew that we were tired and wanted to go home.

The Wood County Community

The Tornado

It was Sunday, June 6, 2010, and my early rising wife came to my bedside and said, "Honey, there has been a terrible tornado in Lake Township. The high school has been destroyed, and so have many houses. Several people have died." Lake Township is about twenty minutes from our home. My only personal experience with tornadoes had been over thirty years ago when one destroyed a mobile home park in my hometown, Willard. Saturday evening, June 5, around eleven fifteen, was to radically change many people's lives. This Sunday was to have been the Lake High School graduation day.

The valedictorian's father had perished in the tornado. The path of the tornado was around eight miles and lasted several minutes. One story told of a woman, an infant, and a man who drove their van into the Lake Township administration parking lot. Safety personnel who had taken cover in a stairwell heard someone frantically pounding on the door. The police officer opened the door and grabbed the baby and man while the lady was sucked into the storm.

Several days after the tornado, I was to pass the Lake High School. It was a mass of twisted steel and broken blocks. I thanked my lucky stars that I was twenty miles away from this tragic act of nature. As I traveled with my wife and son Mark farther east, we saw the wreckage of a large building. Upon further inspection, we found the building was the Lake Township administration building, the same building that the lady had disappeared from while trying to find safe passage for her infant.

The following November, the Black Swamp Humanitarian Awards Committee gave an award to this community. The June 5, 2010, tornado put forth their friends' and neighbors' needs before their own as the death of seven area residents and the destruction of millions of dollars of damage to homes, businesses, the high school, the Lake police department, and the Lake Township building became a stark reality. The Lake Township trustees—Melanie Bowen, Ron Sims, and Richard Welling—accepted the plaque on behalf of the Lake Township residents being honored. The slide presentation on the tornado was difficult to watch for many, but to me, the presence of God was there through the many people who gave help to others in great need of assistance.

An Ongoing Enjoyable Event

Each of us participates in various activities that we find extremely enjoyable in our lives. Shopping at the grocery store has always been one of those activities that has the word "fun" as an appropriate descriptor. While all of us enjoy buying something that is pleasant for us to consume, my greater joy arises from the people I am able to talk to in the many aisles of merchandise available for purchase.

I have found that when I approach people in the aisles, I may or may not know the fellow customers. At times, all I give and receive is a "Hello, how are you today?" I find that rarely does anyone not return my nod. Sometimes I will end up having a pleasant talk with this person whom I wasn't sure I knew. Near the end of 2011, I was with my wife in the checkout line when I spotted a man I thought I had played dartball with many years earlier. I walked up to the man and asked him if he had ever played dartball. He said he had and come to find out he had played on the same church team I had played on, but we were not sure it was at the same time. We both enjoyed a brief conversation.

I began to think back on the people whom I had talked to earlier in the afternoon. A man I had worked with at Wood Lane spotted me, and we had a pleasant talk about some of the other people we had worked with. I turned down another aisle, and there was the mayor of Pemberville. Kathy and I had a pleasant talk and asked the mayor to put us on his newsletter so we could take advantage of some of the overnight trips he organized each year.

I saw a person I had worked with in Wood County many years ago, and he happened to have a piece of equipment I needed for a project. He was very pleasant and promised that he would try to work out something with my needs.

As we were traveling one of the main aisles, Kathy spotted a grandmother of one of her former students. A catch-up session on her family transpired. A wife and husband with their baby offered me the opportunity to see and ask questions about the baby they were proud to have parented. A few other strangers offered me the chance to return a hello.

One of the cautions I must observe in my friendly trip through the Meijer store with my wife is that there is a limited amount of time that we can spend. It is not unusual for my wife to continue her shopping as I continue my conversations. Kathy is pretty good at talking with people for brief periods before moving on. My skill level at conducting short conversations is not as developed as my wife's. To check out at the same time as my wife, I have found that I must conduct more short conversations or fewer long interactions. In either case, I find my trips to the grocery store very uplifting. Yes, the joy of either starting new friendships or continuing existing relationships makes life worth living at a very reasonable price, usually nothing.

Fix It and Stains

Two of my mostly highly developed skills are fixing items and taking stains out of clothing. For years, my children would always bring their broken toys to me. When appliances broke, my wife would single me out to fix it. Likewise, when clothes became stained, I was the one to make the clothing better without stains. A look at these two areas in more detail will now take place.

Fix It

Why is it that some people will throw away a toy or an appliance rather than fix it? I know my father taught me to fix items when possible and try to fix appliances before calling the repairman.

My cap guns were one of the mechanisms that would jam up largely because of the powder from the caps I shot. Cleaning the pistols was easy, and then I was on my way playing cops and robbers. My toy cars would constantly have the rubber tires wear out. Transferring rubber wheels from old cars to newer cars was an easy task. When I was fishing, we used reel-type holders for the fishing line. To properly cast the fishing hook and bobber would at times cause the line to backlash. This would require the skill of unraveling the old fishing line so the backlash was gone, and I could fish again.

Throughout my life, the carburetor on the car, the tires, the muffler, and other more involved mechanisms such as the water pump were constant fix-it items.

As I was writing this section, I remembered that I was to buy new tennis balls for my mother-in-law's walker before they began squeaking. Tennis balls attached to the bottom of the back legs stops the squeaking on hard floors. I had forgotten to purchase the tennis balls, and we were getting ready to go out for the evening. I checked the tennis balls and found they had worn through and were squeaking. The thought hit me that I could rotate the tennis balls, cut a new X on an open side of the tennis ball, and have a squeak-free walker without needing new tennis balls. It worked, and I was lucky this time.

Stains

I have been a recognized remover of stains from clothing for the greater part of my married life. Ballpoint pen marks had been a very common appearance in shirts. I had read where hair spray would take out the marks, and it usually worked for me. Many times it was not known what type of stain had appeared on clothing. I had used a commercial cleaner by soaking the affected clothing, and many times hoping my old stand by Oxi Clean was victorious.

One of the toughest stains we experienced was on our near-white carpet when red nail polish was accidentally spilled on it. I used several combinations of solvents that were to take out nail polish, and after many tries, it did work. The dining room didn't smell good for several days, but the stain was gone.

When I removed some double-sided tape in the back room used to hold down a rubber carpet that collected clay removed from the basement, we had a mess. A solvent and electric shampooer did the trick.

I am sure there will be more challenging stains in the future. I can only hope I get lucky with my bag of anti-stain tricks to once again be successful in my stain removal process. I am the stain-master!

Handling Illness

Everyone in their life has had some forms of either short-term or acute and long-term or chronic illnesses. Some of these illnesses, especially the chronic, have been addressed in previous chapters. I recently had an experience with an acute illness, which was some type of a flu a few days before Christmas in 2010. Being sick a few days before a holiday seems to be a part of my pattern of living. If something major is about to happen that requires my time, illness can appear a few days before these special days.

In the first place, it would be noted that when mild weather changes to cold winter weather, my system adapts poorly to the change in weather. I wear earmuffs, heavy clothes, and gloves, and I try to stay out of the winter weather. It does no good because a bug is going to get me despite my best efforts to avoid them.

You might say, why don't I get a flu shot? Well, two months ago, I did get a flu shot. I guess the explanation is I didn't get the flu shot for the type of flu I was exposed to and contracted.

My mental list of the physical symptoms I displayed were numerous. In fact, the symptoms were growing so fast and were affecting me so severely that I was contemplating a visit to the doctor. I had been fighting some of my flulike symptoms for almost a week with medication around the house that had been successful in the past. This potential move to the doctor forced me to make a list of all that was causing me discomfort.

I started the list with the symptoms as they came to me. An unusual discomfort was that my eyes both itched. The itching was so bad that I needed to rinse both eyes with salt water to stop the itching. Uncontrollable sneezing was next. One, two, three times and more sneezes occurred at a time. I am told that I am not a good sneezer because I will try to stop or reduce the sneeze so that I do not spread germs. This kind of sneezing causes the pressure in my head to back up, and my attempt at stopping the spread of germs in my sneeze may be doing more harm than good.

I began to have some nasal drip into my throat, which I attributed to an active sinus system. Along the same lines, some of the drainage would go into my nose, causing a nasal drip and the frequent use of my handkerchief. A third happening appeared as I began to cough. The cough was usually not severe, but it was periodically present.

The next significant problem area was my ears. At times, it felt as if someone was placing a clamp on my eardrums and slowly applying pressure to them. My ruptured eardrum has always been one of my most susceptible areas of pain in my body.

The next morning after thinking of going to the doctor, I woke with a terrible, terrible headache. I called the doctor's office, and there was an appointment open at five forty-five. It was my first appointment with a nurse practitioner, and I was assured that she could help me. I arrived early at the doctor's office at five thirty. I figured that if I could get in early, I would have a better chance of having my prescription filled that same evening. The pharmacy closed at seven o'clock, and it was over fifteen minutes to my pharmacist. It was five fifty-five, and I was not in the office. I really didn't think I would be called early. I made it in the office around six o'clock.

The nurse practitioner was very good. She worked with me to choose the best antibiotic. Amoxicillin was chosen as the antibiotic since in the past, it had worked the best. I had a nasal spray sample given to me and was encouraged to have an antihistamine. I started the medications that evening, but until they kicked in, I was to get even sicker by being nauseated, dizzy, and nearly vomiting. The next day, I slowly began to feel better, and within a few days, most of the symptoms were under control.

As I was sick and hoping to get better, several thoughts ran through my head. What would happen if I were not to get better and, in fact, had some more serious long-term illness? I also began to think of some of my friends who had gone through, were going through, or would be going through treatment for cancer. I knew people in all three of these categories and thought how very sickening the treatment for cancer could be. Within this timeline, an acquaintance of mine actually died from cancer. I then thought how lucky I would be to get over what I had and not to go through any dramatic treatments such as chemotherapy or radiation.

As I thought of how I treated people who were sick, the realization came to me that I really needed to be more thoughtful, kinder, and generous with my time. I had been blessed and was continuing to be blessed with good health despite my flu symptoms.

Pain

As I lay awake in my bed at four in the morning on the middle of March 2012 with a terrible headache, I could not help but think of the many times I had experienced pain. It happened early in my life with ulcers, my bout with a slight case of a depressive illness, irritable bowel syndrome, a bleeding stomach, the flu, poison ivy, and others. This pain sometimes lasted one day, several days, a week, a month, or longer off and on. The ability to endure for me was that usually I felt it would come to an end. If the medication I had did not help, it may be a trip to the hospital.

I knew that some of my friends endured the pain from cancer or a sore body from a cancer operation. It may be pain from a fractured hip, and the medication prescribed initially did not help. While death was not usually the hoped-for solution for me or my friends, it did happen.

My severe headache this morning was bearable as other previous pain experiences had been much more severe, and a prayer had been an avenue of escape that had been successful. Many times, the hope for relief would motivate me to endure the pain. It would eventually be successful.

One frequent outcome of pain was that the next day, some significant event would be scheduled. It may be an important meeting, a meeting with an employee on a very unpleasant outcome for them, or a public appearance such a speech or a media-related happening. It didn't make it easier to go into any of these events with a lack of sleep, residual symptoms from the night before, or weakness from the lack of sleep. We all usually made it through it by the grace of God or sheer guts. Most of us have experienced these events, and most will experience it again. Hang in there with me, and I with you.

The good part of losing sleep is that the next night, I usually sleep like a baby.

A Revisit of Giving and Love

The gift of friends who can offer useful beliefs to our life is a priceless possession. One of the most important, if not the most important, part of our lives is helping or aiding others to enjoy living. It seems to me that what is important in life is to help other people be successful. In the process of helping others, my father would point out we are helping not only the society but also the world. While helping others benefits us, that was usually not emphasized by either of my parents. Giving is an important part of love. Another related way of analyzing interactions with others is that once you treat others in a positive manner, they will treat you more positively. A positive habit is born. Habit requires work, and anything worthwhile will need energy.

A friend of mine, Chris Clody, did an excellent job of pulling together God, others, and ourselves in love. Chris put forth a few words in an e-mail on January 21, 2010. In a prelude to a poem "To Love," Chris wrote, "But in order to know God you must love others which starts with loving yourself." The words seem simple, but the implications are profound and may be challenging for some to apply.

The conscious presence of a value and the enjoyment of living is dictated by each changing day of the week. Thus, giving to others as in love is a constantly changing variable and one that is not always conscious. On days where meeting one's values is difficult, energy will be needed to try harder to enjoy, give, and realize the good in others and myself.

It is common knowledge that attaining the goal of giving or any other positive values does not always happen. At times, it may even be hard to identify these values in a particular experience because they exist in varying degrees in different circumstances. The energy level is an extremely important element in my life. I have been blessed with an energy level above normal as evidenced by the fact that I am extremely active. This high energy level makes it possible for me to have many more experiences than someone who is not as active, and if my values are positive, more positive values will be exhibited.

Another way of looking at giving is the aspect within giving or loving others is where we pay attention to others. As we have established, it takes energy to give attention, and therefore, it is not easy, and in fact, it can be hard to give others attention. All of us have our own agenda, and giving to others takes time away from our agenda. The paying attention we are talking about is a positive move on our part. Fr. Herb Weber, then pastor of Blessed John XXIII, was delivering a sermon in the summer of 2010 on paying attention to others. In the sermon, he relayed how years ago after Mass, a man came up to him and said giving attention to others is a form of healing. The man went on to say that all of us have many difficult situations in our life, some more than others. When we give people attention, we are helping them to be more positive in healing their lives.

As I reflected on this idea of healing, I had to admit that healing was present in giving others attention. I further had to admit that in helping others, I was helping myself with my difficult situations. It is really a win-win situation that we create for others and ourselves when we give others attention. We usually are not out to hurt people as that can lead to a situation where we feel uncomfortable about having intentional or unintentionally not helped a person make progress in this world. Hurting others causes me to take a step backward because I have to find some way of rectifying or making the situation right to that person. Admitting I am wrong is hard for me and takes me a while to get back on a path that makes me and others feel good.

With this background established, I would like to briefly give you a few cautions. Since all human experiences are not always positive dealing with challenging days and challenging giving, it sometimes stretches one's ability to reach out to others. Trying to practice this value will bring to the forefront the fact that great love and great achievement involve great risk. At times, giving can be challenging because some individuals do not want anything from others as they are often independent people. Independent people can be approached by helping them receive and by receiving what they want to give.

How Do We Treat One Another

It is not hard to find examples of how people treat one another. For example, as I was reviewing some of my experiences, my thoughts went to other people as I listened to a radio show. Several spouses were telling how they were going to treat their spouses better. One wife called in and expressed her commitment to quit nagging her husband about everything he does. Starting that evening, she was going to stop nagging and treat him well by helping him see himself as a good and capable person. She was convinced that if she doesn't just do it, it would not happen. This told me that this everyday negative practice of nagging can be reversed if the nagger says they are going to stop it. This example points out how giving can change at least two people's lives if someone takes the initiative.

As I listened to the overtones of love and commitment that this lady was going to give her husband, I thought that this whole idea of giving does not have to be complicated and may require less energy to change than continuing to do those actions that one feels aren't quite right and make one feel down. The actions by this person reminded me of a saying by Walt Disney: "The way to get started is to quit talking and begin doing." How true this statement is in many examples of our everyday life.

Everyday Experiences in Life

Each day of my life, I miss out on experiences because I am engrossed in another happening, or I am just plain daydreaming, and the world goes by me. While many experiences are not earth-shattering, they could provide me with some wonderful memories and stories about my world. I think you may have similar experiences in your life that could add enrichment to your life and memories. Here are two such enriching experiences that happened in a twelve-hour span in my life.

The Storm and Preceding Evening

I was to attend a training session in Fostoria at St. Wendelin's Catholic Church. The training was on August 23, 2011, and involved evangelization or inviting inactive Catholics or other interested people to the Catholic faith. Our team from Blessed John XXIII is composed of seven people who are committed to this ministry and are experienced in providing this program. Everyone but Kevin met at my house, and we traveled in our van with the remaining six people. The group had worked closely on providing this program as a team and enjoyed their role as a facilitator.

Since Kathy was at her mother's before our departure, I had the pleasure of giving most of the travel group a tour of our century home topped off with some free homegrown tomatoes. The trip down was full of comradeship and stories of our lives. It was hard keeping up with the stories as more than one was being told at a time. We arrived a little early at the meeting site and toured the beautiful church of St. Wendelin. The program was well done, and there was much participation by the audience through group discussion and total group sharing.

When I arrived home, I tried to turn in early, and that rarely works as there is always something to do. I finally settled in bed and was enjoying a deep sleep when I was awakened by lightning, thunder, and a pounding rain around four in the morning. The pounding rain was hitting our vinyl siding so hard I began to wonder if the siding was going to survive the pressure of the rain. I thought Kathy told me she had shut all the windows, but a check seemed in order. As I walked out the bedroom door, the hall light was on. I began checking the windows and noticed Mark was not in bed. The lights were still on in the kitchen. I checked Mark's schedule, and sure enough, he had a double shift. He would be working until 8:00 a.m. I continued my check of the windows and the porch.

As I walked through the house, I suddenly heard an unfamiliar sound. I could not decide if the sound was inside or outside the house. I couldn't solve this question, I was tired, and I made my way to my bedroom and shutting off all the lights.

I lay down noticing the weather was letting up. I couldn't remember if I had checked the back room window. I was up again and checked the back room window; it was closed. Again, I settled in bed. I was about to fall asleep when I heard a noise downstairs like something hit an object and moved it. Chills ran up my leg as I lay motionless listening for another sound. I heard nothing, no more strange sounds. I dozed off to sleep. When I woke the next morning, the first thought that hit me was *If there are spirits in this house, I am glad they are friendly.*

The Railroad Tracks

The same morning as the storm was a day I was to have a day trip with my Kathy; her brother, Dave, and his wife, Diane; her sister, Agnes; and their mother, Laetta. I had a seven o'clock meeting on Special Olympics, but I found it had been postponed. This allowed me to have a little more time to travel to Kathy's mother's near Willard to meet up with everyone for the trip to Lake Erie. I started out allowing myself an extra forty-five minutes in case something went wrong. Kathy was already at her mother's.

Well, something did go wrong. I had passed through the small town of Attica, on Route 4, and had reached the country when I met a double set of CSX railroad tracks. The crossing gates that stopped vehicles from crossing the tracks had just been activated. It looked like a truck and a few cars were ahead of me at the first of the two sets of tracks. I waited and waited, and finally, I saw a small weird-looking railroad car with one driver in the cab coming down the tracks. It had four wheels and looked like it was used to repair the railroad tracks. As it approached the crossing, it blew its whistle.

A few minutes later, the crossing gates remained down, and another small different-looking railroad car came down the track, blowing its whistle when it reached the crossing. Many more came down the track with almost all of them having a different look and probably function. This went on for over a half hour, and each small train car continued to blow its whistle as it approached the crossroad. I counted thirty small utility cars and heard a full-sized train blowing its whistle. I was about to see something I had never seen in my life. The full-sized train came down the track was not coming from the opposite direction of the small cars, but it was going the same direction of the small cars.

After the train and the thirty-third small car went by, I began crossing the tracks. As I passed over the tracks, I noticed the crossing gates were beginning to come down on my van as the warning lights, and sound mechanism began to sound. I quickly went over the tracks and approached the next track a few hundred feet down the road. Sure enough, there was another full-sized train going across the track. As the train went by me, I marveled at the graffiti on the side of the cars, which must have been colored with spray paint. At the second set of tracks, I saw another train ready to go over the first set of tracks. For a person who had lived their childhood around the railroad, I had many unusual happenings this day with both small cars and full-sized trains.

A Busy Weekend Filled with a Big Surprise

Summer weekends are usually filled with activity around our house. On this weekend, we were to be up early and go to Lakeside for its annual antique sale. Lakeside is located on Lake Erie and is a religious community. We arrived in the morning and left about two thirty. We ran into Kathy's sister, Agnes, and her cousin Ron Ruffing and wife, Claudia. The restaurant in Downtown Lakeside provided a delicious pizza meal for most of us. We then saw Mike and Marge back at the antique show.

In a few weeks, my son Joe was to have a surprise fishing party out of Sassy Sal in Port Clinton. This was a good time for us to check out the boat and our accommodations. The plans were so that we would have around fifteen people wishing Joe a happy fortieth birthday party. Joe's wife, Tara, was in charge of the party, and Kathy, Mark, and I were trying to help her out.

Church was at five in the evening in Perrysburg, Ohio, so we needed to get home and change clothes. Immediately following church was a fiftieth anniversary party for Wood Lane Industries in Bowling Green. You may remember that Wood Lane Industries is a sheltered workshop that subcontracts with local industries to provide work for people with developmental disabilities.

After a nice dinner from a restaurant in Wayne, there was a review of the history of Wood Lane Industries. The announcer, Jay Savage, did a great job in giving the background information. I thought I was speaking for Jay because he would tell how he had to announce certain aspects of the program under the helpful direction of his wife's suggestions. Kathy was always there giving me good suggestions as to how I should be handling the program. The progression came to 1985 when I had begun my time and supervision of the day programs at Wood Lane. I was waiting to hear just a word about my influence on the history of the industries when nothing at all was said about me. Everyone else's name was mentioned but not mine. I thought I would get over it and listened to the program. There were a number of awards to be given, six special recognition awards for this year and awards to be given this year and thereafter.

The first few awards were announced for people unable to attend. I was waiting for the next special award when I heard the words "Joe Frederick." I froze. Were they really calling my name? My wife said, "Joe, go up to the platform." I finally did go up and was really in a daze. I was looking for my name to be announced, and here I was, receiving one of the major awards.

As I listened to the reasons for the award, I noted that they had gone back close to forty years and updated my contributions to Wood Lane. It was kind of embarrassing on one hand and a good summary of my relationship to the Wood Lane Industries on the other hand. I later received many comments on how deserving I was of the award. The plaque is beautiful, and my lack of ability to accept praise had to take a second place to accepting the many fine compliments on my awards.

A Great Employment Program

I had over the past few years periodically given my high school friend Bob Bauerle a call so we could catch up on our lives. You might remember that Bob had lost his wife, Mary, several years ago. One of our topics of discussion was our fiftieth Willard High School class reunion to be celebrated on September 14–15, 2012. Another topic of discussion was an employment program Bob was active in his church called the Heart of a Champion. I had generally understood the program but was beginning to have more questions. Bob offered to send me information on the program so I could have a better understanding how it worked. We said our goodbyes.

A few days later, I received a large package from Bob. I opened the packet and began to look it over. A few days later, I got serious about reading the program and was amazed at the professionalism and organization of the program. I also went to the Internet address heartofachampion.net.

The program is a weekly program lasting for nineteen weeks. The comprehensive approach of this program has made it possible for many people to realize the economic success that will help their lives turn around, for example, a job. The success ratio is around 40 percent. I consider that high, and I admire the people who give of their time to attach one of the greatest challenges of our day, being employed and happy.

The Wedding and the Fiftieth Class Reunion

The weekend of September 14 was a busy one. We were to be at Willard High School as the Class of 1962 was to attend and be recognized at the varsity football game. This was not to happen as Kathy and I were very busy pulling together the last arrangements for a wedding in our backyard. A friend of our youngest son, Mark, Scott Danielson, was to be married to Erin Matzgeter the very next day. A sweet autumn clematis was in full bloom over our nine-foot-high-by-twelve-foot-long and eight-foot-deep pergola. The flowers reached a height of four feet over the pergola and extended the entire width and then some of the pergola.

The ceremony went well as did the champagne toast. Providing the champagne to one hundred people went without a hitch. The wine and cheese party with many finger foods also went well. We also provided the homemade wine, which produced many compliments on its taste. The weddings and associated activities were extremely unique, and nothing major or minor went the least bit wrong. All the activities around the wedding and reception at our home went without any hitches.

While the people attending the wedding prepared for the evening's reception, we locked up our home and headed for my fiftieth class reunion in Willard. We were almost on time leaving our home and arrived at the Elk's Club at about the right time. I had been sending out the permission slips to many of my classmates for my book *People + Me*. I was pleased to hear that many people were sending back the slips, allowing me to use their information. My classmates were very supportive of my efforts. It was fun seeing and talking to people whom I had been in high school with fifty years ago. The stories about one another and the teachers we all experienced brought back memories and even a few surprises about high school days.

It seems there were always stories about classmates or other members of my family that surfaced during the times we were able to talk. As I was talking to Sandra Wilkison Atkins, she shared a story about my sister Mary Lu. Sandy's sister is Agnes Wilkinson Bettic and was a friend of my elder sister's when they were in high school. It was popular to buzz Myrtle Avenue, the main street in town, from one end to the other. According to Sandy, Mary Lu and Agnes were going to drive around town in my father's car. They were very concerned about putting on too many miles, so they disconnected the speedometer, did their cruising, and reconnected the speedometer. It must have worked because they really put on the miles that night on Dad's car, and nothing was ever said about the mileage.

The most memorable part of the evening was when Denny Reed set the stage for the meal prayer. Denny gave a tribute to one of our classmates that brought tears of joy. He started out by saying that "There was one classmate that had given him inspiration throughout his life. That person was Danny Kayser, who every day of his life had to do many tasks that others took for granted." Danny had been involved in an auto accident shortly after graduation from high school. He was paralyzed from his waist down because of the accident that happened in the rural Willard area. Being in a mobile chair was something Danny had lived with for around fifty years.

Despite the fact that Danny had dealt with all these challenges in his life, he had become a successful radio broadcaster and had started not one, not two but three Christian broadcast stations. Danny has always been upbeat, smiling, and a real joy to be around. Danny's wife was present to hear this testimonial. As Denny completed his excellent introduction of Danny, the entire group of seventy-one people sprang to their feet to give Danny a well-deserved standing ovation.

Danny gave a few brief remarks to the assembly. The words came from his big heart. Congratulations, Danny, for successfully meeting the difficult challenges in your life.

How Not to Start a Retreat

In the Catholic Church, we have an event called the retreat. It is a time to leave the busy world and take time to spend time with God. I had for three years gone to the Mandresa Jesuit Retreat Home in Bloomfield Hills, Michigan, near Detroit. A friend and our financial consultant, Mel Wicks, had invited me to attend my first retreat there, and I had continued the practice.

This year I had invited my brother from Connecticut, Bob, to attend the retreat. Bob had flown in on Thursday, rented a car, and spent the day with Kathy and me. We had left for the retreat on Friday afternoon on November 30, 2012. Both Bob and I drove to Mel's house in Maumee, and I left my car as Bob would not be coming back to Maumee after the retreat. Mel was to lead us as he had been to the retreat house many times. I rode up with Bob and would ride back with Mel on Sunday after the retreat was done, and Bob was going to the airport.

We were leaving Toledo going into Michigan in heavier traffic than I remembered in the past. A direct result of heavy traffic is stop-and-go traffic. It was at this time that I began having an uncomfortable feeling. I immediately identified the symptoms as car sickness or motion sickness. I adjusted the seat so that I could lay back and rest. For a while, I was feeling a bit better. As we were about a half hour from our destination, I began to feel the motion sickness becoming more acute as we got into heavier traffic and were stopping and starting on a regular basis. We were also on a road that there were few chances to stop, and traffic was everywhere. I told Bob I wasn't feeling well. He advised me to open the window. This did help me for about fifteen minutes.

We were now about fifteen minutes from the retreat house, and I was really sick. My mouth began to water, and I knew what was next. I told Bob I needed to stoop. He gave me a large drinking glass and said he would stop as soon as he could. As soon as he could was not soon enough for me.

I lost my cookies in the drinking glass. I told Bob I wanted to get rid of the unpleasant-smelling contents of the large glass. Luckily or maybe not so luckily, Bob went into the right lane, and there were no cars behind us or even close to us. My calculation was that we were going slow enough for me to discard the contents of the glass. I threw out the contents of the cup and found that my assumption on the speed of the car was incorrect, we were going faster than I thought. The wind immediately threw the contents of the glass against my window and the entire side of the car. Since my right arm was out the window, it also caught the unpleasant contents of the glass. I felt better, but I now had to figure out how to make myself presentable to the registration desk at the retreat house.

We devised a simple plan. I would quickly walk by the registration desk and had Mel and Bob register me and obtain my room number. I could then quickly clean up and go to supper. I walked by the registration table with my suitcase, and Mel and Bob registered me. It worked. In a short time, I was down to the dining room with a clean arm and shirt. I did, however, walk around most of the weekend with the start of a beard. I discovered while packing my electric razor that morning that it needed charged. The razor was charged, but it was not in my suitcase. All three of us were spiritually charged that weekend, and that was all that mattered.

Education and How It Be Useful in Life

Having worked in the area of developmental disabilities, specifically the area of mental retardation, I knew that the subject matter taught was needed by the individual to survive in the world. The areas of communicating in an acceptable manner was important. The ability to prepare and eat the proper food was needed. Keeping the living areas clean and being able to buy or rent the dwelling as well as all related living areas were to be projected in a budget. Yes, living within one's means was essential learning.

My friend Jean Long had recently retired from teaching. In high school, because of legal mandates, she had to abide by different rules regarding the areas taught to her students. She relayed to me that education in public schools is now emphasizing that passing standardized tests is the desired outcome of public education. The practical side of living was not the goal of education. Courses such as budgeting one's money and how to get along with friends and spouses are courses of the past, if they were courses.

As we talked about the many shootings of young children or the inability of people to budget to pay for their homes, it became clear that the public school systems are by and large meeting mandates of legislation with the selection and teaching of course material not meeting the needs of students' everyday needs now and in the future. If public education was teaching how to get along with one's neighbor and when and how much money one needs to buy a house, would our nation be in the trouble it is in these areas? You may say that the everyday needs of children are not the responsibility of the schools. As we look at the many public shootings and the number of bankruptcies caused by the purchase of homes, whoever is to teach overcoming these obstacles must not be doing a good job.

The Fiftieth Wedding Anniversary

My elder brother Walt and Judy, his wife, were married on October 5, 1963. It had long been known that they would have a party to mark their milestone accomplishment. Kathy and I planned to go to North Carolina for the event. Both our sons were more than interested in going. It was decided that they would go by car with us, and they would fly home on Sunday as they both worked that week.

Since I was the best man at the wedding, I was to give a toast and share some info about my brother. I prepared a toast and looked up the poem I gave in my toast. I contacted the matron of honor, Linda Strain, and we coordinated our remarks. I had learned a lesson several years before, and that was to make sure that I notified other similar presenters so that there were no surprises for either of us.

There had been a previous time where I without intent gave a surprise. I had memorized a reading for the wedding Mass. As I started my memorized reading, I could hear a sigh from the other reader that she had not memorized her reading. I was embarrassed for her and me. My thoughtful memorization turned out not to be so thoughtful for the other reader.

I had talked with the master of ceremonies, Pete Frederick, and we had our signals pretty well together. It had been decided that there were to be two parties, one on Friday at the country club for family and church friends and one on Saturday, an informal barbecue for the neighbors and other friends. On Friday morning, I woke up at five thirty at the motel. As I reviewed the script for that evening, it didn't really seem right. All these people were coming in from various points out of and in state to pay tribute to Judy and Walt, and it must have been God telling me to change the script and get more people involved in the program. By the time the dinner came around, Pete, Linda, and I had the potential for involving everyone in the program.

Pete started and outlined the basis of the program of giving and receiving from each other love. With Walt and Judy at the center of the program, Linda told about her relationship to Judy and covered Judy's side of the family and recognized her relatives. A toast to Judy and Walt was given. I walked up to the podium to talk about Walt and his family. I was exactly sure how I was going to address Walt's side of the family. Walt's family was composed of five other children, while Judy had a brother and sister. On my mother's side was sixteen children with representation of several of the brothers and sisters.

I had talked with many of the families and had some cues in words for people to respond with a story and be introduced by their families. Most importantly, I felt God was with me. My aunt Theresa was the first person to be recognized from my mother's family. She overviewed the sixteen children of the Schlotterer family and her relationship to Walt and Judy. She introduced her family who were present, and from there, this section of the presentation took off better than I could have ever hoped. After the stories and introduction of my brothers, I began the story of Walt saving my life. As I tried to beat the train at the crossing, I caught my foot in the railroad tracks. Within a few seconds of a train rolling over me, Walt pulled my foot out of the sandals and rescued the sandals and assured I made it to safety. Ann told the crowd that she never wanted to be in another circumstance even close to that near fateful day that we were going to catechism class. My poem on man and woman's close connection and a toast ended my part.

Pete recognized his brothers and sisters who relayed many fun and serious stories from the family. Jackie, Walt's eldest daughter, led everyone in the night prayers that the family said every evening.

The avalanche of participation caught on so well that before the evening was over, every person had been on their feet and recognized. Some were group recognition and others were individual. The overall recognition of Walt and Judy's giving and receiving to their family, the community, and their church was overwhelming. The 123 people present were into the program, and the smiles on all the faces told me that the stories and testimonials were of a larger, happier family than just the Fredericks and Judy's family, the Kovashs. The evening was priceless and the crowd magnificent. It could not have been better.

Saturday evening was a different crowd honoring Judy and Walt's accomplishment. During the festivities, one of the guests, a friend of my brother, sang a spiritual song with the aid of his daughter and wife. I knew we were in Southern hospitality as the hymn was sung without any musical accompaniment.

On Sunday, we left North Carolina for South Carolina. We stayed close to Myrtle Beach so we could see our friends in Murrells Inlet. Kathy had met Sandy as they both were teachers at Fort Meigs School in Perrysburg. Her husband, Perry, drove us to some great restaurants in the area, and the next day, we went to one of the sculptor gardens. It was interesting finding out more about Perry's different positions in the television industry.

On the second day of our stay, we parted for our last destination, Charleston, South Carolina. We were not prepared for all the city had to offer. We stayed in the old district and were within walking distance of the shops on King and Meeting Streets. We also had the opportunity to visit several specialty shops on the street and in the market. A visit to Magnolia Plantation gave us a new insight into slavery. We were able to see the manner in which fortunes were made with the use of African slaves. The rice plantations and the many beautiful homes and gardens surrounding the properties were examples of cheap labor producing great wealth.

We left the inviting city of Charleston the third day of our visit, and we were convinced that there were many other attractions we would have loved to experience, and hopefully, we could do so another time.

As we casually made our way home, we decided that arriving at one or two o'clock in the morning wasn't worth the inconvenience, so we looked for a motel in West Virginia. The Fairfield Inn in Wilson, North Carolina, had been a very pleasant experience a few days earlier, so we looked for and found a Fairfield Inn in Beckley, West Virginia. We were to have one of the most unusual happenings the next morning as we went to the complimentary breakfast. The preceding evening, Kathy had seen a man who resembled a friend and fellow employee in Tiffin. At breakfast, we saw the man again reading the newspaper. I couldn't see his face well, and we had not seen him recently, but it sure looked like Jerry Johnson. I went up to him and said hello. He did a double take and smiled;, I knew it was Jerry. What were the chances we would run into Jerry in the middle of West Virginia at the very same city and the very same motel? An interesting ending to a great vacation.

Unforgettable People in my Life

Butch Rothschild

From as long as I can remember, Butch has been a constant friend in my life. I grew up with Butch, I have known him throughout my life, and I still know and respect Butch. Butch is a few years older than I am, and he has been like a big brother.

When we were kids, we played together, we rode bikes together, and we fished and trapped together. There was always something going on in Butch's garage on Clark Street, in his yard, or in his house.

In high school, Butch had a 1954 black Chevy, which provided the gang with transportation.

Any trouble we got into, we were also able to gracefully leave. Our younger days of fishing with our fathers is now that we fish with each other, my son Mark, and Butch's son-in-law, Paul.

Although the time we have to spend together is less than when we were younger, we have good quality time. I cannot remember a disagreement we had that was not settled rather easily.

Kathy has encouraged my relationship with Butch and Butch's wife, Phyl. She has always supported our relationship.

There has never been serious competition between us, and our relationship has always been supportive. Butch has and continues to be a good friend.

Fred Eldred

Fred is my brother-in-law, and because of the fact that I lived with him for several summers and one winter, I got to know him well. One of my first experiences with Fred was when I was living with him and my sister Mary Lu. I have previously told the story of shooting a hole in their back porch. I will never forget Fred coming out to the barn when I was hunting rats, and he never mentioned the hole in the wall. Instead, he came into the dark barn, sat beside me, and asked me, "Are you getting any rats?"

On another occasion, I had borrowed his 1957 Ford Fairlane 500 to go to catechism. As I was coming home from church, there was a snowstorm, and I wrecked his car. He never said much about the wreck and allowed me to work off the deductible.

Fred is always cool about anything that happens, and I am aware of many times that he calmly and diplomatically handled issues. Fred is an easy person to be around and usually has a laugh or two for you. Fred could have gone to college and I have no doubt been able to obtain advanced degrees. Like so many others, Fred stayed back to help with the family farm. Fred always was very kind and understanding with all his family but especially both his parents. I have worked with Fred, traveled with Fred, and cried with Fred, and in it all, he is a man I deeply admire.

Conclusion

As we end this book, I would like to remind all of us about another end, the end of our lives. As the saying goes, we should aspire to inspire before we expire. We only have the one shot to get it as right as we can.

I would like to end my stories with the one I began in the introduction of my first book, *People + Me*. You may remember that in July 2008, I was listening to Father Herb as he introduced a member of our parish who was also a sister. In fact, Sr. Pat McClain, principal of Lial Catholic School in Whitehouse, was celebrating that very day her twenty-fifth anniversary in the religious order of the Notre Dame Sisters. Sister Pat was sitting directly in front of Kathy and me with her natural family as well as part of her order, three other Notre Dame sisters. We had ringside seats. As Sister Pat began to review her vows, I was immediately taken in by her words. It was as if she was talking to me as she thanked everyone present for "the opportunity to experience many wonderful people." I had been struggling with the title for the book and knew that I now had one.

Well, the story continues about Sister Pat, who just radiates with joy going to Communion with her family and the other Notre Dame sisters. As she walked down the aisle, I continued to have a front- row seat, and I thought it would be real special to see her take the body of Christ from Father Herb, who was dressed in the beautiful vestments of the season. For your information, Father Herb stands in the middle of the aisle while another lay distributor stands beside him, with two other lay distributors in the side aisles.

I was never to see Sister Pat take Communion from Father Herb that day because as she was approaching Father Herb, the celebrant of the Mass, she turned to her left and took Communion from a lay distributor located on the side. I saw a lesson of humility for all of us as she didn't worry about the limelight but took a road less glitzy yet one where she did serve God.

I began this book many years ago, and I finish this book, it is 2020, in the middle of a COVID-19 pandemic. We lost our son Mark in 2016, and it has never been the same without him. I do have the love of my life, Kathy; my son Joe; and his wife, Tara, and their two sons, Zach and Josh. I hope you have enjoyed this book with the many happenings of a life that *God Keeps On Giving.*